Harbrace College Handbook

4TH EDITION

JOHN C. HODGES

The University of Tennessee

in consultation with

FRANCIS X. CONNOLLY

Fordham University

HARCOURT, BRACE AND COMPANY

New York • Burlingame

[k · 1 · 60]

Printed in the United States of America

▶ To the Instructor

The *Harbrace College Handbook* is both a guide for the individual writer and a text for use in class. It presents its subject matter in a readily usable form, and thus lightens the instructor's task of reading student papers.

Numbers. The book contains only thirty-five major sections, or numbers, referring to errors commonly made in writing. These include (as has been shown by a comprehensive examination of student writing) everything to which instructors normally refer in marking papers. But other errors less frequently made have not been overlooked. They are subordinated logically to the thirty-five primary numbers and may be found readily by reference to the back end papers or to the detailed index. If an instructor wishes to have any of these subordinate errors conveniently before his students, he can have them added in the blanks provided on the chart inside the front cover. With some college students Sections **1-18** may be needed only for review or for occasional reference.

Symbols. Instead of the simplified list of numbers, the instructor may, if he prefers, use the corresponding symbols. Most of these symbols are well known to English teachers; they are entered on both front and back charts.

General Plan. The sections on **Sentence Sense (1)** and **Grammatical Terms (35)** are general sections. The former may be used, whenever needed, as an introduction to the other sections; the latter should be used throughout as a glossary of terms. For correction of specific errors, students will normally be referred to Sections 2-34.

Drill Materials. Exercises are provided both for the major sections and for many subsections, and there are also general exercises applicable to two or more sections. Many of these exercises consist of lively paragraphs instead of conventional groups of unrelated sentences. Many other exercises are of a positive type, in which the student is asked not to correct errors but to compose good sentences to illustrate the principle involved. Some classes may need very little of the drill materials; others may need all of them, or even additional exercises such as those in the *Harbrace College Workbook,* Form 3 (keyed to the *Harbrace College Handbook,* Fourth Edition).

Contemporary Usage. This Fourth Edition of the *Harbrace Handbook* attempts to describe the usual practice of good contemporary writers, and to state that practice as simply as possible. The "rules" are to be interpreted as principles, or descriptions, derived from usage; and they have authority only to the extent that they describe usage. In the illustrations throughout the book, labels such as RIGHT and WRONG indicate what might be expected and what is usually avoided in standard written English.

Acknowledgments. Any English handbook must owe a debt to linguistic scholarship too extensive to be acknowledged in detail. Fortunately this scholarship is now very active. Among the many individuals who have generously offered suggestions for making this handbook more usable, the author wishes especially to thank Professors Francis X. Connolly (Fordham), Robert R. Gross (Bucknell), Gerald A. Smith (Maryland), Grover C. Smith, Jr. (Duke), Francis Lee Utley (Ohio State), and Walter R. Whitney (Maine). For important contributions to Section 33 (**Library Paper**), the author is grateful to Mr. John Dobson and Miss Eleanor Goehring, of the Library Staff (Tennessee), and to Miss Ruby Jean Harris and Mr. Jack Howard Wilson (Tennessee).

Finally, the author is indebted to Professor Bain Tate Stewart and other members of the Freshman Staff at the University of Tennessee for many helpful suggestions. He wishes to express particular thanks to Mr. Roy F. Montgomery, who has prepared most of the new exercise materials.

▶ To the Student

Numbers or Symbols. A number or a symbol written in the margin of your paper indicates an error and calls for a correction. If a number is used, turn directly to the corresponding boldface number at the top of the page in the handbook. If a symbol is used, first consult the alphabetical list of symbols inside the front cover to find the number to which you should turn.

Ordinary References. The ordinary reference will be to the boldface number or symbol standing at the head of one of the thirty-five sections of the handbook. The statement in large boldface at the beginning of each section covers the section as a whole. One of the statements in smaller boldface within the section will usually be needed for the correction of your specific error. Study the section to which you have been referred—the whole of the section if necessary—and master the specific part of the section that explains your error. To prove that you have found the specific principle needed for the correction, write the appropriate letter (**a**, **b**, **c**, etc.) after the number or symbol supplied by your instructor. An *ex* written by the instructor after a number or symbol calls for the writing out of the appropriate exercise.

Specific References. Whenever your instructor wishes to refer you to a specific part of a section, he will add the appropriate letter to the boldface number or symbol.

EXAMPLES **2c** (*or* **frag-c**), **18b** (*or* **sp-b**), **28d** (*or* **ref-d**).

General References. At times your instructor may give you a very general reference from which you are to determine and correct your error. For example, the symbol **gr** will refer you to the whole division on GRAMMAR, including Sections **1-7**; the symbol **m** to the division on MECHANICS, Sections **8-11**; the symbol **p** to the division on PUNCTUATION, Sections **12-17**; and so forth. An obvious error may be called to your attention by the symbol **x**, and general awkwardness by the symbol **k**.

Diagraming. To supplement the explanations, simple diagrams are used occasionally. These diagrams are often limited to parts of sentences—in order to concentrate your attention on the immediate problem and to prevent your becoming more interested in complicated lines than in grammatical relationships.

Additional Help. Some of the principles treated in English handbooks can be mastered only by students who understand the fundamentals of the sentence. A well-developed "sentence sense" is especially helpful in the mastery of Sections **2 (Sentence Fragment)**, **3 (Comma Splice)**, **6 (Agreement)**, **12 (The Comma)**, **14 (The Semicolon)**, **21 (Wordiness)**, **23 (Unity)**, **24 (Subordination)**, **25 (Coherence)**, **26 (Parallelism)**, and **30 (Variety)**. If you have difficulty in understanding these sections, you should first master the fundamentals of the sentence treated in Section **1 (Sentence Sense)**, and then turn again to the principle immediately involved. If you fail to understand any term of grammar used in the handbook, consult the alphabetical list in Section 35 (**Grammatical Terms**).

Revision. After you have mastered the principle underlying the correction of each error, you should make careful revision in the manner recommended by your instructor. One method of revision is explained in Section 8 (**Manuscript Form and Revision**), pages 94-97.

Exercises. The exercises are to be written out on paper, not marked in the book.

▸ Contents

GRAMMAR

MECHANICS

PUNCTUATION

12 The Comma 117

13 Superfluous Commas 135

SPELLING

DICTION

LARGER ELEMENTS

GRAMMAR

▶ Sentence Sense

1

Master the essentials of the sentence as an aid to clear thinking, effective writing, and intelligent reading.

Mastery of sentence sense—a recognition of what *makes* a sentence, and of the proper relationships between its several parts—is your key to good writing and reading. If you lack sentence sense, you cannot effectively communicate your own thoughts, nor effectively and fully comprehend the statements of others.

Sentence sense is prerequisite to the intelligent use of this handbook, especially Sections 2 (Sentence Fragment), 3 (Comma Splice), 6 (Agreement), 12 (The Comma), 14 (The Semicolon), 21 (Wordiness), 23 (Unity), 24 (Subordination), 25 (Coherence), 26 (Parallelism), and 30 (Variety).

The student who lacks a well-developed sentence sense can only with difficulty recognize and avoid the sentence fragment—that is, the failure to complete a thought in the normal fashion of good writers. He will be prone to make comma splices—that is, to link main clauses with only a comma between them—simply because he cannot recognize main clauses; to make errors in agreement because he cannot determine verbs and associate them with their subjects; to misuse the comma because he lacks the ability to distinguish such parts of the sentence as main and subordinate clauses, adverb clauses, adjective clauses, compound predicates, and phrases. Once he has learned how to analyze his sentences, he can make them more effective by applying the principles underlying unity, subordination, coherence, parallelism, and sentence variety. Any student who does not understand the usual and normal construction of the sentence should develop his sentence sense and then study the sections of the handbook concerned with his particular difficulties.

1a Learn to recognize verbs.

The verb ("He *ran* fast"; "you *are* late") is the heart of the sentence. Without a verb any group of words ("after a while," "no advice from anyone," "all waiting for the signal") is only a sentence fragment. A verb is a word (or a group of words) that expresses action, indicates a state of being, or asserts something. It is used (1) in making a statement, (2) in asking a question, or (3) in giving a command.

1. The rain *falls* gently.
2. *Are* you happy?
3. *Walk* carefully.

The verb may consist of one word (as in the three sentences above) or a group of two, three, or four words. The group, called a *verb phrase,* comprises the verb and the auxiliary words often required in English to show inflection; the group is just as much a verb as the single word.

1. The man *will work* faithfully.
2. The man *has been working* faithfully.
3. The man *should have been working* faithfully.

The words that make up a verb phrase are often separated.

1. It *is* not *raining.*
2. It *will* almost certainly *rain* tomorrow.

A verb may be combined with the adverb *not,* or with a contraction of *not.*

1. He *can*not *go.*
2. He *can*'t *go.*
3. It *is*n't cold.
4. He *does*n't *know.*

The student who can find the verb (or verb phrase) and can separate it from other elements has gone a long way toward acquiring sentence sense.

► EXERCISE 1. For each of the following sentences supply an appropriate verb (or verb phrase). Then compose five sentences of your own and underline each verb (or verb phrase).

1. Steve _____ _____ in Baltimore in 1926. 2. His parents _____ six other children, all younger than he. 3. When Steve _____ thirteen, his father _____ _____ in a shipyard accident. 4. With the life-insurance money, Steve's mother _____ to keep the children in school; for she _____ the value of education and _____ _____ _____ any sacrifice to see them graduated. 5. After high school Steve _____ the Navy; and during his last year in service, he _____ his oldest sister to college. 6. When he _____ _____ his period of enlistment, he _____ at the same col-

lege. 7. It ____ there that I first ____ this brother and sister. 8. I ____ never ____ two finer people.

► EXERCISE 2. Underline the fourteen verbs and four verb phrases in the following sentences. Do not underline verbals—participles, gerunds, and infinitives. (For a discussion of verbals, which are derived from verbs but are not regular verbs, see below under **1d**.)

1. Jim angrily called himself a fool, as he had been doing all the way through the woods, for allowing Fred to talk him into this mad idea. 2. What were ghosts and family legends to him, in this year of grace and nuclear fission? 3. He had mysteries enough of his own, of a highly complex electronic sort, to occupy him through the rest of a lifetime. 4. But to be plodding along here, like the Mississippi schoolboy he had been a dozen years before, on a ghost chase in the middle of the night, was preposterous. 5. It was an outrage to everything he stood for; it was lunacy. 6. It was—he swallowed the truth like a bitter pill—frightful! 7. The legend and the ghost had been a horror to him as a child; and they were a horror still. 8. Standing at the edge of the weed-choked, briar-tangled slope, on the top of which the decayed mansion waited evilly, he felt almost sick. 9. The safe, sure things of every day had become distant, childish fantasies. 10. This grotesque night and whatever, ghoulish and monstrous, inhabited it were clammily, horribly real.

► EXERCISE 3. Underline the thirteen verbs and the four verb phrases in the following sentences.

1. Driving his oxen in the face of the dust storm was a wearying task. 2. He buried his face deep in his scarf. 3. Stumbling, he almost fell. 4. "Keep on," he said to himself. 5. His wife called from the wagon, her voice muffled by the roaring storm and by the flapping of the

canvas. 6. Finally he made out what she was saying. 7. "Don't you think that we ought to stop?" she said. 8. "No," he shouted back. 9. There would be time to stop when they reached water, when he could do something for the stumbling oxen, whose anguished bellowing seemed to reproach him. 10. He hoped then to rest, to sleep.

► EXERCISE 4. Underline the twenty-seven verbs or verb phrases in the following sentences.

1. When Falstaff wishes to persuade Mistress Ford of the honesty of his love, he disclaims all likeness to "these lisping hawthorn buds that come like women in men's apparel and smell like Bucklersbury in simple-time." 2. "Simples" are herbs of which medicines are compounded. 3. They were formerly an item of trade in the grocery business. 4. And grocers, as a chronicler of London writing in 1598 tells us, were then found mostly in Bucklersbury. 5. There were two men from Stratford who were partners in a grocery business in London during Shakespeare's time, and their shop was located in Bucklersbury. 6. One of the partners was Richard Quiney, whose brother Thomas was later to become the husband of Shakespeare's younger daughter, Judith. 7. A rather extensive correspondence among the Quineys and some of their family connections in Stratford and London during 1598 frequently mentions Shakespeare and indicates that he was involved with them in several business transactions. 8. More often than not, the transactions were small loans which one or another of his fellow townsmen sought of him, indicating that they regarded him as a person of some means, able and willing to be of service to his friends in their minor emergencies. 9. As H. B. Wheatley has pointed out, there seems no doubt that Shakespeare had occasion to visit the business house of his grocer friends in Bucklersbury. 10. There

seems likewise no reason to doubt that it was the familiar fragrance of the stocks of herbs there which supplied him with the figure of comparison Falstaff used in his love-making.

Note: Ask a competent person to check the accuracy of your spotting of verbs. If you can mark the verbs accurately, you are ready to take up the next exercises. If not, mark verbs in other lists of sentences (such as the exercises at the end of this section) and get assistance in checking the accuracy of your work. Many students confuse verbs with participles, gerunds, and infinitives, which are treated below under **1d**.

1b Learn to recognize the subjects (and objects) of verbs in sentences.

A sentence is a unit of expression that may stand alone. It is followed in speaking by a pause and in writing by a period, a question mark, or an exclamation point. Regularly it has both a verb (called the *predicate*) and its subject, or at least these are implied.[1] In the following sentences the subjects are in *italics* and the predicates (verbs) are in **boldface**.

Complete subject	*Complete predicate*
Men	**work.**
Some *men* on farms	**work** long hours during the summer.
[*You*]	**Walk** carefully.

The subject and the words associated with it ("Some men on farms") are called the *complete subject;* the predicate and the words associated with it ("work long hours during the summer") are called the *complete predicate.*

[1] For a discussion of incomplete sentences, which do not bulk large in written English, see pages 32-33. In this book the word *sentence* will refer to the regular, or complete, sentence.

In order to find the subject, simply ask, in connection with the verb, "Who or what?" In the sentences listed above, who or what *work? Men* work. Who or what *walk? You* walk. No matter how long or how involved the sentence is, the subject can readily be found—if the verb has first been recognized.

> The *airplane,* having reached Miami after a long flight from South America, circles the city before landing at the airport. [Who or what *circles?* The *airplane* circles.]

It is sometimes helpful to make a diagram, or to form a mental picture, of the subject and its verb, thus:

airplane | circles

Any student who can bring the subject and verb together in this way should have little trouble in making the two "agree" (see Section 6); for example, *airplane* circles, *airplanes* circle.

The subject of an interrogative sentence is more readily located when the sentence is recast in the form of a statement.

> Has the *last* of the deserters surrendered?
> The *last* of the deserters has surrendered.

A sentence may have a compound subject (*Mary* and *Jane* played), a compound predicate (*Mary* sang and played), or both compound subject and compound predicate (*Mary* and *Jane* sang and played).

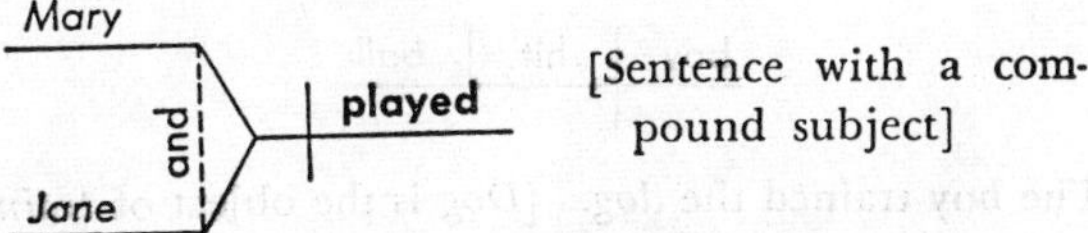

[Sentence with a compound subject]

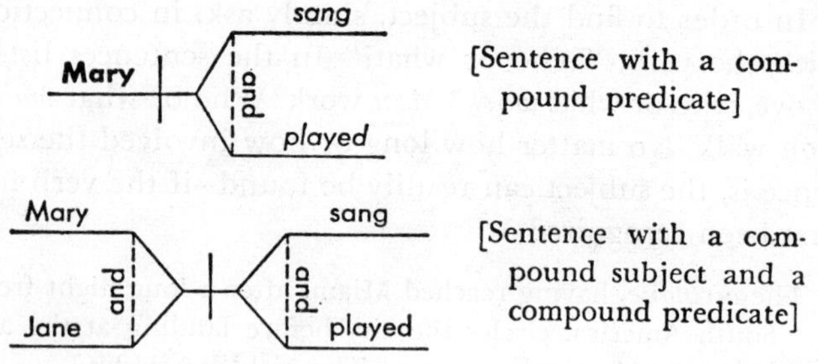

[Sentence with a compound predicate]

[Sentence with a compound subject and a compound predicate]

► EXERCISE 5. Diagram (or point out) the subject and predicate in each of the following sentences. Note that some of the subjects and predicates are compound.

1. Looking out from the attic window, Jim and Ben could see the cattle grazing on the range and hear the bleating of the calves. 2. There were two herds, one of Herefords and one of Angus. 3. Was anything more beautiful than such a sight on a clear spring morning? 4. Jim opened the window and sniffed the air. 5. Quietly, joyfully his eyes embraced the scene: the woods on the left, the creek in the foreground, the range beyond, the corral and bunkhouse on the right. 6. He looked and thought. 7. A thing like this should last forever. 8. If not forever, then it should last for a very long time. 9. Home and the ranch meant a great deal to him that morning. 10. He counted it a golden moment, a golden day, to be treasured against the coming deficit of time.

Some verbs have "objects." A word or group of words that receives the action of a verb is called its *object*.

1. The boy hit the *ball*. [*Ball* is the object of *hit*.]

boy | hit | ball

2. The boy trained the *dog*. [*Dog* is the object of *trained*.]

Note: Sometimes a sentence has both a direct object and an indirect object. The indirect object states the receiver of the direct object.

The boy gave [to] the *dog* a *bone.* [*Dog* is the indirect object of *gave; bone* is the direct object.]

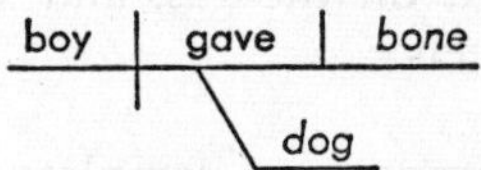

Word Order. In modern English the subject and the object can be determined by the normal order of words in the sentence. A thousand years ago our language was highly inflected, like Latin, with one form of the noun used as the subject and another as the object. With the loss of these inflections we have come to depend on the order of the words to distinguish between subject and object, as in "The dog killed the bear" and "The bear killed the dog." The meaning of these sentences is unmistakable because of our typical language pattern: subject–verb–object.

▶ EXERCISE 6. In the following sentences underline the nineteen subjects once, the twenty-one verbs (or verb phrases) twice, and check the fourteen direct objects of verbs (or verb phrases). Diagram the first three sentences which contain direct objects to show subject, verb, and object.

1. Henry drove up to the gas station. 2. He honked his horn. 3. "Shall I fill her up?" asked the attendant. 4. Henry indicated his assent. 5. He watched the fuel gauge as it fluttered from empty to full. 6. The gasoline pump stopped whirring. 7. "Shall I check your oil?" 8. The attendant grinned at him through the windshield. 9. He lifted the hood and, after fussing with the oil stick and radiator cap, he closed the hood. 10. "You don't

need any oil, but your carburetor is leaking and the points should be cleaned." 11. Henry, anxious to get home, waved a five-dollar bill as a signal that he would discuss the question of major repairs at some other time. 12. As soon as he had pocketed the change, he started the engine, stepped on the gas, and soon rounded the corner on two wheels.

▶ EXERCISE 7. Compose ten complete sentences and underline each verb or verb phrase twice and each subject once. Check each object of a verb.

1c Learn to recognize all the parts of speech.[2]

Words are usually classified into eight "parts of speech" (one could just as well say "parts of writing") according to their uses in the sentence.

Names	*Uses in the sentence*
1. VERBS	Indicators of action or state of being
2. NOUNS (substantives)[3]	Subjects, objects, complements
3. PRONOUNS (*I, you, he,* etc.)	Substitutes for nouns
4. ADJECTIVES	Modifiers of nouns
5. ADVERBS	Modifiers of verbs, adjectives, adverbs
6. PREPOSITIONS (*at, for, in,* etc.)	Words used before substantives to relate them to other words in the sentence

---

[2] For definitions of substantives, complements, and the eight parts of speech, see Section 35.

[3] The word *substantive* is a general term to cover nouns and any words (or groups of words) that are used as nouns. Pronouns, the chief noun-substitutes, function just as nouns do and need little separate attention except that some pronouns have different forms for subjects and objects. Other substantives are phrases and clauses, which are treated below under **1d**.

Names	*Uses in the sentence*
7. CONJUNCTIONS (*and, for, but,* etc.)	Connectives
8. INTERJECTIONS (*oh! alas!* etc.)	Expressions of emotion (without grammatical relationship to the rest of the sentence)

Note how the use of each italicized word below determines its part of speech. Many words can be used as several different parts of speech.

The *sail* is torn. [Noun—a substantive]

It is torn. [Pronoun—a substantive, substituting for the noun *sail*]

I *sail* tomorrow. [Verb—indicator of action]

The *sail* hook is used in sailmaking. [Adjective—modifier of the noun *hook*]

He walks *fast.* [Adverb—modifier of the verb *walks*]

He walks *very* fast. [Adverb—modifier of the adverb *fast*]

This is a *fast* train. [Adjective—modifier of the noun *train*]

A *fast* is sometimes a religious observance. [Noun—subject of the verb *is*]

Fast when you should. [Verb—predicate of *you* understood]

For is usually a conjunction or a preposition. [Noun—subject of the verb *is*]

I rested, *for* I was tired. [Conjunction—connecting the subordinate clause *I was tired* with the main clause *I rested*]

I worked *for* him. [Preposition—showing the relation of the substantive *him* to the verb *worked*]

Oh is commonly used as an interjection. [Noun—subject of *is*]

Oh, I do hope you will go. [Interjection—expression of emotion]

Adjectives and **adverbs** are usually placed in the sentence near the words they modify, and in diagrams they are attached to these words. In the following sentences the adjectives are in boldface and the adverbs in italics.

The *exceedingly* **tall** man walked *very rapidly.*

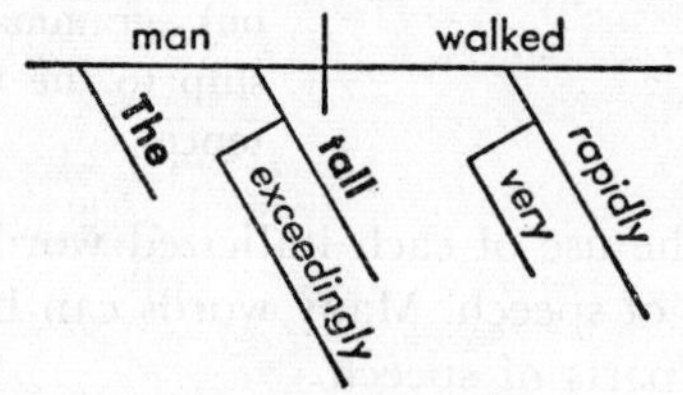

The *predicate adjective,* which helps to complete the meaning of the verb and also to describe the subject, is diagramed thus:

The man is **old.** (He is **an old** man.)

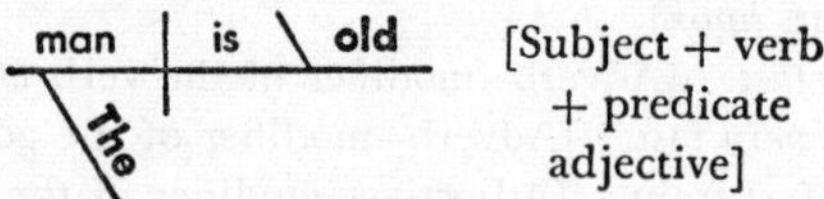

[Subject + verb + predicate adjective]

Some common prepositions are *across, after, as, at, before, between, by, for, from, in, in front of, in regard to, of, on, over, to, together with, under, up, with.* In the following sentence the prepositions are in italics.

The poems *by* Burns express *with* great force his love *of* liberty.

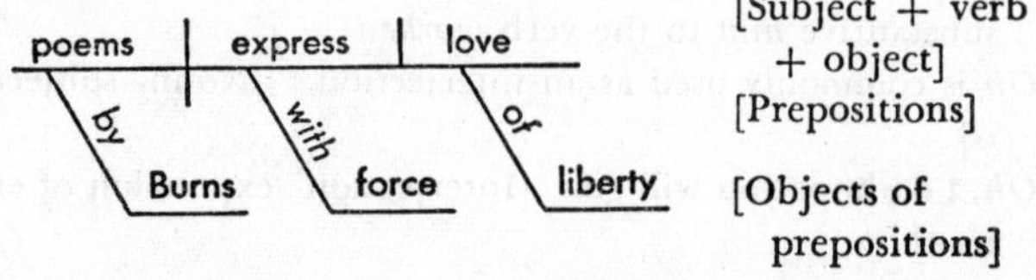

[Subject + verb + object]
[Prepositions]

[Objects of prepositions]

Note: The preposition may follow, rather than precede, the noun or pronoun, and be placed at the end of the sentence.

At times a sentence is most idiomatic or emphatic with the preposition at the end.

UNNATURAL *For* what are you waiting?
NATURAL What are you waiting *for?*
NATURAL We live *by* faith.
NATURAL (*and more emphatic*) Faith is what we live *by.*

Conjunctions fall into two classes: (1) the co-ordinating conjunctions (*and, but, or, nor, for,* and sometimes *so* and *yet*), used to connect words or phrases, or clauses that are of equal rank; and (2) the subordinating conjunctions (such as *after, because, if, since, till, when, where, while*), used to connect subordinate clauses with main clauses. In diagrams, conjunctions are usually placed on broken lines drawn between parts connected by the conjunctions.

When the weather permitted, boys *and* girls played on the lawn *and* walks *and* even in the street.

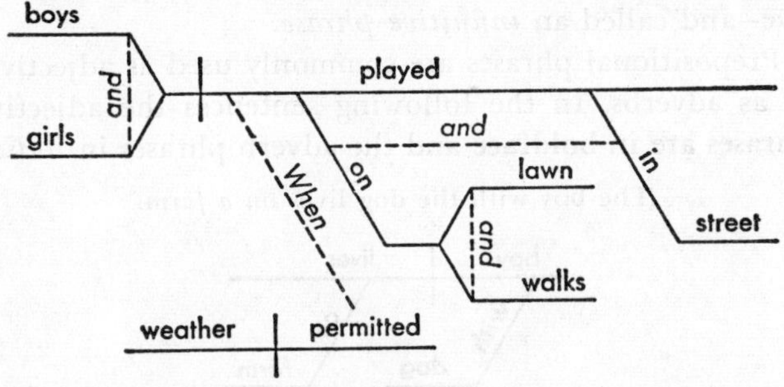

An **interjection** is followed by an exclamation point when the emotion expressed is strong, otherwise by a comma. In diagrams the interjection is set off by itself to indicate its grammatical independence of the rest of the sentence.

Oh, I can hardly believe it.

Oh		[Interjection]
I	can believe	[Subject + predicate]

► EXERCISE 8. Compose and diagram ten sentences to illustrate all the parts of speech.

1d Learn to recognize phrases and clauses.

Phrases

A phrase is a group of related words, without subject and predicate, used as a substantive (called a *noun phrase*) or a modifier (called an *adjective phrase* or an *adverb phrase*). A phrase is connected to the sentence by (1) a preposition—and therefore called a *prepositional phrase,* (2) a participle—and called a *participial phrase,* (3) a gerund—and called a *gerund phrase,* or (4) an infinitive—and called an *infinitive phrase.*

Prepositional phrases are commonly used as adjectives or as adverbs. In the following sentences the adjective phrases are in **boldface** and the adverb phrases in *italics.*

The boy **with the dog** lives *on a farm.*

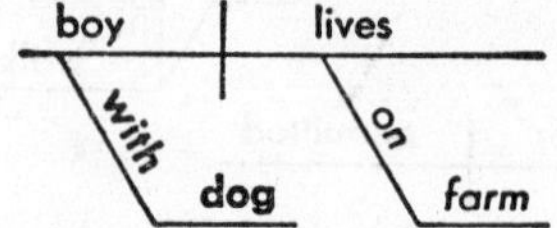

In this sentence *dog* is said to be the object of the preposition *with,* and *farm* the object of the preposition *on.*

Prepositional phrases often come in groups, thus:

The boy **with the dog on a leash** lives *on the farm* **of his grandfather.**

► EXERCISE 9. In Exercise 3, page 4, point out all the prepositional phrases, classifying them as adjective or adverb. (If you prefer, do this exercise by making a simple diagram for each prepositional phrase.)

Verbals. Participles, gerunds, and infinitives are derived from verbs and are therefore called *verbals.* They are much like verbs in that they have different tenses, can take subjects and objects, and can be modified by adverbs. But they are not verbs, for they cannot serve as the heart of a sentence: they cannot make a statement, ask a question, or give a command. Compare the following:

The boy *ate* an apple. Did he *eat* it? *Eat!* [Verbs in complete sentences]

The boy *eating* the apple . . . [Participle (present)—an adjective modifying *boy*]

Eating an apple, the boy . . . [Participle (present)—an adjective modifying *boy*]

The apple *eaten* by the boy . . . [Participle (past)—an adjective modifying *apple*]

Eating an apple is good for the health. [A gerund serving as a noun]

To eat an apple . . . [Infinitive—in a sentence fragment. All verbals are, by themselves, only fragments of sentences.]

Note that the gerund *eating,* like the present participle *eating,* ends in *-ing* and that the two are to be distinguished only by the use in the sentence: the participle is the adjective and the gerund is the noun.

The boy *eating* the apple is happy. [Participle—an adjective]

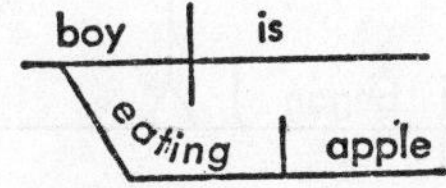

Eating is enjoyable. [Gerund—a noun]

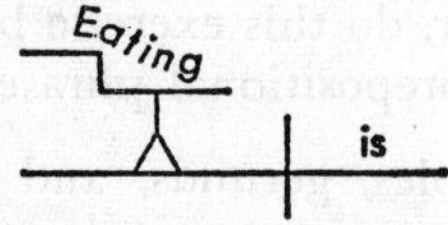

Note that the gerund *eating* in the sentence above is a single word, not part of a phrase. All verbals may be used thus or may be used with related words as part of a verbal phrase.

► EXERCISE 10. In Exercise 3, page 4, point out all participles, showing the noun or pronoun modified by each participle. Point out each gerund in this exercise and show its use in the sentence. (If you prefer, do this exercise by making a simple diagram for each participle and each gerund.)

Infinitive phrases are used as substantives and as modifiers, and may be diagramed thus:

To eat watermelons is enjoyable. [Infinitive phrase used as the subject]

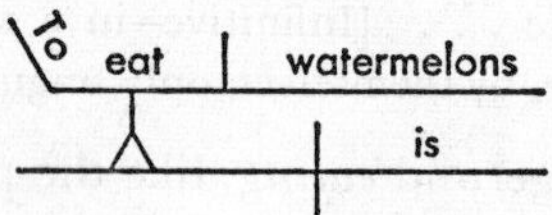

He began *to open the box.* [Infinitive phrase used as the object of the verb]

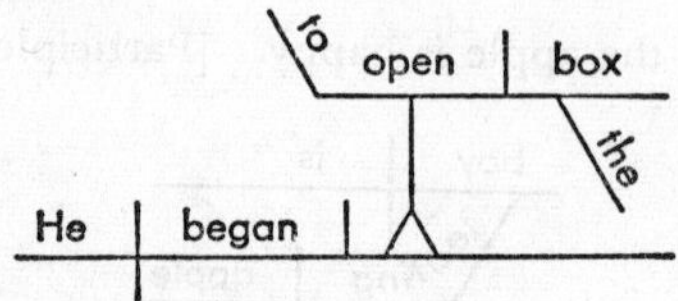

He enlisted *to become an aviator.* [Infinitive phrase used as an adverb]

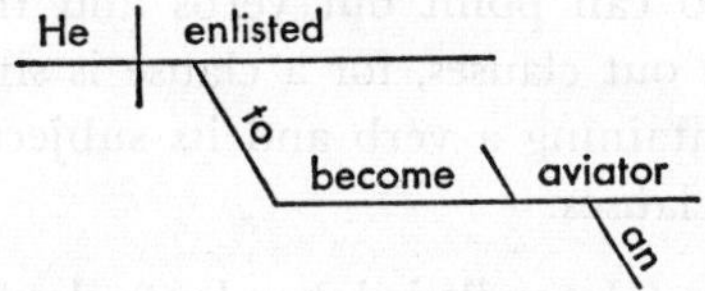

▶ EXERCISE 11. In Exercise 3, page 4, point out each infinitive phrase and show its use in the sentence. (If you prefer, do this exercise by making a simple diagram for each infinitive.)

▶ EXERCISE 12. In the following sentences point out the participial, gerund, and infinitive phrases and show how each is used as an adjective, an adverb, or a noun. (If you prefer, do this exercise by making a simple diagram for each verbal.)

1. Eddie and Cliff had nearly everything they needed to build their diving float. 2. They had spent the whole morning in rolling the eight oil drums from Cliff's back yard down to Eddie's. 3. Now the problem was to find some lumber. 4. Eddie, ransacking his brain, finally thought of a supply. 5. Mr. Kelly had torn down an old barn last fall to build a garage. 6. Going around his paper route only yesterday, Eddie had seen the leftover boards, still piled there and overgrown with weeds. 7. But getting them now, before the Donovan boys found them too, was the important thing. 8. "Get on your feet, boy, and stop wasting our time." 9. Cliff, nudged into movement by a front bicycle wheel, obediently got up. 10. Away they wheeled, pedaling as if the devil himself were after or the Donovans ahead of them. 11. It would be hard to say which might be worse. 12. Coming up to the site, the boys were happy to find the boards safe underneath the weeds.

Clauses

Anyone who can point out verbs and their subjects can also point out clauses, for a clause is simply part of a sentence containing a verb and its subject. There are two kinds of clauses:

1. Subordinate (also called *dependent*) clauses.
2. Main (also called *independent* or *principal*) clauses.

1. SUBORDINATE CLAUSES

A subordinate clause cannot stand alone. It depends upon the rest of the sentence (the main clause) for its meaning, and it is normally introduced by a subordinating conjunction or by a relative pronoun (*who, whom, which, what, that, whoever,* etc.).[4] Subordinate clauses are used as adverbs (called *adverb clauses*), as adjectives (called *adjective clauses*), or as nouns (called *noun clauses*).

EXAMPLES *When it rains,* the work stops. [*When it rains* is a subordinate clause preceding the main clause; it is an adverb clause because it modifies the verb *stops.*]

We can employ all *who will come.* [*Who will come* is a subordinate clause following the main clause; it is an adjective clause because it modifies the pronoun *all.*]

Whoever will come will be welcome. [*Whoever will come* is a noun clause, subject of the verb *will be.*]

---

[4] The subordinate conjunction or the relative pronoun is sometimes omitted: He knew [that] he was going.
We respect men [whom] we can trust.

(a) Adverb Clauses:

Any clause that modifies a verb, adjective, or adverb is an adverb clause. In the following exercise, each subordinate clause modifies the verb of the main clause. Therefore the subordinate clause serves as an adverb and is called an *adverb clause.*

▶ EXERCISE 13. Bracket the adverb clauses in the following sentences.

1. While he was shaving, Mr. Baker began to think of the day ahead. 2. He always began his day's work before he got to the office, though usually it was not this long before. 3. After he got on the train, he nearly always began planning his day. 4. And sometimes he began before the train arrived, if it was a minute or two late. 5. But this morning, as he was shaving the tender place under his chin, details of the day's work began to go clicking through his mind. 6. When he was falling off to sleep last night, he had been reciting these same details. 7. Since he had first been made head accountant, he couldn't remember having brought the job home with him. 8. Whenever anything wasn't as usual with him, he naturally wondered. 9. But suddenly he remembered; while he was rinsing his razor under the hot water, he smiled cheerfully. 10. Today, unless they broke a years-long habit, the state auditors would show up. 11. And because this time he had worked extra carefully to have the books ready for them, he could look forward happily to their coming. 12. Because of all this, after he had finished shaving and while he dressed and listened for his wife's call to breakfast, he was still smiling.

Note the connecting words (subordinating conjunctions) used in these twelve sentences to relate the adverb clauses to the main clauses: *while* (three times), *before* (twice), *though, after* (twice), *if, as, when, since, whenever, unless,* and *because.* Other subordinating conjunctions commonly used to introduce adverb clauses are *although, as soon as, in order that, so that, than, till, until,* and *where.*

▶ EXERCISE 14. Compose five sentences containing adverb clauses introduced by subordinating conjunctions not used in Exercise 13. Bracket each adverb clause.

(*b*) *Adjective Clauses:*

Any clause that modifies a noun or a pronoun is an adjective clause. Adjective clauses are frequently introduced by a relative pronoun such as *who, which,* or *that,* which also serves as the subject of the subordinate clause.

Each subordinate clause in the following exercise modifies a noun or pronoun. In other words, it serves as an adjective. Therefore it is called an *adjective clause.*

▶ EXERCISE 15. Bracket the adjective clauses in the following sentences.

1. William was not at the corner where he usually took the bus. 2. The bus driver, who knew all his regular passengers, commented about it to one of those getting on. 3. The passenger remembered something that William had said one day about beginning his vacation in the middle of the week. 4. That sounded reasonable to the driver, who after all had a schedule to maintain. 5. Edging the big bus back into the traffic that was streaming by, he mentally put William on his "absent with leave" list for the next two weeks.

▶ EXERCISE 16. Compose five sentences containing adjective clauses and bracket the clauses.

(c) Noun Clauses:

Any clause used as a noun is a noun clause.

► EXERCISE 17. Bracket the noun clauses in the following sentences and explain the use of each clause.

1. The repairman said that he would have to take the typewriter in to the shop. 2. What it needed most of all was to be junked. 3. But he remembered that his customer had a sentimental fondness for this old machine. 4. And he had long ago learned that a battered, used-up piece of machinery could be to some people what politics, wife, or religion were to others. 5. What one man loved, other men had to pretend to respect. 6. The repairman wondered whether that saying was in the Bible. 7. He decided that it was.

► EXERCISE 18. Compose five sentences containing noun clauses.

2. MAIN CLAUSES

A main clause (an independent part of a sentence) has both subject and verb and is not introduced by a subordinating conjunction. A main clause does not modify anything. It can stand alone as a simple sentence.

EXAMPLE When it rains, *the work stops.*

The work stops is a main clause; it (1) has both the verb *stops* and its subject *work* and (2) is not introduced by a subordinating conjunction. Therefore it can stand alone as a complete sentence: *The work stops. When it rains* has both a verb and its subject, but it cannot stand alone because it is introduced by the subordinating conjunction *when.*

▶ EXERCISE 19. Point out the main clauses in Exercises 13 and 15.

1e Learn to recognize types of sentences.

Sentences are classified, according to the number and kind of clauses they contain, as (1) simple, (2) compound, (3) complex, or (4) compound-complex.

A **simple sentence** is a sentence made up of one main clause.

EXAMPLE The work stops.

A **compound sentence** is a sentence made up of two (or more) main clauses.

EXAMPLE The work stops, but the tools are kept in readiness.

A **complex sentence** is a sentence made up of one main clause and at least one subordinate clause.

EXAMPLE The work stops when it rains.

A **compound-complex sentence** is a sentence made up of two (or more) main clauses and at least one subordinate clause.

EXAMPLE The work stops when it rains, but the tools are kept in readiness.

▶ EXERCISE 20. In the following compound (or compound-complex) sentences point out the subject and the verb of each main clause and bracket the subordinate clauses. (If you prefer, do this exercise by making simple diagrams as indicated at the top of the next page.)

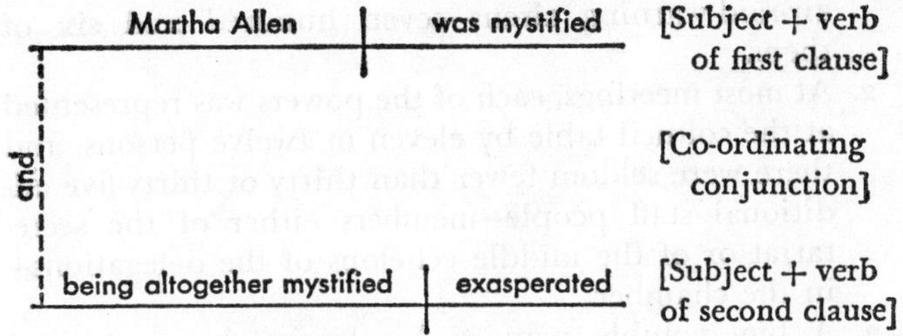

1. Martha Allen was altogether mystified; and being altogether mystified exasperated her. 2. Not two minutes ago she had put down her thimble with her sewing, and now the thimble had utterly disappeared. 3. She turned back to the kitchen to look; but she knew for certain that she wouldn't have worn the thimble to the kitchen. 4. So back again to her sewing she came; and now the scissors were gone! 5. Just then a flapping outside the window made her look out, and there was the children's pet crow flying up to the dead limb in the locust tree. 6. He scrambled about awkwardly in landing, and then Martha saw what was causing his trouble—and her trouble too. 7. Blackie had flown off with her scissors; and that explained the missing thimble as well. 8. In fact, Martha would be much surprised if Blackie wasn't accountable for a great deal of recent mischief; for she remembered now that her thimble and scissors were far from the first of such losses suffered by the household.

► EXERCISE 21. Classify each of the following sentences (selected from the August 6, 1955, issue of *The New Yorker*) as (1) simple, (2) complex, (3) compound, or (4) compound-complex. Be prepared to justify your classification by an analysis of the sentence.

1. Once a month, the local Civil Defense people like to raise a terrible hullabaloo by turning on all their

air-raid-warning sirens—seven hundred and six of them.

2. At most meetings, each of the powers was represented at the council table by eleven or twelve persons, and there were seldom fewer than thirty or thirty-five additional staff people—members either of the secretariat or of the middle echelons of the delegations—in the chamber.
3. A big, voluble man in his forties, he works surrounded by books, filing cabinets, tapes, tape recorders, cameras, pictures, a home developer, a huge record turntable, and an impressive loudspeaker.
4. When I decided to make this trip, I applied to the Guggenheim people for a grant, and got it.
5. While Sprott was blowing away on his harmonica, a friend of his named Harry Rutledge suddenly sprang up and did a buck dance, which is something you never see any more, and the cabin began to go up and down like a ship in a swell.
6. When a big blue convertible with the top up came around the corner at the end of the dusty street, all three looked up.
7. She thought it better not to offer to help with getting supper; instead, she watched and took it easy.
8. His shore home, a local show place, is planted thickly with shrubs that provide excellent covert for a man ducking the public view.
9. He went ahead to explain that his own experience with money was wholly a matter of spending it.
10. Aldrich was at this time twenty-seven himself, but he had an air so paternal, as a result of his precocious achievements, that men twice his age often came to him for advice.
11. Before the dessert arrived, Aldrich had sealed an oral contract with Reed that gave him an excellent salary and a nice percentage of Reed's future gross profits.
12. This summer theatre had been established in 1927

in a structure that had run the gamut of human usefulness.

13. The Provincetown structure also had proved to be injudiciously placed; having been built on a wharf, it departed Provincetown and drifted off to sea one windy afternoon during a high tide.
14. Although Sylvia promises to love him for eternity, she soon goes off and marries somebody else.
15. At the time, it might reasonably have been asked where in the world today the heads of the greatest powers on earth could hope to assemble in privacy and seclusion.

▶ EXERCISE 22. Compose ten sentences and classify each sentence as (1) simple, (2) complex, (3) compound, or (4) compound-complex. Write at least two sentences of each type.

▶ EXERCISE 23. Analyze the following sentences (selected from *Fortune*) according to instructions given for Exercise 21.

1. That the United States could well afford to switch some of its production to defense seemed clear.
2. The pioneering days, whether territorial or industrial, are over; and although many deny that the United States has reached maturity, all agree that it is out of its infancy.
3. There is pleasant talk, as the elections draw nearer, of tax reduction.
4. Surveying the dismal option before the British electorate, the London *Economist* recently called for a new party to represent "the extreme center."
5. The experience in Pittsburgh, where industry finally helped the city back into the light after a century of smoggy darkness, is an example of what can be performed when business puts itself behind a civic effort.

6. Generally speaking, therefore, it can be said that the medical services of the United States, while adequate, or nearly so, in certain wealthy areas of the country, fall in other areas far below any standard that an American could conscientiously defend.
7. The test of the dynamic businessman is how much he is doing with what he has to work with.
8. The talent for self-examination is another intangible asset.
9. Like his perfumes, he is a volatile essence in a small, stylish package.
10. As the motorist emerges from the Holland Tunnel, Jersey City proudly puts its worst foot forward.
11. There is nothing particularly sententious to say about this city street, except that it is lacking in the amenities.
12. Looking backward through an autumn haze of imperfect memory, he catches seductive glimpses of a world that never was, a world that nonetheless he wants desperately to return.
13. Conservatism may be defined as the system of thought and habit opposed to innovation in the institutions and mores of our established society.
14. A true conservative must have "a sound sense for the pace of historical change."
15. Looked at from the long view of history, the American capitalist, however "sound" his views on politics, family, or religion, has been the most marvelous agent of social change the world has ever known.

► EXERCISE 24. Compose ten varied sentences and analyze them as directed by the instructor.

► EXERCISE 25. Analyze the following sentences of the Gettysburg Address as directed by the instructor.

1. Fourscore and seven years ago our fathers brought forth on this continent a new nation, conceived in

liberty, and dedicated to the proposition that all men are created equal.

2. Now we are engaged in a great civil war, testing whether that nation, or any nation so conceived and so dedicated, can long endure.
3. We are met on a great battlefield of that war.
4. We have come to dedicate a portion of that field as a final resting place for those who here gave their lives that that nation might live.
5. It is altogether fitting and proper that we should do this.
6. But in a larger sense we cannot dedicate, we cannot consecrate, we cannot hallow this ground.
7. The brave men, living and dead, who struggled here, have consecrated it far above our power to add or detract.
8. The world will little note, nor long remember, what we say here; but it can never forget what they did here.
9. It is for us, the living, rather to be dedicated here to the unfinished work which they who fought here have thus far so nobly advanced.
10. It is rather for us to be here dedicated to the great task remaining before us, that from these honored dead we take increased devotion to that cause for which they gave the last full measure of devotion; that we here highly resolve that these dead shall not have died in vain; that this nation, under God, shall have a new birth of freedom, and that government of the people, by the people, for the people shall not perish from the earth.

2 frag

▶ Sentence Fragment

2

Do not carelessly write a sentence fragment—a phrase or a subordinate clause—as if it were a complete sentence.

Caution: Can you distinguish between phrases and clauses, and between main and subordinate clauses? Until you can do so, you are likely to write careless sentence fragments. You may need to master the fundamentals of the sentence treated in Section **1**, **Sentence Sense,** especially **1d**, before you can understand Section **2**.

A sentence fragment—a phrase or a subordinate clause—should not be set off as if it were a complete sentence. The fragment should be (1) included in the sentence, that is, attached to the main clause, or (2) rewritten to form a sentence by itself.

WRONG He registered for the summer session. Hoping thus to graduate ahead of his class. [We have here one sentence and one fragment, a participial phrase.]

RIGHT He registered for the summer session, hoping thus to graduate ahead of his class. [Participial phrase included in the sentence]

RIGHT He registered for the summer session. By this means he hoped to graduate ahead of his class. [Participial phrase made into a sentence]

WRONG He registered for the summer session. Because he hoped thus to graduate ahead of his class. [We have here one sentence and one fragment, a subordinate clause.]

RIGHT He registered for the summer session because he hoped thus to graduate ahead of his class. [Subordinate clause included in the sentence]

RIGHT By registering for the summer session, he hoped to graduate ahead of his class.

RIGHT He registered for the summer session. By this means he hoped to graduate ahead of his class. [Subordinate clause made into a sentence]

A TEST FOR SENTENCE COMPLETENESS

The sentence fragment is characterized by its incompleteness of meaning. This incompleteness is usually obvious; however, it may be tested (1) by searching for the verb and its subject and (2) by determining whether this verb and subject are introduced by a subordinating conjunction. If the supposed sentence does not have a verb and its subject, it may be identified at once as a phrase. *Hoping thus to graduate ahead of his class,* for example, has no verb. *Hoping* is a participle and *to graduate* is an infinitive, but there is no verb. Even when both verb and subject are present, they may be introduced by a subordinating conjunction and thus constitute a subordinate clause. *Because he hoped to graduate ahead of his class* has the verb *hoped* and the subject *he.* But since these words are introduced by the subordinating conjunction *because,* the group of words is a subordinate clause—still a sentence fragment.

Make a diagram, or at least form a mental picture, of the core of each sentence: its subject + its verb (predicate). Then if you find that subject and verb are not introduced by a subordinating conjunction such as *because, since, if,* or *when,* you may be reasonably sure that the sentence is grammatically complete. (For logical completeness see Section 23c.)

He registered for the summer session.

He | registered [Subject + verb]

The diagram shows subject and verb, and there is no subordinating conjunction: the sentence is complete.

2a Do not carelessly write a phrase (participial, prepositional, or infinitive) as a complete sentence.

WRONG I made little progress. *Finally giving up all my efforts.* [Participial phrase]

RIGHT I made so little progress that I finally gave up all my efforts. [Fragment included with the sentence]

RIGHT I made little progress. Finally I gave up all my efforts. [Fragment made into a sentence]

WRONG Soon I began to work for the company. *First in the rock pit and later on the highway.* [Prepositional phrases]

RIGHT Soon I began to work for the company, first in the rock pit and later on the highway. [Fragment included with the sentence]

WRONG He will have an opportunity to visit his home town. *And to talk with many of his old friends.* [Infinitive phrase]

RIGHT He will have an opportunity to visit his home town and to talk with many of his old friends. [Fragment included with the sentence]

2b Do not carelessly write a subordinate clause as a complete sentence.

WRONG A railway control board should be constructed with care. *Because from this board trains are moved through a system of tracks and switches.* [Subordinate clause]

RIGHT A railway control board should be constructed with care, because from this board trains are moved through a system of tracks and switches. [Fragment included with the sentence]

WRONG I had some definite ideas about college. *Although I had never before been on a college campus.* [Subordinate clause]

RIGHT I had some definite ideas about college although I had never before been on a college campus. [Fragment included with the sentence]

2c Do not carelessly write as a complete sentence any other fragment, such as an appositive or a member of a compound predicate.

WRONG My father was born in Cartersville. *A little country town where everyone knows everyone else.* [Appositive]

RIGHT My father was born in Cartersville, a little country town where everyone knows everyone else.

WRONG At school Paul ran into many new problems. *Such as handling his pocket money and choosing his friends.* [Appositive]

RIGHT At school Paul ran into many new problems, such as handling his pocket money and choosing his friends.

WRONG William was elected president of his class. *And was made a member of the National Honor Society.* [Detached member of a compound predicate]

RIGHT William was elected president of his class and was made a member of the National Honor Society.

Note: At times sentences may be grammatically incomplete and yet clear because omitted words can be readily supplied by the reader. Such elliptical expressions occur in commands, in exclamations, and in questions and answers, especially in dialogue. But these expressions are not real fragments since the completion is unmistakably implied.

COMMANDS Come nearer. [You come nearer.]
Open the door. [You open the door.]
Please enter. [You will please enter.]

EXCLAMATIONS Too bad! [That is too bad!]
What a pity! [What a pity it is!]

QUESTIONS AND ANSWERS Why did he go? Because his friends were going. [He went because his friends were going.]
"Will you play with me? A lot?" ["Will you play with me a lot?"]
"Perhaps." ["Perhaps I will."]

Real fragments are sometimes used intentionally by professional writers, especially in fiction. In the following passages, from Aldous Huxley,[1] the intentional fragments are in italics.

"He wasn't a gorilla. *Just the cutest little baboon.* And the garbage wasn't garbage. It was ice cream. *A genuine strawberry and fish-guts sundae."*

From corned beef hash Pamela turned to the latest starlet. *Five feet five and a half. One hundred and seventeen pounds.*

[1] "Voices," *Atlantic Monthly*, July, 1955, pp. 35, 42.

But such fragments are employed consciously, for rhetorical effect, by experienced writers. And besides, such fragments are not common in expository writing emphasized in college. Students are usually advised to learn the fundamentals of English composition and the accepted style of expository writing before permitting themselves the liberties taken by experienced craftsmen.

► EXERCISES ON THE SENTENCE FRAGMENT

A. Test each of the following for sentence completeness as suggested on pages 29-30. As an aid in your analysis underline each verb (*not* verbal) in a main clause twice and its subject once, and bracket each subordinate clause. Write *C* after each numbered item which contains no fragment. Attach each fragment to an existing sentence or make it into an independent sentence.

1. There were no eclipses visible in England in 1604 and 1606. Although there were three in 1605.
2. The festival beginning on the twentieth of June and continuing through the month of July.
3. It was all I could do to keep my mouth shut. Finally I did speak out.
4. Since the party was made up of twelve men, nine of whom had been members of the previous year's expedition.
5. The hydraulic lift raises the plows out of the ground. And lowers them again.
6. I had a feeling that some sinister spirit of evil brooded over the place. A feeling that I could not analyze. But that was impossible to disregard or reason away.
7. Our stay at the Halcombs' cottage was altogether delightful. Except for the mosquitoes, which nothing seemed to discourage.

8. To watch Dempsey in the ring was to watch a perfectly engineered machine operated with exact precision.
9. To anyone who knew him in 1840, it would have seemed ridiculous beyond belief. To predict that one day this rawboned frontier lawyer would be President of the United States.
10. The time when you are young and enthusiastic. That's when you should work. Leave dreams to old men.
11. This was the nightmare that haunted her, the dread of the inevitable surrender.
12. I am often told to do things I don't like. Such as getting out of bed.
13. He was still angry with me. His eyes glaring fiercely.
14. He killed three ducks with one shot. Against the law of averages but possible.
15. She dressed exactly like the Hollywood starlets. Since she wanted to become one of them herself.

B. Identify each fragment; determine whether it falls under the rule for 2a, 2b, or 2c; then make the appropriate correction. Write *C* in place of each numbered item which contains no fragment.

1. I knew that he was asking for trouble. As soon as I heard of his buying that motorcycle.
2. He let me believe that I had first chance at the job. But without definitely committing himself.
3. Unless I can get a lower berth, I prefer to go by coach.
4. By noon we already had our bag limit. More birds than we had ever seen during the first half of the season.
5. That lion was in just about as bad a spot as a lion can be in. Until his faithful little friend the mouse came along and found him there.

6. Andy was here just a minute ago. You may find him in the poolroom next door.
7. There is my pride, my joy, and my dependable money-maker. That herd of fat black Anguses.
8. At least he stays sober on the job. Which is more than I can say for the last agent we had here.
9. Early in life he decided upon a simple philosophy. From which grew all his subsequent opinions.
10. Sheriff Nolan took no deputy along with him. Believing that he could handle the prisoner easily enough alone.
11. Let's take a ten-minute break. But see that you don't make it twenty.
12. Wilson is one of the most capable men we have. Besides being one of the most even-tempered.
13. The painter asked us to be careful about touching the walls. Since it would take all night for the paint to harden.
14. Doc Potter is exactly what you said he would be. A thoroughly profane and thoroughly entertaining old reprobate.
15. He picked up the revolver by thrusting a pencil into its muzzle. In order to avoid smearing any prints which might be on it.

C. Follow directions given under A or B, or under both A and B, as your instructor may direct. In writing your revision, omit the numbers.

1. Very late in *The Merry Wives of Windsor,* Shakespeare introduces an incident which is altogether extraneous to either of the plot lines in the play. 2. And which advances the action in no way whatsoever. 3. Bardolph in a very brief scene with the Host announces that "the Germans" desire three of the Host's horses. 4. So that they may go to meet "the Duke," who is to be at court on the next day. 5. The Host seems to know

so little of these Germans that he must ask if they speak English. 6. A highly improbable ignorance on his part, for in his next lines he states that they have been already a week at his tavern. 7. But he lets them have the horses. 8. Insisting, however, that they must pay for them. 9. Two scenes later Bardolph returns to the tavern with the report that the villainous Germans have handled him roughly on the road. 10. Thrown him into a puddle, and run off with the horses. 11. Immediately on his heels, in come first Sir Hugh and then Dr. Caius. 12. With rumors confirming Bardolph's assurance of the evil character of the Germans. 13. So that the Host is at last alarmed. 14. He is convinced now that the Germans have indeed cozened him of a week's board bill. 15. And stolen his horses in the bargain.

[See other exercises on sentence fragments at the end of Section 3.]

▶ Comma Splice and Fused Sentence

3

Do not carelessly link two main clauses with only a comma between them (comma splice), or, worse, without any punctuation (fused sentence).

Caution: If you cannot recognize main clauses, study Section 1, **Sentence Sense,** especially **1d,** before trying to apply the following instructions to your writing.

COMMA SPLICE The current was swift, he could not swim to shore. [Two main clauses linked only by a comma]

FUSED SENTENCE The current was swift he could not swim to shore. [Omission of the comma makes an even worse error than the comma splice.]

Note: The fused sentence is corrected in exactly the same way as the comma splice. Hence all the methods of correction given below apply equally to comma splices and fused sentences.

3a Usually the comma splice is best corrected by some method of subordination.[1]

WRONG The current was swift, he could not swim to shore. [Comma splice]

RIGHT Since the current was swift, he could not swim to

[1] See also Section 24, **Subordination.**

shore. [First main clause changed to a subordinate clause]

RIGHT The current was so swift that he could not swim to shore. [Second main clause changed to a subordinate clause]

RIGHT Because of the swift current he could not swim to shore. [First main clause changed to a prepositional phrase]

RIGHT The swiftness of the current prevented his swimming to shore. [The two main clauses changed to one simple sentence]

3b Sometimes the comma splice is best corrected by some method of co-ordination.

Co-ordination is preferable when the writer wishes to give equal weight to the ideas in the two main clauses. If these ideas are sufficiently independent, the clauses may be made into separate sentences.

WRONG The hunting instinct in man is deep, it is universal. [Comma splice]

RIGHT The hunting instinct in man is deep. It is universal. [Each main clause made into a sentence]

—NEW YORK TIMES MAGAZINE

WRONG Hiking is great fun, you should try it. [Comma splice]

RIGHT Hiking is great fun. You should try it. [Each main clause made into a sentence]

If the ideas in the main clauses are closely related, the clauses may be separated (1) by a semicolon instead of a comma or (2) by a comma + a co-ordinate conjunction (*and, but, or, nor,* or *for*).

WRONG He dared not retract, money and fame were at stake. [Comma splice]

RIGHT He dared not retract; money and fame were at stake. [Main clauses separated by a semicolon]
—SATURDAY REVIEW OF LITERATURE

WRONG I thought about that, I found the answer. [Comma splice]

RIGHT I thought about that, and I found the answer. [Main clauses separated by a comma + *and*]
—ATLANTIC MONTHLY

WRONG He kept no old friends, he made lots of shiny new friends. [Comma splice]

RIGHT He kept no old friends, but he made lots of shiny new friends. [Main clauses separated by a comma + *but*]
—ATLANTIC MONTHLY

3c *Caution:* Do not let a conjunctive adverb, a transitional or a parenthetical expression, or a divided quotation trick you into making a comma splice.

When a conjunctive adverb (such as *accordingly, also, anyhow, besides, consequently, furthermore, hence, however, indeed, instead, likewise, moreover, nevertheless, still, then, therefore, thus*) or a transitional expression (such as *for example, in fact, namely, on the contrary, on the other hand, that is*) is used to connect main clauses, a semicolon is commonly used between the clauses.

WRONG The two teams line up for the kickoff, then comes the thrill. [Comma splice]

RIGHT The two teams line up for the kickoff; then comes the thrill. [Semicolon used instead of comma]

RIGHT The two teams line up for the kickoff, and then comes the thrill. [Co-ordinating conjunction inserted after the comma]

WRONG The story was not true, however, it was interesting. [Comma splice]

RIGHT The story was not true; however, it was interesting. [Semicolon used instead of comma]

RIGHT The story was not true, but it was interesting. [Co-ordinating conjunction substituted]

WRONG Bears in the park are very tame, in fact, they will eat food from one's hands. [Comma splice]

RIGHT Bears in the park are very tame; in fact, they will eat food from one's hands. [Semicolon used]

Divided Quotations:

WRONG "Your answer is wrong," he said, "correct it."

RIGHT "Your answer is wrong," he said. "Correct it."

WRONG "What are you looking for?" she asked, "may I help you?"

RIGHT "What are you looking for?" she asked. "May I help you?"

Exceptions: Short co-ordinate clauses in series, parallel in form and unified in thought, may be separated by commas:

RIGHT I came, I saw, I conquered.

ALSO RIGHT I came; I saw; I conquered.

The comma is also used to separate a statement from the echo question and sometimes to set off a main clause when subordination is implied:

You can come, can't you? [Statement echoed by question]

I must confess, [that] I did not want to go. [Implied subordination of the second clause]

Main clauses separated only by commas are fairly common in some informal types of writing. Occasionally examples are found in more formal writing, chiefly when there is a balance or contrast between the clauses.

But this was better, this was much more satisfying.
—ALDOUS HUXLEY

The English of those days did not paint broadly, they filled in with deft touches. —BONAMY DOBRÉE

They were unprepared, their people were divided and demoralized. —WALTER LIPPMANN

But the immature writer is much more likely to produce an ordinary comma splice than an effective sentence of this sort. He will do well to make sure that main clauses in his sentences are separated (1) by a comma + a co-ordinate conjunction or (2) by a semicolon.

► EXERCISES ON THE COMMA SPLICE

A. Determine which of the following sentences contain comma splices. As an aid to your analysis (1) underline each verb of a main clause twice and its subject once, (2) bracket each subordinate clause, and (3) place an inverted caret (v) between main clauses, drawing a wavy line under the co-ordinating conjunction (if any) that connects the main clauses. Write *C* after each sentence that needs no revision. Correct each comma splice in the most appropriate way.

1. Some athletes strive for mere delight in competition, Jim Thorpe was one of these.
2. There used to be alligators in that lake, I remember seeing them when I was a boy.
3. "This is the way you do it," he explained, "you step on the clutch and the brake and press the starter."
4. We were lucky in our choice of a day for the trip, though it had been raining at bedtime, the weather cleared during the night.
5. There was no coffee, no bacon, no bread, and the milk had begun to sour, therefore my breakfast consisted of marmalade and four limp crackers.

6. Walt calls that place of his a "farm," "weed patch" would describe it better.
7. Jay was the fastest first baseman I ever saw, if his batting eye had been a little better, he could have gone all the way up.
8. The hut was built to house eight men, nevertheless, there were sixteen in it when I arrived.
9. The large table is always reserved for Mr. Mansfield and his guests, but his secretary has just phoned that he will not be able to come today.
10. I wouldn't carry that gun into the house loaded, son, you're not going to shoot anybody in there, are you?
11. Jefferson's political views became more and more democratic, but his opponents did not cease reminding him of his wealth.
12. Typhus used to kill far more soldiers than warfare itself did, however, this disease is little heard of now.
13. Washington Irving was one of the first American writers to exploit local legends, by writing "Rip Van Winkle," he helped to start America's folklore tradition.
14. To earn money by baby-sitting, a co-ed must know the rudiments of domestic science, for example, she should know how to warm a bottle and burp the baby.
15. Florida depends upon tourists for much of its income, visitors spend many millions at hotels, restaurants, race tracks, and "palaces" of entertainment.

B. Revise each comma splice (or fused sentence) by some method of subordination. Write *C* in place of any sentence that needs no revision.

1. Frantically I wound and jerked the starting cord a tow of gravel barges was bearing directly down upon me.

2. Sheila has her mind made up, nothing you can say will change it.
3. We have enough bricks we can build a barbecue pit.
4. I spoke of the Rufus Kane matter to Chief Kelly, he recalled the case quite clearly.
5. The plaster hardens rapidly it should not be mixed in large quantities.
6. When you come to a red brick church across from a filling station, turn left and go exactly one block.
7. There is a roadside market on the Maryville highway you can buy all the berries you want there.
8. At farrowing, her pigs weighed slightly over three pounds apiece, this is a little above average weight.
9. We do not plan to come back in the fall, therefore we are giving up our apartment.
10. One man was digging at the bottom of the well, the other stayed at the top to haul up the loose dirt.

C. Revise each comma splice (or fused sentence) by the method that seems most appropriate. Be ready to explain and justify the method used. Write *C* in place of any sentence that needs no revision. (Some students may find it helpful to analyze the sentences as directed in Exercise A.)

1. Let me know at least a week before you expect to be here, I will need that long to get your cabin ready.
2. You must first preheat your oven then you put your rolls in to bake.
3. The winters here are quite mild, however I cannot say the same for the summers.
4. I could have sworn I had an extra pair of shoelaces in this drawer, I surely can't find them now.
5. I have never been able to understand why there is no traffic light on this corner.
6. "Don't unsaddle him," George called from the door-

way, "I'll want to ride down after the mail in a minute or two."

7. The Santa Gertrudis is an American breed of cattle, it was developed to combine the heat-resistance of the Brahma with the meat-producing qualities of the Shorthorn.
8. In 1728 William Byrd was a member of a party of surveyors, they were charged with the task of determining the proper boundary between Virginia and North Carolina.
9. The bay was far too rough to venture upon, therefore we decided to walk around by land.
10. The Red Cross opened its blood bank to the survivors, as a result, many lives were saved.

D. Copy from a book or magazine (1) five sentences in which main clauses are separated by a semicolon and (2) five sentences in which main clauses are separated by a comma + a co-ordinating conjunction.

▶ EXERCISES ON THE SENTENCE FRAGMENT AND COMMA SPLICE

E. Test the following for sentence fragments and comma splices (or fused sentences) and make appropriate corrections. Write *C* in place of any numbered item that needs no revision.

1. International misunderstanding is a great calamity, however there is advantage to those who fish in troubled waters.
2. There is probably no more efficient fund-raising device in the United States than a clear-eyed, neatly uniformed Boy Scout who is patriotically seeking adult help in doing his daily good turn.
3. It was the kind of day to inspire an adventure a warm wind blew across the lake.

4. Dine at the Campus Cookery. Where the beans taste like caviar.
5. A lifeboat wallowed alongside the raft, grappled for the lifeboat, and finally made it fast.
6. A few hundred feet out in the lake, drifting away in the offshore wind, was a derelict canoe.
7. The teacher's friendliness impressed me. Nothing like that having been expected.
8. Night and cold closed down on the field, thus we could search no longer.
9. On top of the hill is a windmill, after you pass that, you will see the town in the valley below.
10. The peasants remember many periods of inflation, therefore they prefer to keep their produce rather than exchange it for paper currency.
11. "You will soon be needed," he said, "how long will you be gone?"
12. Edgar Allan Poe attended West Point, there he was not a success.
13. Just to stand up in the face of life's problems. That takes courage.
14. Certainly there is no reason for our becoming panicky, on the other hand, there is no reason for our failing to take due precautions.

F. Follow directions given under E.

1. Under the law the Speaker of the House is next to the Vice-President in line of succession he precedes the Secretary of State.
2. The silver iodide smoke ascends into the clouds, this causes condensation, and thus artificial rainfall is produced.
3. Hour after hour Coast Guard boats methodically zigzagged over the area, sweeping the water with searchlights.

4. Learn to recognize the need for good manners philosophers say that good manners are the outward signs of good morals.
5. Arizona is blessed with a fine climate, therefore many sanatoria are located there.
6. Strange-sounding names and faraway places. Travel brings you to them.
7. Some students claim that Walt Whitman is the best American poet, their opinion of his works, however, is far too favorable, according to the admirers of Lowell, Longfellow, Whittier, and Emily Dickinson.
8. Some of the most beautiful scenery in Canada is in the Maritime Provinces. The forests, the rivers, and the sea in combination.
9. There is some pessimism about our steel supply, since the resources of the Mesabi Range have been depleted, there is no comparable source of iron ore in the United States.
10. I hope to learn English in one year. Since I am now living with people who speak the language.
11. "Don't sell your freshman textbooks," Jim advised, "they will be helpful throughout the rest of your college course."
12. I came here for two reasons. To see you and to be seen by you.

G. Rewrite the paragraph, correcting each fragment and comma splice by the method that seems most suitable. Be ready to explain and justify the method used. (Not all the sentences in the exercise are faulty ones.) In making the revision, omit the numbers.

1. When Boyd and Nancy were preparing to move to Pennsylvania. 2. Nancy asked me if I knew anybody who would want a cigar box full of cat bones. 3. These were the dismantled parts of a cat skeleton. 4. Which she had used when teaching a science course in the

local school. 5. I told her that I would be delighted to have them. 6. Feeling quite sure that the day would come when I should find them useful. 7. In this way one former cat, retired from teaching, found a home with me, then I went on my vacation, and while I was away, my landlady decided to refinish the floor of my room. 8. I suppose I should count it among my blessings. 9. That I wasn't around to hear what she had to say about the miscellaneous gear I have accumulated during my residence here. 10. But she was very kind about it all. 11. And had nothing to say when I came back. 12. Except that she hoped I liked the new floor. 13. The floor was quite elegant, her rearrangement of my goods and chattels is a puzzle that I haven't yet altogether untangled. 14. I am still finding, in all sorts of odd places, things that I had long ago forgotten. 15. But search as I will, I cannot find those cat bones, I wish I had the nerve to ask what she did with them.

H. Follow directions given under G.

1. At half-past nine that morning I went out and got into the car. 2. Intending to drive across town to Fielding's Garden Shop to see about some tulip bulbs I had ordered. 3. The traffic had just cleared. 4. Letting me turn left at the main intersection, then I first heard the siren. 5. It made me think of an air raid. 6. And of a bomb that might drop right on top of me. 7. A bomb couldn't have done any more to me than that fire truck did. 8. Does anybody want to buy the gear-shift knob of what was once an automobile? 9. I'll ask the nurse to get it, the ambulance driver had to take it away from me. 10. When he hauled me in here. 11. It seems that I thought it was a tulip bulb. 12. One that I had to plant.

▸ Adjectives and Adverbs

4

Distinguish between adjectives and adverbs and use the appropriate forms.

Adjectives and adverbs modify—that is, they make clearer and more specific—the meaning of other words. Adjectives modify nouns; adverbs modify chiefly verbs, adjectives, and other adverbs. In the following sentences the adjectives are in **boldface** and the adverbs are in *italics.*

Boys like toys. [No modifiers]
Young boys *usually* like **colored** toys.
Very **young** boys *almost always* like *brightly* **colored** toys.

FORMS OF ADJECTIVES AND ADVERBS

A good dictionary shows the appropriate form for adjective or adverb, but only the use to which the word is put in the sentence determines whether the adjective or the adverb form is required. The dictionary shows, for example, that the form *beautiful* is used only as an adjective and *beautifully* only as an adverb: The **beautiful** woman sang *beautifully.* In this sentence *beautiful* is the required form as modifier of the noun *woman,* and *beautifully* is the required form as modifier of the verb *sang.*

Although the *-ly* ending is the usual sign for the adverb, the dictionary shows that a few words in *-ly* (such as *manly, saintly, womanly*) are adjectives. A few others in *-ly* (such as *only, early, cowardly*) may be either adjectives or adverbs, and the same is true for a considerable number of common words not ending in *-ly* (such as *far, fast, late, little, near, right, straight, well*).

Adjective	*Adverb*
The early bird gets the worm.	He rose *early* to go to work.
He came on a late train.	He came *late*.
I have little energy.	He was a *little* ambitious.
He is well. He feels well.	He works *well*. He plays *well*.

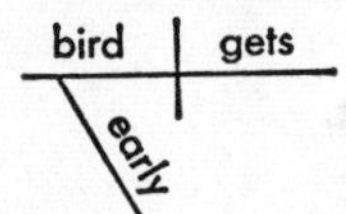

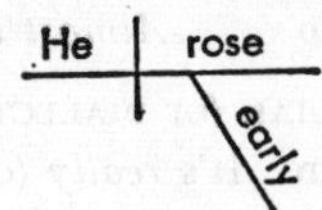

► EXERCISE 1. Compose sentences to illustrate each of the following words (1) as an adjective and (2) as an adverb: *only, cowardly, far, fast, near, right, straight*.

Most adjectives and adverbs have distinct forms which must be used with care.

4a Use the adverb form for modifiers of verbs, adjectives, and other adverbs.

(1) Modifiers of verbs

WRONG His clothes fit him *perfect*. [The adjective *perfect* cannot modify the verb *fit*.]

RIGHT His clothes fit him *perfectly*.

WRONG One can drown in a pool as *easy* as in a lake. [The adjective *easy* cannot modify the verb *can drown*.]

RIGHT One can drown in a pool as *easily* as in a lake.

WRONG He ran *good* for the first half mile. [The adjective *good* cannot modify the verb *ran.*]

RIGHT He ran *well* for the first half mile.

(2) Modifiers of adjectives

WRONG The farmer has a *reasonable* secure future. [The adjective *reasonable* cannot modify the adjective *secure.*]

RIGHT The farmer has a *reasonably* secure future.

WRONG The plane was a *special* built fighter.

RIGHT The plane was a *specially* built fighter.

COLLOQUIAL[1] *Most* all men

STANDARD *Almost* all men

COLLOQUIAL (or DIALECTAL) It's *real* hot.

STANDARD It's *really* (or *very*) hot.

(3) Modifiers of adverbs

COLLOQUIAL She was *most* always late.

STANDARD She was *almost* always late. [*Almost* is the regular adverb.]

4b As a rule use the adjective form after *is, was, seems, becomes,* and the verbs pertaining to the senses (*feel, look, smell, sound, taste*).

RIGHT The man is *old.* [*Old* is an adjective modifying *man:* The man is an *old* man.]

RIGHT The girl was *excited.* [An *excited* girl]

RIGHT The town seems *deserted.* [A *deserted* town]

RIGHT The Indian became *hostile.* [A *hostile* Indian]

---

[1] For the distinction between colloquial and standard usage see Section 19.

RIGHT The boy felt *lonesome.* [A *lonesome* boy]
RIGHT The flower smells *sweet.* [A *sweet* flower]
RIGHT The milk tastes *sour.* [The *sour* milk]
RIGHT The woman looked *angry.* [An *angry* woman]
RIGHT I feel *well.* [*Well,* the form for either adjective or adverb, is here the adjective meaning "not sick." The adjective *good* should not be used with this meaning.]

Exception: The modifier is an adverb when it refers to the action of the verb.

RIGHT The blind beggar felt *cautiously* along the wall. [The adverb *cautiously* qualifies the verb *felt.*]
RIGHT The woman looked *angrily* at him. [The adverb *angrily* qualifies the verb *looked.*]

Note: A modifier following a verb and its direct object is an adjective when it refers to the object rather than to the action of the verb.

RIGHT Dig the hole *deep.* [*Deep* is an adjective: *deep* hole.]
RIGHT The hole was dug *deep.* [*Deep* hole]
RIGHT Dig *deeply* into the ground. [*Deeply* is an adverb modifying the verb *dig.*]

4c Standard English tends to prefer the adverb in -ly.

Some adverbs have a form identical with that of the adjective (*loud, quick, slow*) and also another form in *-ly* (*loudly, quickly, slowly*). For such adverbs, standard English generally prefers the form in *-ly.* The shorter form is very common in commands: "Drive slow," "Move quick," "Speak loud."

STANDARD He shouted as *loudly* as he could.
The sword hung *loosely* at his side.

4d Use the appropriate forms for the comparative and the superlative.

In general the shorter adjectives (and a few adverbs) form the comparative degree by adding *-er* and the superlative by adding *-est;* the longer adjectives and most adverbs form the comparative by the use of *more* (*less*) and the superlative by the use of *most* (*least*). Some adjectives, such as *good* and *bad,* and some adverbs, such as *well* and *badly,* have an irregular comparison. But these are among our common words and are seldom confused.

	Positive	*Comparative*	*Superlative*
ADJECTIVES	warm	warmer	warmest
	tired	more tired	most tired
	good	better	best
	bad	worse	worst
ADVERBS	warmly	more warmly	most warmly
	well	better	best
	badly	worse	worst

(1) Use the comparative degree for two persons or things.

RIGHT Today is *warmer* than yesterday.

RIGHT James was the *taller* of the two boys. [The superlative is occasionally used in such sentences, especially in informal speaking and writing.]

(2) Use the superlative degree for three or more persons or things.

RIGHT Today is the *warmest* day of the year.

RIGHT William was the *tallest* of the three boys.

Usage tends to ignore the fact that such adjectives as *round, square, perfect,* and *unique* express a complete thing or idea and are therefore logically incapable of comparison.

ILLOGICAL This hoop is *rounder* than that.

LOGICAL This hoop is *more nearly round* than that. [Preferred by some careful writers]

4e Avoid any awkward or ambiguous use of a noun form as an adjective.

Although many noun forms (*boat* race, *show* business, *opera* tickets, etc.) are used effectively, especially when no appropriate adjective is available, such forms should be avoided when they are either awkward or ambiguous.

AWKWARD The man sometimes forgets his *gentleman* habits.

BETTER The man sometimes forgets his *gentlemanly* habits. [The regular adjective form substituted]

AMBIGUOUS Recently I was involved in a *race* argument.

BETTER Recently I was involved in an argument *concerning race* (or *about racing*).

► EXERCISES ON ADJECTIVES AND ADVERBS

A. In the following sentences choose the standard form of the modifier within parentheses. Justify your choice by a simple diagram or by analysis of the sentence. Use your dictionary to distinguish between standard and informal usage.

1. The plans, (beautiful, beautifully) drawn, were presented in all their (careful, carefully) elaborated detail.
2. The (older, oldest) of the two brothers had the (brighter, brightest) red hair, but the (smaller, smallest) one (easy, easily) outnumbered him in freckles.

3. We sold the house at a (considerable, considerably) higher price than we had paid for it.
4. His (nightmare, nightmarish) tales made me feel (glum, glumly).
5. Now you pull (steady, steadily) on the knob until I lock the door.
6. (Most, almost) all students fall short of their possibilities; I (sure, surely) have.
7. I want someone who can do the work (prompt and efficient, promptly and efficiently) and still behave (courteous, courteously) toward the customers.
8. Do you realize how (bad, badly) your mother will feel if you do not work (steady, steadily) or (serious, seriously) enough?
9. The horse trotted (rapid, rapidly) and won the race (easy, easily).
10. Dave is (uncommon, uncommonly) light on his feet for such a (heavy, heavily) built man.
11. It was a (fair, fairly), warm day in April.
12. It was a (fair, fairly) warm day in April.
13. Mr. Porter was so excited that he could not play his part (good, well).
14. Visitors to the cavern never fail to comment upon the (awful, awfully) quiet of the place.
15. It is (awful, awfully) dark in there.
16. The wind blew (fierce, fiercely) and the snow fell (continuous, continuously) all the long night.
17. The next few weeks passed very (rapid, rapidly).
18. I am afraid that the good woman is (some, somewhat) confused.
19. Under our new (department, departmental) arrangement, Mr. Willoughby's time is taken up almost wholly with (administration, administrative) work.
20. If you study (consistent, consistently) and (regular, regularly), you should overcome (most, almost) any handicap.

B. Rewrite the following sentences to provide the proper adjectives or adverbs in accordance with standard English usage. Write *C* for each sentence that needs no revision.

1. Henry, I do wish you wouldn't stop so sudden.
2. We began to eat more often and plentiful, and everything went along smooth for a while.
3. I can't tell which smells more sweetly, the roses or the honeysuckle.
4. I have tried both brands, and I still can't decide which I like best.
5. He rang the bell loud; loudly it sounded through hall and yard.
6. William, the oldest of the two brothers, always got along good with his studies.
7. Uncle Ben spends all his leisure time working in the garden.
8. If you want to catch him, you had better be quick about it.
9. We felt sure we had acted quick enough.
10. The boys played good last Saturday and won the game very easy.
11. Remember, if you do bad in this test, you may not have another chance.
12. Timmy felt sleepily under his pillow to see if the tooth was still there.
13. If you didn't snore so noisy, you wouldn't keep waking yourself up.
14. Without careful study no student can make good grades consistently.
15. A good hog has short legs and a reasonable wide body.
16. The author pictures the scene so vivid that the reader is eager to know what happens next.

C. Compose sentences in which each of the following words is used (1) as an adjective and (2) as an adverb: *well, near, daily, even, ill, fast, hard, high, straight.*

▶ Case

5

Use the proper case form to show the function of each noun or pronoun in the sentence as subject, possessor, or object.[1]

Nouns have a common form for the subject (*boy, dog*) and the object (*boy, dog*) and a distinctive form only for the possessor (*boy's, dog's*).

> The *boy* (subject) bought the *dog* (object).
> The *dog* (subject) followed the *boy* (object).
> The *boy's* (possessor) dog; the *dog's* (possessor) collar

Six of our common pronouns have one form for the subject (*I, he, she, we, they, who*), another for the possessor (*my* or *mine, his, her* or *hers, our* or *ours, their* or *theirs, whose*), and a third form for the object (*me, him, her, us, them, whom*). Therefore these pronouns must be used with special care.

NOUN

	Subjective	*Possessive*	*Objective*
SINGULAR	boy	boy's	boy
PLURAL	boys	boys'	boys

1 The subject is said to be in the subjective or nominative case, the possessor in the possessive or genitive case, and the object in the objective or accusative case.

	PRONOUN		
	Singular		
	Subjective	*Possessive*	*Objective*
FIRST PERSON	I	my, mine	me
SECOND PERSON	you	your, yours	you
THIRD PERSON	he, she, it	his, her, hers, its	him, her, it
	Plural		
FIRST PERSON	we	our, ours	us
SECOND PERSON	you	your, yours	you
THIRD PERSON	they	their, theirs	them
SINGULAR / PLURAL	who	whose	whom

Note on appositives: An appositive has the same case as the noun or pronoun with which it is in apposition.

RIGHT We—*John* and *I*—are responsible for the damage. [The appositives *John* and *I* are in the subjective case, in agreement with *we.*]

RIGHT The damage was caused by us—*John* and *me.* [The appositives *John* and *me* are in the objective case, in agreement with *us.*]

Subjective Case

5a Use the subjective case for subjects of verbs. (See 5g for subjects of infinitives.)

RIGHT *He* is old. *She* is kind. *They* work diligently.

In certain types of sentences care must be taken to prevent mistaking the subject for the object:

(1) Do not allow the subjective *who* (*whoever, whosoever*) to be incorrectly changed to *whom* (*whomever, whomsoever*) by

a following parenthetical expression such as *I think* or *he says.* (Note that such parenthetical expressions may be omitted without destroying the sense of the sentence.)

WRONG She is a very dependable person *whom* I think will prove worthy of every trust.

RIGHT She is a very dependable person *who* I think will prove worthy of every trust.

who | will prove

WRONG Jones is a man *whom* we know is dependable.

RIGHT Jones is a man *who* we know is dependable.

(2) The subject of a noun clause is always in the subjective case, even when the whole noun clause is the object of a verb or a preposition.

WRONG Employ *whomever* is willing to work.

RIGHT Employ *whoever* is willing to work. [*Whoever* is the subject of *is willing*. The object of *employ* is the whole clause *whoever is willing to work.*]

WRONG He had respect for *whomever* was in power.

RIGHT He had respect for *whoever* was in power. [The complete clause, not merely the pronoun *whoever,* is the object of the preposition *for.*]

(3) Use the subjective case after the conjunctions *than* or *as* if the pronoun is the subject of an implied verb.

RIGHT He is older than *I* [am].

RIGHT He is as wise as *they* [are].

RIGHT He likes you better than *I* [like you].

RIGHT He likes you as well as *I* [like you].

(See 5f(3) for the use of the objective case after *than* or *as.*)

► EXERCISE 1. Compose ten sentences to illustrate the appropriate use of pronouns in the subjective case as explained in 5a, (1), (2), (3). Underline each pronoun in the subjective case and explain why it is properly used.

5b Use the subjective case for the predicate (subjective) complement.

RIGHT It is *I* (*he, she, we, they*).

Note: Informal usage accepts *It is me* (*It's me*) but not *It is him* (*her, us, them*).

► EXERCISE 2. Select from your reading ten sentences to illustrate the various uses of pronouns in the subjective case.

Possessive Case

5c Use the apostrophe to form the possessive of nouns and indefinite pronouns, but not the possessive of personal pronouns (*my, mine, your, yours, his, hers, its, our, ours, their, theirs*) nor of the relative-interrogative pronoun *whose*.[2]

Apostrophe carelessly omitted:

WRONG my *sons* wife; both *sons* wives; *everyones* wife
RIGHT my *son's* wife; both *sons'* wives; *everyone's* wife

Apostrophe wrongly used:

WRONG Virtue is *it's* own reward. The hat is *her's.*
RIGHT Virtue is *its* own reward. The hat is *hers.*

[2] See further details for forming the possessive case under Section 15.

Remember that the possessive *it's* or *her's* or *our's* or *their's* is just as incorrect as *hi's*—an error no one would make. Of course *it's* is correct as a contraction of *it is:* "*It's* cold today."

5d A pronoun immediately preceding the gerund is usually in the possessive case.

RIGHT My brother approved of *my* (*her, our, your, their*) going to the fair.

When a pronoun (*this, that*) has no common possessive form, or when either a noun or a pronoun is separated from the gerund, the use of the possessive would be awkward or incorrect.

RIGHT I cannot approve of *this* (*that*) being done.

RIGHT The chance of *anyone* in the party *falling* out was remote.

Nouns immediately preceding the gerund are often in the possessive case, but they are also common in the objective case, especially when the emphasis falls on the noun rather than on the gerund.

RIGHT I was pleased by *John's* asking me to dinner.

RIGHT Just imagine *Mary* being on time. [Emphasis on *Mary*]

COLLOQUIAL Just imagine *him* being on time.

5e An *of* phrase is sometimes preferred to the possessive in *'s*.

(1) For inanimate objects

UNUSUAL The house's roof; the wall's surface; the property's value

BETTER The roof of the house; the surface of the wall; the value of the property

Note: Usage justifies many exceptions, especially to indicate time or measure (*month's leave, day's work, hour's delay, year's end, stone's throw*) or personification (*love's song, pity's sake, mercy's plea*).

(2) To avoid awkwardness

RIGHT The wagon *of the boy* who lives next door was stolen (not "The boy's wagon who lives next door. . . ." or "The boy who lives next door's wagon. . . .").

RIGHT As soon as the tourists were assembled, the officers examined the papers *of each* (not *each's*). [Some of the indefinite pronouns—such as *each, any, all, some, most,* and *few*—are not used with *'s*.]

Objective Case

5f Use the objective case for the object of a verb, a verbal, or a preposition.

RIGHT All of *us* (not *we*) students gave *him money*. [*Us* is the object of the preposition *of; him* is the indirect object of the verb *gave; money* is the direct object of the verb *gave*.]

RIGHT By opposing *him* we offended *her*. [*Him* is the object of the verbal *opposing; her* is the object of the verb *offended*.]

(1) Who and whom

Informal English is tending more and more to avoid the use of the objective *whom,* except when it comes immediately after a preposition; but in formal writing *whom* is still generally used for the objective case.

WRONG For *who* did you vote? [*Who* immediately follows the preposition *for,* of which it is the object.]

RIGHT For *whom* did you vote?

RIGHT *Whom* did you vote for? [Somewhat formal]

RIGHT *Who* did you vote for? [Informal use of *who* when it does not follow the preposition]

FORMAL The artist and the model *whom* he loved had a quarrel. [*Whom* is the object of *loved.*]

INFORMAL The artist and the model he loved had a quarrel. [*Whom* is avoided.]

(2) Pronouns following the conjunction *and*

WRONG Last summer my father took Tom and *I* on a camping trip.

RIGHT Last summer my father took Tom and *me* on a camping trip. [*Me* is an object of the verb *took.*]

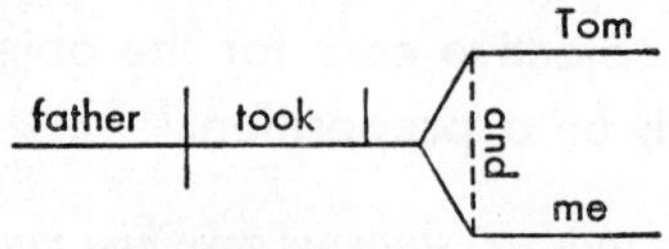

WRONG This is a secret between you and *I.*

RIGHT This is a secret between you and *me.* [*Me* is an object of the preposition *between.*]

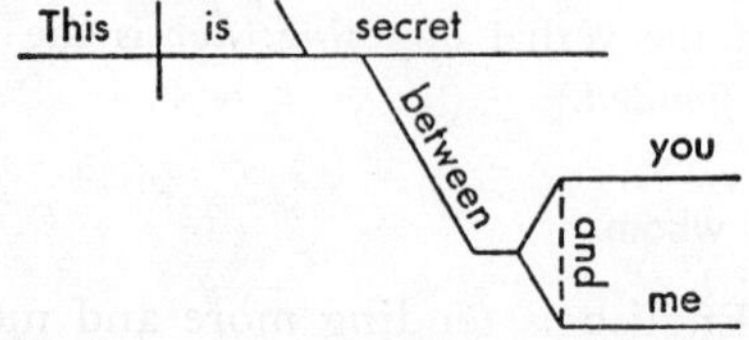

(3) Pronouns following the conjunctions *than* or *as*

Use the objective case when the pronoun following *than* or *as* is the object of an implied verb.

RIGHT He likes you better than [he likes] *me.*
RIGHT He likes you as well as [he likes] *me.*

(See 5a(3) for the use of the subjective case after *than* or *as.*)

5g Use the objective case for the subject, the object, or the complement of an infinitive.

RIGHT *Whom* do you think *him* to be? [*Whom* is the complement and *him* the subject of the infinitive *to be. Him to be whom* is the object of the verb *do think.*]
RIGHT He asked *me* to help *him.* [*Me* is the subject and *him* the object of the infinitive *to help.*]

► EXERCISES ON CASE

A. In the following passage select the word in parentheses that is in the proper case and give the reason for your choice.

1. Miss Adams, will you ask (whoever, whomever) calls for me while I'm away to talk to Dr. Knight instead? 2. There is one patient (who, whom) I believe may phone —a Mrs. Abell—but Dr. Knight can take care of her as well as (I, me). 3. It was (she, her) who phoned just now about her little (boys, boy's, boys') foot. 4. And if Mrs. Watson comes in about the (twins, twins') prescription, that is (theirs, their's, theirs') on the corner of my desk. 5. Caution her that (its, it's) to be given exactly according to directions and that she must report promptly on (them, their) showing any skin reaction. 6. Tell her to keep the bottle on the (refrigerator's lower shelf, lower shelf of the refrigerator). 7. And will you phone Dr. (Browns, Brown's) mother and tell her that all of (we, us)

here wish her a happy birthday. 8. Ask her in (whose, who's) care we should address letters to him now.

B. In the following passage, choose between the pronouns in parentheses and justify your choice.

1. Sheriff Comstock, to (who, whom) I introduced myself, had on his desk the records of the three men (who, whom) he believed were capable of committing a burglary such as that in East Dover Heights. 2. His deputy, Abe Phillips, with (who, whom) I had worked on the Berryman jewel theft a few years earlier, came into the office.

3. "(Whoever, Whomever) we find out did this job, it won't be Joey Piper," Phillips said. 4. "I've just talked to the superintendent of Davis Polyclinic, (who, whom) tells me that Joey has been there for three weeks, in a plaster cast up to his waist."

5. "You'd better get (whoever, whomever) is out that way on the case to check on Joey," the sheriff said. 6. He turned to me. "Between you and (I, me), I wouldn't trust Joey Piper's dead body in a lead coffin. 7. You must get me to tell you sometime about the troubles we have had —Joey and (I, me)."

8. "You think it mightn't be (he, him) out at Davis?" I suggested.

9. "I think that (whoever, whomever) takes Piper for granted is a fool," he said.

10. The sheriff turned to his deputy. "Abe, (who, whom) do you think should check on Piper out at Davis? . . . Flamm? Good. Have Flamm get me a complete case history, along with X rays of all Joey's injuries. 11. (They, Them) should be new X rays—made today."

12. Sheriff Comstock moved the Piper file to one side. "Well," he said, "(he, him) we can forget for a while. 13. But even if Piper is clear, that still leaves you and (I, me) two others (who, whom) are just as capable of this sort of job as (he, him).

▶ Agreement

6

Make every verb agree in number with its subject; make every pronoun agree in number with its antecedent.[1]

Caution: Can you easily distinguish verbs and relate them to their subjects? Can you readily find the antecedents of pronouns? Until you can do so, you may continue to have difficulty with agreement. If necessary, master first the fundamentals of the sentence treated in Section **1, Sentence Sense,** especially **1a, 1b,** and **1c;** then study Section **6.**

Singular subjects require singular verbs; plural subjects require plural verbs. Pronouns agree with their antecedents (the words to which they refer) in the same way. Note that in the subject the *s* ending is the sign of the plural, that in the verb it is the sign of the singular.

RIGHT The *engine runs* smoothly. [Singular subject—singular verb]

RIGHT The *engines run* smoothly. [Plural subject—plural verb]

RIGHT The *woman* washes *her* clothes. [Singular antecedent—singular pronoun]

RIGHT The *women* wash *their* clothes. [Plural antecedent—plural pronoun]

[1] For other kinds of agreement see Section 27.

Make a diagram, or at least form a mental picture, of each subject and its verb

(engine | runs   engines | run)

and of each antecedent and its pronoun (*woman* ← *her*, *women* ← *their*). This practice will make it easy to avoid errors in agreement.

6a Make every verb agree in number with its subject.

(1) Do not be misled (a) by nouns or pronouns intervening between the subject and the verb or (b) by careless pronunciation of nouns ending in *st*.

WRONG The *recurrence* of like sounds *help* to stir the emotions.
RIGHT The *recurrence* of like sounds *helps* to stir the emotions.

WRONG His *interest were* many and varied. The *Communist are* . . . *Scientist are* . . .
RIGHT His *interests were* many and varied. The *Communists are* . . . *Scientists are* . . .

Most writers feel that the number of the subject is not changed by the addition of parenthetical expressions introduced by such words as *with*, *together with*, *as well as*, *no less than*, *including*, *accompanied by*.

RIGHT *John*, together with James and William, *was drafted* into the Army.
RIGHT *Thomas*, like his two brothers, *was* often in debt.

(2) Subjects joined by *and* usually take a plural verb.

RIGHT A hammer and a saw *are* useful tools.
RIGHT Mary, Jane, and I *were* tired after our morning's work.

Exceptions: A compound subject referring to a single person, or to two or more things considered as a unit, takes a singular verb.

RIGHT My best friend and adviser *has gone.* [A single individual was both friend and adviser.]

RIGHT The tumult and the shouting *dies.*—KIPLING. [Two nouns considered a single entity]

Each or *every* preceding singular subjects joined by *and* calls for a singular verb.

RIGHT Each boy and each girl *is* to work independently.

RIGHT Every boy and girl *has been urged* to attend the play.

(3) Singular subjects joined by *or, nor, either . . . or, neither . . . nor* usually take a singular verb.

RIGHT Neither the boy nor the girl *is* to blame for the accident.

RIGHT Either the man or his wife *knows* the exact truth of the matter.

When the meaning is felt to be plural, informal English occasionally uses the plural verb: "Neither she nor I *were* dancing, for we felt weary."

If one subject is singular and one plural, the verb usually agrees with the nearer.

PERMISSIBLE Neither teacher nor pupils *are* in the building.

PERMISSIBLE Neither pupils nor teacher *is* in the building.

PERMISSIBLE Either you or I *am* mistaken.

BETTER Either you *are* mistaken or I *am.*

(4) When the subject follows the verb (as in sentences beginning with *there is, there are*) special care is needed to determine the subject and to make sure that it agrees with the verb.

RIGHT According to the rules, there *are* to be at least three *contestants* for each prize.

contestants	are

RIGHT There *are* many possible *candidates.*
RIGHT There *is* only one good *candidate.*

Before a compound subject the first member of which is singular, a singular verb is sometimes used: "In the basement there *is* a restaurant, which serves delicious food, and a poolroom and two barber shops."

Note: The expletive *it* is always followed by a singular verb: "It *is* the *woman* who suffers." "It *is* the *women* who suffer."

(5) A relative pronoun used as a subject takes a plural or singular verb to accord with its antecedent.

RIGHT *Boys* who *work* . . . A *boy* who *works* . . .
RIGHT Mary is among the *students* who *have done* honor to the college. [*Students* is the antecedent of *who.*]
RIGHT Mary is the only *one* of our students who *has achieved* national recognition. [*One,* not *students,* is the antecedent of *who.* The sentence means, "Of all our students Mary is the only *one* who *has achieved* national recognition."]

(6) *Each, either, neither, another, anyone, anybody, anything, someone, somebody, something, one, everyone, everybody, everything, nobody, nothing* regularly take singular verbs.

RIGHT Each *takes* his turn at rowing.
RIGHT Neither *likes* the friends of the other.
RIGHT Someone *is* likely to hear the signal.
RIGHT Everyone *has* his prejudices.
RIGHT Nobody *cares* to listen to worries.

None is plural or singular, depending upon the other words in the sentence or in the immediately surrounding sentences (the context) which condition its meaning.

RIGHT None *are* so blind as those who will not see.
RIGHT None *is* so blind as he who will not see.

(*Any, all, more, most* and *some* are used with plural or singular verbs in much the same way as *none.*)

(7) Collective nouns (and numbers denoting fixed quantity) usually take singular verbs because the group or quantity is usually regarded as a unit.

RIGHT The whole family *is* concerned. [The common use: *family* regarded as a unit]

RIGHT The family *have gone* about their several duties. [Less common: individuals of the family regarded separately]

RIGHT A thousand bushels *is* a good yield. [A unit]

RIGHT A thousand bushels of apples *were crated.* [Individual bushels]

RIGHT One third of the crop *was ruined.* [A fraction followed by a singular object in the *of* phrase is usually singular]

RIGHT One third of the peaches *were ruined.* [A fraction followed by a plural object in the *of* phrase is usually plural]

RIGHT The public *is aroused.* [A unit]

RIGHT The public *have been warned.* [Regarded as a group of individuals]

RIGHT The number in the class *was* small. [*The number* is regularly taken as a unit.]

RIGHT A number of the class *were* sick. [*A number* refers to individuals.]

RIGHT The data *is* sound. [A unit]

RIGHT The data *have been* carefully *collected.* [Individual items]

(8) A verb usually agrees with its subject, not with its predicate noun.

RIGHT His chief support *is* his brother and sister.

RIGHT His brother and sister *are* his chief support.

But such sentences are often better recast so as to avoid the disagreement in number between subject and predicate noun.

BETTER His support came chiefly from his brother and sister.

(9) Nouns plural in form but singular in meaning usually take singular verbs. In all doubtful cases a good dictionary should be consulted.

Regularly singular: aesthetics, civics, economics, linguistics, logistics, mathematics, measles, mumps, news, physics, semantics

RIGHT Mathematics *is* exact. The news *is* good.

Regularly plural: oats, pliers, scissors, trousers

RIGHT Pliers *are* useful. The trousers *are* new.

Means and *headquarters* may be either singular or plural. Some nouns ending in *-ics*, such as *acoustics* and *statistics*, are considered singular when referring to an organized body of knowledge and plural when referring to activities, qualities, or individual facts.

RIGHT Acoustics *is* an interesting study.
RIGHT The acoustics of the hall *are* good.

RIGHT Statistics *is* a science.
RIGHT The statistics *were* easily *assembled.*

(10) A title of a single work or a word spoken of as a word, even when plural in form, takes a singular verb.

RIGHT *Twice-Told Tales was written* by Hawthorne.
RIGHT The New York *Times has* a wide circulation.
RIGHT *They is* a pronoun.

► EXERCISE 1. In the following sentences, find each verb and relate it to its subject. Then rewrite each sentence to secure agreement of subject and verb. Justify every change. Write *C* in place of each sentence that needs no revision.

1. The King's eldest son and heir apparent were then only six years old.
2. Do each of you know where to go if the alarm should sound?

3. This book, a collection of recent articles published by the editor and others, give you a comprehensive view of a many-sided question.
4. There come to my mind now three men who might have qualified, but none of the three was given the chance.
5. Everybody one met in the streets that summer were excitedly talking about Essex's homecoming.
6. The significance of words are taught by simply breaking them up into suffixes, prefixes, and roots.
7. A majority of delinquent children are from broken homes.
8. A simple majority is sufficient to elect a candidate to office.
9. Application exercises for each chapter enables the student to practice the principles which the various chapters set forth.
10. His one ambition was to get well and get back to work.
11. His aging parents and the provision he might make for them were his one principal concern.

► EXERCISE 2. Rewrite the following *correct* sentences as directed. Change verbs to secure agreement and make any additional changes required for good sentence sense.

1. Certain portions of our collection are kept in an underground, air-conditioned vault and are never placed on exhibit. [Insert *One* before *Certain*.] 2. Each piece in the exhibit has to be carefully dusted and polished once a day and then put back in place. [Change *each piece* to *the pieces*.] 3. I might mention that this particular specimen has a distinguished place in history. [Change *this* to *these*.] 4. Our staff takes great pride in the efficient cataloguing system which we have developed here. [Insert *members* after *staff*.] 5. In this room is my assistant, who is cataloguing a newly arrived shipment. [Change *assistant* to *assistants*.] 6. One of our research parties has just returned from the field and is to be meeting with the directors during the remainder of

the week. [Change *One* to *Two*.] 7. A detachment of four men has been left behind to maintain a permanent camp at the excavation site. [Omit *A detachment of*.] 8. Eaton Murray, the leader of the expedition and an especially capable man, is among the four. [Insert *John Wade* after *and*.] 9. Neither of the others is known to us here. [Change *is known* to *are unknown*.] 10. Both, however, were selected for particular abilities which they have shown. [Change *they* to *he*.]

6b Make each pronoun agree in number with its antecedent.

A singular antecedent (the word to which a pronoun refers) takes a singular verb and is also referred to by a singular pronoun; a plural antecedent takes a plural verb and is referred to by a plural pronoun.

(1) In standard[2] English use a singular pronoun to refer to such antecedents as *man, woman, person, one, anyone, anybody, someone, somebody, everyone, everybody, each, kind, sort, either, neither, no one, nobody*. See also **6a(6)**.

WRONG	An outstanding trait of primitive *man* was *their* belief in superstitions.
RIGHT	An outstanding trait of primitive *man* was *his* belief in superstitions.
STANDARD	Each of the sons had planned to follow *his* father's occupation.
COLLOQUIAL	Each of the sons had planned to follow *their* father's occupation.
STANDARD	Everybody stood on *his* chair.
COLLOQUIAL	Everybody stood on *their* chairs.

[2] See pages 196-99 for the distinction between standard and colloquial English.

(2) Two or more antecedents joined by *and* are referred to by a plural pronoun; two or more singular antecedents joined by *or* or *nor* are referred to by a singular pronoun. If one of two antecedents joined by *or* is singular and one plural, the pronoun usually agrees with the nearer. See also 6a(2),(3).

RIGHT Henry and James have completed *their* work.

RIGHT Neither Henry nor James has completed *his* work.

WRONG When a *boy or girl* enters college, *they* find it different from high school.

RIGHT BUT CLUMSY When a *boy or girl* enters college, *he or she* finds it different from high school.

BETTER When *boys and girls* enter college, *they* find it different from high school.

RIGHT Neither the *master* nor the *servants* were aware of *their* danger. [The plural *servants* is the nearer antecedent.]

RIGHT Neither the *servants* nor the *master* was aware of *his* danger.

(3) Collective nouns are referred to by singular or plural pronouns depending on whether the collective noun is considered singular or plural. See also 6a(7).

Special care should be taken to avoid making a collective noun *both* singular and plural within the same sentence.

WRONG If the board of directors *controls* the company, *they* may vote themselves bonuses. [*Board* is first singular with *controls*, then plural with *they*.]

RIGHT If the board of directors *control* the company, *they* may vote themselves bonuses. [Made plural throughout as demanded by the last half of the sentence]

RIGHT If the board of directors *controls* the company, *it* may vote itself a bonus. [Last half of the sentence changed to agree with the first]

► EXERCISE 3. In the following sentences select the pronoun in parentheses that agrees with its antecedent in accordance with standard English usage. Note also any pronouns that would be acceptable in conversation or familiar writing but not in formal writing.

1. The foreman unlocked the shed and everybody went in and got (his, their) tools. 2. Each man, and Charlie too, left (his, their) lunch pail inside. 3. Roy and Dave were tearing out concrete forms, and (he, each, they) took a section apiece and went to work. 4. One or another would yell for the helpers to clear away the salvage lumber (he was, they were) tearing out. 5. The helpers were supposed to pile the lumber outside the foundation, where Andy was cleaning (it, them) up and stacking (it, them) for re-use. 6. Every few minutes someone would call out for the water boy to bring (him, them) a drink. 7. The crew was small, but (its, their) thirst was large. 8. Charlie, the water boy, had all he could do to keep (it, them) satisfied. 9. "If anybody here ever drank water when (he was, they were) off the job," he grumbled, "I'd be proud to shake (him, them) by the hand." 10. But nobody volunteered (his, their) hand to be shaken. 11. Every minute, instead, somebody new would be yelling for water, and Charlie would trudge off toward (him, them). 12. It was either Roy or Dave who was whooping for (his, their) ninetieth drink when the noon whistle blew. 13. Nobody was so ready to stop where (he was, they were) as Charlie. 14. "Whoever wants a drink knows where (he, they) can get it," he let it be known, and emptied his bucket out on the ground.

► EXERCISE 4. In Exercise 3 make each change as directed below and then complete the sentence so as to secure agreement of pronoun with its antecedent. In Sentence 1, change *everybody* to *the workmen.* In 4, change *One or another* to *Both.* In 9, change *anybody here* to *these men.* In 11, change *somebody new* to *two or three more.*

► EXERCISE ON AGREEMENT

In the following passage correct each italicized word which needs correcting. Explain whether the correction is necessary to secure agreement between (1) subject and verb or between (2) pronoun and antecedent. Justify each italicized word which you would leave as it is.

1. Everybody, I suppose, is entitled to *their* own opinion about Major McIntyre and the Confederate gold. 2. Anyhow, there *is* all sorts of opinions to be heard if a person has patience enough in *their* being to hear them all. 3. This wagonload of gold, most of it in bars, *were* being moved from the capital to keep *them* from being captured when the capital fell. 4. Or at least, so one of the stories *go*. 5. Some *says* that there *was* two wagonloads and that Abel or one of the younger McIntyre boys *were* driving the second one. 6. And some few of us *haven't* decided to put any belief in the tales at all. 7. But nearly everybody else *are* agreed that the gold got this far, because while it was being moved, one or another of the McIntyre brothers *were* captured and shot at the family home near here. 8. You can still see the ruins of the house, which *were* burned after the soldiers had ransacked it. 9. All the family *were* deeply involved in the war and couldn't afford to risk *their* lives by staying where *they* could easily be found. 10. So the house had been standing empty when the Major, or Abel, *were* captured there that night. 11. All the McIntyre slaves but one *were* scared off when the soldiers surrounded the place, and this one couldn't say which of the brothers *was* captured. 12. He saw someone dragged out and shot and *their* body thrown back into the burning house, but there *wasn't* enough left of the body afterward to tell whose it was. 13. And neither the Major nor Abel nor the gold *were* ever seen again.

▶ Tense

Mood; *Shall* and *Will*

7

Use the appropriate form of the verb.

Tense

7a Use the appropriate tense form.

Tense, from the Latin word meaning "time," refers to changes in the form of the verb to indicate the time of the action. But tense and time do not always agree. The present tense, for example, is by no means limited to action in the present time. It may be used also to recall vividly the events of the past, as in the "historical present," or to refer to future action: "I leave for Chicago tomorrow morning." English verbs have six tenses.

1. PRESENT—present action: "He *sees* me now"; customary action: "He *sees* me daily"; and other uses such as: "Napoleon *opens* the campaign brilliantly" [historical present, used instead of the past tense]; "*I start* my vacation a week from Friday" [used instead of the future tense]; "Some early philosophers knew that the earth

is round" [timeless truth, expressed in the present even when the main verb is in the past].

2. PAST—past action not extending to the present: "He *saw* me at the game yesterday."
3. FUTURE—action at some time after the present: "He *will see* me next month in New York." The future is frequently expressed by the phrase *is going to:* "He *is going to see* me next month in New York."
4. PRESENT PERFECT—past action extending to the present: "He *has seen* me many times."
5. PAST PERFECT—past action completed before some indicated time in the past: "My friend *had seen* me before the game started." "I *had* already *decided* to talk with him before I left the house." [Sometimes put in the simple past tense: "My friend *saw* me before the game started." But note that "I *decided* to talk with him before I left the house" would be a change of meaning.]
6. FUTURE PERFECT—action to be completed before some indicated time in the future: "He *will have seen* me again before my departure tomorrow." [Commonly put in the simple future tense: "He *will see* me again before my departure tomorrow." The future perfect tense is seldom used.]

These six tenses are built on three forms, called **principal parts:** (1) the present stem (infinitive)—*see, use,* (2) the past tense—*saw, used,* and (3) the past participle—*seen, used.* Most English verbs, like *use,* are **regular;** that is, they form both the past tense (*used*) and the past participle (*used*) by adding *-d* or *-ed* to the present stem (*use*). Other verbs, like *see,* are **irregular** because they change the present stem (*see*) to form the past tense (*saw*) and the past participle (*seen*). It will be noted in the conjugation on the following pages that the present stem is the basis for both present and future tenses; the past, for the past tense alone; and the past participle, for the present perfect, past perfect, and future perfect tenses.

CONJUGATION OF THE VERB *TO SEE*

(Principal Parts: *see, saw, seen*)

INDICATIVE MOOD [1]

	Active Voice		*Passive Voice*	
	PRESENT TENSE			
	Singular	*Plural*	*Singular*	*Plural*
1.	I see	we see	I am seen	we are seen
2.	you see	you see	you are seen	you are seen
3.	he (she, it) sees	they see	he (she, it) is seen	they are seen
	PAST TENSE			
1.	I saw	we saw	I was seen	we were seen
2.	you saw	you saw	you were seen	you were seen
3.	he saw	they saw	he was seen	they were seen
	FUTURE TENSE			
1.	I shall see	we shall see	I shall be seen	we shall be seen
2.	you will see	you will see	you will be seen	you will be seen
3.	he will see	they will see	he will be seen	they will be seen
	PRESENT PERFECT TENSE			
1.	I have seen	we have seen	I have been seen	we have been seen
2.	you have seen	you have seen	you have been seen	you have been seen
3.	he has seen	they have seen	he has been seen	they have been seen
	PAST PERFECT TENSE			
1.	I had seen	we had seen	I had been seen	we had been seen
2.	you had seen	you had seen	you had been seen	you had been seen
3.	he had seen	they had seen	he had been seen	they had been seen
	FUTURE PERFECT TENSE (seldom used)			
1.	I shall have seen	we shall have seen	I shall have been seen	we shall have been seen
2.	you will have seen	you will have seen	you will have been seen	you will have been seen
3.	he will have seen	they will have seen	he will have been seen	they will have been seen

---

[1] Such terms as *mood, indicative, subjunctive,* and *voice* are explained in Section 35, Grammatical Terms.

SUBJUNCTIVE MOOD

Active Voice	*Passive Voice*
PRESENT TENSE	
Singular: if I, you, he see	if I, you, he be seen
Plural: if we, you, they see	if we, you, they be seen
PAST TENSE	
Singular: if I, you, he saw	if I, you, he were seen
Plural: if we, you, they saw	if we, you, they were seen
PRESENT PERFECT TENSE	
Singular: if I, you, he have seen	if I, you, he have been seen
Plural: if we, you, they have seen	if we, you, they have been seen
PAST PERFECT TENSE	
(Same as the Indicative)	

IMPERATIVE MOOD

PRESENT TENSE	
see	be seen

INFINITIVES

PRESENT TENSE	
to see	to be seen
PRESENT PERFECT TENSE	
to have seen	to have been seen

PARTICIPLES

PRESENT TENSE	
seeing	being seen
PAST TENSE	
seen	been seen
PRESENT PERFECT TENSE	
having seen	having been seen

GERUNDS

Active Voice	*Passive Voice*
PRESENT TENSE	
seeing	being seen
PRESENT PERFECT TENSE	
having seen	having been seen

In addition to the simple verb forms illustrated above, English uses a "progressive" form to show action in progress and a "do" form for (1) emphatic statements, (2) questions, or (3) negations.

SIMPLE FORM I see, he sees; I saw, he saw; I am seen.
PROGRESSIVE FORM I am seeing, he is seeing; I was seeing, he was seeing; I am being seen.
"DO" FORM (1) I do see, he does see; I did see, he did see.
(2) Does he see her? Did he see her?
(3) He does not see her. He did not see her.

Principal Parts

The writer usually knows the tense needed to express his ideas. He can determine the correct form of this tense by consulting his dictionary for the principal parts of the verb. In the dictionary every irregular verb is listed by its infinitive or present stem; for example, *see*. Then follow the past tense (*saw*), the past participle (*seen*), and the present participle (*seeing*). *See*, *saw*, and *seen* are the principal parts from which the writer can readily derive the proper form for any of the six tenses. For regular verbs (such as *use*) the past tense and the past participle, when not given, are understood to be formed by adding *-d* or *-ed*.

WRONG The boy *seen* where the bullet had entered. [Past tense needed; the dictionary gives *saw* as the correct form.]
RIGHT The boy *saw* where the bullet had entered.

WRONG I *use* to live in the country. [Past tense needed]
RIGHT I *used* to live in the country.

► EXERCISE 1. Some verbs are frequently confused because of similarity in spelling or meaning. Master the principal parts of the following verbs. Then compose sentences (three to illustrate each verb) in which each verb is correctly used (1) in the past tense, (2) in the present perfect tense, and (3) in the present tense (progressive form, using the present participle).

Present stem (infinitive)	*Past tense*	*Past participle*	*Present participle*
lie (to recline)	lay	lain	lying
lay (to cause to lie)	laid	laid	laying
sit (to be seated)	sat	sat	sitting
set (to place or put)	set	set	setting

WRONG He *layed* (or *laid*) down on the bed. [Past tense of the intransitive verb *lie* needed]
RIGHT He *lay* down on the bed.

WRONG He *lay* the book on the table. [Past tense of the transitive verb *lay* needed]
RIGHT He *laid* the book on the table.
RIGHT The book is *lying* (not *laying*) on the table.

WRONG He *set* in the chair. [Past tense of the intransitive verb *sit* needed]
RIGHT He *sat* in the chair.
RIGHT He *set* the bucket on the table. [Transitive]
RIGHT The man is *sitting* (not *setting*) in the chair.

► EXERCISE 2. Principal parts of other difficult verbs are listed on the following pages. *Add the principal parts of all verbs that you have used incorrectly in your writing.* Then master the whole list and compose sentences to illustrate the correct use of each principal part (as assigned, perhaps in groups of ten, by the instructor).

Present stem	*Past tense*	*Past participle*
begin	began	begun
bid (offer)	bid	bid
bid (order)	bade	bidden
bite	bit	bitten, bit
blow	blew	blown
break	broke	broken
bring	brought	brought
burst	burst	burst
catch	caught	caught
choose	chose	chosen
come	came	come
dive	dived, dove	dived
do	did	done
drag	dragged	dragged
draw	drew	drawn
drink	drank	drunk
eat	ate	eaten
fall	fell	fallen
flee	fled	fled
fly	flew	flown
forget	forgot	forgotten, forgot
freeze	froze	frozen
get	got	got, gotten
go	went	gone
grow	grew	grown
know	knew	known
lead	led	led
lose	lost	lost
raise	raised	raised
ride	rode	ridden
ring	rang, rung	rung
rise	rose	risen

Present stem	*Past tense*	*Past participle*
run	ran	run
see	saw	seen
shrink	shrank, shrunk	shrunk, shrunken
sing	sang, sung	sung
speak	spoke	spoken
spring	sprang, sprung	sprung
steal	stole	stolen
swim	swam	swum
swing	swung	swung
take	took	taken
tear	tore	torn
write	wrote	written

Sequence of Tenses

7b Make a verb in a subordinate clause or an infinitive or a participle agree logically (naturally) with the verb in the main clause.

1. *Verbs*

RIGHT The audience *rises* as the speaker *enters.* [The present *enters* follows the present *rises.*]

RIGHT The audience *rose* as the speaker *entered.* [The past *entered* follows the past *rose.*]

RIGHT I *have ceased* worrying because I *have heard* no more rumors. [The present perfect follows the present perfect.]

RIGHT I *believed* (or *had believed*) that the letter *had* (not *has*) *been lost.* [The past perfect in the subordinate clause follows the past or past perfect in the main clause.]

RIGHT I *believe* (or *will believe, have believed*) that the letter *has* (not *had*) *been lost.* [The present perfect in the subordinate clause follows present, future, or present perfect in the main clause.]

RIGHT You *will find* that he *will have done* well. [The future perfect in the subordinate clause is used only with the future in the main clause.]

POOR I *hoped* that I *could have gone.*

BETTER I *hoped* that I *could go.* [In the past time indicated by *hoped* I was still anticipating going.]

POOR When I *was* at camp four weeks, I *received* word that my father *had died.*

BETTER When I *had been* at camp four weeks, I *received* word that my father *had died.* [The past perfect *had been* or *had died* indicates a time prior to that of the main verb *received.*]

2. *Infinitives*

Use the present infinitive to express action contemporaneous with, or future to, that of the governing verb; use the perfect infinitive for action prior to that of the governing verb.

RIGHT I was happy *to find* (not *to have found*) you at home. [The finding and the happiness were contemporaneous.]

RIGHT I hoped *to go* (not *to have gone*). I hope *to go.* [Present infinitives. At the time indicated by the verbs I was still hoping *to go*, not *to have gone.*]

RIGHT I should like *to have lived* in Shakespeare's time. [Perfect infinitive—expressing time prior to that of the governing verb. Simpler: I wish I had lived in Shakespeare's time.]

RIGHT I should have liked *to live* (not *to have lived*) in Shakespeare's time. [Present infinitive—for time contemporaneous with that of the governing verb]

3. *Participles*

Use the present participle to express action contemporaneous with that of the governing verb; use the perfect participle for action prior to that of the governing verb.

RIGHT *Walking* along the streets, he met many old friends. [The walking and the meeting were contemporaneous.]

RIGHT *Having walked* all the way home, he found himself tired. [The walking was prior to the finding.]

Caution: Do not confuse gerunds and participles.

RIGHT After *walking* home he found himself tired. [Gerund]

RIGHT *Having walked* (not *After having walked*) home, he found himself tired. [Participle. *After* would be redundant.]

Subjunctive Mood

7c The subjunctive mood is still required in a few types of expressions, and may be used in others.

The subjunctive mood has been largely displaced by the indicative. Distinctive forms for the subjunctive occur only in the third person singular of the present tense (*I demand that he* **see** *a physician* instead of the indicative *he sees a physician*) and in the verb *to be* as indicated by boldface below.

Present indicative		*Present subjunctive*	
I am	we are	if I **be**	if we **be**
you are	you are	if you **be**	if you **be**
he is	they are	if he (she, it) **be**	if they **be**

Past indicative		*Past subjunctive*	
I was	we were	if I **were**	if we were
you were	you were	if you were	if you were
he was	they were	if he (she, it) **were**	if they were

The subjunctive is regularly used (1) in *that* clauses of motions, resolutions, recommendations, orders, or demands and (2) in a few idiomatic expressions.

RIGHT I move that the report *be* approved.
Resolved, that dues for the coming year *be* doubled.

I recommend (order, demand) that the prisoner *be* released.

I demand (request, insist) that the messenger *go* alone.

If need *be*; *suffice* it to say; *come* what may; etc. [Idiomatic expressions in which the subjunctive is fixed]

Most writers prefer the subjunctive in contrary-to-fact conditions and in expressions of doubts, wishes, or regrets.

STANDARD If the apple *were* ripe, it would be delicious. [Subjunctive]

COLLOQUIAL If the apple *was* ripe, it would be delicious. [Indicative]

RIGHT If the apple *is* ripe, I will eat it. [The indicative is regularly used in conditions not contrary to fact.]

STANDARD The man looks as if he *were* sick. [Subjunctive]

COLLOQUIAL The man looks as if he *was* sick. [Indicative]

STANDARD I wish that he *were* here. [Subjunctive]

COLLOQUIAL I wish that he *was* here. [Indicative]

► EXERCISE 3. Choose the proper form for the subjunctive mood in the parentheses below.

1. We insist that he (be, is) punished.
2. I wish that James (was, were) here.
3. We have talked of a trip to Madrid as though it (was, were) impossible.
4. Present-day problems demand that we (be, are) ready for any emergency.
5. "A good idea," one of the members said, "but I propose that the suggestion (be, is) tabled for the present."
6. Our purpose, (suffice it, it suffices) to say, is to win the confidence of our patrons.
7. If there (was, were) time, I could finish my report.
8. We ought to refuse consideration of this idea lest the prospective trip to Europe (prove, proves) too much a distraction to our immediate business.
9. "If this (be, is) treason, make the most of it."

10. I demand that he (make, makes) an explanation.
11. I wish he (was, were) present to explain his continued neglect of his duties.
12. If he (was, were) here, he might explain everything to our full satisfaction.
13. The principal urged that everyone (stay, stays) until the end of the meeting.

► EXERCISE 4. Compose five sentences in which the subjunctive is required. Compose three other sentences in which either the subjunctive or the indicative may be used, giving the indicative (colloquial) form in parentheses.

Shifts in Tense or Mood

7d Avoid needless shifts in tense or mood.[2]

WRONG He *came* to the river and *pays* a man to ferry him across. [Contradictory use of tenses within one sentence]

RIGHT He *came* to the river and *paid* a man to ferry him across.

INCONSISTENT It is necessary to restrain an occasional foolhardy park visitor lest a mother bear *mistake* his friendly intentions and *supposes* him a menace to her cubs. [Mood shifts improperly from subjunctive to indicative within the compound predicate.] But females with cubs *were* only one of the dangers. [A correct enough sentence if standing alone, but here inconsistent with present tense of preceding one, and therefore misleading] One *has* to remember that all bears *were* wild animals and not domesticated pets. [Inconsistent and misleading shift of tense from present in main clause to past in subordinate clause] Though a bear *may* seem altogether peaceable and harmless, he *might* not remain peaceable and he is never harmless. [Tense shifts improperly from present in introductory clause to past in main clause.] It *is*

[2] See also Section 27, **Shifts in Point of View.**

therefore an important part of the park ranger's duty *to watch* the tourists, and above all *don't* let anybody try to feed the bears. [Inconsistent. Mood shifts needlessly from indicative to imperative.]

IMPROVED It is necessary to restrain an occasional foolhardy park visitor lest a mother bear *mistake* his friendly intentions and *suppose* him a menace to her cubs. But females with cubs *are* only one of the dangers. One *has* to remember that all bears *are* wild animals and not domesticated pets. Though a bear *may* seem altogether peaceable and harmless, he *may* not remain peaceable and he is never harmless. It *is* therefore an important part of the park ranger's duty *to watch* the tourists and above all not *to let* anybody try to feed the bears.

► EXERCISE 5. In the following passage correct all errors and inconsistencies in tense and mood and any other errors in verb usage. Write *C* in place of any sentence which is satisfactory as it stands.

1. Across the Thames from Shakespeare's London lay the area known as the Bankside, probably as rough and unsavory a neighborhood as ever laid across the river from any city. 2. And yet it was to such a place that Shakespeare and his company had to have gone to build their new theater. 3. For the Puritan government of the City had set up all sorts of prohibitions against theatrical entertainment within the city walls. 4. When it became necessary, therefore, for the Company to have moved their playhouse from its old location north of the city, they obtain a lease to a tract on the Bankside. 5. Other theatrical companies had went there before them, and it seemed reasonable to have supposed that Shakespeare and his partners would prosper in the new location. 6. Apparently the Puritans of the City had no law against anyone's moving cartloads of lumber through the public streets. 7. There is no record that the Company met with difficulty while the timbers of the dismantled playhouse are being hauled to the new site. 8.

One difficulty the partners had foresaw and forestalled, and that is the effort that their old landlord might make to have stopped their removing the building. 9. Lest his presence complicate their task and would perhaps defeat its working altogether, they waited until he had gone out of town. 10. And when he came back, his lot was bare, the building's timbers were all in stacks on the far side of the river, and the theater is waiting only to be put together. 11. It is a matter of general knowledge that on the Bankside Shakespeare continued his successful career as a showman and went on to enjoy even greater prosperity after he had made the move than before.

Shall *and* Will

7e Observe such distinctions as exist between *shall* (*should*) and *will* (*would*).

(1) Use *should* in all persons to express an obligation (in the sense "ought to") or a condition.

RIGHT I (You, He, We, They) *should* (i.e., *ought to*) help the needy.

RIGHT If I (you, he, we, they) *should* resign, the program would not be continued.

(2) Use *would* in all persons to express a wish or a customary action.

RIGHT *Would* that I (you, he, we, they) had received the message!

RIGHT I (You, He, We, They) *would* spend hours by the seashore during the summer months.

Shall is generally used for the first person in asking questions (*Shall* I enter?), and it is often used in all persons for special emphasis. Except for these uses of *shall*, and for the use of *should* to express an obligation or condition, informal English tends to use *will* and *would* in all persons.

(3) Some careful writers distinguish between *shall* and *will*:

(a) By using *shall* in the first person and *will* in the second and third to express the simple future or expectation (I *shall* plan to stay; he *will* probably stay).

(b) By using *will* in the first person and *shall* in the second and third to express determination, threat, command, prophecy, promise, or willingness (I *will* stay; you and he *shall* stay).

(c) By using in a question the same form expected in the answer (*Will* you stay? Expected answer: I *will* stay).

► EXERCISE 6. Select the form in parentheses that is consistent with contemporary usage. Justify your choice.

1. To save time we (should, would) fly to the coast.
2. No totalitarian tyrant (will, shall) treat us with contempt.
3. (Will, Shall) I go on the early train?
4. Very often during those years we (should, would) go to the country for relaxation.
5. At school we learn what we (should, would) do throughout life.

► EXERCISE 7. Compose five sentences to illustrate the chief distinctions in the use of *shall*, *should*, and *would*. Explain the meaning of each sentence.

MECHANICS

▶ Manuscript Form and Revision; Syllabication

8

Put your manuscript in acceptable form. Make revisions with care.

8a Use the proper materials.

(1) **Paper.** Unless you are given other instructions, use standard theme paper, size 8½ by 11 inches, with lines about half an inch apart, and write only on the ruled side of the paper. (The usual notebook paper, even if it is the standard size, should not be used because the narrow spaces between lines make for hard reading and allow insufficient space for corrections.) For typewritten papers use the unruled side of theme paper; or, if you prefer, regular typewriter paper, size 8½ by 11 inches.

(2) **Ink.** Use black or blue-black ink.

(3) **Typewriter.** Submit typewritten papers only if you do your own typewriting. Use a black ribbon and make sure that the type is clean.

8b Arrange your writing in clear and orderly fashion on the page.

(1) **Margins.** Leave sufficient margins—about an inch and a half at the left and top, an inch at the right and bottom—to prevent a crowded appearance. The ruled lines on theme paper indicate the proper margins at the left and top.

(2) **Indention.** Indent the first lines of paragraphs uniformly, about an inch in longhand and five spaces in typewritten copy.

(3) **Paging.** Use Arabic numerals—without parentheses or period—in the upper right-hand corner to mark all pages after the first.

(4) **The Title.** Center the title on the page about an inch and a half from the top or on the first ruled line. Leave the next line blank and begin the first paragraph on the third line. In this way the title will be made to stand off from the text. Capitalize the first word of the title and all succeeding words except articles and short conjunctions and prepositions. *Do not put quotation marks around the title or underline it* (unless it is a quotation or the title of a book), and use no period after the title.

(5) **Poetry.** Quoted lines of poetry should be arranged and indented as in the original. In typing, use single spacing. (See also Section **16a.**)

(6) **Punctuation.** Never begin a line with a comma, a colon, a semicolon, or a terminal mark of punctuation; never end a line with opening quotation marks, bracket, or parenthesis.

(7) **Endorsement.** Papers are endorsed in the way prescribed by the instructor to facilitate handling. Usually papers carry the name of the student, the date, and the number of the theme.

8c Write legibly, so that your writing may be read easily and accurately.

(1) Spacing for Legibility. Adequate space between lines and between the words in the line is essential to easy reading. In typewritten copy use double space between lines. Single-spaced copy is difficult for the instructor to read and even more difficult for the student to revise. Leave one space after a comma or semicolon, one or two after a colon, and two or three after a period, a question mark, or an exclamation point. In longhand make each word a distinct unit: join all the letters of a word and leave adequate space in the line before beginning the next word.

(2) Shaping for Legibility. Shape each letter distinctly. Avoid flourishes. Many pages of manuscript, though artistic and attractive to the eye, are almost illegible. Dot the *i*, not some other letter nearby. Cross the *t*, not the adjoining *h* or some other letter. Make dots and periods real dots, not small circles. Let all capitals stand out distinctly as capitals and keep all small letters down to the average of other small letters. Remember that you will not be present to tell the reader which letters you intend for capitals, which for small letters.

8d Revise the manuscript with care.[1]

(1) Revising the paper before submitting it to the instructor. If time permits, the writer should put the paper aside for a day or more after completing his first draft. Then he will be able to read the paper more objectively, to see what parts need to be expanded, what to be excised.

---

[1] For marks used in correcting proofs for the printer see *Webster's New Collegiate Dictionary*, pp. 1208-09, or *The American College Dictionary*, Text Edition, p. xxxv.

If extensive revisions are necessary, he should make a completely new copy to submit to the instructor. If only a few changes are needed, the paper may be handed in—after corrections have been made—without rewriting. The changes should be made as follows:

(a) Draw one line horizontally through any word to be deleted. Do not put it in parentheses or make an unsightly erasure.

(b) In case of a short addition of one line or less, place a caret (∧) in the line where the addition comes and write just above the caret the part to be added.

CHECK LIST FOR REVISION

1. Have I stated by central idea clearly, and have I developed it adequately in the paper? (See Section **32.**)
2. Is the manuscript form correct? (See Section **8.**)
3. Are grammar and mechanics correct? (See Sections **1-7; 9-11.**)
4. Is the punctuation correct? (See Sections **12-17.**)
5. Is the spelling correct? (See Section **18.**)
6. Is the diction standard, exact, concise? (See Sections **19-22.**)
7. Are the sentences as effective as possible? (See Sections **23-30.**)
8. Are the paragraphs properly developed? (See Section **31.**)
9. Does the outline follow exactly the final version of the paper? (If not, revise the outline to fit the paper. See Section **32.**)
10. What do my answers to the foregoing questions show my chief defects to be? (Review intensively the sections of this book which deal with your defects. Observe the same procedure for additional defects noted by your instructor.)

(2) Revising the paper after the instructor has criticized it. The best way to learn to write is by correcting one's own errors. Corrections made by another are of comparatively little value. Therefore the instructor points out the errors but *allows the student to make the actual revision for himself.*

The instructor usually indicates a necessary correction by a number or a symbol from the handbook marked in the margin of the paper opposite the error. For example, if he finds a fragmentary sentence, he will write either the number **2** or the symbol **frag.** The student should then find in the text the specific part (**a**, **b**, or **c**) of Section **2** that deals with his error, should correct the error in red, and write the appropriate letter after the instructor's number or symbol in the margin. (See the example paragraph on page 96.)

The comma. After the number **12** in the margin the student should take special care to supply the appropriate letter (**a**, **b**, **c**, or **d**) to show why the comma is needed. The act of inserting a comma teaches little; understanding why it is required in a particular situation is a definite step toward mastery of the comma.

The following pages reproduce a student paragraph and show, on the first page, the instructor's markings (for grammar and other details) and, on the second page, the same paragraph after it has been corrected by the student. These corrections should be in red to make them stand out distinctly from the original paragraph and the markings of the instructor.

(For three student papers, with the instructor's comments on content and organization, see pages 383-89 at the end of Section **32**. The content, or subject matter, of a paper is first in importance, but a paper must also stand the test of the "Check List" on page 94.)

Marked by the Instructor—with Numbers

3 Making photographs for newspapers is hard work,
12 it is not the romantic carefree adventure glorified
in motion pictures and fiction books. For every
18 great moment recorded by the stareing eye of the
camera, there are twenty routine assignments that
28 must be handled in the same efficient manner. He
must often overcome great hardships. The work con-
24 tinues for long hours. It must meet the deadline.
At times he is called upon to risk his own life to
2 secure a picture. To the newspaper photographer,
getting his picture being the most important thing.

Marked by the Instructor—with Symbols

cs Making photographs for newspapers is hard work,
,/ it is not the romantic carefree adventure glorified
in motion pictures and fiction books. For every
sp great moment recorded by the stareing eye of the
camera, there are twenty routine assignments that
ref must be handled in the same efficient manner. He
must often overcome great hardships. The work con-
sub tinues for long hours. It must meet the deadline.
At times he is called upon to risk his own life to
frag secure a picture. To the newspaper photographer,
getting his picture being the most important thing.

Corrected by the Student—in Red

3b Making photographs for newspapers is hard work~~,~~;
12c it is not the romantic, carefree adventure glorified
in motion pictures and fiction books. For every
18d great moment recorded by the ~~stareing~~ staring eye of the
camera, there are twenty routine assignments that
28c must be handled in the same efficient manner. ~~He~~ The
newspaper photographer must often overcome great
~~must often overcome great hardships. The work con-~~
24a hardships and works long hours to meet the deadline.
~~tinues for long hours. It must meet the deadline.~~
At times he is called upon to risk his own life to
secure a picture. To the newspaper photographer,
2a getting his picture ~~being~~ is the most important thing.

---

cs-b Making photographs for newspapers is hard work~~,~~;
,/c it is not the romantic, carefree adventure glorified
in motion pictures and fiction books. For every
sp-d great moment recorded by the ~~stareing~~ staring eye of the
camera, there are twenty routine assignments that
ref-c must be handled in the same efficient manner. ~~He~~ The
newspaper photographer must often overcome great
~~must often overcome great hardships. The work con-~~
sub-a hardships and work long hours to meet the deadline.
~~tinues for long hours. It must meet the deadline.~~
At times he is called upon to risk his own life to
frag-a secure a picture. To the newspaper photographer,
getting his picture ~~being~~ is the most important thing.

8e Keep a record of your errors to check the improvement in your writing.

A clear record on a single sheet of paper will show at a glance the progress you are making from paper to paper. In each paper try to avoid mistakes already pointed out. Master the spelling of any word incorrectly spelled in order to avoid misspelling it a second time. *Be sure that you have made, and that you understand fully, every correction on your last paper before you write the next.* If you follow this plan consistently throughout the year, your writing will show marked improvement.

One simple but useful way to record your errors is to write them down in the order in which they occur in each paper, grouping them in columns according to the seven major divisions of the handbook as illustrated below. In the spaces for Paper Number 1 are recorded the errors from the student paragraph on the preceding page. In the spelling column appears the misspelled word with the correct spelling, and in other columns the section number with the letter to indicate the specific error made.

RECORD OF ERRORS

Paper No.	Grammar 1—7	Mechanics 8—11	Punctuation 12—17	Words Misspelled 18	Diction 19—22	Effectiveness 23—30	Larger Elements 31—34
1	3b 2a		12c	Staring		28c 24a	
2							

8f Divide words only between syllables (parts naturally pronounced as separate units of the word), and never set off a syllable made up of a single letter. (For hyphenated words see Section 18f.)

If the writer leaves a reasonable right-hand margin, he will seldom need to divide words, especially short ones. The reader will object less to an uneven margin than to a number of broken words.

WRONG ignit-ion, sentin-el [Words not divided between syllables. Whenever you are uncertain about the proper syllabication of a word, consult a good dictionary.]

RIGHT ig-nition (*or* igni-tion), sen-tinel (*or* senti-nel)

RIGHT can-ning, com-mit-ting [Double consonants are usually divided except when they come at the end of a simple word: kill-ing.]

WRONG enjoy-ed, gleam-ed, watch-ed, remember-ed [Never confuse the reader by setting off an *-ed* pronounced as part of the preceding syllable.]

WRONG e-nough, a-gainst, e-vade [The saving of space is not sufficient to justify the break. Begin the word on the next line.]

WRONG man-y, show-y, dyspepsi-a [The final letter can be written as readily as the hyphen.]

WRONG fire-eat-er, mass-pro-duced, Pre-Raphael-ite

RIGHT fire-eater, mass-produced, Pre-Raphaelite [Divide hyphenated words only where the hyphen comes in the regular spelling.]

► EXERCISE. With the aid of your dictionary write out the following words by syllables, grouping (1) those that may properly be divided at the end of a line, and (2) those that may not be divided: *affection, against, alone, combed, decadent, erase, immense, levy, looked, nature, rainy, thought, through, transient, treaty, troller, trolley, vary, veiled, walked, weary, willing, willow, wily, windy.*

▸ Capitals

9

Capitalize words in accordance with general usage. Avoid unnecessary capitals.

9a Capitalize proper names and, generally, derivatives of proper names and abbreviations of them.[1]

1. SPECIFIC PERSONS OR PLACES: Milton, Miltonic; California, Californian, Cal.; the South (referring to a specific section of the country); the Orient, an Oriental custom
2. ORGANIZATIONS OF ALL KINDS: Rotarians, Quakers, the Standard Oil Company, the Republican Party, Communist (a member of the Communist Party), the Senate, the Air Service, the United Nations, the Atomic Energy Commission, the Freshman Class (*but* a freshman)

---

[1] In general, abbreviations are capitalized or not according to the capitalization of the word abbreviated. One important exception is *No.* for *number.* For a more detailed discussion of capitalization of words and abbreviations see the *Style Manual* of the United States Government Printing Office, 1953, pp. 17-50, or *A Manual of Style,* the University of Chicago Press, 1949, pp. 23-45. Capitalization of individual words may well be checked in a good dictionary, such as *The American College Dictionary* or *Webster's New World Dictionary* (in the main vocabulary) or *Webster's New Collegiate Dictionary* (in the main vocabulary and also in a special section, pp. 998-1007).

3. RACES, PEOPLES, AND LANGUAGES: Caucasian, Indian, Negro, Dutch, Norwegian, Pole, Polish, Spanish
4. DAYS OF THE WEEK, MONTHS, SPECIAL DAYS: Friday, June, Christmas, Easter, Labor Day
5. HISTORICAL PERIODS, EVENTS, OR DOCUMENTS: the Dark Ages, the Stone Age, the Spanish War, the Revolution, the Magna Carta, the Declaration of Independence
6. WORDS PERTAINING TO DEITY: God the Father, the Lord, the Saviour, the Trinity, the Almighty, the Creator
7. PERSONIFICATIONS:

   Can Honor's voice provoke the silent dust,
   Or Flattery soothe the dull cold ear of Death?

   —GRAY

8. ADJECTIVES DERIVED FROM PROPER NOUNS: Southern or Western (referring to the South or the West, specific sections of the country), an English ship, an Italic custom (but italic type because this common adjective is no longer closely associated with the source). In case of doubt, consult a recent dictionary.

9b Capitalize titles preceding the name, or other words used as an essential part of a proper name.

RIGHT Mr. Brown, Judge White, King George, Aunt Mary

(1) Titles immediately following the name, or used alone as a substitute for the name, are capitalized only to indicate pre-eminence or high distinction: Dwight D. Eisenhower, President of the United States; the President of the United States; the President. On the other hand, ordinary titles are usually not capitalized: William Smith, president of the First National Bank; the president of the bank.

(2) Words denoting family relationship (*father*, *mother*, *brother*, *aunt*, *cousin*) are generally capitalized when used as

titles or alone in place of the name, but not when preceded by a possessive: Brother William; Sister Mary;[2] Mary, my sister; my brother; my sister; a trip with Father; a trip with my father; a letter from Mother; a letter from my mother.

(3) Such words as *college*, *high school*, *club*, *lake*, *river*, *park*, *building*, *street*, *pike*, *county*, *railroad*, and *society* are (except in newspapers) usually capitalized when they are an essential part of a proper name, but not when used alone as a substitute for the name: Knox College, the college; Central High School, the high school; Madison Street, the street; the Pennsylvania Railroad, the railroad.

► EXERCISE 1. In the following sentences supply capitals wherever needed. State the reason for the use of each capital.

1. Very gradually the prince's position changed. 2. He began to find the study of politics less uninteresting than he had supposed. 3. He read blackstone, and took lessons in english law; he was occasionally present when the queen interviewed her ministers. 4. At lord melbourne's suggestion he was shown all the despatches relating to foreign affairs. 5. Sometimes he would commit his views to paper, and read them aloud to the prime minister, who, infinitely kind and courteous, listened with attention, but seldom made any reply. 6. An important step was taken when, before the birth of the princess royal, the prince, without any opposition in parliament, was appointed regent in case of the death of the queen. 7. Stockmar, owing to whose intervention with the tories this happy result had been brought about, now felt himself at liberty to take a holiday with his family in coburg. 8. But his solicitude, poured out in innumerable letters, still watched over his pupil from afar. 9. "Dear prince," he wrote, "I am satisfied with the news you have sent me. 10. Mistakes, misunderstandings,

[2] This rule also applies to names of members of religious orders.

obstructions, which come in vexatious opposition to one's views, are always to be taken for just what they are—namely, natural phenomena of life, which represent one of its sides and that the shady one."[3]

► EXERCISE 2. Copy the following sentences, supplying capitals wherever needed. State the reason for the use of each capital.

1. We invited judge green to meet uncle henry at the cosmos club to make plans for the annual community chest drive.
2. This club meets every monday in the madison state bank building on walnut street.
3. We invited mother and aunt bertha to attend our class play at parker high school.
4. Both my mother and my aunt had graduated from the same high school.
5. Before the end of the summer, perhaps during july, the president of the first national bank will take a vacation in florida.
6. The pacific ocean was discovered in 1513 by a spaniard named balboa.
7. When I returned to my work after labor day, I met mr. morgan, president of the liberty trust company.
8. The sussex riding club has bought a large tract of land near sand lake.
9. The president of this club is also president of the second national bank.
10. We are expecting father and uncle robert to visit us during the easter vacation.
11. After William was graduated from westview high school, he entered simpson college.
12. This high school has sent more than one hundred of its graduates to harvard during the past twenty years.

---

[3] Adapted from *Queen Victoria*, by Lytton Strachey, copyright 1921, by Harcourt, Brace and Company, Inc.; renewed, 1949, by James Strachey. Reprinted by permission of the publishers.

13. As soon as mother met uncle james, she told him that she had seen major white at the claiborne county fair.
14. Young northerners are sometimes advised to settle in the south or in the west, and many of them do go south or west.
15. Many new englanders go south for part of the winter, but usually they are back in the north before easter.
16. It is difficult to say whether southerners or westerners are more hospitable.
17. Some indians still live in the everglades of florida.
18. Many americans in the northwest are of polish or scandinavian descent.
19. Most of our high schools open the week after labor day, but west high school will open a week later.

9c In titles of books, plays, student papers, etc., capitalize the first word and all succeeding words except articles (*a, an, the*) and short conjunctions or prepositions.

RIGHT *Crime and Punishment*, *To Have and to Hold*, *Midnight on the Desert*, *The Man Without a Country* [A conjunction or preposition of five or more letters (*without*) is usually capitalized.]

9d Capitalize the pronoun *I* and the interjection O (but not *oh*).

RIGHT If *I* forget thee, *O* Jerusalem, let my right hand forget her cunning. —PSALMS

9e Capitalize the first word of every sentence (including quoted sentences and direct questions) and the first word of every line of poetry.[4]

[4] Except poetry originally printed without initial capitals.

RIGHT He said, "The work is almost finished."

RIGHT He said that the work was "almost finished." [A fragmentary quotation does not begin with a capital.]

RIGHT The question is, Shall we go?

RIGHT But I was one-and-twenty,
No use to talk to me. —HOUSMAN

Capitals after the colon. A quoted sentence after the colon regularly begins with a capital, but other sentences are usually not capitalized if they are closely related to the preceding clause. For examples see Section **17d.**

9f Avoid unnecessary capitals.

Many students err in using too many rather than too few capitals. If you have a tendency to overuse capitals, you should study the five principles treated above (**9a, b, c, d, e**) and use a capital letter only when you can justify it.

WRONG He went farther South for the winter. [Mere direction —*south, southwest, north, east*—is not capitalized.]

RIGHT He went south for the winter, *or* He lived in the South during the winter.

RIGHT Winter, spring, summer, and autumn are the four seasons. [Names of the seasons are usually not capitalized.]

RIGHT I studied History 2, geography, Spanish, and mathematics. [It is preferable to capitalize the name of a study only when it is specific—*History* 2—or when it is derived from a proper name—*Spanish.*]

RIGHT I went to high school, to college, to the library (*or* to Dover High School, to Oberlin College, to Wade Memorial Library).

RIGHT Gum arabic; italic type. [Words from proper nouns that have acquired general meanings are not capitalized. When in doubt, consult your dictionary.]

► EXERCISE 3. Indicate which of the capitals in the following sentences should be changed to small letters and which small letters changed to capitals. State your reasons.

1. According to traditions now perhaps forever impossible to verify, Shakespeare wrote *The merry Wives Of Windsor* at the desire of queen Elizabeth, who commanded that it be finished in a fortnight and that it show Falstaff in Love. 2. One may believe these Tales or not, as he chooses. 3. but suppose they are true. 4. Two weeks is an uncomfortably short time, and a Dramatist pressed to fill such an order would quite imaginably summon up every short cut in his Bag of Tricks to meet the deadline. 5. First a plot of some sort must be pieced together, with falstaff in it, in love. 6. But suppose that done, or at least begun. 7. Now if the dialogue were in Prose, some writing time might possibly be saved. 8. And if here and there another Character besides Falstaff, already created for another Play, could be worked in, there might be an added saving. 9. Lines might be written, too, in a wild skimble-scamble of Rant, Cant, Jargon, and Malapropism; to have the mouths of half the characters filled with such Nonsense might be overdoing it, but that would have to be risked. 10. And if, to piece out the Plot with Incident, the Ragbag of recent gossip—windsor gossip especially—were tumbled out and ransacked, a play of sorts might conceivably be rigged out in time. 11. Any or all of these short cuts might do to try—Still assuming, of course, that the traditions are correct and that by Hook or by Crook a play was going to have to be ready within the Fortnight as ordered.

▶ Italics

10

Italicize (underline) titles of publications, foreign words, names of ships, titles of works of art, and words spoken of as words. Use italics sparingly for emphasis.

In longhand or typewritten papers, italics are indicated by underlining. The printer sets all underlined words in italic type.

TYPEWRITTEN In David Copperfield Dickens writes of his own boyhood.

PRINT In *David Copperfield* Dickens writes of his own boyhood.

10a Titles of separate publications—such as books, bulletins, magazines, newspapers, musical productions—are italicized (underlined) when mentioned in writing.

Occasionally quotation marks are used instead of italics for titles of separate publications. The usual practice, however, reserves quotation marks for short stories, short poems, one-act plays, articles from periodicals, and subdivisions of books. See Section **16b.**

RIGHT *David Copperfield* opens with a chapter entitled "I Am Born."

RIGHT Many people still enjoy Mark Twain's *Roughing It.* [Note that the author's name is not italicized.]

RIGHT We read *The Comedy of Errors,* which is based on the *Menaechmi* of Plautus. [An initial, *a, an,* or *the* is capitalized and italicized only when it belongs to the title.]

RIGHT Mozart's *Don Giovanni;* Beethoven's *Fifth Symphony*

RIGHT He pored over *Time,* the *Atlantic Monthly,* the *Saturday Evening Post,* and the *New York Times* (or: New York *Times*). [Italics are not commonly used for articles standing first in the titles of periodicals, and sometimes not used for the name of the city in the titles of newspapers. Many periodicals omit all italics for titles, but students are usually cautioned against this informal practice.]

10b Foreign words and phrases not yet Anglicized are usually italicized (underlined).

Such words are indicated in *Webster's New Collegiate Dictionary* by parallel bars (‖), and in *Webster's New World Dictionary* by a double dagger (‡), immediately before the words; in *The American College Dictionary,* by the italicized name of the language immediately after the words.

RIGHT She had a *joie de vivre* distinctly her own.

RIGHT Mexico is sometimes called the land of *mañana.*

RIGHT The *Weltansicht* of despots is often discolored by their ambitions.

RIGHT We heartily wish him *bon voyage.*

► EXERCISE 1. With the aid of your dictionary list and underline five foreign words or phrases that are generally written in italics. List five other foreign words or phrases (such as "apropos," "bona fide," "ex officio") that no longer require italics.

10c Names of ships and aircraft and titles of works of art are italicized (underlined).

RIGHT The *Queen Mary* and the *Princess Elizabeth* sailed from New York.

RIGHT Rodin's *The Thinker* stands in one of the Parisian gardens.

10d Words, letters, or figures spoken of as such or used as illustrations are usually italicized (underlined). (See also **16c.**)

RIGHT The article *the* has lost much of its demonstrative force. In England an *elevator* is called a *lift*. [Sometimes quotation marks ("the," "elevator," "lift") are used instead of italics.]

RIGHT The final *e* in *stone* is silent.

RIGHT The first *3* and the final *o* of the serial number are barely legible.

► EXERCISE 2. Copy the following sentences, italicizing (underlining) as necessary.

1. Galsworthy's The Man of Property, In Chancery, and To Let were published separately as novels between 1906 and 1921, before they were issued in one volume entitled The Forsyte Saga.
2. To Let was completed in September, 1920, before Galsworthy sailed from Liverpool on the Empress of France to spend the winter in America.
3. Galsworthy's novels have been reviewed in such periodicals as Harper's Magazine, the Saturday Review of Literature, and the New York Herald Tribune.
4. According to Greenough and Kittredge, in their book entitled Words and Their Ways in English Speech, "it is more natural for us to say divide (from L. divido) than cleave (from A.S. cleofan); travel than fare; river than stream; castle than burg; residence than dwelling;

remain than abide; expect than ween; pupil or scholar than learner."

5. A Manual of Style, published by the University of Chicago Press, recommends that such Latin words or abbreviations as vide, idem, ibid., and op. cit. be italicized when used in literary references.

10e As a rule do not use italics (underlining) to give special emphasis to a word or a group of words. Do not underline the title of your own paper.

Frequent use of italics for emphasis defeats its own purpose and becomes merely an annoyance to the reader. This use of italics has been largely abandoned by good contemporary writers. Emphasis on a given word or phrase is usually best secured by careful arrangement of the sentence. See Section 29.

Note: A title is not italicized when it stands at the head of a book or an article. Accordingly, a student should not italicize (underline) the title standing at the head of his own paper (unless the title happens to be also the title of a book).

▶ EXERCISE ON ITALICS

Copy the following passage, underscoring all words that should be italicized.

1. I was returning home on the America when I happened to see a copy of Euripides' Medea. 2. The play was of course in translation, by Murray, I believe; it was reprinted in Riley's Great Plays of Greece and Rome. 3. I admire Medea the play and Medea the woman. 4. Both of them have a quality of atrocitas which our contemporary primitivism misses. 5. Characters in modern plays are neurotic; Medea was sublimely and savagely mad.

▶ Abbreviations and Numbers

11

In ordinary writing avoid abbreviations (with a few well-known exceptions), and write out numbers whenever they can be expressed in one or two words.

Abbreviations

11a In ordinary writing spell out all titles except *Mr., Messrs., Mrs., Mmes., Dr.,* and *St.* (*saint,* not *street*). Spell out even these titles when not followed by proper names.

WRONG The Dr. made his report to the Maj.
RIGHT The doctor (*or* Dr. Smith) made his report to the major (*or* to Major Brown).

In informal writing *Hon.* and *Rev.* may be used before the surname when it is preceded by the Christian name or initials, never before the surname alone.

WRONG Hon. Smith, Rev. Jones
RIGHT Hon. George Smith, Hon. G. E. Smith, Rev. Thomas Jones, Rev. T. E. Jones
RIGHT (more formal) The Honorable George Edward Smith, the Reverend Thomas Everett Jones, the Reverend Mr. Jones

For forms of address in writing or speaking to officials and other dignitaries of church and state see *Webster's New World Dictionary*, pages 1717-19.

11b In ordinary writing spell out names of states, countries, months, and days of the week.

WRONG He left Ia. on the last Sun. in Jul.
RIGHT He left Iowa on the last Sunday in July.

WRONG James will go to Mex. in Oct.
RIGHT James will go to Mexico in October.

11c In ordinary writing spell out *Street, Road, Park, Company,* and similar words used as part of a proper name.

WRONG The procession moved down Lee St. between Central Pk. and the neon signs of the Ford Motor Co.
RIGHT The procession moved down Lee Street between Central Park and the neon signs of the Ford Motor Company.

Avoid the use of & (for *and*) and such abbreviations as *Bros.* or *Inc.* except in copying official titles: A & P; Goldsmith Bros.; Best & Co., Inc.; Doubleday & Company, Inc.

11d In ordinary writing spell out the words *volume, chapter,* and *page* and the names of subjects.

WRONG The notes on chem. are taken from ch. 9, p. 46.
RIGHT The notes on chemistry are taken from chapter 9, page 46.

Many abbreviations not acceptable in the text are preferable in footnotes. See Section 33.

11e In ordinary writing spell out Christian names.

WRONG Jas. Smith, Geo. White
RIGHT James Smith, George White

Permissible Abbreviations: In addition to the abbreviations mentioned in **11a,** the following are permissible and usually desirable.

1. *After proper names:* Jr., Sr., Esq., and degrees such as D.D., LL.D., M.A., M.D.

   RIGHT Mr. Sam Jones, Sr.; Sam Jones, Jr.; Thomas Jones, M.D.

2. *With dates or numerals:* A.D., B.C., A.M., P.M. (*or* a.m., p.m.), No., $

   RIGHT In 450 B.C., at 9:30 A.M.; in room No. 6; for $365

   WRONG Early this A.M. he asked the No. of your room. [The abbreviations are correct only with the numerals.]

   RIGHT Early this morning he asked the number of your room.

3. *For names of organizations and government agencies usually referred to by their initials:* DAR, ECA, GOP, RFC, TVA, WAC

4. *In general use, but often spelled out in formal writing as indicated in parentheses:* i.e. (*that is*), e.g. (*for example*), viz. (*namely*), cf. (*compare*), etc. (*and so forth*), vs. (*versus*)

Note: Use *etc.* sparingly. Never write *and etc.* The abbreviation comes from *et cetera,* of which *et* means *and.*

Special Exceptions: Many abbreviations are desirable in footnotes, in tabulations, and in certain types of technical writing. In such special writing the student should follow the practice of the better publications in the field. If he has any doubt regarding the spelling or capitalization of any abbreviation, he should consult a good dictionary such as *Webster's New Collegiate Dictionary* (in a special section, pages 998-1007) or *The American College Dictionary* or *Webster's New World Dictionary* (in the main vocabulary).

Numbers

11f Although usage varies, writers tend to spell out numbers that require only one or two words; they regularly use figures for other numbers.

RIGHT twenty years; a sum of four dollars; fifty thousand dollars; a million dollars

RIGHT after 124 years; a sum of $2.27; only 187 votes; exactly 4,568,305 votes [Note the commas used to separate millions, thousands, hundreds.]

Special Usage Regarding Numbers:

1. *Use figures for dates.*

RIGHT May 1, 1951; 1 May 1951; July 12, 1763

The letters *st*, *nd*, *rd*, *th* should not be added to the day of the month when the year follows; they need not be added even when the year is omitted.

CORRECT May 1, July 2

When the year is omitted, the day of the month may be written out.

CORRECT May first, July second

Ordinal numbers to designate the day of the month may be written out or expressed in figures.

CORRECT He came on the fifth (*or* 5th) of May.

But the year is never written out except in very formal social announcements or invitations.

2. *Use figures for street numbers, for pages and divisions of a book, for decimals and percentages, and for the hour of the day when used with* A.M. *or* P.M.

RIGHT 26 Main Avenue, 460 Fourth Street
RIGHT The quotation is from page 80.
RIGHT The bar is .63 of an inch thick.
RIGHT She gets 10 per cent of the profits.
RIGHT He arrived at 4:30 P.M.

3. *Be consistent in spelling out or using figures. Normally use figures for a series of numbers.*

RIGHT The garden plot was 125 feet long and 50 feet wide and contained an asparagus bed 12 feet square.

RIGHT He earned $60 weekly, spent $15 for room rent, $17.50 for board, $12 for incidentals, and saved $15.50.

4. *Normally spell out any numeral at the beginning of a sentence. If necessary, recast the sentence.*

WRONG 25 boys made the trip.
RIGHT Twenty-five boys made the trip.

WRONG 993 freshmen entered the college last year.
RIGHT Last year 993 freshmen entered the college.

5. *The practice of repeating in parentheses a number that is spelled out (now generally reserved for legal and commercial writing) should be used logically if at all.*

ILLOGICAL I enclose twenty ($20) dollars.
LOGICAL I enclose twenty (20) dollars.
LOGICAL I enclose twenty dollars ($20).

► EXERCISES ON ABBREVIATIONS AND NUMBERS

A. Correct the abbreviations and numbers in the following letter. Where necessary, substitute a word or phrase for abbreviations improperly used. Justify all corrections.

1. Dear Rev. Peabody 2. I left the State Ref. and arrived at home last Sat. A.M. 3. The family, etc., were very kind, as you said they would be. 4. Early tomorrow I'm going to 27 Jackson Blvd. to tell the Dr. how sorry I am. 5. I'll pay him the $475 I stole as soon as I have the $.

B. Consult your dictionary to find out what the following abbreviations mean.

1. R.F.D.	5. S.P.C.A.	9. A.A.U.P.	13. AAF
2. AAA	6. UNESCO	10. P.H.	14. Ph.C.
3. A.D., A.D.	7. B.C., B.C.	11. viz.	15. D.V.
4. chm.	8. i.e.	12. ex lib.	16. C.I.F.

C. In the following sentences correct all errors in the use of abbreviations and numbers.

1. My father moved to Cal. about 10 years ago.
2. He is now living at sixty-five Sandusky St. in Frisco.
3. Geo. Washington, our first Pres., was born in seventeen hundred and thirty-two.
4. When he was 20 years old, he inherited Mt. Vernon from his half bro.
5. He assumed command of the Continental armies in Cambridge, Mass., on Jul. 3, 1775.
6. 125 men were stationed in the mts. to serve as guides.
7. These one hundred and twenty-five men have been in service for nearly 5 years.
8. Our class in math. did not meet last Wed.
9. Do you know the No. of the prof's office?
10. Rev. Williams will preach next Sun.

PUNCTUATION

▶ The Comma

12

Use the comma where it is demanded by the structure of the sentence.

The many different uses of the comma may be grouped under a very few principles and mastered with comparative ease by anyone who understands the structure of the sentence.[1] These principles, which cover the normal practice of the best contemporary writers, are adequate for the needs of the average college student. He may note that skilled writers sometimes employ the comma in unusual ways to express delicate shades of meaning. Such variations can safely be made by the writer who has first learned to apply the following major principles:

---

[1] *Caution:* Mastery of the comma is almost impossible for anyone who does not understand the structure of the sentence. If a student cannot readily distinguish main clauses, subordinate clauses, and the various kinds of phrases, he should study Section **1, Sentence Sense,** especially **1d**, before trying to use this section. (Mastery of Section **12** will help to eliminate one of the two most common errors in the average student paper.)

a. To separate main clauses joined by *and, but, or, nor,* or *for.*
b. To separate an introductory clause (or a long phrase) from the main clause.
c. To separate items in a series (and co-ordinate adjectives modifying the same noun).
d. To set off nonrestrictive and other parenthetical elements.

Main Clauses

12a Main clauses joined by one of the co-ordinating conjunctions (*and, but, or, nor, for*)[2] are separated by a comma.

[If the conjunction is omitted, the main clauses must be separated by a semicolon—or broken into distinct sentences and separated by a period. See Sections 3 and **14.**]

RIGHT Other ages have produced inspiring discussions of the nature of the good life**,** but the people of the twentieth century have not been satisfied with reflection and discussion. —SUMNER H. SLICHTER

ages | have produced **,** but people | have been satisfied

RIGHT The ranchmen from the valley in the foothills rode in on saddles decorated with silver**,** and their sons demonstrated their skill with unbroken horses. —JOHN STEINBECK[3]

ranchmen | rode **,** and sons | demonstrated

---

[2] *Yet* is occasionally used as a co-ordinating conjunction equivalent to *but.* Informal writing frequently uses *so* as a co-ordinating conjunction, but careful writers usually avoid the *so*-sentence by subordinating one of the clauses.

[3] "Always Something to Do in Salinas," *Holiday,* June, 1955, p. 58.

Caution: Do not confuse the compound sentence (two main clauses) with the simple sentence (one main clause) containing a compound predicate.

RIGHT The ranchmen rode with their families into the little town and encouraged their sons to demonstrate their skill with unbroken horses.

ranchmen | rode and encouraged [No comma before *and*]

Even more objectionable than the comma between parts of the compound predicate would be the use of a comma before a conjunction which joins merely two words (*men* and *women*, *white* and *black*) or two phrases (*out of the pan* and *into the fire*, *to see* and *to believe*).

At times the comma is used to set off what seems to be merely the second part of a compound predicate, or even a phrase. Closer examination usually discloses, however, that such a word or phrase is actually a regular main clause with some words "understood." Note the following sentences, in which the implied matter is inserted in brackets:

There is no other way for the world's living standards to be raised to anything like our level, and [there is] no other way to link or merge the economies of the free nations. —FORTUNE

The number of high school graduates has been increasing since 1890 about thirteen times as fast as the population, and the number of college graduates [has been increasing] six times as fast. —THE ATLANTIC MONTHLY

We are proud of this tradition, and [we are] not [proud] without good cause. —FORTUNE

***Exceptions to* 12a:**

1. *Omission of the comma:*

When the main clauses are short, the comma is frequently omitted before *and* or *or*, less frequently before *but.*

Before *for* the comma is needed to prevent confusion with the preposition *for*. (In colloquial style, especially in narrative writing, the comma is frequently omitted even when the clauses are longer.)

RIGHT The brown earth turned dark and the trees glistened.
—JOHN STEINBECK

2. *Use of the semicolon instead of the comma:*

Sometimes the co-ordinating conjunction is preceded by a semicolon instead of the usual comma, especially when the main clauses have internal punctuation or reveal a striking contrast. See also Section **14a.**

RIGHT It was childish, of course; for any disturbance, any sudden intruding noise, would make the creatures stop.
—ALDOUS HUXLEY [4]

RIGHT The visit will have had a certain ritualistic value; but it will not have brightened the man's life, caught his fancy, stirred his soul, or fired a brand-new passion.
—WALTER KERR [5]

► EXERCISE 1. In each of the following sentences find the main clauses. Then explain why the main clauses should be (1) separated by a comma, (2) separated by a semicolon, or (3) left without any punctuation.

1. The governor proclaimed a state of civil emergency for the water supply was dangerously low. 2. The days passed and the drought grew steadily worse. 3. The state fire marshal ordered all parks closed but forest fires broke out in spite of all precautions. 4. City-dwellers watched their gardens shrivel and die and industrial workers were laid off as electric-power output failed. 5. But perhaps the worst afflicted were the farmers for there was no hope of

[4] "Voices," *Atlantic Monthly*, July, 1955, p. 33.
[5] "Killing Off the Theatre," *Harper's Magazine*, April, 1955, p. 55.

saving their crops and even their livestock had to be sold on a glutted market or else left to die in the fields.

6. Our first night at the camp I remember very well for I thought I should never live to tell the story.
7. The bus stopped and the children got off.
8. It was a difficult year but I managed to graduate with my class.
9. It was a difficult year, filled with interruptions, new instructors, and shifting schedules but I budgeted my time so carefully that I was able to hold my place on the team and also to graduate with my class.

► EXERCISE 2. Compose six sentences (two to illustrate each type) in which main clauses are (1) separated by a comma, (2) separated by a semicolon, and (3) left without any punctuation.

Introductory Clauses

12b A subordinate clause (or a long phrase) preceding the main clause is usually followed by a comma.

RIGHT *Although I am not a member of the club*, I know much of its history. [Subordinate clause preceding the main clause]

RIGHT *At the critical moments in this sad history*, there have been men worth listening to who warned the people against their mistakes. —WALTER LIPPMANN [6]

Introductory phrases containing a gerund, a participle, or an infinitive, even though short, must often be followed by a comma to prevent misreading.

RIGHT *Before leaving*, the soldiers demolished the fort.

RIGHT *Because of his effort to escape*, his punishment was increased.

---

[6] "The Decline of Western Democracy," *Atlantic Monthly*, February, 1955, p. 33.

Short introductory prepositional phrases, except when they are transitional expressions (such as *in fact, on the other hand,* and especially *for example, generally speaking, in the light of these facts*), are seldom followed by a comma.

RIGHT *During the night* he heard many noises.
RIGHT *Within the next few days* I hope to leave.
RIGHT *In fact,* I hope to leave tomorrow. [Transitional expression]

Many writers omit the comma after short introductory clauses, and sometimes after longer ones, when the omission does not make for difficult reading. In the following sentences the commas may be used or omitted at the option of the writer:

When you arrive(,) you will find me waiting for you.
When *he* comes to the end of the lane(,) *he* should turn to the left. [When the subject of the introductory clause is repeated in the main clause, the comma is usually unnecessary.]
If we do not go(,) we may be sorry.

Adverb clauses following the main clause. Each introductory clause illustrated above is an adverb clause—i.e., it modifies the verb of the main clause. When the adverb clause *follows* the main clause, the comma is usually omitted. (*Example:* The comma is usually omitted *when the adverb clause follows the main clause.*) But such clauses are set off by a comma if they are nonrestrictive or loosely connected with the rest of the sentence, especially if the subordinating conjunction seems equivalent to a co-ordinating conjunction.

RIGHT Henry is now in good health, although he has been an invalid most of his life. [*Although* is equivalent to *but.*]
RIGHT He stayed until Sunday, when he packed his trunk and went home. [*When* is equivalent to *and then.*]

▶ EXERCISE 3. In each of the following sentences find the main clause and identify the preceding element as a subordinate clause or a phrase. Then determine whether to use or omit a comma after the introductory element. Justify your decision.

1. In order to pay his way through college George worked at nights in an iron foundry. 2. During this time he became acquainted with all the company's operations. 3. At the end of four years' observation of George's work the foundry owner offered George a position as manager. 4. Although George had planned to attend medical school and enter his father's profession he found now that the kind of work he had been doing had a far greater appeal for him. 5. Without hesitation he accepted the offer.

Items in Series

12c Words, phrases, or clauses in a series (and coordinate adjectives modifying the same noun) are separated by commas.

(1) Words, phrases, or clauses in a series

RIGHT The room is *bright*, *clean*, *quiet*. [Form *a*, *b*, *c*]
RIGHT The room is *bright*, *clean*, and *quiet*. [Form *a*, *b*, and *c*]
RIGHT The room is *bright* and *clean* and *quiet*. [Form *a* and *b* and *c*. Commas are omitted when *and* is used throughout the series]

RIGHT He walked *up the steps*, *across the porch*, and *through the doorway*. [Phrases in a series]

RIGHT We protested *that the engine used too much oil*, *that the brakes were worn out*, and *that the tires were dangerous*. [Subordinate clauses in a series]

The final comma is often omitted, especially by newspapers, when the series takes the form *a*, *b*, and *c*. But students are usually advised to follow the practice of the more conservative books and periodicals in using the comma throughout the series, if only because the comma is sometimes needed to prevent confusion.

CONFUSING The natives ate beans, onions, rice and honey. [Was the rice and honey a mixture?]

CLEAR The natives ate beans, onions, rice, and honey; *or* The natives ate beans, onions, and rice and honey.

(2) Co-ordinate adjectives

RIGHT a *clean*, *quiet* room; a *bright*, *clean*, *quiet* room; a *keen*, *watchful* man. [*Clean* and *quiet* are co-ordinate—that is, of equal grammatical rank—and modify the same noun, *room*.]

RIGHT a *clean* and *quiet* room; a *bright* and *clean* and *quiet* room; a *keen* and *watchful* man. [The adjectives are co-ordinate, as shown by the easy substitution of *and* for the comma.]

RIGHT a *deep*, *malevolent* satisfaction. —ALDOUS HUXLEY [7]

The comma is omitted between adjectives not truly co-ordinate, as when the second adjective is thought of as a part of the noun.

RIGHT a *quiet* dining room [*Dining room* has the force of a single noun, like *bedroom*. *Quiet* and *dining* are not co-ordinate; instead, *quiet* modifies *dining room*.]

RIGHT a *keen* old man; *beautiful* blue eyes; *ambitious* young men [*Old man*, *blue eyes*, and *young men* have the force of single nouns. *And* cannot be used between the adjectives.]

But in "young, ambitious men" or "blue, beautiful eyes" the adjectives are co-ordinate, as shown by the possibility of writing "young *and* ambitious men" or "blue *and* beautiful eyes."

---

[7] "Voices," *Atlantic Monthly*, July, 1955, p. 33.

Caution: A comma is not used between the adjective and the noun.

WRONG a clean, quiet, room.
RIGHT a clean, quiet room.

► EXERCISE 4. In the following sentences distinguish each series and each group of co-ordinate adjectives, inserting commas where needed. Justify each comma used.

1. Do you remember Pete Moore and that old battered lunch pail he used to carry? 2. He would go past our house every morning wait on the corner for his ride hand his lunch pail up to one of the men on the truck climb up himself and go rolling away. 3. Year after year—spring summer fall and winter—Pete and his lunch pail would wait on that corner. 4. And every year they both got a little older a little more battered a little nearer used up. 5. My brothers my sisters and I used to make bets about which would wear out first. 6. Then one awful day we heard the blast at the plant saw the sky black with smoke and watched the streets fill with frightened hurrying people. 7. That day was the end of old Pete of his battered lunch pail and of the jokes we made about them.

► EXERCISE 5. Compose six sentences to illustrate punctuation of co-ordinate adjectives and different types of items in series.

12d Nonrestrictive clauses (or phrases) and other parenthetical elements ("interrupters") are set off by commas. Restrictive clauses (or phrases) are not set off.

To *set off* means to put a comma after a parenthetical element at the beginning of a sentence, before a parenthetical element at the end, and both before and after one within a sentence. ***Caution:*** When two commas are needed to set off a parenthetical element within the sentence, as in the third and sixth sentences below, the omission of one of the two commas is usually more objectionable than the omission of both.

EXAMPLES *My friends*, we have no alternative.
We have no alternative, *my friends.*
We have, *my friends*, no alternative.

He said, "The story has been told."
"The story has been told," *he said.*
"The story," *he said*, "has been told."

(1) Nonrestrictive clauses and phrases are set off by commas. Restrictive clauses and phrases are not set off.

Adjective clauses introduced by *who* or *which* are nonrestrictive (set off by commas) when they merely add information about a word already identified. Such clauses are parenthetical; they are not essential to the meaning of the main clause and may be omitted.

My mother, *who is visiting me*, is on her way to New York.
Henry Smith, *who is lazy*, will lose his job.
Florence, *which he visited next*, was then torn by rival factions.

Adjective clauses introduced by *who*, *which*, or *that* are restrictive (not set off by commas) when they are needed for identification of the word they modify. Such clauses limit or qualify the meaning of the sentence and cannot be omitted.

A mother *who does not love her son* is unnatural.
A boy *who is lazy* deserves to lose his job.
The city *that he visited next* was Florence.

Anyone who has difficulty in distinguishing between restrictive and nonrestrictive clauses should read aloud the illustrative sentences above, noting the lack of pause before restrictive clauses and the definite pauses setting off nonrestrictive clauses. The "pause" test may prove helpful, but a more conclusive test is to read the sentence without the clause.

NONRESTRICTIVE CLAUSE Our newest boat, *which is painted red and white*, has sprung a leak. [The *which* clause, adding information about a boat already identified, is parenthetical. It is not essential to the main clause, *Our newest boat has sprung a leak.*]

NONRESTRICTIVE PHRASE Our newest boat, *painted red and white*, has sprung a leak.

RESTRICTIVE CLAUSE (NO COMMAS) A boat *that leaks* is of little use. [The clause *that leaks* is essential to the meaning of the main clause.]

RESTRICTIVE PHRASE (NO COMMAS) A boat *with a leak* is of little use.

NONRESTRICTIVE CLAUSE My new car, *which is parked across the street*, is ready. [Clause adding information about a car already identified]

NONRESTRICTIVE PHRASE My new car, *parked across the street*, is ready.

RESTRICTIVE CLAUSE (NO COMMAS) The car *which is parked across the street* is ready. [Clause essential to the identification]

RESTRICTIVE PHRASE (NO COMMAS) The car *parked across the street* is ready.

Sometimes a clause (or phrase) may be either restrictive or nonrestrictive; the writer signifies his meaning by the proper use of the comma.

NONRESTRICTIVE He spent hours caring for the Indian guides, who were sick with malaria. [He cared for all the Indian guides. All of them were sick with malaria.]

RESTRICTIVE (NO COMMA) He spent hours caring for the Indian guides who were sick with malaria. [Some of the Indian guides were sick with malaria. He cared for the sick ones.]

► EXERCISE 6. In the following sentences determine whether each clause (or phrase) is restrictive or nonrestrictive. Set off only the nonrestrictive clauses (or phrases).

1. The James Lee who owns the bank is a grandson of the one who founded it.
2. James Lee who owns this bank and five others is one of the wealthiest men in the state.
3. The coach called out to Higgins who got up from the bench and trotted over to him.
4. Higgins had an ankle which sometimes gave him trouble.
5. The coach who chewed on cigars but never lighted them threw one away and reached for another.
6. Anyone who saw him could tell that something was troubling him.
7. All banks which fail to report will be closed.
8. All banks failing to report will be closed.
9. The law permitted banks to borrow money from the Federal Reserve Banks which were twelve in number.
10. Henry betrayed the man who had helped him build his fortune.
11. James White who had helped Henry build his fortune died yesterday.
12. My father hoping that I would remain at home offered me a share in his business.

► EXERCISE 7. Compose and punctuate five sentences containing nonrestrictive clauses or phrases. Compose five sentences containing restrictive clauses or phrases and underline the restrictive elements.

(2) Nonrestrictive appositives, contrasted elements, geographical names, and items in dates and addresses are set off by commas.

Note that most appositives may be readily expanded into nonrestrictive clauses. In other words, the principle underlying the use of commas to set off nonrestrictive clauses also applies here.

APPOSITIVES AND CONTRASTED ELEMENTS

RIGHT Jesse, *the caretaker*, is a good fellow. [The appositive *caretaker* is equivalent to the nonrestrictive clause *who is the caretaker*.]

RIGHT Sandburg, *the biographer of Lincoln*, was awarded the Pulitzer Prize. [The appositive is equivalent to the nonrestrictive clause *who is the biographer of Lincoln*.]

RIGHT My companions were James White, *Esq.*, William Smith, *M.D.*, and Rufus L. Black, *Ph.D.* [Abbreviated titles after a name are treated as appositives.]

RIGHT The cook, *not the caretaker*, will assist you. [The contrasted element is a sort of negative appositive.]

RIGHT Our failures, *not our successes*, will be remembered.

RIGHT Trade comes with peace, *not with war*.

Appositives are usually nonrestrictive (parenthetical), merely adding information about a person or thing already identified. Such appositives are set off by commas. But when an appositive is restrictive, commas are usually omitted.

RIGHT The poet Sandburg has written a biography. [*Sandburg* restricts the meaning, telling what poet has written a biography.]

RIGHT His son James is sick. [*James*, not his son *William*]

RIGHT William the Conqueror invaded England in 1066. [An appositive that is part of a title is restrictive.]

RIGHT The word *malapropism* is derived from Sheridan's *The Rivals*.

RIGHT Do you refer to Samuel Butler the poet or to Samuel Butler the novelist?

Note: The "pause" test and the "omission" test will prove helpful. See pages 126-27.

► EXERCISE 8. Copy the following sentences, using commas to set off contrasted elements and nonrestrictive appositives. Underline restrictive appositives.

1. When the three-master *Pharaon* put into Marseilles on February 28, 1815, she was commanded by nineteen-year-old Edmond Dantes not her captain but her first mate. 2. When M. Morrel the owner heard that the old captain had died at sea, he promised the post to Edmond, who went off gaily to see his father and his beloved the Catalan girl Mercedes. 3. Meantime Danglars the supercargo an offensive man of twenty-six who disliked Dantes was informing M. Morrel that Edmond had stopped at the Isle of Elba on the voyage. 4. Edmond found that his father had lived on almost nothing for three months, having paid the tailor Caderousse some money which Dantes owed. 5. The youth then hurried to the beautiful Mercedes, whom he found with her cousin Fernand Mondego a twenty-one-year-old fisherman. 6. While Edmond and Mercedes made hurried preparations for their marriage, Fernand and Danglars plotted together. 7. They wrote an anonymous letter to Ferard de Villefort the deputy *procureur de roi* saying that Dantes was carrying a letter from Napoleon to the Bonapartists in Paris.[8]

► EXERCISE 9. Compose ten sentences to illustrate the punctuation of appositives and contrasted elements.

GEOGRAPHICAL NAMES, ITEMS IN DATES AND ADDRESSES

RIGHT Pasadena, California, is the site of the Rose Bowl. [*California* may be thought of as equivalent to the nonrestrictive clause *which is in California*.]

---

[8] Adapted from *Plot Outlines of 100 Famous Novels*, ed. Roland A. Goodman, by permission of Garden City Books. Copyright, 1942, by Doubleday & Company, Inc.

RIGHT My friends live near the Charles River at 24 Radcliff Road, Waban 68, Massachusetts. [Postal zone numbers are not separated by a comma from the name of the city.]

RIGHT Tuesday, May 8, 1956, in Chicago; 8 May 1956; May, 1956, in Boston *or* May 1956 in Boston. [Commas are often omitted when the day of the month is not given, or when the day of the month precedes rather than follows the month. Students are usually advised not to follow the less conservative practice of dropping the comma after the year, as in "May 8, 1956 in Chicago."]

► EXERCISE 10. Copy the following sentences, inserting commas where they are needed.

1. Their son was born on Friday June 18 1954 at Baptist Hospital Knoxville Tennessee.
2. Manuscripts should be mailed to the Managing Editor 109 Parrington Hall University of Washington Seattle 5 Washington.
3. He was inducted into the army at Fort Oglethorpe Georgia on 30 September 1942.
4. William Congreve was born in Bardsey England on January 24 1670.
5. The accident occurred in De Soto Parish Louisiana on Monday September 9 1950.
6. Please send all communications to 383 Madison Avenue New York 17 New York.

(3) Parenthetical words, phrases, or clauses (inserted expressions), words in direct address (vocatives), absolute phrases, and mild interjections are set off by commas.

PARENTHETICAL EXPRESSIONS

As a matter of fact, the term "parenthetical" is correctly applied to everything discussed under **12d**; but the term is more commonly applied to such expressions as *on the other* *hand*, *in the first place*, *in fact*, *to tell the truth*, *etc.*, *however*, *that is*, *for example*, *I hope*, *I report*, *he says*. The term would apply equally well to expressions inserted in dialogue: *he said*, *he observed*, *he protested*, etc.

RIGHT You will, *then*, accept our offer?
RIGHT *To tell the truth*, we anticipated bad luck.
RIGHT The work is, *on the whole*, very satisfactory.
RIGHT "We believe," *he replied*, "that you are correct."
RIGHT We believe, *however*, that you should go. [When *however* means "nevertheless," it is usually set off by commas. But when *however* means "no matter how," it is not parenthetical and is therefore not set off by commas: "The trip will be hard *however* you go.]

Some parenthetical expressions causing little if any pause in reading are frequently not set off by commas: *also*, *too*, *indeed*, *perhaps*, *at least*, *likewise*, etc. The writer must use his judgment.

RIGHT I am *also* of that opinion.
RIGHT He is *perhaps* the best swimmer on the team.
RIGHT Your efforts will *of course* be appreciated; *or*, Your efforts will, *of course*, be appreciated.

DIRECT ADDRESS

RIGHT Come here, *Mary*, and help us.
RIGHT I refuse, *sir*, to believe the report.
RIGHT This, *my friends*, is the whole truth.

ABSOLUTE PHRASES [9]

RIGHT *Everything being in readiness*, we departed promptly.
RIGHT He ran swiftly, *the dog in front of him*, and plunged into the forest.
RIGHT I fear the encounter, *his temper being what it is*.

---

[9] See Section 35, **Grammatical Terms.**

MILD INTERJECTIONS

RIGHT *Well*, let him try if he insists.
RIGHT *Ah*, that is my idea of a good meal.

[Strong interjections call for the exclamation point. See Section **17c**.]

12e Note: Occasionally a comma, though not called for by any of the major principles already discussed, may be needed to prevent misreading.

Use **12e** sparingly, if at all, to justify your commas. In a general sense, nearly all commas are used to prevent misreading or to make reading easier. Your mastery of the comma will come through the application of the more specific major principles (**a, b, c, d**) to the structure of your sentences.

CONFUSING Inside the room was gaily decorated. [*Inside* may be at first mistaken for the preposition.]
CLEAR Inside, the room was gaily decorated. [*Inside* clearly the adverb]

CONFUSING After all the conquest of malaria is a fascinating story.
CLEAR After all, the conquest of malaria is a fascinating story.

► EXERCISES ON THE COMMA

A. Copy the following passage, using commas to set off appositives, parenthetical expressions, words in direct address, absolute phrases, and mild interjections.

1. Gentlemen shall I tell you what you have done? 2. You have sent me a man broken in spirit to an untimely grave. 3. Ah do not think that I shudder at the thought of the grave. 4. On the contrary I welcome it. 5. Even as

a hurt child to the arms of a comforting mother I fly to it as my only refuge. 6. My wound being mortal where else should I fly? 7. Man and boy have I not served you on bloody fields of battle and in the halls of the Congress itself? 8. Is this then to be the mark of your gratitude? 9. Must I after a life of selfless service hear my dearest friends question my integrity in this manner? 10. Can it be possible I ask myself that those friends would even listen to the foul slanders spread by my opponent?

B. Copy the following passage, inserting all commas needed.

1. After a night spent in fever and sleeplessness I forced myself to take a long tramp the next day through the hilly country which was covered with pine woods. 2. It all looked dreary and desolate and I could not think what I should do there. 3. Returning in the afternoon I stretched myself dead tired on a hard couch awaiting the long-desired hour of sleep. 4. It did not come; but I fell into a kind of somnolent state in which I suddenly felt as though I were sinking in swiftly flowing water. 5. The rushing sound formed itself in my brain into a musical sound the chord of E-flat major which continually re-echoed in broken forms; these broken chords seemed to be melodic passages of increasing motion yet the pure triad of E-flat major never changed but seemed by its continuance to impart infinite significance to the element in which I was sinking. 6. I awoke in sudden terror from my doze feeling as though the waves were rushing high above my head. 7. I at once recognized that the orchestral overture to the *Rheingold* which must long have lain latent within me though it had been unable to find definite form had at last been revealed to me.

—RICHARD WAGNER

[*See the general exercises on the comma and the semicolon following Section* 14; *on capitals, italics, and all marks of punctuation following Section* 17.]

▶ Superfluous Commas

13

Do not use superfluous commas.

If you have a tendency to use unnecessary commas, consider every comma you are tempted to use and omit it unless you can justify its use by one of the principles treated under Section 12.

Another way to avoid unnecessary commas is to observe the following rules:

13a Do not use a comma to separate the subject and its verb, the verb and its object, or an adjective and its noun.

WRONG Rain at frequent intervals, is productive of mosquitoes. [Needless separation of subject and verb]

RIGHT Rain at frequent intervals is productive of mosquitoes.

Note, however, that a comma before the verb sometimes makes for clarity when the subject is heavily modified.

EXAMPLE Rain coming at frequent intervals and in sufficient amounts to fill the ponds, the cisterns, and the many small containers near the house, is productive of mosquitoes.

In the following sentences the commas in parentheses should be omitted:

He learned at an early age(,) the necessity of economizing. [Needless separation of verb and object]
The book says(,) that members of the crew deserted. [Indirect discourse: needless separation of verb and object]
He was a bad, deceitful, unruly(,) boy. [Incorrect separation of adjective and its noun]

13b Do not use a comma to separate two words or two phrases joined by a co-ordinating conjunction.

In the following sentences the commas in parentheses should be omitted:

The poem has nobility of sentiment(,) and dignity of style.
The players work together(,) and gain a victory. [Compound predicate: *and* joins two verbs.]
He had decided to work(,) and to save his money. [*And* joins two infinitive phrases.]

13c Do not use commas to set off words or short phrases (especially introductory ones) that are not parenthetical or that are very slightly so.

In the following sentences the commas in parentheses should be omitted:

On last Monday(,) I went to a baseball game.
Maybe(,) he had a better reason for leaving.
The center passes the ball(,) through his legs(,) to a man in the backfield.
In our age(,) it is easy to talk(,) by wire(,) to any continent.

13d Do not use commas to set off restrictive clauses, restrictive phrases, or restrictive appositives.

In the following sentences the commas in parentheses should be omitted:

A man(,) *who hopes to succeed*(,) must work hard. [Restrictive clause]

A man(,) *disinclined to work*(,) cannot succeed. [Restrictive phrase]

That man(,) *Jones*(,) will outwit his opponents. [Restrictive appositive]

13e Do not put a comma before the first item of a series, after the last item of a series, or after a conjunction.

In the following sentences the commas in parentheses should be omitted:

I enjoy the study of(,) history, geography, and geology. [Needless comma before the first item of a series. A colon here would be even worse—since there is no formal introduction. See **17d.**]

History, geography, and geology(,) are interesting subjects.

I enjoy these subjects, but(,) for others I have less appreciation.

Field work is required in a few sciences, such as(,) botany and geology.

► EXERCISE ON SUPERFLUOUS COMMAS

In the following passages (adapted from Francis Parkman) some of the commas are needed and some are superfluous. Strike out all commas that would usually be omitted in good contemporary writing. Justify each comma that you allow to stand.

1. In opening this plan of treachery, Pontiac spoke rather as a counselor, than as a commander. 2. Haughty as he was, he had too much sagacity to wound the pride of a body of men, over whom he had no other control, than that derived from his personal character and influence. 3. No one was hardy enough, to venture opposition to the proposal of their great leader. 4. His plan, was eagerly adopted. 5. Hoarse ejaculations, of applause, echoed his speech; and, gathering their blankets around them, the chiefs withdrew, to their respective villages, to prepare for the destruction of the unsuspecting garrison.

1. The twelve canoes, had reached the western end of the Lake, of St. Peter, where it is filled, with innumerable islands. 2. The forest was close, on their right; they kept near the shore, to avoid the current, and the shallow water, before them, was covered with a dense growth, of tall bulrushes. 3. Suddenly, the silence was frightfully broken. 4. The war-whoop rose, from among the rushes, mingled, with the reports of guns, and the whistling of bullets; and several Iroquois canoes, filled, with warriors, pushed out, from their concealment, and bore down upon Jogues and his companions. 5. The Hurons, in the rear, were seized with a shameful panic. 6. They leaped ashore; left canoes, baggage, and, weapons; and, fled into the woods. 7. The French, and the Christian Hurons, made fight, for a time; but, when they saw another fleet of canoes approaching, from the opposite shores, or islands, they lost heart, and those escaped, who could.

▸ The Semicolon

14

Use the semicolon (a) between two main clauses not joined by *and, but, or, nor,* or *for* and (b) between co-ordinate elements containing commas. (Use the semicolon only between parts of equal rank.)

Caution: Your understanding of this section will depend upon your ability to distinguish clauses and phrases, main clauses and subordinate clauses. You may need to master Section **1, Sentence Sense,** especially **1d** and **1e,** before studying Section **14.**

14a Use the semicolon between two main clauses not joined by one of the simple co-ordinating conjunctions (*and, but, or, nor, for*).

RIGHT The semicolon is a much stronger mark of separation than the comma; it is almost as strong as the period. [The use of a comma in such a sentence would be a *comma splice.* See Section 3.]

RIGHT With educated people, I suppose, punctuation is a matter of rule; with me it is a matter of feeling. But I must say I have a great respect for the semicolon; it's a useful little chap. —ABRAHAM LINCOLN

RIGHT We didn't abolish truth; even we couldn't do that.
—WILLIAM FAULKNER [1]

Conjunctive adverbs (such as *accordingly*, *also*, *anyhow*, *besides*, *consequently*, *furthermore*, *hence*, *however*, *indeed*, *instead*, *likewise*, *moreover*, *nevertheless*, *still*, *then*, *therefore*, *thus*) cannot be used in place of co-ordinating conjunctions. Thus, in accordance with the rule, main clauses joined by these adverbs should be separated by the semicolon.

RIGHT I carried a letter of introduction with me; therefore I had no difficulty in getting an interview. [But usually such sentences are better revised according to the principles of **Subordination,** Section 24: Since I carried a letter of introduction with me, I had no difficulty in getting an interview.]

Explanatory expressions (such as *for example*, *in fact*, *namely*, *on the contrary*, *on the other hand*, *that is*) are similar in use to conjunctive adverbs; that is, main clauses joined by them are usually separated by the semicolon.

RIGHT He is coming today; in fact, he is due here now.

Note: Such conjunctive adverbs or explanatory expressions as *therefore* and *in fact*, when used after the semicolon, are or are not followed by a comma, depending on how parenthetical the writer feels them to be. See Section **12d**(3).

Co-ordinating conjunctions between main clauses are often preceded by a semicolon (instead of the usual comma) if the clauses have internal punctuation or reveal a striking contrast. See also Section **12a.**

RIGHT American education may be sometimes slapdash and fantastic, with its short-story and saxophone courses, its strange fraternities and sororities, its musical-comedy

[1] "On Privacy," *Harper's Magazine*, July, 1955, p. 36.

co-ed atmosphere, its heavily solemn games departments; but at least it has never departed from the fine medieval tradition of the poor scholar. —JOSEPH PRIESTLEY

14b The semicolon is used to separate a series of equal elements which themselves contain commas.

This use of the semicolon makes for clarity, showing the reader at a glance the main divisions, which would otherwise be obscured by the commas.

RIGHT Her best friends were Laura Bagley, her sorority sister; John Bagley, Laura's brother; and James White, the president of the class. [Semicolons separating a series of nouns]

RIGHT It is well known that Mr. Fadiman is an exceedingly clever, witty, and nimble writer; that he has read widely and remembered well; and that he is wonderfully adept at communicating his appreciation to others. [Semicolons separating a series of noun clauses]

—CHARLES J. ROLO[2]

RIGHT He is not cantankerous, sour, spiteful, parochial, or fanatical; not arrogant, patronizing, or reactionary; not sanctimonious, glibly inspirational, nice-Nellyish, or mushy. [Semicolons separating a series of adjective groups] —IBID.

14c *Caution:* Do not use the semicolon between parts of unequal rank, such as a clause and a phrase or a main clause and a subordinate clause.

---

[2] From "Reader's Choice" by Charles J. Rolo, *Atlantic Monthly*, July 1955. By permission.

WRONG A bitter wind swept the dead leaves along the street; casting them high in the air and against the buildings. [Main clause; phrase]

RIGHT A bitter wind swept the dead leaves along the street, casting them high in the air and against the buildings.

WRONG I hope to spend my vacation in Canada; where I enjoy the fishing. [Main clause; subordinate clause]

RIGHT I hope to spend my vacation in Canada, where I enjoy the fishing.

► EXERCISES ON THE SEMICOLON

A. Copy the following sentences, inserting semicolons where they are needed. Do not allow a semicolon to stand between parts of unequal rank. Write *C* in place of each sentence that needs no revision.

1. We first knew the Martinellis in St. Louis; when they were living next door to us.
2. Mac goes around in par now, he has trimmed several strokes off his game since we played together last.
3. I hear it said by the people hereabouts that the old mansion is haunted, in fact, there are some who swear that it is.
4. Hank had dismantled his motor; intending to give it a complete overhaul for the following week's races.
5. He is fairly even-tempered most of the time, and you should have no difficulty getting along with him but whatever you do, don't ever let him get you into a political argument.
6. He lamented that he had no suggestions to offer, however, he spent the next forty minutes offering them.
7. It's all right for you to be here, I crashed this party myself.
8. I went to the address you gave me; if your brother lives there, he lives upstairs over a vacant lot.
9. In our unit at that time there were Lieutenant Holmes, who was a criminologist by profession and a university

lecturer on penology, Captain Sturm, in peacetime a U.S. Steel executive, two old majors, previously retired and now still writing their memoirs, Lieutenant Colonel Beale, a Mississippi cotton planter, and Colonel Quincy, who was, I think, some sort of tycoon in the peanut butter industry.

10. If you expect me to be here in time, or even to get back at all; you had better send somebody to help me.

B. From your reading, copy any five sentences in which the semicolon is properly used. Explain the reason for each semicolon.

C. Compose five sentences to illustrate the proper use of the semicolon.

[*See also the general exercises immediately following; also the general exercises following Section* **17**.]

► GENERAL EXERCISES ON THE COMMA AND THE SEMICOLON

A. Commas are used correctly in the following sentences. Explain each comma by writing above it the appropriate letter from Section **12**: **a, b, c,** or **d.** [Instead of using these letters for this and the following exercises, you may prefer to use meaningful abbreviations: *m* (main clauses), *i* (introductory clauses, phrases), *ser* (series), *c-ad* (co-ordinate adjectives), *nonr* (nonrestrictive), *app* (appositives, etc.), *par* (parenthetical).]

1. After crossing the river we built no more fires, for we were now in hostile Indian country.
2. Having nothing very important to do, I simply did nothing at all.
3. Well, all I have to say is that you didn't try very hard.
4. If he says he'll be there, he'll be there.
5. The smith straightened up, the horse's hoof still between his knees, and then he bent back to his work.

6. Although there are a few adjustments yet to be made, the main part of the work is finished, and the next few days should see it completed altogether.
7. The panting, tormented bull lowered his head for another charge.
8. The doctor, after a brief examination of the patient, gave orders to have him prepared for surgery.
9. The kit contains cement, balsa, paper, and instructions for assembly.
10. You will, I suppose, be back tomorrow.
11. The old opera house, which has stood unused for years, will finally be torn down.
12. Our class meets at ten on Mondays, Wednesdays, and Fridays.
13. The Executive Mansion is located at 1600 Pennsylvania Avenue, Washington, D. C.
14. To tell the truth, I am not quite sure where I was on November 18, 1955.
15. It was a long, hot, tiresome trip, and I was sorry that I had promised to go.

B. Explain each comma used in Section **1**, Exercise 21. Follow the directions given under A.

C. Explain each comma used in Section **1**, Exercise 23. Follow directions given under A.

D. Explain each comma used in Section **1**, Exercise 25. Follow directions given under A.

E. In the following sentences insert all necessary commas and semicolons. Then explain each comma by writing above it the appropriate letter from Section **12: a, b, c,** or **d** (or the abbreviations suggested in Exercise A).

1. Yes if you feel that you must go I hope you will not delay longer.
2. There is so far as I can see no reason why you should not.

3. If I were in your position however I would be extremely cautious about believing what I heard.
4. Taking everything into consideration I believe that Robinson should have a better season this year than ever before however you understand that this is only an opinion and that I reserve the right to amend it after I have seen him work out a few times.
5. After we wash the dishes we must wash the towels.
6. There were four letters for Marian but not a single one for me.
7. Two or three scrawny mangy-looking hounds lay sprawled in the shade of the cabin.
8. Have I your permission sir to continue?
9. While Frank was unpacking the cooking gear and Gene was chopping firewood I began to put up our shelter Phil meanwhile had gone down to the lake to try to get a few bass for our supper.
10. A small Christmas tree would cost very little perhaps we should buy one.
11. After perhaps an hour or so of waiting they may go away but don't expect them to go far and don't think they aren't still watching.
12. Bales of cotton hogsheads of sugar and salted meats barrels of flour and cases and crates of goods of every kind imaginable crowded the busy landing as far up and down the river as the eye could reach.
13. In complete disregard of the machine-gun bullets which were nipping through the grass tops all around us Jerry wriggled on his belly all the way out to where I was put a tourniquet on my leg and then began dragging me back to the shelter of the ditch.
14. "Tim you old reprobate" he shouted "it's good to see your ugly face again."
15. If I am expected to arrive by eleven o'clock someone should volunteer to wake me up otherwise I shall probably sleep until noon.

▸ The Apostrophe

15

Use the apostrophe to indicate the possessive case (except for personal pronouns), to mark omissions, and to form the plurals of letters and figures.

15a Do not carelessly omit the apostrophe in the possessive case of nouns and indefinite pronouns.

(1) If the ending (either singular or plural) is not in an *s* or *z* sound, add the apostrophe and *s*.

RIGHT The man's hat; the boy's shoes; a dollar's worth; today's problems [Singular]
RIGHT Men's hats; women's dresses [Plural]
RIGHT One's hat; another's coat; someone's shirt; anybody's room [Indefinite pronouns—singular]

(2) If the plural ends in an *s* or *z* sound, add only the apostrophe.

RIGHT Ladies' hats (hats for ladies); boys' shoes (shoes for boys); the Joneses' boys (the boys of the Joneses); three dollars' worth; Farmers' (*or* Farmers) Co-operative Society [The names of organizations frequently omit the apostrophe. Cf. Teachers College.]

(3) If the singular ends in an *s* or *z* sound, add the apostrophe and *s* for words of one syllable. Add only the apostrophe for words of more than one syllable unless you expect the pronunciation of the second *s* or *z* sound.

RIGHT James's book; Moses' law; Xerxes' army; Hortense's coat

(4) Compounds or nouns in joint possession show the possessive in the last word only. But if there is individual (or separate) possession, each noun takes the possessive form.

RIGHT My brother-in-law's house; my brothers-in-law's houses; someone else's hat

RIGHT Helen and Mary's piano [Joint ownership]

RIGHT Helen's and Mary's clothes [Individual ownership]

Although usage sanctions the apostrophe with compounds to indicate possession, an *of* phrase is frequently more pleasing: the house of my father-in-law; the car of the president of the bank (the president of the bank's car). For the use of an *of* phrase with inanimate objects see Section **5e**.

► EXERCISE 1. Copy the following, inserting apostrophes to indicate the possessive case:

1. everybodys business
2. the girls (*sing.*) coat
3. the girls (*pl.*) coats
4. Williams book
5. a months pay
6. two months pay
7. a turkeys nest
8. two turkeys nests
9. a fairys wand
10. fairies wands
11. the childs toys
12. the childrens toys

► EXERCISE 2. Rewrite the following as possessives with the apostrophe:

1. the home of my neighbor
2. homes of my neighbors
3. a book for a boy
4. books for boys
5. the car of my sister

6. the cars of my sisters
7. the ideas of a woman
8. the ideas of women
9. the boat of Robert and Jim
10. the boats of Robert and Jim (individual possession)
11. the hat of the lady
12. the hats of the ladies

15b Do not use the apostrophe with the personal pronouns (*his, hers, its, ours, yours, theirs*) or with the relative-interrogative pronoun *whose*.

WRONG He met *hi's* friend. [An error no one would make]
RIGHT He met *his* friend.

WRONG Virtue is *it's* own reward. [Fully as wrong as *hi's*. *It's* means "it is."]
RIGHT Virtue is *its* own reward.

WRONG her's, hers', it's (possessive), its', our's, ours', your's, yours', their's, theirs', who's (possessive), who'se
RIGHT hers, its (possessive), it's (meaning "it is," as in "It's cold today"), ours, yours, theirs, whose, who's (meaning "who is," as in "Who's going to the game?")

15c Use an apostrophe to mark omissions in contracted words or numerals.

RIGHT Can't; didn't; he's (he is); it's (it is); you're; o'clock (of the clock); the class of '55 (1955)

Caution: Place the apostrophe exactly where the omission occurs: isn't, haven't (*not* is'nt, have'nt).

15d Use the apostrophe and *s* to form the plural of letters, figures, symbols, and words referred to as words.

RIGHT Congreve seldom crossed his *t*'s, his *7*'s looked like *9*'s, and his *and*'s were usually *&*'s.

Note: This apostrophe is sometimes omitted when there is no danger of ambiguity: the 1930's, or the 1930s; two *B*'s and three *C*'s, or two *B*s and three *C*s.

► EXERCISES ON THE APOSTROPHE

A. Write the possessive singular and the possessive plural of each of the following words.

1. goose	7. lawyer	13. brother-in-law
2. father	8. princess	14. fox
3. lackey	9. jockey	15. genius
4. milkman	10. witch	16. army
5. other	11. mouse	17. Brooks
6. family	12. sailor	18. Morris

B. Copy the following sentences, inserting necessary apostrophes and omitting needless or faulty ones. Underline each possessive once and each contraction twice.

1. Who's going to do the dishes? Who's turn is it?
2. The choice is our's to make, not your's.
3. Shes writing copy for a new program on one of the local station's.
4. On Thursday's the childrens' department does'nt open.
5. That boys one of the worlds' worst; whats he doing now?
6. Its a ladys' world despite the saying's to the contrary.
7. *Ifs*, *buts*, and *maybes* wont satisfy a young swains ardent proposal.
8. Its not her's to give away.
9. They have'nt said the property is theirs'.
10. I did'nt go to sleep until after two oclock.
11. I cant go on Monday's and you wont go on Friday's.
12. Its a mans right to see that he gets his dollars worth.
13. Theyre not coming to see Freds' new house.
14. The books format is it's best feature.
15. Who'se idea was it? It must have been your's.

▶ Quotation Marks (and Quotations)

16

Use quotation marks to set off all direct quotations, some titles, and words used in a special sense. Place other marks of punctuation in proper relation to quotation marks.

Quotations usually consist of (1) passages borrowed from the written work of others or (2) the direct speech of individuals, especially in conversation (dialogue).

Caution: Be careful not to omit the second set of quotation marks: the first set, marking the beginning of the part quoted, must be followed by another set to mark the end. Note that the verb of saying used with a quotation is always outside the quotation marks and is regularly set off by commas.

WRONG "I have no intention of staying, he replied.
RIGHT "I have no intention of staying," he replied.

WRONG "I do not object, he said, to the tenor of the report."
RIGHT "I do not object," he said, "to the tenor of the report." [Two parts are quoted. Each must be enclosed, leaving *he said* outside of the quotation marks.]

16a Use double quotation marks to enclose direct (but not indirect) quotations; for a quotation within a quotation, use single marks.

RIGHT He said, "I have no intention of staying." [Direct quotation—the exact words spoken]

RIGHT He said that he had "no intention of staying." [Direct quotation of a fragment of the speech]

WRONG He said "that he had not intended to stay." [Indirect quotation—should not be enclosed in quotation marks]

RIGHT He said that he had not intended to stay.

RIGHT "It took courage," the speaker said, "for a man to affirm in those days: 'I endorse every word of Patrick Henry's sentiment, "Give me liberty or give me death!" ' "—WILLIAM LEWIN. [Note that a quotation within a quotation is enclosed by single quotation marks; one within that, by double marks.]

(1) **Long quotations (not dialogue).** Quoted passages of ten or more lines [1] are usually set off from the other matter, without quotation marks, by means of smaller type. In typewritten papers such quoted passages are single-spaced and indented, as in the example on page 437.[2]

(2) **Poetry.** Quoted lines of poetry are sufficiently marked by the verse form without the aid of quotation marks. But poetry must be quoted line for line, not written as prose.

(3) **Dialogue (conversation).** Written dialogue represents the directly quoted speech of two or more persons talking together. Standard practice is to write each person's speech, no matter how short, as a separate paragraph. Verbs of saying, as well as closely related bits of narrative, are included in the paragraph along with the speech.

---

1 Recommended by "The MLA Style Sheet," *Publications of the Modern Language Association of America*, LXVI (April, 1951), pp. 9-10.

2 When quotation marks—instead of the usual smaller type or indention—are used for a passage of two or more paragraphs, the quotation marks come before each paragraph and at the end of the last; they do not come at the end of intermediate paragraphs.

RIGHT "You remember Kate Stoddard, Mother?" Georgia asked. "This is Kate to pay us a little visit."

Mrs. Stanton rocked and closed her eyes. "What's everybody shouting for?" she asked.

"Sit down, Kate," Georgia said.

Mrs. Stoddard pulled a chair close to Mrs. Stanton. "Well, I will, but I can't stay. I came for a reason."

"We paid our yearly dues," Georgia said.

"I don't know what makes you say that," Mrs. Stoddard said. "I don't think you've ever known me to solicit *personally*. I came about quite another matter. I wanted you to look at this." She fished in her bag and brought out the diary, which she held out rather grudgingly to Georgia. "Be careful of it! It's quite old!"

—SALLY BENSON [8]

In the last paragraph, note that although a narrative passage interrupts the dialogue, the speaker is Mrs. Stoddard throughout.

► EXERCISE 1. Compose five sentences to illustrate the proper use of double and single quotation marks.

16b Use quotation marks for minor titles (short stories, one-act plays, short poems, articles from magazines) and for subdivisions of books.

RIGHT The February, 1955, issue of the *Atlantic Monthly* contains a short story entitled "The Portrait" by Wolf Mankowitz, a poem called "Winter Leaves" by Claire McAllister, and an article on "The Decline of Western Democracy" by Walter Lippmann.

---

[8] From "Spirit of '76" by Sally Benson. Originally published in *The New Yorker*, December 25, 1954.

RIGHT Stevenson's *Treasure Island* is divided into six parts, the last of which, called "Captain Silver," opens with a chapter entitled "In the Enemy's Camp."

Note: Quotation marks are sometimes used to enclose titles of books, magazines, and newspapers, but italics are usually preferred. See Section **10a.**

► EXERCISE 2. Compose five sentences showing use of quotation marks with minor titles and subdivisions of books.

16c Words used in a special sense are sometimes enclosed in quotation marks.

RIGHT The printer must see that quotation marks are "cleared" —that is, kept within the margins.

RIGHT "Sympathy" means "to suffer with." [Also right: *Sympathy* means *to suffer with; Sympathy* means "to suffer with." See also Section **10d.**]

16d Do not overuse quotation marks.

Do not use quotation marks to enclose titles of themes or to mark bits of humor. In general do not enclose in quotation marks common nicknames, well-known phrases and technical terms, or slang used in informal writing. Above all, do not use quotation marks for emphasis.

NEEDLESS PUNCTUATION "Old Hickory" was wrought up over the loss of his friend.

BETTER Old Hickory was wrought up over the loss of his friend.

16e In using marks of punctuation with quoted words, phrases, or sentences, follow the arbitrary printers' rules by placing:

16e ”/

(1) **The period and the comma always within the quotation marks.**

(2) **The colon and the semicolon always outside the quotation marks.**

(3) **The dash, the question mark, and the exclamation point within the quotation marks when they apply to the quoted matter only; outside when they refer to the whole sentence.**

RIGHT “I will go,” he insisted. “I am needed.” [Comma and period always inside quotation marks]

RIGHT He spoke of his “old log house”; he might have called it a mansion. [Semicolon (and colon) always outside quotation marks]

RIGHT He asked, “When did you arrive?” [Here the question mark applies only to the part of the sentence within quotation marks.]

RIGHT What is the meaning of “the open door”? [Here the question mark applies to the whole sentence.]

RIGHT The captain shouted, “Halt!” [Here the exclamation point applies only to the quotation.]

RIGHT Save us from his “mercy”! [Here the exclamation point applies to the whole sentence.]

► EXERCISE 3. Compose six sentences to illustrate the proper placing of the period, the comma, the colon, the semicolon, the dash, the question mark, and the exclamation point in relation to quotation marks.

► EXERCISE ON QUOTATION MARKS AND QUOTATIONS

Insert quotation marks where they are needed in the following sentences. Then rewrite the passage, following standard procedures for paragraphing of dialogue and omitting sentence numbers.

1. Young Herman Ponsonby-Jett's countenance was an open page, one upon which might be read a tale of contending emotions. 2. Your countenance, Herman, his

Uncle Rodney observed, is an open page, one upon which may be read a tale of contending emotions. 3. Oof, Herman seemed to assent. 4. Or perhaps it was nff. 5. Did you say oof? 6. Or was it nff? 7. The acoustics in here aren't all they might be, considering the club dues one pays. 8. Oof, Herman clarified the matter. 9. Thank you. 10. Oof it is. 11. I like to take care of these little things as they arise. 12. Keeps the picture sharp and clear, so to speak. 13. Am I to gather that the picture at present is not one which sends you into transports of delight? 14. Nff. 15. Not even the faulty acoustics could obscure Herman's meaning. 16. There ought to be a manual published to help the troubled soul out of its plights in times like these—a book with some such chapter as How To Notify a Former Beloved That She Has Been Supplanted, Uncle Rodney said. 17. Herman's silence said eloquently that he found little more solace in what ought to be than in what was. 18. Have you thought of addressing a note to the erstwhile fairest, beginning, let us say, When in the course of human events? 19. Nff; the young man's discourse seemed to be running lately to nff's. 20. Your discourse, young man, seems to be running lately to nff's, remarked Uncle Rodney, ever alert to a gathering trend. 21. I may assume, then, that you had thought of the note and dismissed it as unfeasible? 22. Herman's reply suffered an encounter with the acoustics, concerning which his uncle forebore to comment. 23. Uncle Rodney went on, I deplore our society's abandonment of the art of composing verse. 24. This might be an occasion for sending 'round a few stanzas—perhaps in the manner of Dowson's To Cynara, with the refrain going I shall be true to you, Rosabella! in my fashion. 25. He cast a tentative eye Hermanward. 26. Or, he continued, you could always face the young lady candidly and make a clean—that is, deliver the tidings in so many words, the manly way. 27. I wonder, though, he mused if at these times any of us is really a man at all—or what we are. 28. Mice, said Herman.

▶ The Period and Other Marks

17

Use the period, the question mark, the exclamation point, the dash, the colon, parentheses, and brackets in accordance with accepted usage.

The Period (.)

17a Use the period after declarative and mildly imperative sentences, after indirect questions, and after most abbreviations. Use the ellipsis mark (three spaced periods) to indicate omissions from quoted passages.

(1) Use the period to mark the end of a declarative sentence, a mildly imperative sentence, or an indirect question.

DECLARATIVE They changed the rules.
MILDLY IMPERATIVE Change the rules. Let's change the rules.
INDIRECT QUESTION He asked whether the rules had been changed.

(2) Use periods to follow most abbreviations.

RIGHT Mr. Dr., M.D., etc., *i.e.*, A.D., B.C., A.M., P.M., *viz.*, Jr.

Periods are not used after such contractions as *I've*, *can't*, *2nd*, *15th*, and usually not with such abbreviations of national or international agencies as *ECA*, *FBI*, *NATO*, *TVA*, *UN*, *WAC*. If you have any doubt about the punctuation of a given abbreviation, consult a good dictionary such as *Webster's New Collegiate Dictionary* (in a special section, pages 998-1007) or *The American College Dictionary* or *Webster's New World Dictionary* (in the main vocabulary).

(3) Use the ellipsis mark (three spaced periods) to indicate omissions from quoted passages.

Three spaced periods are used to mark an omission of one or more words within the quoted passage. If the omission ends with a period, this period precedes the usual ellipsis mark to serve as the normal end of the sentence.

RIGHT "The fundamental justification for poetry on the stage . . . lies in the play itself, in the illusion the play undertakes to create. . . . To go far one must go by art."

—ARCHIBALD MACLEISH[1]

The Question Mark (?)

17b Use the question mark to follow direct (but not indirect) questions.

RIGHT Who started the riot? [Direct question]

RIGHT He asked who started the riot. He asked whether the riot had been quelled. [Indirect questions, followed by periods]

RIGHT Did he ask who started the riot? [The sentence as a whole is a direct question despite the indirect question at the end.]

1 "The Poet as Playwright," *Atlantic Monthly*, February, 1955, p. 52.

RIGHT "Who started the riot?" he asked.

RIGHT He asked, "Who started the riot?"

RIGHT You started the riot? [Question in the form of a declarative sentence]

RIGHT You told me—did I hear you correctly?—that you started the riot. [Interpolated question]

RIGHT To ask who started the riot is unnecessary. [Indirect question, requiring no question mark]

RIGHT Did you hear him say, "What right have you to ask about the riot?" [Double direct question followed by a single question mark]

RIGHT Did he plan the riot, employ assistants, and give the signal to begin? *Or:* Did he plan the riot? employ assistants? give the signal to begin? [Question marks used between the parts of the series cause full stops and throw emphasis on each part.]

OTHER USES

A question mark (within parentheses) is used to express the writer's uncertainty as to the correctness of the preceding word, figure, or date: "Chaucer was born in 1340(?) and died in 1400." But the question mark is not a desirable means of expressing the author's wit or sarcasm.

QUESTIONABLE "This kind (?) proposal caused Gulliver to take refuge in nearby Blefuscu." [Omit the question mark. If the context does not make the irony clear, either revise your sentence or give up your attempt to strike an ironic note.]

Courtesy questions common to business letters may be followed by question marks but are usually followed by periods: "Will you (= Please) write me again if I can be of further service."

Caution: Do not use a comma or a period after a question mark.

WRONG "Are you ready?," he asked.

RIGHT "Are you ready?" he asked.

The Exclamation Point (!)

17c Use the exclamation point after an emphatic interjection and after a phrase, clause, or sentence to express a high degree of surprise, incredulity, or other strong emotion.

RIGHT What! I cannot believe it! How beautiful! [*What* and *how* often begin exclamations.]

RIGHT Oh! You have finally come! (*Or:* Oh, you have finally come!)

RIGHT March! Halt! Get out of this house! [Sharp commands—vigorous imperatives]

RIGHT Forbid it, Almighty God! I know not what course others may take, but as for me, give me liberty, or give me death! —PATRICK HENRY

Caution 1: Avoid overuse of the exclamation point. Use a comma after mild interjections, and end mildly exclamatory sentences with a period.

RIGHT Well, you are to be congratulated.

Caution 2: Do not use a comma or a period after the exclamation point.

WRONG "Halt!," cried the corporal.
RIGHT "Halt!" cried the corporal.

► EXERCISE 1. Compose ten sentences to illustrate the chief uses of the period, the question mark, and the exclamation point.

► EXERCISE 2. Copy the following passage, supplying needed periods, question marks, exclamation points, and commas—in proper relation to quotation marks. See **16e**.

1. "Now Jane" said Mrs. Colonel Wugsby turning to one of the girls "what is it" 2. "I came to ask ma whether I might dance with the youngest Mr. Crawley" whispered

the prettier and younger of the two 3. "Good God Jane how can you think of such things" replied the mamma indignantly 4. "Haven't you repeatedly heard that his father has eight hundred a year which dies with him 5. I am ashamed of you 6. Not on any account" 7. "Ma" whispered the other who was much older than her sister and very insipid and artificial "Lord Mutanhed has been introduced to me 8. I said I *thought* I wasn't engaged ma" 9. "You're a sweet pet my love" replied Mrs. Colonel Wugsby tapping her daughter's cheek with her fan "and are always to be trusted 10. He's immensely rich my dear 11. Bless you" 12. With these words Mrs. Colonel Wugsby kissed her eldest daughter most affectionately and frowning in a warning manner upon the other sorted her cards

—CHARLES DICKENS

The Colon (:)

17d Use the colon after a formal introductory statement to direct attention to what is to follow. Avoid needless colons.

The colon and the semicolon, notwithstanding the similarity of the names, differ greatly in use. The semicolon (see Section 14) is a strong *separator* almost equal to a period, and is used only between equal parts. The colon is an *introducer*, calling attention to something that is to follow. It has the meaning of *as follows*.

(1) The colon may direct attention to an appositive (or a series of appositives) at the end of a sentence, to a formal list or explanation, or to a long quotation.

RIGHT All her thoughts were centered on one objective: marriage. [A dash or a comma, which might be used instead of the colon, would be less formal.]

RIGHT We may divide poems into three classes: narrative, lyric, and dramatic. [A dash might be used instead of the colon; because of the series a comma would be confusing.]

RIGHT At any rate, this much can be said: The Council is not the vital organ it is supposed to be.
—THE ATLANTIC MONTHLY

RIGHT Competition in the steel industry is described by one of the Corporation's competitors as follows: "Your ability to win when competition for business gets tough comes in the entire setup of your operation, the quality of your management, . . . and so on. You have to play a judgment game. This is no 2-cent poker." —FORTUNE

(2) The colon may separate two main clauses when the second clause explains or amplifies the first.

RIGHT Webster definitely undervalued the area: with prime ribs at 85 cents a pound, any acreage that can fatten steers has its purpose. —NEW YORK TIMES MAGAZINE

RIGHT We have one chance for escape: we may retreat through the mountain pass. [The second clause explains the first.]

RIGHT The case for fly-fishing can be briefly put: First, trout fishing is a sport—one of the finest man knows.
—NEW YORK TIMES MAGAZINE

[For capitalization after the colon see Section **9e**.]

(3) The colon may direct attention to a business letter following the salutation, to the verse following the Biblical chapter, or to the minute following the hour.

EXAMPLES Dear Sir:
Matthew 6:10; 9:30 A.M.

(4) Avoid needless colons.

When there is no formal introduction or summarizing word, the colon is usually a needless interruption of the sentence.

NEEDLESS All her thoughts were centered on: marriage.
BETTER All her thoughts were centered on marriage.

NEEDLESS Three kinds of poems are: narratives, lyrics, and dramas. [Awkward separation of verb and its complement]
BETTER Three kinds of poems are narratives, lyrics, and dramas.

► EXERCISE 3. Compose ten sentences to illustrate the various uses of the colon.

The Dash (—)

17e Use the dash to mark a sudden break in thought, to set off a summary, or to set off a parenthetical element that is very abrupt or that has commas within it.

[For a comparison of the dash, the comma, and parentheses, see Section **17f**. On the typewriter the dash is made by two hyphens without spacing before or after.]

(1) Use the dash to mark a sudden break in thought.

RIGHT But you think that I—
RIGHT We shall need—let's see, what shall we need?
RIGHT He was now at peace—in his grave.

(2) Use the dash to set off a brief summary.

RIGHT We need three tools—hammer, saw, and chisel.
RIGHT A hammer, a saw, and a chisel—all these we shall need.

(3) Use dashes to set off a parenthetical element that is very abrupt or that has commas within it.

RIGHT He will return—can you believe it?—a major.

RIGHT He stood up—small, frail, and tense—staring toward things in his homeland. —NORA WALN

Caution: The dash should be used sparingly in formal writing. It is more in keeping with an informal style, but even there it becomes ineffective when overused.

Parentheses ( )

17f Use parentheses (1) to enclose figures, as in this rule, and (2) to set off parenthetical, supplementary, or illustrative matter.

Parentheses, dashes, commas—all are used to set off parenthetical matter. Parentheses set off parts loosely joined to the sentence and tend to minimize the parts thus set off. Dashes set off sharply abrupt parts and tend to emphasize them. Commas are the mildest, most commonly used separators and tend to leave the parts more closely connected with the sentence. Parentheses and dashes should be used sparingly, only when commas will not serve equally well. (For the use of the comma to set off parenthetical matter, see Section **12d**; for the use of the dash, see Section **17e.**)

RIGHT Dashes are used (1) to mark breaks, (2) to set off summaries, and (3) to set off parenthetical elements. [Parentheses enclose figures used to enumerate items.]

RIGHT Mr. Brown's horses (the best, no doubt, in the whole state) were exhibited at the fair. [Dashes would be used if the writer wished to emphasize the parenthetical matter.]

RIGHT It is strange (as one reviews all the memories of that good friend and master) to think that there is now a new generation beginning at Haverford that will never know his spell. —CHRISTOPHER MORLEY

When the sentence demands other marks of punctuation with the parenthetical matter, these marks are placed after the second parenthesis. The comma is never used before the first parenthesis.

Caution: Do not use parentheses or brackets to indicate deletions. Draw a line through any word that you wish to delete.

► EXERCISE 4. Compose ten sentences to illustrate the various uses of the dash and parentheses.

► EXERCISE 5. Copy the following sentences, supplying colons, dashes, or parentheses where needed. Justify each mark of punctuation used.

1. I quote now from my opponent "I am wholly opposed to wasteful spending but why go into that?"
2. This organization needs more of everything more money, brains, initiative.
3. Our course embraced three projects first, the close reading of Shakespeare's tragedies; second, the writing of critiques on various aspects of these tragedies; and third, the formulation of a tentative theory of tragedy.
4. Two questions well worth asking yourself every day are these What must I do? Have I done it?
5. If our potential enemies I need not be specific insist upon slandering America's good name, we have recourse to two methods of reply words and action.
6. "Dearest" his voice broke and he could say no more.

Brackets [ ]

17g Use brackets to set off corrections or interpolations made in a quotation by the person using the quotation.

RIGHT At the office he found a note from the janitor: "Last night i [*sic*] found the door unlocked." [A bracketed *sic* (meaning *thus*) tells the reader that the error appears in the original—is not merely a misprint.]

RIGHT Every man who loved our vanished friend [Professor Gummere] must know with what realization of shamed incapacity one lays down the tributary pen.

—CHRISTOPHER MORLEY

► EXERCISE 6. Compose three sentences to illustrate the proper use of brackets.

► GENERAL EXERCISES ON CAPITALS, ITALICS, AND MARKS OF PUNCTUATION

A. Copy the following sentences, entering all necessary capitals, italics (underlining), and marks of punctuation. Change unnecessary capitals to small letters. Justify each change made. Write *C* in place of each correct sentence. (If so directed by your instructor, explain each change by writing above it the appropriate number and subhead.)

1. As for macaulay's point of view everyone knows it was the whig one. 2. In reality this is simplifying too much but however we may describe it there can be no doubt that macaulays vision was singularly alien to the england of the latter years of the seventeenth century like Gibbon, like michelet like the later carlyle he did not to put it succinctly understand what he was talking about. 3. Charles II James II that whole strange age in which religion debauchery intellect faction wit and brutality seethed and bubbled together in such an extraordinary olla podrida escaped him. 4. He could see parts of it but he could not see into the depths and so much the better he had his point of view. 5. The definiteness the fixity of his position is what is remarkable. 6. he seems to have been created en bloc 7. His manner never changed as soon as he could write at all at the age of eight he wrote in the style of his history 8. The three main factors in his mental growth the clapham

sect cambridge holland house were not so much influences as suitable environments for the development of a predetermined personality. 9. Whatever had happened to him, he would always have been a middle-class intellectual with whig views. 10. It is possible however that he may actually have gained something from holland house.[2]

B. Follow directions given under A.

1. "Well Babbitt crossed the floor slowly ponderously seeming a little old 2. "I've always wanted you to have a college degree." 3. he meditatively stamped across the floor again 4. "But I've never now for heavens sake dont repeat this to your mother or shed remove what little hair ive got left but practically ive never done a single thing Ive wanted to do in my whole life 5. I dont knows Ive accomplished anything except just get along 6. I figure out I've made about a quarter of an inch out of a possible hundred rods. 7. Well maybe youll carry things on further I dont know but I do get a kind of sneaking pleasure out of the fact that you knew what you wanted to do and did it 8. Well those folks in there will try to bully you and tame you down. 9. Tell em to go to the devil Ill back you 10. Take your factory job if you want to dont be scared of the family no nor all of zenith nor of yourself the way Ive been 11. go ahead old man the world is yours" 12. arms about each others' shoulders the babbitt men marched into the living-room and faced the swooping family [3]

---

[2] Adapted from *Literary Essays*, by Lytton Strachey. Reprinted by permission of Harcourt, Brace and Company, Inc.

[3] Adapted from *Babbitt*, by Sinclair Lewis, copyright, 1922, by Harcourt, Brace and Company, Inc.; renewed, 1950, by Sinclair Lewis. Reprinted by permission of the publishers.

SPELLING

▶ Spelling

18

Spell every word according to established usage as shown by a good dictionary.[1]

When one of your misspelled words is pointed out, do not guess at the correct spelling or ask a friend. Consult the dictionary for the correct spelling and write it down in your INDIVIDUAL SPELLING LIST. By keeping a list of all the words you misspell throughout your first college year, and by analyzing and mastering these words as they are called to your attention, you can make steady improvement in your spelling.

The college student cannot count upon much, if any, class time devoted to spelling. Correct spelling is his individual responsibility. If he will follow the program outlined in this section, he can improve his spelling tremendously. *Ignorance of the correct spelling of ordinary words is now, and will probably continue to be, the one universally accepted sign of the uneducated man.*

[1] Careful study of Section **18** will help to eliminate one of the two most common errors in the average student theme.

In order to fix the correct spelling of the word in your memory, use the following:

THE EYE Look carefully at the word (1) as it appears in the dictionary and (2) as you write it *correctly* in your spelling list. Photograph the word with your eye so that you may visualize it later.

THE EAR Pronounce the word aloud several times, clearly and distinctly, in accordance with the phonetic spelling in the dictionary. Note any difference between the pronunciation and the spelling. Careful pronunciation and an awareness of the difference between spelling and pronunciation help in the spelling of many words.

THE HAND After you are sure of the correct picture and the correct pronunciation, write the word several times—at least once by syllables carefully pronounced. See the correct picture of the word and listen to your pronunciation of it as you write it down. Writing out the word is definitely helpful to many persons as the final step in fixing the correct spelling in the memory.

18a Do not allow mispronunciation to cause misspelling.

► EXERCISE 1. In the four lists below determine which words you tend to mispronounce—and to misspell.

(1) Careless omission

Pronounce this first list distinctly, making it a point *not to omit* the italicized letters

acciden*tal*ly	car*ry*ing	gen*e*rally
ar*c*tic	consid*er*able	g*e*ography
bound*a*ry	fam*i*ly	gover*n*ment
can*d*idate	Feb*r*uary	li*a*ble

library	recognize	use*d*
liter*a*ture	represen*ta*tive	us*u*ally
occasion*al*ly	soph*o*more	valu*a*ble
prob*a*bly	stric*t*ly	vet*e*ran
quan*t*ity	temper*a*ment	visu*a*lize

(2) Careless addition

Pronounce this second list distinctly, making it a point *not to add* any syllable or letter.

disastrous	grievous	mischievous
drowned	handling	remembrance
elm	height	similar
entrance	hindrance	suffrage
genuine	lightning	umbrella

(3) Careless change

Pronounce this third list distinctly, making it a point *not to change* letters, particularly letters in italics.

accum*u*late	form*er*ly	pre*j*udice
acc*u*rate	int*ro*duce	prep*a*ration
cav*i*ty	math*e*matics	priv*i*lege
d*i*vide	opt*i*mistic	temp*o*rary
exist*e*nce	partic*u*lar	th*e*n (*not* than)

(4) Careless transpositions of letters

Pronounce this fourth list distinctly, making it a point *not to transpose* italicized letters.

cav*al*ry	irre*le*vant	p*re*fer
child*re*n	p*er*haps	p*re*scription
hund*re*d	p*er*spiration	p*re*serve

Add to your INDIVIDUAL SPELLING LIST any of the words in the four lists that you have a tendency to misspell. (If there is no class test on these word lists, or on other lists in Section **18,** students may pair themselves outside of class to test one another.)

18b Distinguish between words of similar sound and spelling, and use the spelling demanded by the meaning.

► EXERCISE 2. Study the following list, perhaps ten word groups at a time, to improve your ability to select the word needed to express your meaning. With the aid of your dictionary compose a sentence to illustrate the correct use of each word. Add to your INDIVIDUAL SPELLING LIST any word that you tend to misspell.

accent, ascent, assent
accept, except
advice, advise
affect, effect
all ready, already
all together, altogether
allusive, elusive, illusive
altar, alter
berth, birth
born, borne

capital, capitol
choose, chose
cite, sight, site
coarse, course
complement, compliment
conscience, conscious
council, counsel, consul
decent, descent, dissent
desert, dessert
device, devise

dual, duel
dyeing, dying
fair, fare
formally, formerly
forth, fourth
freshman, freshmen
hear, here
holy, wholly
instance, instants
irrelevant, irreverent

its, it's
know, no
later, latter
lead, led
lessen, lesson
lose, loose
moral, morale
of, off
passed, past
peace, piece

personal, personnel
plain, plane
precede, proceed
presence, presents
principal, principle
prophecy, prophesy
quiet, quite
respectfully, respectively
right, rite, wright, write
sense, since
shone, shown
stationary, stationery
statue, stature, statute
there, their, they're
threw, through
to, too, two
weak, week
weather, whether
whose, who's
your, you're

18c Distinguish between the prefix and the root.

The root is the base to which prefix or suffix is added. Take care not to double the last letter of the prefix (as in *disappear*) when it is different from the first letter of the root or to drop the last letter of the prefix when the root begins with the same letter (as in *immortal* and *unnecessary*).

dis- (prefix) + appear (root) = disappear
grand- + daughter = granddaughter
im- + mortal = immortal
un- + necessary = unnecessary

18d Apply the rules for spelling in adding suffixes.

[For more detailed rules consult *Webster's New International Dictionary*, Second Edition, pages lxxix-lxxx or *Webster's New Collegiate Dictionary*, pages 1195-97 (1949), 1145-47 (1953).]

(1) Drop the final e before a suffix beginning with a vowel but not before a suffix beginning with a consonant.

Drop the final *e* before a suffix beginning with a vowel.

bride + -al = bridal
combine + -ation = combination

come	+ -ing	= coming
fame	+ -ous	= famous
plume	+ -age	= plumage
precede	+ -ence	= precedence
prime	+ -ary	= primary

Retain the final *e* before a suffix beginning with a consonant.

care	+ -ful	= careful
care	+ -less	= careless
entire	+ -ly	= entirely
place	+ -ment	= placement
rude	+ -ness	= rudeness
stale	+ -mate	= stalemate
state	+ -craft	= statecraft
sure	+ -ty	= surety

Some Exceptions: *due, duly; awe, awful; hoe, hoeing; singe, singeing.* After *c* or *g* the final *e* is retained before suffixes beginning with *a* or *o*: *notice, noticeable; courage, courageous.*

► EXERCISE 3. Explain in each case why the final *e* should be dropped or retained.

1. confine + -ing
2. confine + -ment
3. arrange + -ing
4. arrange + -ment
5. love + -ing
6. love + -ly
7. peruse + -al
8. like + -ness
9. like + -ing
10. like + -ly

(2) Double a final single consonant before a suffix beginning with a vowel (a) if the consonant ends a word of one syllable or an accented syllable and (b) if the consonant is preceded by a single vowel. Otherwise, do not double the consonant.

drop, dro*pp*ing [In a word of one syllable preceded by a single vowel. But preceded by a double vowel: *droop, drooping.*]

admit, admi*tt*ed [In accented syllable, preceded by a single vowel. But in unaccented syllable: *benefit. benefited.*]

► EXERCISE 4. Note the importance of the last rule in forming the present participle and the past tense of verbs. Example: *regret, regretting, regretted.* Supply the present participle for each of the following verbs, justifying the spelling by the rule: *appear, compel, differ, kidnap, occur, plan, profit, remit, scoop, ship.*

(3) Except before a suffix beginning with *i*, final *y* is usually changed to *i*.

defy + -ance = defiance
happy + -ness = happiness
mercy + -ful = merciful
modify + -er = modifier
modify + -ing = modifying [Not changed before *i*]

Note: Verbs ending in *y* preceded by a vowel do not change the *y* to form the third person singular of the present tense or the past participle: *array, arrays, arrayed.* Exceptions: *lay, laid; pay, paid; say, said.*

► EXERCISE 5. Explain why the final *y* has, or has not, been retained before the suffixes of the following words: *alloys, craftiness, employed, employs, fanciful, fancying, studied, studying, volleys, volleying.*

(4) Form the plural by adding *s* to the singular, but by adding *es* if the plural makes an extra syllable.

boy, boy*s;* cap, cap*s*
bush, bush*es;* match, match*es* [The plural makes an extra syllable.]

Exceptions:

a. If the noun ends in *y* preceded by a consonant, change the *y* to *i* and add *es: sky, skies; comedy, comedies.* But after a vowel the *y* is retained and only *s* is added: *joy, joys.*

b. If the noun ends in *fe*, change the *fe* to *ve* and add *s: knife, knives.*

c. If the noun ends in *o* preceded by a vowel, add *s: radio, radios.*

For other plurals formed irregularly, consult your dictionary.

Note: Add *'s* to form the plurals of letters, signs, and figures. See also **15d** above.

► EXERCISE 6. Supply plural forms for words listed below. If words are not covered by the rules given under **18d,** consult your dictionary.

cup	army	foot	passer-by
wife	cameo	son-in-law	room
box	marsh	valley	leaf
child	ox	alumnus	goose
key	sheep	radius	mouse

18e Apply the rules for spelling to avoid confusion of *ei* and *ie*.

When the sound is *ee*, write *ie* (except after *c*, in which case write *ei*).

		(after *c*)
chief	pierce	ceiling
field	relief	conceit
grief	wield	deceive
niece	yield	perceive

When the sound is other than *ee*, usually write *ei.*

eight	heir	sleigh
foreign	neighbor	weigh
height	reign	vein
deign	feign	stein

Exceptions: Fiery, financier, leisure, seize, species, weird.

► EXERCISE 7. Write out the following words, filling out the blanks with *ei* or *ie*. Justify your choice for each word.

bes—ge	dec—t	fr—ght	r—gned	s—ve
conc—ve	f—nd	pr—st	s—ne	th—f

Hyphenated Words

18f Hyphenate words chiefly to express a unit idea or to avoid ambiguity. (For division of words at the end of a line, see Section 8f.)

A hyphenated word may be either a new coinage made by the writer to fit the occasion or two words still in the process of becoming one word. In the latter case a recent dictionary will assist in determining current usage. Many words now written as one were originally separate words and later hyphenated in the transitional stage. For example, *post man* first became *post-man* and then *postman.* More recently *basket ball* has passed through the transitional *basket-ball* to *basketball.* The use of the hyphen in compounding is in such a state of flux that authorities often disagree. Some of the more generally accepted uses are listed below.

(1) The hyphen may be used to join two or more words serving as a single adjective before a noun.

[The dictionary ordinarily cannot help with this use of the hyphen. The writer joins recognized words to coin a new unit idea to fit the occasion.]

RIGHT A well-paved road, a know-it-all expression, a bluish-green dress

But the hyphen is omitted when the first word of the compound is an adverb ending in *-ly* or when the words follow the noun.

RIGHT A slightly elevated walk, a gently sloping terrace
RIGHT The road was well paved.
RIGHT His expression suggested that he knew it all.
RIGHT The dress was a bluish green.

(2) The hyphen is used with compound numbers from twenty-one to ninety-nine.

RIGHT twenty-two, forty-five, ninety-eight, one hundred twenty, one hundred twenty-six

(3) The hyphen is used to avoid ambiguity or an awkward union of letters or syllables between prefix or suffix and root.

RIGHT His re-creation of the setting was perfect.
RIGHT Fishing is good recreation.

RIGHT He re-covered the leaky roof.
RIGHT He recovered his health.

RIGHT Micro-organism, re-enter, semi-independent, shell-like, thrill-less, sub-subcommittee.

(4) The hyphen is used with the prefixes ex-, *self-*, *all-*, and the suffix -*elect*.

RIGHT ex-governor, self-made, all-American, mayor-elect

► EXERCISES ON SPELLING

A. First on the GENERAL SPELLING LIST
B. Then on your INDIVIDUAL SPELLING LIST

The general list of words most frequently misspelled is made up of 654 (651 + *it's*, *too*, *two*) common words that everyone needs in his business and social life. The list is drawn, by kind permission of Dean Thomas Clark Pollock, from his recent study of 31,375 misspellings in the written work of college students.[2] In the list as given below the words *its, it's* and *to, too, two* are treated as word groups; all other words are listed individually, usually omitting any word that is spelled the same as a part of a longer word. For example, the list includes *definitely* but not *definite, existence* but not *exist, performance* but not *perform.* Each of the first hundred words in the general list below was misspelled more than forty-three times (or more than an *average* of forty-three times in the case of words grouped in Dean Pollock's report). The letters which caused the greatest difficulty are indicated by italics.

A. With the aid of your dictionary study the words in the general list in small units (perhaps fifty words at a time) until you feel sure (1) of the meaning and (2) of the spelling of each word. Then without the aid of your dictionary test yourself by writing sentences in which each word is correctly used and spelled. Add to your INDIVIDUAL SPELLING LIST each word that you tend to misspell.

GENERAL SPELLING LIST

I. The Hundred Words Most Frequently Misspelled[3]

1. accom*m*odate
2. achi*e*vement
3. a*c*quire
4. al*l* right
5. am*ong*
6. ap*p*ar*e*nt
7. argu*m*ent
8. argu*i*ng
9. bel*i*ef *
10. bel*ie*ve *
11. ben*e*ficial
12. ben*e*fi*t*ed
13. cat*e*gory
14. com*i*ng
15. compar*a*tive
16. cons*cious*
17. contr*o*versy
18. contr*o*ver*s*ial
19. de*f*ini*t*ely
20. de*f*ini*t*ion
21. de*f*ine
22. de*s*cribe
23. de*s*cri*p*tion
24. disas*tr*ous

[2] See Thomas Clark Pollock, "Spelling Report," *College English,* XVI (November, 1954), 102-09; and Thomas Clark Pollock and William D. Baker, *The University Spelling Book,* Prentice-Hall, Inc., New York, 1955, pp. 6-12.

[3] An asterisk indicates the most frequently misspelled words among the first hundred. The most troublesome letters for all 654 words are indicated by italics.

25. *eff*ect
26. embar*rass*
27. envir*on*ment
28. exa*gg*erate
29. ex*i*st*e*nce *
30. ex*i*st*e*nt *
31. experi*e*nce
32. expl*an*ation
33. fa*s*cinate
34. he*i*ght
35. *i*nt*e*rest
36. i*ts* (i*t's*)
37. *le*d
38. lo*s*e
39. lo*s*ing
40. marr*ia*ge
41. me*re*
42. ne*cess*ary
43. o*cc*a*s*ion *
44. occu*rr*ed
45. occu*rr*ing
46. occu*rre*nce
47. o*p*inion
48. o*pp*or*t*unity
49. pa*i*d
50. particul*a*r
51. p*e*rform*a*nce
52. person*al*
53. perso*nnel*
54. po*ss*e*ss*ion
55. po*ss*ible
56. practic*al*
57. prec*ede* *
58. pre*j*udice
59. prepa*re*
60. prev*a*lent
61. princip*al*
62. princip*le*
63. privi*l*eg*e* *
64. prob*ab*ly
65. proc*ee*d
66. proc*e*dure
67. pro*f*essor
68. pro*f*ession
69. promin*e*nt
70. p*u*rsue
71. qui*e*t
72. rec*ei*ve *
73. rec*ei*ving *
74. reco*mm*end
75. refe*rr*ing *
76. rep*e*tition
77. r*h*ythm
78. sen*s*e
79. sep*a*rate *
80. sep*a*ration *
81. shi*n*ing
82. simil*a*r *
83. stud*y*ing
84. su*cc*eed
85. su*cc*ession
86. su*r*prise
87. te*ch*ni*que*
88. th*a*n
89. th*e*n
90. th*ei*r *
91. th*ere* *
92. they*'re* *
93. th*o*rough
94. transfe*rr*ed
95. *to* * (*too*, * *two* *)
96. un*n*e*c*e*ss*ary
97. vill*ai*n
98. wom*a*n
99. *write*
100. wri*t*ing

II. The Next 551 Words Most Frequently Misspelled

101. ab*s*ence
102. ab*u*nd*a*nce
103. ab*u*nd*a*nt
104. aca*d*e*m*ic
105. aca*d*emica*lly*
106. acad*e*my
107. *a*ccept*a*ble
108. *a*ccept*a*nce
109. *a*ccepting
110. acces*si*ble
111. a*cc*idental
112. a*cc*ident*a*lly
113. a*cc*laim
114. accomp*a*ni*e*d
115. accomp*anies*
116. accomp*a*n*i*ment
117. accomp*any*ing
118. acco*mpl*ish
119. a*cc*ura*cy*
120. a*cc*u*r*ate
121. a*cc*urat*e*ly
122. a*cc*us*er*
123. a*cc*u*s*es
124. a*cc*us*i*ng
125. a*cc*u*s*tom
126. a*cq*uaint*a*nce
127. a*cr*oss

128. actuality
129. actually
130. adequately
131. admission
132. admittance
133. adolescence
134. adolescent
135. advantageous
136. advertisement
137. advertiser
138. advertising
139. advice
140. advise
141. affect
142. afraid
143. against
144. aggravate
145. aggressive
146. alleviate
147. allotted
148. allotment
149. allowed
150. allows

151. already
152. altar
153. all together
154. altogether
155. amateur
156. amount
157. analysis
158. analyze
159. and
160. another
161. annually
162. anticipated
163. apologetically
164. apologized
165. apology
166. apparatus
167. appearance
168. applies
169. applying
170. appreciate
171. appreciation
172. approaches
173. appropriate
174. approximate
175. area
176. arise
177. arising
178. arouse
179. arousing
180. arrangement
181. article
182. atheist
183. athlete
184. athletic
185. attack
186. attempts
187. attendance
188. attendant
189. attended
190. attitude
191. audience
192. authoritative
193. authority
194. available
195. bargain
196. basically
197. basis
198. beauteous
199. beautified
200. beautiful

201. beauty
202. become
203. becoming
204. before
205. began
206. beginner
207. beginning
208. behavior
209. bigger
210. biggest
211. boundary
212. breath
213. breathe
214. brilliance
215. brilliant
216. Britain
217. Britannica
218. burial
219. buried
220. bury
221. business
222. busy
223. calendar
224. capitalism
225. career
226. careful
227. careless
228. carried
229. carrier
230. carries
231. carrying
232. cemetery
233. certainly
234. challenge
235. changeable
236. changing
237. characteristic
238. characterized
239. chief

240. child*ren*
241. C*h*rist*ian*
242. C*h*rist*ian*ity
243. choi*c*e
244. ch*oo*se
245. ch*o*se
246. cig*arette*
247. *cite*
248. clo*th*es
249. co*m*mer*c*ial
250. co*m*mis*s*ion
251. co*m*mit*tee*
252. co*m*munist
253. compan*ies*
254. compat*i*ble
255. compe*t*ition
256. compe*tit*ive
257. compe*tit*or
258. comple*te*ly
259. conc*e*de
260. conc*ei*v*a*ble
261. conc*ei*ve
262. con*c*entrate
263. con*c*ern
264. condem*n*
265. confu*s*e
266. confu*s*ion
267. co*nn*otation
268. co*nn*ote
269. con*sc*ience
270. con*sc*ien*t*ious
271. con*s*equen*tly*
272. con*sid*er*a*bly
273. consist*e*ncy
274. consist*e*nt
275. contem*p*or*a*ry
276. contin*u*ous(ly)
277. contro*ll*ed
278. contro*ll*ing
279. conv*enie*nce
280. conv*enie*nt
281. co*rr*elate
282. coun*cil*
283. coun*s*el*o*r
284. countr*ie*s
285. creat*e*
286. critic*ism*
287. critic*ize*
288. cruel*ly*
289. cru*elty*
290. c*uri*osity
291. c*urious*
292. c*urr*iculum
293. de*a*lt
294. dec*ei*ve
295. de*c*ided
296. de*c*ision
297. depend*e*nt
298. desir*a*bility
299. des*i*re
300. desp*air*
301. de*s*truction
302. detr*i*men*t*
303. dev*as*tating
304. devi*c*e
305. di*ff*eren*c*e
306. di*ff*erent
307. di*ff*icult
308. d*i*le*mm*a
309. d*i*ligence
310. di*n*ing
311. disa*pp*oint
312. dis*c*iple
313. dis*ci*pline
314. d*i*scrimi*n*ation
315. d*i*s*c*us*s*ion
316. d*i*sease
317. disg*us*ted
318. dis*ill*usioned
319. di*ss*atisfied
320. d*i*vide
321. d*i*vine
322. do*esn't*
323. domin*ant*
324. dro*pp*ed
325. du*e*
326. du*r*ing
327. e*a*ger
328. eas*i*ly
329. effi*cie*ncy
330. effi*cie*nt
331. eig*hth*
332. e*liminate*
333. emper*o*r
334. emph*asize*
335. *e*ncour*a*ge
336. end*eavo*r
337. *e*njoy
338. enou*gh*
339. *e*nterpri*s*e
340. *e*ntertain
341. *e*nterta*i*nment
342. *e*nt*i*rely
343. ent*r*ance
344. equi*p*ment
345. equi*pp*ed
346. e*s*cap*a*de
347. e*s*cape
348. es*pec*ially
349. e*tc.*
350. everything

351. evident*ly*
352. excel*le*nce
353. excel*le*nt
354. *exc*ept
355. exci*ta*ble
356. e*x*er*c*ise
357. expen*s*e
358. exper*i*ment
359. extrem*e*ly
360. fal*la*cy
361. famil*ia*r
362. famil*ie*s
363. fanta*sie*s
364. fanta*sy*
365. fa*sh*ions
366. favor*ite*
367. fict*i*tious
368. f*ie*ld
369. final*ly*
370. fin*a*ncial*ly*
371. financ*ie*r
372. for*ei*gners
373. for*t*y
374. for*w*ard
375. fo*u*rth
376. fr*ie*ndl*i*ness
377. fu*l*fill
378. fund*a*ment*ally*
379. furth*e*r
380. gai*e*ty
381. genera*lly*
382. gen*ius*
383. gover*n*ment
384. gover*n*or
385. gramm*a*r
386. gra*mm*atically
387. gr*ou*p
388. guarant*ee*d
389. guid*a*nce
390. gui*d*ing
391. hand*l*ed
392. happ*e*ned
393. ha*pp*iness
394. h*ea*r
395. h*ere*
396. hero*es*
397. her*o*ic
398. her*oi*ne
399. hin*dr*ance
400. hop*e*less

401. ho*p*ing
402. hospit*a*lization
403. hug*e*
404. hum*o*rist
405. hum*orous*
406. hund*re*d
407. hung*e*r
408. hung*ri*ly
409. hung*ry*
410. hypocr*i*sy
411. hypocrit*e*
412. idea*lly*
413. ign*o*rance
414. ignor*a*nt
415. imagin*a*ry
416. *im*agination
417. imagin*e*
418. imm*e*diately
419. *imm*ense
420. import*a*n*c*e
421. inc*i*dent*ally*
422. *increase*
423. indefin*i*te
424. independ*e*nce
425. independ*e*nt
426. ind*i*spens*a*ble
427. indivi*dually*
428. industr*ie*s
429. *i*nevi*t*able
430. in*flue*nce
431. in*fl*uent*i*al
432. *i*ngen*io*us
433. ingred*ie*nt
434. initi*a*tive
435. int*ell*ect
436. inte*ll*igence
437. inte*ll*igent
438. interfer*e*nce
439. interpr*et*ation
440. inte*rr*upt
441. *i*nvolve
442. irre*lev*ant
443. irr*e*sist*i*ble
444. ir*ri*table
445. jeal*ousy*
446. kno*w*le*d*ge
447. lab*o*ratory
448. labor*e*r
449. labor*i*ously
450. la*i*d

451. la*t*er
452. le*i*sur*e*ly
453. length*en*ing
454. li*c*ense
455. lik*e*lihood
456. lik*e*ly
457. lik*e*ness
458. list*e*ner
459. li*t*er*ary*
460. lit*era*ture
461. liv*e*liest
462. livel*i*hood

463. liv*e*liness
464. li*v*es
465. lon*e*liness
466. lon*e*ly
467. l*oose*
468. lo*ss*
469. lux*ur*y
470. mag*a*zine
471. magnifi*ce*nce
472. magnific*e*nt
473. maint*e*nance
474. man*age*ment
475. man*eu*ver
476. ma*nne*r
477. manufact*urers*
478. materi*a*l
479. math*e*matics
480. ma*tt*er
481. ma*y*be
482. me*a*nt
483. me*ch*anics
484. med*i*cal
485. med*i*cine
486. medi*eva*l
487. mel*a*nc*h*oly
488. meth*ods*
489. mini*a*ture
490. min*ute*s
491. misch*ief*
492. mora*l*
493. moral*e*
494. mora*lly*
495. m*y*sterious
496. na*rra*tive
497. natur*ally*
498. Negro*e*s
499. nin*e*ty
500. nob*le*
501. notic*e*able
502. noti*c*ing
503. num*er*ous
504. obst*a*cle
505. o*ff*
506. o*m*it
507. o*p*erate
508. o*pp*ose
509. o*pp*onent
510. o*pp*osite
511. opt*i*mism
512. organ*i*zation
513. orig*i*nal
514. *p*amphlets
515. par*allel*
516. parl*ia*ment
517. paral*y*zed
518. pa*ss*ed
519. pas*t*
520. p*eace*
521. pecul*iar*
522. perc*ei*ve
523. perm*a*n*e*nt
524. permi*t*
525. persist*e*nt
526. pe*r*suad*e*
527. pe*r*tain
528. *phas*e
529. phenom*e*non
530. ph*i*loso*ph*y
531. p*h*ysical
532. p*ie*ce
533. pla*nn*ed
534. plaus*i*ble
535. playwri*ght*
536. pl*ea*sant
537. politic*ia*n
538. politic*a*l
539. practi*c*e
540. predomin*ant*
541. prefe*rr*ed
542. pre*s*en*c*e
543. prest*i*ge
544. prim*i*t*i*ve
545. pris*o*ners
546. prop*a*ganda
547. prop*a*gate
548. prophe*c*y
549. psyc*h*oanalysis
550. psyc*h*ology
551. psyc*h*opathic
552. psyc*h*osomatic
553. quan*t*ity
554. re*ally*
555. re*a*lize
556. rebe*l*
557. re*cog*nize
558. re*g*ard
559. rel*a*tive
560. rel*ie*ve
561. rel*i*gion
562. rem*em*ber
563. reminis*c*e
564. rep*re*sent
565. reso*ur*ces
566. respon*s*e
567. rev*ea*led
568. r*i*dicule
569. r*i*diculous
570. room*m*ate
571. sacr*i*fice
572. saf*e*ty
573. sat*i*re
574. satisf*ie*d
575. satisf*y*

576. sc*e*ne
577. s*ch*edul*e*
578. s*ei*ze
579. sent*e*nce
580. serg*ea*nt
581. sev*era*l
582. shep*h*erd
583. signific*ance*
584. simil*e*
585. simp*le*
586. sim*p*ly
587. s*i*nce
588. sincer*e*ly
589. soci*o*logy
590. soph*o*more
591. sour*c*e
592. sp*ea*king
593. sp*ee*ch
594. spons*or*
595. stab*i*lization
596. ste*pp*ed
597. stor*ie*s
598. stor*y*
599. str*ai*ght
600. stren*gth*
601. str*et*ch
602. stri*ct*
603. stu*b*born
604. substan*t*ial
605. su*bt*le
606. su*ff*icient
607. su*mm*ary
608. su*mm*ed
609. su*pp*ose
610. su*pp*ress
611. su*rrou*nding
612. suscept*i*ble
613. suspen*s*e
614. swi*mm*ing
615. symb*ol*
616. synon*y*mous
617. temper*a*ment
618. tend*e*ncy
619. themsel*ves*
620. theor*ie*s
621. theor*y*
622. therefor*e*
623. tho*se*
624. though*t*
625. tog*e*ther
626. to*morr*ow
627. trag*edy*
628. trem*e*nd*o*us
629. tr*ie*d
630. tr*ie*s
631. tyra*nn*y
632. undoubt*ed*ly
633. unus*ually*
634. us*e*ful
635. us*e*less
636. us*i*ng
637. va*cuu*m
638. val*ua*ble
639. var*i*es
640. var*i*ous
641. v*ie*w
642. veng*ea*nce
643. warr*a*nt
644. *wea*ther
645. w*ei*rd
646. w*h*ere
647. w*he*ther
648. *w*hole
649. who*se*
650. y*ie*ld
651. you'r*e*

B. Analyze your INDIVIDUAL SPELLING LIST *to learn why you misspell words and how you can most readily improve your spelling.*

Spelling is an individual matter. No two persons make exactly the same errors in spelling. Therefore it is important that you compile and master your INDIVIDUAL SPELLING LIST. Once you analyze this list to determine why you misspell words, you can concentrate on the part of Section **18** (**a, b, c, d, e,** or **f**) that treats your difficulty.

When each misspelled word is first called to your attention, consult your dictionary and copy down the correct spelling as directed at the opening of Section **18.** Then write out the word by syllables, underline the trouble spot, and indicate why you misspelled the word, by using the letter **a** (omission, addition, change, or transposition), **b** (confusion of words similar in sound), **c** (failure to distinguish prefix from root), **d** (confusion of *ei* and *ie*), **e** (error in adding suffix), **f** (error in hyphenation), or **g** (any other reason for misspelling).

EXAMPLES:

Word (correctly spelled)	*Word (spelled by syllables)—with trouble spots underlined*	*Reason for error*
1. candidate	can di date	**a** (letter omitted)
2. athlete	ath lete	**a** (letter added)
3. prejudice	prej u dice	**a** (letter changed)
4. marriage	mar riage	**a** (letters transposed)
5. among	a mong	**b** (confused with *young*)
6. its	its	**b** (confused with *it's*)
7. misspell	mis spell	**c** (prefix not distinguished)
8. bridal	brid al	**d** (drop final *e* before vowel)
9. careful	care ful	**d** (retain final *e* before consonant)
10. duly	du ly	**d** (exception to the rule)
11. occurred	oc curred	**d** (before a vowel double final single consonant after a single vowel in accented syllable)
12. merciful	mer ci ful	**d** (change final *y* to i except before *i*)
13. believe	be lieve	**e** (*ie* when the sound is *ee*)
14. receive	re ceive	**e** (*ei* when the sound is *ee* after *c*)
15. forty-five	for ty-five	**f** (hyphen with compound number)

DICTION

▸ Good Use—Glossary

19

When in doubt about the meaning of a word, consult a good dictionary. Select the word most appropriate to the occasion. In standard writing employ only words in general and approved use.

Words are the coinage of thought, the medium by which men exchange ideas. To possess a large and varied vocabulary is to possess intellectual wealth. This wealth is not the private property of the few, but a common fund from which anyone may draw as much as he needs. The treasury of language is a good dictionary.

19a Use only a good dictionary, and be sure to use it intelligently.

A good dictionary of the English language is based upon the scientific examination of the writing and speaking habits of the English-speaking world; it records the origin, development, and changing use of words. Any dictionary is reliable only to the extent that it is based on usage. There can be no perfect dictionary, as Dr. Johnson recognized long ago. Among the full or unabridged dictionaries, the following are especially useful:

Webster's New International Dictionary. Second Edition; Springfield, Massachusetts: G. & C. Merriam Company, 1934, 1950.

New Century Dictionary. 2 vols. New York: D. Appleton-Century Company, 1948.

New Standard Dictionary. New York: Funk & Wagnalls Company, 1947.

A New English Dictionary on Historical Principles. 10 vols. and Supplement. Oxford: Clarendon Press, 1888-1933. (A corrected reissue in twelve volumes and one supplementary volume appeared in 1933 under the title *The Oxford English Dictionary.*)

Most students must consult these large dictionaries in the library. But even if a student possesses a large dictionary, he will still find indispensable, for more convenient use, one of the smaller dictionaries on the college or adult level, such as the following:

American College Dictionary (Text Edition, 1948)
New College Standard Dictionary (1947)
Webster's New Collegiate Dictionary (1956)
Webster's New World Dictionary (1953)

Note: Dictionaries are usually kept up to date by frequent slight revisions, sometimes with supplementary pages for new words. Long periods elapse between thorough revisions.

Intelligent use of a dictionary requires some knowledge of its plan and special abbreviations as given in the introductory matter. Let us take, for example:

ex·pel (ĭk spĕl′), *v.t.*, **-pelled, -pelling. 1.** to drive or force out or away; discharge or eject: *to expel air from the lungs, an invader from a country.* **2.** to cut off from membership or relations: *to expel a student from a college.* [ME *expelle(n)*, t. L: m. *expellere* drive out] **—ex·pel′la·ble,** *adj.* **—ex·pel′ler,** *n.* **—Syn. 2.** oust, dismiss.

ex·pel′ (ĕks·pĕl′; ĭks-), *v. t.;* EX·PELLED′ (-pĕld′); EX·PEL′LING. [L. *expellere, expulsum*, fr. *ex* out + *pellere* to drive.] **1.** To drive or force out; to eject. **2.** To cut off from membership in or the privileges of an institution or society; as, to *expel* a student from college. — **Syn.** See EJECT. — **ex·pel′la·ble,** *adj.*

ex·pel (ik-spel′), *v.t.* [EXPELLED (-speld′), EXPELLING], [ME. *expellen;* L. *expellere; ex-*, out + *pellere*, to thrust, drive], 1. to drive out by force; make leave; eject. 2. to dismiss or send away by authority; deprive of rights, membership, etc.: as, he was *expelled* from school because of misconduct. —*SYN.* see **eject.**

(1) Spelling and pronunciation. The spelling of *expel* (by syllables separated by a dot) is given first, with pronunciation indicated (within parentheses) immediately following. The sound of each letter is shown by the key to pronunciation at the bottom of the page or on one of the inside covers. *Webster's* (*Webster's New Collegiate Dictionary*) gives two acceptable pronunciations for the first syllable; *ACD* (*American College Dictionary*) and *WNWD* (*Webster's New World Dictionary*) give only one. The accent on *expel,* as shown by the mark (′), falls on the last syllable.

(2) Grammatical information comes next: *v. t.* classifies *expel* as a "verb, transitive"; the words in boldface (*ACD*) or in small capitals (*Webster's* and *WNWD*) give the forms for the past participle and the present participle; other parts of speech formed from the base word are listed toward the end of the entry.

(3) Meanings (including synonyms and antonyms). Two separate meanings of *expel* are shown after the numbers *1* and *2*. In *Webster's* and in *WNWD* such definitions are arranged in the historical order of development, thus enabling the reader to see at a glance something of the history of the word. *But he should note that the meaning which developed first, and is consequently placed first, may no longer be the most common.* For example, *Webster's* and *WNWD,* in defining *prevent,* begin with the original but obsolete meaning "to anticipate" and come later to the present meaning "to hinder." The *ACD,* which puts the most common meaning first, begins with "to hinder" and comes later to the obsolete meaning. With *expel,* as with many words, the meaning that first developed is still the more common of the two.

The meaning is made clearer by comparing the word with other words of similar meaning (synonyms, abbreviated **Syn.**) or opposite meaning (antonyms, abbreviated **Ant.**). The *ACD* lists for *expel* the two synonyms *oust* and *dismiss; Webster's* and *WNWD* refer to another word *eject* under which a helpful special paragraph compares *expel* with *eject* and other synonyms.

For more detailed information about *expel* the student may consult one of the unabridged dictionaries in the library. In *Webster's New International Dictionary* the entry for this word is more than twice as long as that in the *Collegiate* or the *ACD,* and includes a quotation from Spenser to illustrate the use of the word. *The Oxford English Dictionary,* the most detailed of all dictionaries of the English language, quotes some fifty English writers of the past five or six hundred years to show the exact meaning of *expel* at each stage of its history. The following passage (about one third of the complete entry) illustrates the method used by the *OED.*

Expel (ekspe·l), *v.* Forms: 4–5 expelle, 6–7 expell, 6– expel. [ad. L. *expell-ĕre*, f. *ex-* out + *pellĕre* to drive, thrust: cf. COMPEL. OF. had *espellir*, and in 15th c. *expeller*.]

1. *trans.* To drive or thrust out; to eject by force. Const. *from* (rarely *out of*) also with double obj. (by omission of *from*).

a. With obj. a person, etc.: To eject, dislodge by force from a position; to banish from, compel to quit, a place or country.

c 1489 CAXTON *Sonnes of Aymon* xx. 446 Reynawde and his brethern were thus expelled out of it [mountalban]. 1532 MORE *Confut. Tindale* Wks. 819/2 God.. expelled those heretikes and scismatikes out of heauen. 1577 tr. *Bullinger's Decades* (1592) 838 The Apostles receiued power from the Lord..that they should expell and cast them [the devils] out. 1628 HOBBES *Thucyd.* (1822) 8 The Bœotians ..expelld Arne by the Thessalians seated themselues in that Country [Bœotia]. *c* 1710 C. FIENNES *Diary* (1888) 266 Such a State takes Care..to Expel him their Dominions by proclamation. 1749 WEST tr. *Pindar's Olympic Odes* xii. 36 Sedition's Civil Broils Expell'd thee from thy native Crete. 1754 HUME *Hist. Eng.* I. xi. 229 He sent.. two knights..to expel them the convent. 1863 FR. A. KEMBLE *Resid. Georgia* 31 Bidding the elder boys..expel the poultry.

b. With a material thing as obj.: To drive out from a receptacle, etc. by mechanical force; to discharge, send off (*e.g.* a bullet from a gun, † an arrow from a bow); to drive off or dislodge (a substance) from a chemical compound, mixture, solution, etc. Also, † *To expel forth.*

1669 STURMY *Mariner's Mag.* v. xii. 80 The Shot is.. expelled with no other thing, than by the Air's exaltation. 1695 WOODWARD *Nat. Hist. Earth* III. (1723) 151 It [water] is usualy expelled forth in vast Quantities. *a* 1700 DRYDEN (J.), The virgin huntress was not slow T'expel the shaft from her contracted bow. *c* 1790 IMISON *Sch. Art* I. 74 Expelling the water into the bason. 1807 T. THOMSON *Chem.* (ed. 3) II. 394 Alcohol..absorbs about its own weight of nitrous gas, which cannot afterwards be expelled by heat. 1838 — *Chem. Org. Bodies* 168 Not capable of being expelled by a stronger base. 1860 MAURY *Phys. Geog. Sea* xi. § 512 If still more heat be applied.. the air will be entirely expelled. 1878 HUXLEY *Physiogr.* 77 The matter.. thus expelled from the powder by heat.

(4) Origin; development of the language. The origin of the word—also called *derivation* or *etymology*—is shown in square brackets, as in the *ACD:* [ME *expelle(n)*, t. L: m. *expellere* drive out]. This bracketed information means that *expel* was used in English during the Middle English (ME.) period, A.D. 1100-1500, with the spelling *expelle(n)*; that it was taken from (t.) Latin (L.) and is a modification of (m.) the Latin word *expellere* meaning "to drive out." *Webster's* does not give the Middle English form of *expel,* but it does break down the Latin source *expellere* into *ex* "out" + *pellere* "to drive." The original Latin, meaning "to drive out," supplies the basic definition of the English word. Frequently the origins of words give special insight into meanings. *Automobile,* for example, originally signified "self-moving"; *to sympathize* was "to suffer with"; *to telegraph* was "to write far off." Any student who wishes to get at the heart of a word cannot afford to ignore its origin.

Common prefixes (such as *ex-,* out, *ad-,* to, *circum-,* around, *de-,* from or down, *dis-,* from, *inter-,* between, *pre-,* before, *re-,* back, *sub-,* under, *sur-,* over, and *trans-,* across), suffixes (such as *-able,* capable of being, *-age,* amount of, *-al,* pertaining to, *-ation,* act of, *-ic* or *-ical,* like, *-ile,* of or suited for, *-ish,* of the nature of, *-ive,* given to, *-ous,* full of, and *-ty* or *-ity,* state of), and combining forms (such as *tele-,* far off, *grapho-,* writing, and *phono-,* sound) are listed separately in the dictionary and are well worth study because they make up a part of the meaning of many English words.

The bracketed information given by a good dictionary is especially rich in meaning when associated with the historical development of our language. English is one of the Indo-European (IE.) [1] languages, which apparently had at one time, thousands of years ago, a common vocabulary. In the recorded Indo-European languages, many of the more familiar words are remarkably alike.

---

1 The parenthetical abbreviations for languages here and on the next few pages are those commonly used in the bracketed derivations in dictionaries.

Our word *mother,* for example, is *mater* in Latin (L.), *meter* in Greek (Gk.), and *matar* in the ancient Persian and in the Sanskrit of India. Our pronoun *me* is exactly the same in Latin, in Greek, in Persian, and in Sanskrit. Words in different languages which apparently go back to a parent language are called *cognates.* The large numbers of these cognates make it seem probable that at one time, perhaps three thousand years before Christ, the Indo-Europeans lived in one region and spoke a common language. By the opening of the Christian era they had spread themselves over Europe and as far east as India. Of the eight or nine language groups into which they had developed (see the inside back cover of the *WNWD* or the entry "Indo-European languages" in *Webster's*), English is chiefly concerned with the Greek (on the eastern Mediterranean), with the Latin (on the central and western Mediterranean), and with the Germanic (in northwestern Europe), from which English is descended.

Two thousand years ago the Greek, the Latin, and the Germanic each comprised a more or less unified language group. After the fall of the Roman Empire in the fifth century, the several Latin-speaking divisions developed independently into the modern Romance languages, chief of which are Italian, French, and Spanish. Long before the fall of Rome the Germanic group was breaking up into three groups: (1) East Germanic, represented by the Goths, who were to play a large part in the last century of the Roman Empire before losing themselves in its ruins; (2) North Germanic, represented by Old Norse (ON.), or Viking, from which we have modern Danish (Dan.) and Swedish (Swed.), Norwegian (Norw.) and Icelandic (Icel.); and (3) West Germanic, the direct ancestor of English, Dutch, and German.

The English language may be said to have begun about 450 A.D. when the Jutes, Angles, and Saxons, West Germanic tribes, began the conquest of what is now England and either absorbed or drove out the Celtic-speaking inhabitants. The next six or seven hundred years are known as the Old English (OE.) or Anglo-Saxon (AS.) period of the English language. The fifty or sixty thousand words then in the language were chiefly Anglo-Saxon, with a small mixture of Old Norse words as a result of the Danish (Viking) conquests of England beginning in the eighth century. But the Old Norse words were so much like the Anglo-Saxon that they cannot always be distinguished.

The transitional period—about 1100 to 1500—from Old English to Modern English is known as Middle English (ME.). Changes already under way were accelerated by the Norman Conquest beginning in 1066. The Normans or "Northmen" had settled in northern France during the Viking invasions and had adopted the Old French (OF.) in place of their native Old Norse. The Normans, coming over to England by thousands, made French the language of the King's court in London and of the ruling classes (both French and English) throughout the land, while the masses continued to speak English. But the language that emerged toward the end of the fifteenth century had lost most of its Anglo-Saxon inflections and had taken on thousands of French words (derived originally from Latin). The language, however, was still basically English, not French, in its structure. The marked and steady development of the language (until it was partly stabilized by the beginning of printing in London in 1476) is suggested by the following passages, two from Old English and two from Middle English.

Hē ǣrst gescēop eorðan bearnum
He first created for earth's children

heofon tō hrōfe, hālig scippend.
heaven as a roof, holy creator.

[From the so-called "Hymn of Cædmon," Middle of the Old English Period.]

Ēalā, hū lēas and hū unwrest is þysses middan-eardes
Alas! how false and how unstable is this midworld's

wēla. Sē þe wæs ǣrur rīce cyng and maniges landes
weal! He that was before powerful king and of many lands

hlāford, hē næfde þā ealles landes būton seofon fōt mǣl.
lord, he had not then of all land but seven foot space.

[From the *Anglo-Saxon Chronicle,* A.D. 1087. End of the Old English Period.]

A knight ther was, and that a worthy man,
That fro the tyme that he first bigan
To ryden out, he loved chivalrye,
Trouthe and honour, fredom and curteisye.

[From Chaucer's Prologue to the *Canterbury Tales,* about 1385.]

Thenne within two yeres king Uther felle seke of a grete maladye. And in the meane whyle hys enemyes usurpped upon hym, and dyd a grete bataylle upon his men, and slewe many of his peple.

[From Sir Thomas Malory's *Morte Darthur,* printed 1485.]

► EXERCISE 1. With the aid of your dictionary select the five words in the passage from Malory's *Morte Darthur* that were taken into English—after the Norman Conquest, of course—from the Old French. Copy both the Old French word and the Latin source (if given). (Note that in this passage from Malory all words of one syllable are from Anglo-Saxon. The preposition *upon* may be a combination of two Anglo-Saxon words, *up* and *on,* but more probably it was taken from the Old Norse during the Danish invasions of Britain during the ninth century.)

Although Sir Thomas Malory wrote nearly five hundred years ago, we can still read his *Morte Darthur* with relative ease. William Caxton, who printed Malory's book in 1485, observed that "our language as now used varieth far from that which was used and spoken when I was born." The books he was printing, with millions that have followed since, have helped greatly to stabilize the language.

A striking feature of Modern English (since 1500) is its immense vocabulary. Old English used perhaps fifty thousand words, very largely native Anglo-Saxon; Middle English used perhaps a hundred thousand, many taken through the French from Latin and others directly from Latin; and now our unabridged dictionaries list over half a million. To make up this tremendous word hoard, we have borrowed most heavily from the Latin, but we have drawn some words from almost every known language. English writers of the sixteenth century were especially eager to interlard their works with words from Latin authors; and as Englishmen pushed out to colonize and to trade in many parts of the globe, they brought home new words as well as goods. Modern science and technology have drawn heavily from the Greek. The result of all this borrowing is that English has become the richest, most cosmopolitan of all languages.

In the process of enlarging our vocabulary we have lost most of our original Anglo-Saxon words. But the eight or ten thousand that are left make up the most familiar, most useful part of our vocabulary. Practically all of our simple verbs, our articles, conjunctions, prepositions, and pronouns are native Anglo-Saxon; and so are many of our familiar nouns, adjectives, and adverbs. Every speaker and writer uses these native words over and over, much more frequently than the borrowed words. If every word is counted every time it is used, the percentage of native words runs very high, usually between 70 and 90 per cent. Milton's percentage was 81, Tennyson's 88, Shakespeare's about 90, and that of the King James Bible about 94. English has been enriched by its extensive borrowings without losing its individuality; it is still fundamentally the *English* language.

► EXERCISE 2. Note the origins of the words on a typical page (or on several typical pages) of your dictionary. Copy down examples of words derived from (1) Anglo-Saxon; (2) Old French or Latin through Old French; (3) Latin directly; (4) Greek through Latin; (5) Greek directly; (6) other languages.

(5) Dictionary labels—levels of usage. An unabridged English dictionary attempts to define the half million or more words that have been used by English writers during the Modern English period (since about 1500). The better abridged dictionaries for adults—such as *Webster's, ACD,* or *WNWD*—list between 100,000 and 150,000 words. The dictionary uses labels (*Colloq., Slang, Dial., Obs., Archaic, Eccl., Naut.,* etc.) to show the standing or special use of a word. Any word, or any meaning of a word, that does not have one of these labels is said to be "standard"; that is, it belongs to the general vocabulary and may be used whenever appropriate to the writer's meaning and style. Labeled words, or labeled meanings of words, should be used with appropriate care as suggested below in the "Outline for Dictionary Labels" and treated further under **19 b, c, d, e, f, g,** and **h** on pages 202-06.

Note that none of the three entries illustrated on page 187 gives a label before either of the two meanings for *expel.* Thus we see that the word is fully standard. But let us note *Webster's* entry for *impose,* in which three of the meanings are labeled.

> **im·pose′** (ĭm·pōz′), *v. t.* [F. *imposer*, fr. *im-* in + *poser* to place.] **1.** To subject (one) *to* a charge, penalty, or the like. **2.** To lay as a charge, duty, command, etc.; hence, to levy; inflict; as, to *impose* burdens or a penalty. **3.** *Eccl.* To lay on (the hands), as in confirmation. **4.** *Archaic.* To place; deposit. **5.** To pass or palm off; as, to *impose* inferior goods on a buyer. **6.** To obtrude; as, to *impose* oneself upon others. **7.** *Print.* To arrange in order on a table of stone or metal (**imposing stone** *or* **table**) and lock up in a chase. — *v. i.* **1.** To impress oneself or itself, esp. obnoxiously; presume; as, to *impose* upon good nature. **2.** To practice tricks or deception; — with *on* or *upon.* — **im·pos′er** (-pōz′ẽr), *n.*

For the transitive verb *impose* seven different meanings are given, of which the first, second, fifth, and sixth are unlabeled and therefore standard. The third, labeled *Eccl.,* is a technical word in ecclesiastical usage; the fourth, labeled *Archaic,* is antiquated—no longer used in ordinary writing; and the seventh, labeled *Print.,* is a technical term used in printing. Neither of the two meanings of the intransitive verb *impose* is labeled, and therefore both are standard.

OUTLINE FOR DICTIONARY LABELS

(*a*) *Standard words*—not labeled by the dictionary.

(Used freely to suit the purpose and style of the writer —usually the commonest word that will express the exact meaning.)

FORMAL He has none. It is impossible. We should consider the essentials.

INFORMAL He hasn't any. It's impossible. Let's consider essentials.

(*b*) *Colloquialisms*—labeled *Colloq.*

(Used freely in conversation and in very informal writing.)

EXAMPLES He *hasn't got* any. It's *no go.* Let's get down to *brass tacks.*

(*c*) *Slang*—labeled *Slang.*

(Used only with special care, and never in formal writing.)

EXAMPLES He had been *done in* (for *done away with* or *killed*).

The speech was all *hooey* (for *nonsense*).

(*d*) *Dialectal words* (*localisms, provincialisms*)—labeled *Dial., Scot., South African,* etc.

(Generally avoided in writing because the words may be known only in a limited region.)

EXAMPLE The sheep were kept in a *kraal* (for *enclosure*).

(*e*) *Illiteracies* (*vulgarisms*)—labeled *Illit.* or *Vulgar* (if included in the dictionary at all).

(Always avoided except to illustrate illiterate speech in written dialogue.)

EXAMPLE He ain't got none.

(*f*) *Obsolete and archaic words*—labeled *Obs., Archaic.*

(No longer used, but retained in the dictionary to explain older writings.)

EXAMPLE Edward was he *hight* (for *called*).

(*g*) *Technical words*—labeled *Law, Med.*[2] (medicine), *Naut.* (nautical), *Phar.* (pharmacy), *Surg.* (surgery), *Zool.* (zoology), etc.

(Generally limited in use to writing or speaking for specialized groups.)

EXAMPLE The *hyperemia* (for *increase in blood*) in the left arm is difficult to explain.

(*h*) *Poetic words*—labeled *Poetic.*

(Avoided in general writing and speaking.)

EXAMPLE The man sat *oft* (for *often*) in the moonlight.

The labeling or classification of words is often difficult, for the language is constantly changing and many words are on the borderline, as between slang and colloquial or between colloquial and standard; and it is to be expected that good dictionaries will frequently differ in classifying such words. Although classes of words (especially standard, colloquial, illiterate) are commonly referred to as "levels," we are not to think of one class as always higher or better than another. Actually any one of the eight classes may be the best for a given occasion. Even the illiterate word is best when the writer is trying to illustrate the speech of the uneducated. Technical language is often best in speech and writing addressed to those in one's profession. The occasion and the purpose of the writer or speaker will determine the best words to select. The standard (unlabeled) words which make up the bulk of the English vocabulary are usually best for general writing and, along with colloquialisms, for

---

[2] The *WNWD* writes "in *law,*" "in *medicine,*" etc., and thus avoids abbreviations.

conversation. Our standard words range from the very learned to the very simple and are adequate for the most dignified or the most informal style.

► EXERCISE 3. Classify according to the labels of your dictionary the thirty-three words beginning with *hunky*. *Example:* The thirty-three words in *Webster's New Collegiate Dictionary* preceding *hunky* (beginning with *hummingbird*) may be classified as indicated below. *Italics* indicate that a word belongs in the class in respect to one or more, but not all, of its meanings.

a. STANDARD (not labeled) hummingbird, *hummock, humor,* humorist, humoristic, *humorous, hump,* humpback, humpbacked, humped, humph, humpy, humus, Hun, *hunch,* hunchback, hunchbacked, *hundred,* hundredfold, hundred-percenter, hundredth, hundredweight, hung, *Hungarian,* hunger, hungeringly, hunger strike, *hungry,* hunks
b. COLLOQUIAL *hunch,* hunk
c. SLANG *hump, Hungarian*
d. DIALECTAL *hummock, hump,* hunkers
e. ILLITERATE (None listed)
f. OBSOLETE (or ARCHAIC) *humor, humorous, hunch, Hungarian,* hungerly, *hungry*
g. TECHNICAL *humor,* humoresque, *humorous, hundred*
h. POETIC (None listed)

► FURTHER EXERCISES ON THE USE OF THE DICTIONARY

► EXERCISE 4. What were the original meanings of the following words?

adjective	conjunction	dialogue	monarchy
aristocracy	democracy	emperor	oligarchy

▶ EXERCISE 5. What were the original meanings of the following words? What meanings developed later?

amateur	inspiration	nebulous	sanguine
doom	knave	proper	Yankee

▶ EXERCISE 6. List synonyms for each of the following words. (For synonyms and antonyms you may find that your dictionary should be supplemented by a book of synonyms such as *Roget's International Thesaurus,* New York, 1936, which is available also in a pocketbook size.)

act	change	fight	see
anger	eat	go	think

▶ EXERCISE 7. List antonyms for each of the following words.

awkward	clever	gallantry	quiet
clear	fast	greed	study

▶ EXERCISE 8. Study the following pairs of words in your dictionary (in the special paragraphs, if any, that compare and contrast the pairs) and write sentences to illustrate the shades of difference in meaning.

cause–reason	help–aid	push–shove
freedom–liberty	position–situation	valid–sound

▶ EXERCISE 9. Determine the preferred American spelling of the following words: *connexion, gypsy, labour.* Which of the following words should be written separately, which should be written solid, and which should be hyphenated?

cropeared	girlscout	heartfelt	toiletwater
cubbyhole	heartbroken	heartfree	vestpocket

▶ EXERCISE 10. Determine the pronunciation for each of the following words. Which of the words change the accent to indicate a change in grammatical function?

absent	exquisite	Montaigne	vehement
contest	impious	object	Viet-Nam

▶ EXERCISE 11. Classify each of the following words as a verb (transitive or intransitive), a noun, an adjective, an adverb, a preposition, or a conjunction. Give the principal parts of each verb, the plural (or plurals) of each noun, and the comparative and superlative of each adjective or adverb. (Note that some words are used as two or more parts of speech.)

bad	drag	often	since	stratum
bite	into	sheep	sing	tomato

▶ EXERCISE 12. Which of the following words are always capitalized? Which are capitalized only for certain meanings?

easter	italic	platonic	spanish
italian	liberian	roman	stoical

▶ EXERCISE 13. Divide the following words into syllables.

analytic	industrious	liberty	vindictive
indistinguishable	laboriously	supplement	vocabulary

▶ EXERCISE 14. Get from your dictionary specific information about each of the following. Note the source of information as (a) general vocabulary, (b) list of abbreviations, (c) gazetteer, (d) biographical list, or (e) appendix.

Annam	Esau	Melpomene	*vive le roi*
Connecticut College	Escorial	Louis Pasteur	WAC

19b Colloquialisms are generally avoided in standard (formal) writing.

Colloquial words or expressions (labeled *Colloq.*) are appropriate to conversation and to informal writing. For these purposes colloquialisms often give a desirable tone of informality. But colloquial expressions tend to bring a discordant note into expository or other formal types of writing and should usually be avoided in formal writing.

COLLOQUIAL The cabin was very *homey.*
STANDARD The cabin was very *homelike.*

COLLOQUIAL The man never had a fair *show.*
STANDARD The man never had a fair *chance.*

COLLOQUIAL The boys gave a good *show.*
STANDARD The boys gave a good *performance.*

Contracted forms (*won't, I'd, she'll, hasn't*) are perfectly proper in informal writing and equally proper in all but the most extremely formal speech. But they are to be avoided in formal expository writing. Write them out—*will not, I would, I had,* etc.

INFORMAL *It's* really too bad that *he's* been detained and *can't* be here for our opening.
FORMAL *It is* really too bad that *he has* been detained and *cannot* be here for our opening.

► EXERCISE 15. Consult your dictionary for *colloquial* meanings of the following words: *brass, dig, fizzle, kick, way.* For each word compose a sentence in which the word is used with the colloquial meaning. Then in each sentence substitute a standard word with the same meaning.

19c Slang and jargon should be used sparingly if at all in standard speech and writing.

Slang, according to *The American College Dictionary,* is "language of a markedly colloquial character, regarded as below the standard of cultivated speech." Some slang words have a pungent quality: *slob,* which derives from an Irish word for *mud,* along with *jive, goon,* and *jitter,* may soon join *mob, van, sham,* and *banter* as standard members of the English language. But much slang is trite and tasteless, and is used in an ineffective attempt to mask an inadequate vocabulary. Some people describe everything as "swell" or "lousy," when they really want to say *excellent, generous, satisfying, distinguished,* or *contemptible, foolish, inadequate.*

The objection to slang, then, is not based upon arbitrary *don'ts,* but upon slang's habitual alliance with lazy thinking. Slang is the sluggard's way of avoiding the search for the exact, meaningful word.

For the same reason *jargon*—language which is meaningless, or at least very confusing except to a special group—should be avoided. Almost every trade or occupation has its own jargon. A man with recent military experience might write the following jargon about his first day in college:

> The mustering-in was snafu, and the old man blew his top.

This sentence would be easily understood by his army friends; other readers might require a formal statement:

> The registration was confused, and the dean lost his temper.

A particularly confusing type of jargon is found in much government writing.[3]

---

[3] Bureaucratic jargon is also wordy. See Section 21a.

BUREAUCRATIC JARGON All personnel functioning in the capacity of clerks will indicate that they have had opportunity to take due cognizance of this notice by transmitting signed acknowledgment of receipt of same.

IMPROVED All clerks will acknowledge in writing the receipt of this notice.

19d Dialectal words should generally be avoided.

Dialectal words (also called *localisms* or *provincialisms*) should normally be avoided in speaking and writing because they are often meaningless outside the limited region where they are current. Speakers and writers may, however, safely use dialectal words known to the audience they are addressing.

DIALECT He filled the *poke* with potatoes.
STANDARD He filled the *bag* with potatoes.

DIALECT The *highhole* has flown away.
STANDARD The *flicker* has flown away.

DIALECT I *reckon* he will come.
STANDARD I *suppose* he will come.

19e Illiteracies and improprieties should be avoided.

Illiteracies (also called *vulgarisms*) are the crude expressions of uneducated people, usually not listed in the dictionary.

ILLITERATE He *ain't* going. *They's* no use asking him.
STANDARD He *isn't* going. *There's* no use asking him.

An *impropriety* is a good word used with the wrong sense or function.

WRONG I *except* your invitation. [Wrong meaning]
RIGHT I *accept* your invitation.
ILLITERATE (or COLLOQUIAL) She sang *good.* [Wrong function —adjective used as adverb]
STANDARD She sang *well.*

19f Obsolete, archaic, or obsolescent words should be avoided.

All dictionaries list words (and meanings for words) that have long since passed out of general use. Such words as *parfit* (perfect), *ort* (fragment of food left at a meal), *yestreen* (last evening), *waxen* (to grow or become) are still found in dictionaries because these words were once the standard vocabulary of great authors and must be defined for the modern reader.

Some archaic words—like *wight, methinks,* and *quoth*—have been used for purposes of humor. Modern practice tends to label such usage as juvenile.

19g Technical words should be avoided in nontechnical speaking and writing.

When you are writing for the general reader, avoid all unnecessary technical language. Since the ideal of the good writer is to make his thought clear to as many people as possible, he will not describe an apple tree as a *Malus pumila* or a high fever as *hyperpyrexia.* (Of course technical language, with its greater precision, is highly desirable when one is addressing an audience that can understand it.)

Sometimes, however, even though the dictionary labels

words as technical expressions (*electron* and *atomic theory,* for example), the words are well enough known to justify their general use.

19h Avoid (1) "fine writing," (2) "poetic" expressions, and (3) unpleasing combinations of sound.

(1) **Avoid "fine writing."** "Fine writing" is the unnecessary use of ornate words and expressions. It is generally fuzzy and repetitious; it tends to emphasize words rather than ideas. A simple, direct statement like "From childhood I have looked forward to a journey" can become by fine writing something like this: "From the halcyon days of early youth I have always anticipated with eagerness and pleasure the exciting vistas of distant climes and mysterious horizons."

(2) **Avoid "poetic" expressions.** Genuine poetry has its very proper place, and the vivid language of simile and metaphor enriches even colloquial prose. But the sham poetry of faded imagery (*eye of night* for *moon*) and inappropriate expressions like *oft, eftsoons, 'twas,* and *'neath* are misplaced in the usual prose style.

(3) **Avoid unpleasing combinations of sound.** Good prose has rhythm, but it does not rhyme. If you write, "In foreign relations, the western nations are subject to dictation," you distract the reader's attention from your meaning. Equally offensive to the average reader is the awkward combination of consonants, as in "Some people shun the seashore."

► EXERCISES ON USAGE

A. In the following list check any sentence that requires no revision, even for standard writing. Write *Colloq.* for

24. Her folks live in the country ten miles outside the city limits.
25. He calculated he could win out in the election.

B. Rewrite the following passage in standard informal English.

1. I know, Dean, I'm over a barrel good this time. 2. You wouldn't of made all this hullabaloo if you wasn't plenty peeved. 3. So I'm on the hook. 4. Well, I won't try to put the monkey on somebody else's back—pass the buck, that is. 5. I done what the prof says I done, and I can't say as I blame him for being some aggravated over it. 6. I guess I'd be doing flips if I was him. 7. And, like I say, you maybe got a right to be provoked with me too, especially after that hassle with the law over the parking meters last winter. 8. But I never painted up them nickel nabbers, Dean, honest I didn't. 9. The cops just hauled me in because, the way the papers been riding City Hall, they had to put the snag on somebody and I sort of happened to be handy. 10. I was clean as Monday's wash on that deal, Dean. 11. Still, you've got the whole thing on the poop-sheet there—I mean on my record—and that's as black a eye as I need, especially with this Zo lab rhubarb on top of it. 12. I guess that little ruckus sounded pretty bad by the time it got to the top brass. 13. But it wasn't any worse as a lot of things you never hear a peep about. 14. Sure, I know us guys had no business horsing around like that, but you know how guys are. 15. So when them two caught me logging a little sack time before lab and started putting frogs up my britches legs and then tipped my chair over backward—I told you I'd pay for that busted chair, didn't I, Dean, even if I didn't bust it myself? 16. Well, when I come up with my pants full of frogs and there was this cat barrel I like to have fell in, I just grabbed me a cat and heaved it. 17. How'd I know the prof was going to

barge in right then and get it smash in the smush? 18. I know it don't sound too funny to hear tell it, but I wisht you'd a seen him. 19. Honest, Dean, you'd a laid right down and died.

C. Rewrite the following passages of bureaucratic, legal, or academic jargon[4] in simple standard English.

1. It is obvious from the difference in elevation with relation to the short depth of the property that the contour is such as to preclude any reasonable developmental potential for active recreation.
2. Verbal contact with Mr. Blank regarding the attached notification of promotion has elicited the attached representation intimating that he prefers to decline the assignment.
3. Voucherable expenditures necessary to provide adequate dental treatment required as adjunct to medical treatment being rendered a pay patient in in-patient status may be incurred as required at the expense of the Public Health Service.
4. I hereby give and convey to you, all and singular, my estate and interests, right, title, claim and advantages of and in said orange, together with all rind, juice, pulp and pits, and all rights and advantages therein.
5. I prefer an abbreviated phraseology, distinguished for its lucidity.
6. Realization has grown that the curriculum or the experiences of learners change and improve only as those who are most directly involved examine their goals, improve their understandings and increase their skill in performing the tasks necessary to reach newly defined goals.

---

[4] Quoted, by permission, from Stuart Chase's *Power of Words,* Harcourt, Brace and Company, New York, 1953, pp. 250-53.

▶ Glossary of Usage

19i Consult this list to determine the standing of a word or phrase and its appropriateness to your purpose.[5] (If the word you are looking for is not included, or if you need more information about any word in the list, consult a good dictionary—preferably one of the unabridged dictionaries in the library.)

A, an. Use *a* before a consonant sound, *an* before a vowel sound. Examples: *a* band, *a* well, *a* yard, *a* unit [*y* sound], *a* one [*w* sound], *a* hammer, *a* history; *an* apple, *an* olive, *an* hour [silent *h* before the vowel]

Accept, except. Do not confuse. The verb *accept* means "to receive." *Except* means "to exclude."

RIGHT Mary accepted (*not* excepted) an invitation to dinner.

RIGHT They excepted (*not* accepted) Mary from the invitation.

Ad. Colloquial shortening of *advertisement.* Use the full word in standard speech and writing.

---

[5] Before attempting to use this list, the student should read pages 195-206 above for distinctions between STANDARD (both FORMAL and INFORMAL) and COLLOQUIAL **(19b)**, SLANG **(19c)**, DIALECTAL **(19d)**, ILLITERATE or VULGAR **(19e)**, OBSOLETE and ARCHAIC **(19f)**, TECHNICAL **(19g)**, and POETIC **(19h)**.

Affect, effect. Do not confuse. *Affect* (a verb) means "to influence." "The attack affected the morale of the troops." *Effect* is both a verb and a noun. As a verb it means "to bring to pass." "The medicine effected a complete cure." As a noun *effect* means "result." "The effect of the medicine was instantaneous."

Aggravate. Means "to intensify, to increase." "Lack of water aggravated the suffering." Colloquially it means "to irritate, exasperate, provoke, annoy."

COLLOQUIAL He was extremely aggravated by the delay.
STANDARD He was extremely annoyed by the delay.

Agree to, agree with. One agrees *to* a plan but *with* a person.

A half a. Redundant. See **Half a, a half, a half a.**

Ain't. An illiterate or dialectal contraction. In conversation and in informal writing the following contractions may be used: *I'm not, you* (*we, they*) *aren't, he* (*she, it*) *isn't.* In formal writing the words are usually written out: *I am not,* etc.

Alibi. Colloquial for *excuse.* Standard English accepts the word only in its technical legal sense.

Allude, refer. Do not confuse. *Allude* means "to refer to indirectly." "When he mentioned dictators, we knew that he was alluding to Hitler and Mussolini." *Refer* means "to mention something specifically." "I refer you to the third act of *Hamlet.*"

Allusion, illusion. Do not confuse *allusion,* "an indirect reference," with *illusion,* "an unreal image or false impression."

Already, all ready. *Already* (one word) means "prior to some specified time, either present, past, or future." "By noon the theater was already full." *All ready* (two words) means "completely ready." "I am all ready to go."

Alright. Incorrect spelling. Use *all right.*

Also. A weak connective. *And* is a better connective. "I met Harry and Tom (*not* also Tom)."

Altogether, all together. *Altogether* (one word) means "wholly, thoroughly, in all." "The report is altogether true." *All together* (two words) means "in a group, collectively." "The packages were all together on the table."

Alumnus, alumna. *Alumnus,* a male graduate; *alumni,* two or more male graduates. *Alumna,* a female graduate; *alumnae,* two or more female graduates. *Alumni,* male and female graduates grouped together.

A.M., P.M. (also **a.m., p.m.**). Use only with figures. "He came at 10:00 A.M. (*not* in the A.M.) and left at 4:00 P.M." "He came in the morning and left in the afternoon (*not* in the P.M.)."

Among, between. *Among* always implies more than two. "Joseph's brethren divided the spoils among them." *Between* literally implies only two. "I divided the cake between John and Mary." But *between* is used for more than two to indicate a reciprocal relation. "A treaty was concluded between the three nations."

Amount, number. Use *amount* to refer to things in bulk or mass, *number* to refer to countable objects. "A large amount of grain; a number of watermelons."

An, a. See **A, an.**

And etc. Never place *and* before *etc.* The *and* is redundant since *etc.* is an abbreviation of *et* (and) + *cetera* (other things).

And which, but which. Do not thwart subordination by inserting *and* or *but* before a subordinate clause. "Law enforcement is a current problem which (*not* and which) is hard to solve." "The college needs new dormitories which (*not* but which) cannot be erected until funds are provided." But *and* or *but* may be used before *which* to join two *which* clauses. "Law enforcement is a problem which is current and which is hard to solve."

Ante-, anti-. *Ante-* means "before," as in *antebellum. Anti-* means "against," as in *anti-British.* The hyphen is used after *anti-* before capital letters and before *i,* as in *anti-imperialist.*

Anyone, everyone, someone. Distinguish from *any one, every one, some one. Anyone* (one word) means "any person, anybody." *Any one* (two words) means "any single person or thing." Similarly with *everyone, someone.*

Anyways. Dialectal for *in any case, anyway.*

STANDARD I may not get the pass I have requested, but I am planning to go anyway (*not* anyways).

Anywheres. Illiterate for *anywhere.*

Apt. See **Likely, liable, apt.**

Around. Colloquial in the sense of "about, near."

COLLOQUIAL To come around noon; to stay around the house.

STANDARD To come about noon; to stay near (*or* about) the house.

As. (1) Generally avoid *as* in the sense of "because." *For* or *since* is usually clearer.

VAGUE He worked steadily as the day was cool.
CLEARER He worked steadily, for the day was cool.

(2) In standard English do not use *as* in place of *that* or *whether.*

COLLOQUIAL I feel as I should go.
STANDARD I feel that I should go.

(3) In negative statements careful writers prefer *so . . . as* to *as . . . as.* "I am not so strong as I used to be." "He will go only so far as he is forced to go."
See also **Like, as, as if.**

At. Redundant and usually illiterate in such sentences as the following:

REDUNDANT Where does he live at? Where are you at now?
IMPROVED Where does he live? Where are you now?

At about. *About* is preferable.

WORDY He arrived at about noon.
BETTER He arrived about noon.

Awful. Colloquial in the sense of "very bad, ugly, shocking."

COLLOQUIAL The suit was awful.
STANDARD The suit was very ugly.

Awhile, a while. Distinguish between the adverb *awhile* and the article and noun *a while*. "Rest awhile before leaving." "Rest for a while (*not* awhile) before leaving."

Bank on, take stock in. Colloquial expressions for *rely on, trust in.*

Because. Do not use *because* to introduce a noun clause.

POOR Because he was sick was no excuse.
BETTER The fact that he was sick was no excuse, *or* His sickness was no excuse.

See also **Reason is because.**

Being as, being that. Substandard for *since, because.*

Beside, besides. Do not confuse. *Beside* is a preposition meaning "by the side of." "Sit beside me." *Besides,* used chiefly as an adverb, means "in addition to." "We ate apples and other fruit besides."

Better. See **Had better, had rather, would rather.**

Between, among. See **Among, between.**

Bunch. Colloquial for *group of people.*

COLLOQUIAL A bunch of boys, a bunch of farmers
STANDARD A group of boys, a group of farmers; a bunch of carrots

Bust, busted, bursted. Illiterate forms of the verb *burst,* which uses the same form for all its principal parts: *burst, burst, burst.*

But, only, hardly, scarcely. These words, negative in implication, should not be used with another negative.

POOR He didn't have but one hat.
BETTER He had but one hat; *or,* He had only one hat.

POOR He wasn't sick only three days.
BETTER He was sick only three days.

POOR I don't hardly (scarcely) know.
BETTER I hardly (scarcely) know.

But what. Colloquial for *that.*

COLLOQUIAL He had no doubt *but what* he would succeed.
STANDARD He had no doubt *that* he would succeed.

But which, and which. See **And which, but which.**

Calculate. Colloquial or dialectal for *think, guess, plan.*

Can, may. In formal usage *can* denotes ability and *may* denotes possibility or permission. The use of *can* to denote permission is colloquial.

COLLOQUIAL Can I go?
FORMAL May I go?

Can't hardly. A double negative in implication. Use *can hardly.* See **But, only, hardly, scarcely.**

Case, line. Often used in wordy expressions. Say "Jones had good intentions," not "In the case of Jones there were good intentions." Say "Get some fruit," not "Get something in the line of fruit."

Cause of. Do not say that the *cause of* something was *on account of.* Complete the expression with a predicate noun or a noun clause.

LOGICAL The cause of my inability to work was a bad headache (*not* on account of a bad headache). [Predicate noun]
LOGICAL The cause of my inability to work was that I had a bad headache. [Noun clause]

Censure, criticize. See **Criticize, censure.**

Common, mutual. That thing is *common* in which two or more share equally or alike, as in "a common purpose." That thing is *mutual* which is reciprocally given and received, as in "mutual assistance."

Company. A colloquial expression for *guests, visitors, escort.*

Compare to, compare with. "One object is *compared with* another when set side by side with it in order to show their relative value or excellence; *to* another when it it formally represented as like it." (*Webster's*)

RIGHT He compared the book with the manuscript.
RIGHT He compared the earth to a ball.

Complected. Dialectal or colloquial for *complexioned.*

STANDARD He was a light-complexioned (*not* light-complected) man.
STANDARD He was a man of light complexion.

Considerable. An adjective; colloquial as a noun; illiterate as an adverb.

COLLOQUIAL He lost considerable in the depression.
STANDARD He lost a considerable amount of property during the depression.
ILLITERATE He was considerable touched by the girl's plea.
STANDARD He was considerably touched by the girl's plea.

Continual, continuous. *Continual* means "occurring in steady, rapid, but not unbroken succession." "The rehearsal was hampered by continual interruptions." *Continuous* means "without cessation." "The continuous roar of the waterfall was disturbing."

Could of. Illiterate corruption of *could have.*

Criticize, censure. In standard English, *criticize* means "to examine and judge as a critic," not necessarily "to censure." *Censure* means "to find fault with" or "to condemn as wrong."

Cunning. Means "shrewd." Colloquial for *attractive.*

Cute. Colloquial for *clever, shrewd, attractive, petite.*

Data, strata, phenomena. Plurals of *datum, stratum, phenomenon.* "These data, these strata, these phenomena, this stratum, this phenomenon." *Stratum* and *phenomenon* have alternative plurals in *s.* The singular *datum* is seldom used. The plural *data* is often construed as a collective noun taking a singular verb: "This data is new."

Date. Colloquial for *appointment, engagement; to make an appointment.*

Deal. Colloquial or commercial term for *transaction, bargain.*

Didn't ought. See **Had ought, hadn't ought, didn't ought.**

Differ from, differ with. Do not confuse. *Differ from* means "to stand apart because of unlikeness." "The Caucasian race differs from the Mongolian race in color, stature, and customs." *Differ with* means "to disagree." "On that point I differ with you."

Done. The past participle of the verb *to do. I do, I did, I have done. Done* is illiterate for *did* or for the adverb *already.*

ILLITERATE He done well.
RIGHT He did well.

ILLITERATE He has done sold the dog.
RIGHT He has already sold the dog; *or,* He has sold the dog.

Don't. A contraction for *do not,* but not for *does not.*

WRONG He don't smoke. [He do not smoke.]
RIGHT He doesn't smoke. [He does not smoke.]
PROPER CONTRACTIONS I don't, we don't, you don't, they don't. [do not]
He doesn't, she doesn't, it doesn't. [does not]

Due to. A prepositional phrase beginning with *due to* is universally approved as an adjective modifier, as in "His tardiness was due to an accident," in which the prepositional phrase modifies the noun *tardiness.* There is increasing use of *due to* in adverbial constructions, as in "Due to an accident he arrived late," in which the prepositional phrase modifies the verb *arrived.* But for this adverbial construction many writers prefer *because of* or *on account of.* "Because of an accident he arrived late."

Each other, one another. Used interchangeably. Some writers prefer *each other* when referring to only two, and *one another* when referring to more than two.

Effect, affect. See **Affect, effect.**

Elegant. Means *polished, fastidious, refined.* Used colloquially for *delicious, good.*

STANDARD This food is delicious (*not* elegant).

Emigrate, immigrate. *Emigrate* means "to leave a place of abode for residence in another country." *Immigrate* means "to come for permanent residence into a country of which one is not a native."

Enthuse. Colloquial for *to make enthusiastic, to become enthusiastic.*

COLLOQUIAL She enthuses over anything.
STANDARD She becomes enthusiastic about anything.

Equally as good. The *as* is redundant. Say "equally good" or "as good as."

Etc. See **And etc.**

Every bit. Colloquial for *entirely, in every way.*

Everyone, anyone, someone. See **Anyone, everyone, someone.**

Everywheres. Dialectal for *everywhere.*

Exam. Colloquial shortening of *examination.* For formal purposes, use the full word.

Except, accept. See **Accept, except.**

Expect. Colloquial if used to mean "suppose."

COLLOQUIAL I expect the report is true.
STANDARD I suppose the report is true.

Farther, further. *Farther* is often preferred to express geographic distance. "They went even farther the next day." *Further* is regularly preferred to express the meaning, "more, in addition." "Further reports came."

Faze. Colloquial for *worry, disconcert.*

Fellow. Colloquial for *man.*

Fewer, less. *Fewer* refers especially to number. "Fewer than twenty persons attended." *Less* refers especially to value, degree, or amount. "The suit costs less than the overcoat."

Fine. The adjective *fine* is much overused as a vague word of approval. Choose an expression to fit the meaning exactly.

Fine is colloquial or dialectal when used as an adverb meaning "well, excellently."

COLLOQUIAL	She plays the organ fine.
STANDARD	She plays the organ well.

Flunk. Colloquial for *fail.*

Folks. Colloquial for *parents, relatives, persons of one's own family.*

Former. Refers to the first named of two. Not properly used when three or more are named.

Foul up. Colloquial for *confuse, entangle, bungle.*

Funny. Colloquial for *strange, queer, odd.* In standard usage *funny* means "amusing."

Further, farther. See **Farther, further.**

Gent. Illiterate (or humorous) for *gentleman, man.* "The store advertises men's (*not* gents') suits.

Gentleman, lady. Generally preferable: *man, woman.* Use *gentleman, lady* when your purpose is to distinguish persons of refinement and culture from the ill-bred. Use the plural forms in addressing an audience: "Ladies and Gentlemen."

QUESTIONABLE	Lady preacher, saleslady, lady clerk, cleaning lady, ladies' colleges
BETTER	Woman preacher, saleswoman, woman clerk, cleaning woman, women's colleges

Get, got. The verb *to get* is one of the most useful words in standard English. It is common in such good idioms as *get along with* (someone), *get the better of* (someone), *get at* (information), *get up* (a dance), *get on* (a horse), or *get over* (sickness). But *get* or *got* is also used in expressions that are colloquial or slangy. Examples (with standard equivalents in parentheses):

COLLOQUIAL	He has got to (is obliged to, must) go.
	This work gets (puzzles, irritates) me.
	The bullet got (killed) him.

Good. Not generally recognized as an adverb.

QUESTIONABLE He reads good. He works good.
STANDARD He reads well. He works well; *or,* He does good work.

Gotten. Past participle of *get,* the principal parts of which are *get* (present), *got* (past), *got,* or *gotten* (past participle). In England *gotten* is now archaic, but in the United States both *got* and *gotten* are in general use.

Grand. Avoid the vague colloquial use of *grand* to mean "excellent." Select the exact word to fit the meaning.

LOOSE We had a grand trip.
BETTER We had a delightful (pleasant, exciting) trip.

Guy. Slang for *man, boy, fellow.*

Had better, had rather, would rather. Good idioms used to express advisability (with *better*) or preference (with *rather*). *Better* is a colloquial shortening of *had better.*

COLLOQUIAL He better listen to reason.
STANDARD He had better listen to reason.

Had of. Illiterate for *had.*

ILLITERATE I wish I had of gone.
STANDARD I wish I had gone.

Had ought, hadn't ought, didn't ought. Illiterate combinations.

ILLITERATE He hadn't ought to have gone.
STANDARD He ought not to have gone.

Half a, a half, a half a. Use *half a* or *a half,* but avoid the redundant *a half a.*

REDUNDANT He worked a half a day.
STANDARD He worked half a day.
STANDARD He worked a half day. [Perhaps more formal and more specific]

Hardly. See **But, only, hardly, scarcely.**

Healthful, healthy. *Healthful* means "giving health," as in "healthful climate, healthful food." *Healthy* means "having health," as in "healthy boy, healthy woman, healthy people."

Himself, myself, yourself. See **Myself, himself, yourself.**

Hisself. Illiterate for *himself.*

Homey. Colloquial for *homelike, intimate.*

Honorable, Reverend. See **Reverend, Honorable.**

If, whether. Some writers prefer *whether* to *if* after such verbs as *say, learn, know, understand, doubt,* especially when followed by *or.* "I did not know whether he would ride or walk."

Illusion, allusion. See **Allusion, illusion.**

Immigrate, emigrate. See **Emigrate, immigrate.**

Imply, infer. See **Infer, imply.**

In, into. Do not confuse. *In* indicates "location within." "He was in the room." *Into* indicates "motion or direction to a point within." "He came into the room."

In-, un-. See **Un-, in-.**

Incredible, incredulous. *Incredible* means "too extraordinary to admit of belief." *Incredulous* means "inclined not to believe on slight evidence."

Individual, party, person. *Individual* refers to a single person, animal, or thing. *Party* refers to a group, never to a single person (except in colloquial or legal usage). *Person* is the preferred word for general reference to a human being.

COLLOQUIAL He is the interested party.
STANDARD He is the interested person.

Infer, imply. *Infer* means "to arrive at through reasoning." "From his statement I infer that he will resign." *Imply* means "to hint or suggest." "His statement implies that he will resign."

Ingenious, ingenuous. *Ingenious* means "clever, resourceful," as "an ingenious device." *Ingenuous* means "open, frank, artless," as "ingenuous actions."

In regards to. Use either of the correct idioms, *in regard to* or *as regards.*

Into, in. See **In, into.**

Invite. Slang when used as a noun.

Its, it's. Do not confuse the possessive *its* and the contraction *it's* (= *it is*).

Just. Colloquial for *completely, simply, quite.*

COLLOQUIAL He was just tired out.
STANDARD He was completely tired out.

Kind, sort. Singular forms, modified by singular adjectives.

COLLOQUIAL OR ILLITERATE I like these kind (*or* sort) of shoes.
STANDARD I like this kind (*or* sort) of shoes.

Kind of, sort of. Loosely colloquial when used as an adverb to mean "somewhat, rather, after a fashion."

COLLOQUIAL I was kind of (sort of) tired.
STANDARD I was somewhat tired.

COLLOQUIAL I kind of (sort of) thought you would go.
STANDARD I rather thought you would go.

Kind of a, sort of a. Omit the *a* in standard writing.

STANDARD What kind of (*not* kind of a) car does he drive?
What sort of (*not* sort of a) car does he drive?

Lady, gentleman. See **Gentleman, lady.**

Later, latter. Do not confuse. *Later* is the comparative of late and means "more late." *Latter* refers to the last named of two. If more than two are named, use *last* or *last-mentioned* instead of *latter.*

Lay, lie. Do not confuse. See Section 7a, page 81.

Lead, led. Present tense and past tense of the verb. Do not confuse with the noun *lead* (pronounced *led*), the name of the metal.

Learn, teach. *Learn* means "to acquire knowledge"; *teach* means "to impart knowledge." "She taught (*not* learned) him his lesson."

Leave, let. Do not use *leave* for *let. Leave* means "to depart from"; *let* means "to permit." But "Leave (*or* Let) me alone" is a standard idiom.

SLANG I will not leave you go today.
STANDARD I will not let you go today.

Less, fewer. See **Fewer, less.**

Let's us. *Let's* is the contraction of *let us.* Therefore *Let's us go* is redundant for *Let's go. Let's don't stay* is redundant for *Let's not stay.*

Lie, lay. Do not confuse. See Section 7a, page 81.

Like, as, as if. Use *like* as a preposition; use *as* or *as if* as a conjunction. *Like* is much used colloquially as a conjunction, but this use is generally avoided in standard writing.

STANDARD He worked like a man. Do as (*not* like) I do. It looks as if (*not* like) it might rain.

Likely, liable, apt. Standard writing tends to use *likely* to express mere probability; to use *liable* to suggest, in addition, the idea of harm or responsibility. "My friends are likely to arrive tomorrow." [Mere probability] "The boy is liable to cut his foot with the ax." [Probability + the idea of harm] "The hotel will not be liable for stolen property." [Responsibility] *Apt* implies a predisposition or dexterity. "He is apt to worry." "He is an apt pupil." [Associate *apt* with *aptitude; liable* with *liability*] In colloquial usage *likely, liable,* and *apt* are interchangeable.

Line, case. See **Case, line.**

Locate. Colloquial for *settle.*

STANDARD He settled (*not* located) in Texas.

Lose, loose. Do not confuse. *Lose* means "to cease having." *Loose* (verb) means "to set free." *Loose* (adjective) means "free, not fastened."

Lot, lots of. Colloquial for *much, many, a great deal.*

Lovely. Avoid the vague colloquial use of *lovely* to mean "very pleasing." Select the exact word to fit the meaning.

Mad. Means "insane." Colloquial for *angry.*

May be, maybe. Do not confuse the verb form *may be* with the adverb *maybe,* meaning "perhaps." "He may be waiting for my letter." "Maybe he will come tomorrow."

May, can. See **Can, may.**

May of. Illiterate corruption of *may have.*

Mean. Colloquial for *ill-tempered, indisposed, ashamed.*

Might of. Illiterate corruption of *might have.*

Mighty. Colloquial for *very.*

Most. Standard English does not recognize the adjective *most* as a substitute for the adverb *almost.*

COLLOQUIAL	The trains arrive most every hour.
STANDARD	The trains arrive almost every hour.
STANDARD	The trains are most crowded during the holidays. [*Most* is correctly used as an adverb to form the superlative.]

Must of. Illiterate corruption of *must have.*

Mutual. See **Common, mutual.**

Myself, himself, yourself. Properly intensive or reflexive pronouns. "I myself will go; I will see for myself." In general *myself* is not a proper substitute for *I* or *me;* but it is substituted colloquially (1) for *I* after comparisons with *than* or *as* ("Everyone worked as well as myself") or (2) for *me* when it is the second member of a compound object ("He allowed my brother and myself to go home").

Nice. In formal writing, means "precise" or "exact." Do not overwork *nice* as a vague word of approval. Find an exact word.

VAGUE	It was a nice day.
SPECIFIC	It was a bright (mild, sunny) day.

No account, no good. Colloquial for *worthless, of no value.*

No place. Colloquial for *nowhere.*

Nowhere near. Colloquial for *not nearly.*

Nowheres. Dialectal for *nowhere.*

Number. See **Amount, number.**

O, oh. Interjections. *O* is used especially in very formal direct address, is always capitalized, and is never followed by any mark of punctuation. "O God, deliver us!" *Oh* is used to express grief, surprise, or a wish, and is followed by a comma or an exclamation point. "Oh, I hope so."

Of. See **Could of, Had of, Ought to of.**

Off of. *Of* is superfluous. "He fell off (*not* off of) the platform."

One another, each other. See **Each other, one another.**

Only. See **But, only, hardly, scarcely.**

Other times. Use *at other times.*

Ought. See **Had ought.**

Ought to of. Illiterate corruption of *ought to have.*

Out loud. Colloquial for *aloud.*

Outside of. Colloquial in the sense of "except."

STANDARD Except (*not* outside of) James, nobody went with him.

Party, person, individual. See **Individual, party, person.**

Per. Used especially in commercial writing. In standard English some authors use *per* only with Latin words, such as *diem, annum.*

COMMERCIAL His salary was four thousand dollars per year.

STANDARD His salary was four thousand dollars a year.

Per cent (or percent). Means "by the hundred." Use only after a numeral: "10 per cent, 20 per cent." In other situations *per cent* is colloquial for *percentage.* "A large percentage, a small percentage." Do not overwork *percentage* for *portion, part.*

Person, party, individual. See **Individual, party, person.**

Phenomena. Plural of *phenomenon.* See **Data, strata, phenomena.**

Phone. Colloquial shortening of *telephone.* Use the full word in formal writing.

Photo. Colloquial shortening of *photograph.* Use the full word in standard writing.

Piece. Dialectal for *short distance.*

Plenty. Colloquial when used as an adverb.

COLLOQUIAL It is plenty good enough.
STANDARD It is quite good enough.

P.M., A.M. See **A.M., P.M.**

Practical, practicable. *Practical* means "useful, sensible," not "theoretical." *Practicable* means "feasible, capable of being put into practice." "The sponsors are practical men, and their plans are practicable."

Prefer. Not to be followed by *than,* but by *to, before, above, rather than.*

UNIDIOMATIC I should prefer that than anything else.
IDIOMATIC I should prefer that to anything else.

Principal, principle. Distinguish between *principal,* an adjective or noun meaning "chief" or "chief official," and the noun *principle,* meaning "fundamental truth."

Proposition. Properly "a thing proposed." Colloquial with the meaning "a project involving action, venture, difficulty."

STANDARD The mine was a paying venture (*not* proposition) from the first.

Quite. An adverb meaning "entirely, positively." Used colloquially to mean "to a great extent, very."

COLLOQUIAL The lake is quite near.
STANDARD The lake is rather near.
STANDARD His guess was quite wrong.

Quite, quiet. Do not confuse. *Quite* is an adverb meaning "entirely." *Quiet* is an adjective meaning "calm."

Quite a few, quite a bit, quite a little, quite a good deal. Colloquial for *a good many, a considerable number, a considerable amount.*

Raise, rear. Some writers prefer *rear* to *raise* in the sense of "bringing up children." "He reared (*not* raised) the boy from infancy."

Raise, rise. See **Rise, raise.**

each sentence approved for informal use only. Label each violation of good usage. Then rewrite all sentences (except those checked) to make them conform to standard English.

1. If I had of known you was coming, I would of waited longer.
2. Everyone suspicioned the old man of stealing our apples.
3. The ad in the paper was sort of hazy.
4. The sifting snow screened our view of the highway.
5. George was not dumb, though he looked like he was.
6. The profs dished out more than we could take.
7. Has your neighbor done sold his house?
8. The boy had a keen desire to win the game.
9. You do things different from anybody I know.
10. We filled the bucket with H_2O.
11. The poor man was in a sad fix.
12. I suppose that your findings are correct.
13. "You are goofy," I yelled. "Now scram!"
14. I am terribly aggravated with your doings.
15. Ten miles is all the farther that I can live away from my store.
16. Where do you live at now?
17. The general was completely sold on the private who had some spunk.
18. 'Twas a clear, cool eve, and the moon shed an effulgent glow.
19. A first-rate farmer raises heaps of farm produce.
20. I am kind of late today, for I do not feel so good.
21. He took and snatched the parcel from her hands although he knew that he hadn't ought.
22. Since Richard hopes to become a musician, he is taking piano lessons.
23. Due to the depression he lost considerable in his business.

Real. Colloquial or dialectal for *very* or *really.*

STANDARD She was very (*not* real) brave.

Rear. See **Raise, rear.**

Reason is because. Formal English usually completes the construction *The reason is* (*was*) with a *that* clause or recasts the sentence.

COLLOQUIAL The reason why he missed his class was because (*or* on account of) he overslept.
STANDARD The reason why he missed his class was that he overslept.
STANDARD He missed his class because he overslept.

Reckon. Colloquial or dialectal for *think, suppose.*

Refer. See **Allude, refer.**

Respectfully, respectively. Do not confuse. *Respectfully* means "in a manner showing respect." "Yours respectfully." *Respectively* means "each in the order given." "The President respectfully paid tribute to the Army, Navy, and Air Force, respectively."

Reverend, Honorable. To be followed by the first name, the initials, or some title of the person referred to as well as the surname. See Section **11e.**

Right. Colloquial or dialectal as an adverb meaning "very, extremely."

STANDARD I am very (*not* right) glad to see you.

Right along. Colloquial for *continuously.*

STANDARD The clock struck continuously (*not* right along).
I knew it all the time (*not* right along).

Rise, raise. Do not confuse. *Rise* is an intransitive verb. "I rise every morning." "I rose at four o'clock." "I have risen at four o'clock for many months." *Raise* is a transitive verb. "I raise vegetables." "I raised vegetables last year." "I have raised vegetables for many years."

Said. The adjective *said,* meaning "before-mentioned," should be used only in legal documents.

Same, said, such. Except in legal documents, not used as substitutes for *it, this,* or *that.*

QUESTIONABLE	When said coat was returned, same was found to be badly torn.
BETTER	When this coat was returned, it was found to be badly torn.

Say. Colloquial for *give orders.*

COLLOQUIAL	The teacher said to go home.
STANDARD	The teacher told us to go home.

Says. Illiterate for *said.*

ILLITERATE	He says to her, "I am tired."
STANDARD	He said to her, "I am tired."

Scarcely. See **But, only, hardly, scarcely.**

Seldom ever, seldom or ever. Unidiomatic expressions for *seldom if ever, hardly ever.*

Should of. Illiterate corruption of *should have.*

Show. Colloquial for *play, opera, motion picture.*

Sight. Colloquial for *a great deal.*

STANDARD "He left a great deal (*not* a sight) of money."

Sit, set. Do not confuse. See Section 7a, page 81.

So. An overworked word. Do not overwork *so* to join co-ordinate clauses.

COLLOQUIAL	The work had tired him, so he did not begin his journey the next day.
STANDARD	Since the work had tired him, he did not begin his journey the next day.

In clauses denoting purpose, *so that* is usually preferred to *so.*

QUESTIONABLE	He came early so he might see a friend.
BETTER	He came early so that he might see a friend.

Some. Slang when used as an intensive. "He is making an excellent (*not* some) race."

Someone, anyone, everyone. See **Anyone, everyone, someone.**

Someplace. Colloquial for *somewhere.*

Somewheres. Illiterate for *somewhere.*

Sort. See **Kind, sort.**

Sort of. See **Kind of, sort of.**

Sort of a. See **Kind of a, sort of a.**

Strata. Plural of *stratum.* See **Data, strata, phenomena.**

Such. Note carefully the use of *such* in the dictionary. When *such* is followed by a relative clause, the proper relative is *as.* "I shall give such aid as I think best." When *such* is completed by a result clause, it should be followed by *that.* "There was such a rain that we could not drive." Avoid the weak and vague use of *such.* "We had a good (*not* such a good) time."

Such, same, said. See **Same, said, such.**

Sure. Colloquial for *surely, certainly.*

STANDARD This is certainly (*not* sure) a quiet place.

Sure and. See **Try and.**

Suspicion. Dialectal when used as a verb in place of *suspect.*

DIALECTAL I did not suspicion anything.
STANDARD I did not suspect anything.

Swell. The adjective is slang for *excellent, first-rate.*

STANDARD Our last symphony concert was first-rate (*not* swell).

Take and. Dialectal or illiterate.

STANDARD He knocked (*not* took and knocked) the ball over the base line.

Take stock in. See **Bank on, take stock in.**

Tasty. Colloquial for *savory* or *tasteful.*

Teach. See **Learn, teach.**

Terrible, terribly. Colloquial for *extremely bad.*

That. Used colloquially as an adverb.

COLLOQUIAL I can approach only that near.
STANDARD I can approach only so near.

Theirselves. Illiterate for *themselves.*

These kind, these sort. See **Kind, sort.**

This here, that there, these here, them there. Illiterate expressions. Use *this, that, these, those.*

Try and, sure and. Colloquial for *try to, sure to.*

STANDARD Try to (*not* and) calm yourself. Be sure to (*not* and) come early.

Ugly. Colloquial for *ill-tempered.*

STANDARD He was never in an ill-tempered (*not* ugly) mood.

Un-, in-. Do not confuse. The prefix *un-* (from AS. *un-,* not) is used regularly with words derived from Anglo-Saxon (*undo, untie*); *in-* (from L. *in-,* not) is used with either Anglo-Saxon or Latin derivatives. (But distinguish *in-,* not, from the other Latin prefix *in-,* in or into, as in *inbreed, induct.*)

United States. When used as a noun, always *the United States,* with the article.

Used to could. Illiterate or facetious for *used to be able.*

Very. Some careful writers avoid using *very* to modify a past participle that has not yet established itself as an adjective. They insert some appropriate adverb—such as *much, greatly, deeply*—between *very* and the past participle.

QUESTIONABLE His singing was very appreciated.
BETTER His singing was very greatly appreciated.

Wait on. Means *to attend, to serve.* Colloquial for *wait for.*

STANDARD "I waited for (*not* waited on) him to begin."

Want. Cannot take a clause as its object.

ILLITERATE I want that he should have a chance.
STANDARD I want him to have a chance.

Want in, out, down, up, off, through. Dialectal for *want to come in* or *get in, out, down, up, off, through.*

Ways. Colloquial for *distance.*

STANDARD A long distance (*not* ways).

Where. Improperly used for *that.*

POOR I saw in the newspaper where the strike had been settled.

BETTER I saw in the newspaper that the strike had been settled.

Where at. Illiterate.

ILLITERATE Where is she at?

STANDARD Where is she?

Which, who. Use *who* or *that* instead of *which* or *what* to refer to persons. "Mr. Jones was the man who (*not* which) helped me."

While. Do not overuse this conjunction. In general do not substitute *while* for *and, but, though,* or *whereas.*

Who, which. See **Which, who.**

Worst kind, sort, way. Dialectal for *very much.*

Would of. Illiterate corruption of *would have.*

Would rather. See **Had better, had rather, would rather.**

You all. A Southern colloquialism for *you* (plural).

You was. Illiterate for *you were.*

Yourself, myself, himself. See **Myself, himself, yourself.**

▸ Exactness

Idiom; Freshness

20

Select words that are exact, idiomatic, and fresh.

A word is exact when it expresses the precise idea or conveys the emotional suggestion intended by the writer. By this definition the measures of a right word will be the purpose of the writer, the subject he has selected, and his attitude toward his subject and his readers.

20a Consult a good dictionary for the exact word needed to express the idea.

Before you use a word, know exactly what it means. Do not confuse words that are similar in spelling or meaning. Above all, train yourself to be specific.

WRONG The bell rang *continually* for five minutes.
RIGHT The bell rang *continuously* for five minutes.

WRONG He *contributes* his success to sound preparation.
RIGHT He *attributes* his success to sound preparation.

WRONG She seemed scarcely *conscience* of what she was doing.
RIGHT She seemed scarcely *conscious* of what she was doing.

VAGUE *The thing about it is* that we are destitute.
SPECIFIC *The truth of the matter* is that we are destitute.

► EXERCISE 1. Review the first twenty word groups in the list of similar words in Section 18, Exercise 2, consulting your dictionary as necessary to make sure that you can use each word with its exact meaning.

► EXERCISE 2. Review in the same way the second twenty word groups in the list.

► EXERCISE 3. Review in the same way the third (last) twenty word groups in the list.

Be careful to use the right conjunction to express the exact relation between words, phrases, and clauses.

WRONG There were other candidates, *and* he was elected.
RIGHT There were other candidates, *but* he was elected. [*And* adds or continues; *but* contrasts.]

WRONG I read in the paper *where* you had arrived.
RIGHT I read in the paper *that* you had arrived.

(1) ***Denotation and Connotation.*** **Select the word with the denotation and connotation proper to the idea you wish to express.**

The denotation of a word is what the word actually points to. (Thus *cow* stands for the milk-giving quadruped.) The connotation of a word is what the word suggests or implies. (Thus *cow,* when applied to a human being, suggests awkwardness.) Connotation includes the aura of emotion or association that surrounds some words. For example, *street, avenue, boulevard, lane, place, alley, promenade, prospect* all denote much the same thing to a postman. But to various readers, and in various contexts, each word may have a special connotation. *Street* may suggest city pavements; *avenue,* a broad passageway bordered on each side by trees; *boulevard,* a broad highway; *lane,* a rustic walk; *place,* a secluded corner in a large city; *alley,* a city slum; *promenade,* a street for the display of elegance, fashion, and so forth; *prospect,* an avenue commanding a splendid view. Similarly, *highway, road, route, drive, trail, concourse, path, turnpike*—all denote a passage for travel, but each word carries a variety of connotations.

A word may be right in one situation, wrong in another. *Female parent,* for instance, is a proper expression, but it would be very inappropriate to say "John wept for the death of his female parent." *Female parent* used in this sense is literally correct, but the connotation is wrong. The more appropriate word, *mother,* not only conveys the meaning denoted by *female parent;* it also conveys the reason why John wept. The first expression simply implies a biological relationship; the second is full of imaginative and emotional suggestions.

► EXERCISE 4. Distinguish between the denotation and the connotation of the following pairs of words. Select phrases from your reading to illustrate proper usage of the words.

cabin—hut	foggy—murky	palace—mansion
dirt—soil	healthy—robust	steed—nag
fire—conflagration	joy—felicity	wealth—opulence

► EXERCISE 5. Show why the italicized words in the following sentences, although literally correct, might be inappropriate because of their connotations.

1. Miss Kincaid's exotic costume won the admiration of everyone at the party, and even the hostess remarked several times how *outlandish* she looked.

2. For the *enlightenment* of the other ladies, Mrs. Bromley measured upon her *belly* the area of her recent operation.
3. Robin Roberts *excogitated* each pitch.
4. Homer squeezed a quantity of *chlorophyllaceous extrusion* onto his toothbrush.
5. The army *scampered* home at full speed.
6. The librarian catalogued her books with *dauntless* energy.
7. We are building our new home on the rim of a most delightful little *gulch*.
8. Heifetz *tucked* his *fiddle* under his chin.

► EXERCISE 6. Explain the denotations and connotations of the italicized words in the following selections. Note how context in some instances intensifies the connotative power of a simple, everyday word; in other instances, it determines which of several differing connotations the word will carry. For each italicized word substitute a word of nearly the same denotation and consider its relative effectiveness in the sentence.

1. My good *blade* carves the *casques* of men.—TENNYSON
2. Thy soul was like a star and dwelt *apart*.
   —WORDSWORTH
3. O what can *ail* thee, knight at arms,
   Alone and *palely* loitering? —KEATS
4. They also serve who *only* stand and *wait*. —MILTON
5. The barge she sat in, like a *burnished* throne,
   Burned on the water. —SHAKESPEARE
6. He had a thin *vague* beard. —BEERBOHM
7. It was a chill, *rain-washed* afternoon. —SAKI
8. He had *flaxen* hair, *weak* blue eyes, and the general demeanor of a saintly but timid *codfish*.
   —P. G. WODEHOUSE
9. By *midnight*, the *peace* of *Christmas*, a special *intimate* kind of *wonder*, had *descended* upon them.
   —PAUL HORGAN

10. A little man, dry like a chip and agile like a monkey, *clambered* up. —CONRAD
11. A Poor *Relation* is the most *irrelevant* thing in Nature, a piece of *impertinent correspondency,* an odious *approximation.* —LAMB
12. But in a larger sense we cannot *dedicate,* we cannot *consecrate,* we cannot *hallow* this ground. —ABRAHAM LINCOLN

► EXERCISE 7. Substitute more suggestive, homely words for the italicized expressions in the following sentences.

1. The family *came together* around the *chimney place* at Christmas.
2. Tex Gray was a *herder of cattle* for a *stockman.*
3. The old *servant* sang a *song* to the *infant.*
4. The salesman *presented* a *plausible appearance.*
5. The *flowers* on the trellis reminded her of her *farmhouse* home in Kentucky.

(2) *Concreteness.* Select the specific word instead of the vague word.

Avoid vague generalities. General expressions are necessary in science, literature, and philosophy, as the common use of such terms as *deduction, empiricism, diction, style* testify. But the purpose of most writing is to communicate specific observations and practical instructions. Consequently the safest rule is—Be as specific as you can.

Instead of writing *went* consider the possibility of *rode, walked, trudged, slouched, hobbled, sprinted.* When you are tempted to say a *fine* young man, ask yourself whether *brave, daring, plucky, vigorous, energetic, spirited,* or *loyal* would not be more appropriate. Do not be satisfied with the colorless *ask* when you can choose among *beg, pray, entreat, beseech, implore.* The word *try* is ineffective in most situations when *struggle, fight, battle, strive* are available.

The test for the specific word is contained in six words —*who, what, where, when, how, why.* Notice how the following sentences are improved by asking the questions Who? What? Where? When? How? or Why? about one or more elements in the sentence.

VAGUE The Dean spoke about student life and that sort of thing. [*Who* spoke about *what?*]

IMPROVED Dean Jones spoke about the social advantages of the student union.

VAGUE My brother is going away to have a good time. [*Where* is he going? *How* will he have a good time?]

IMPROVED My brother is going to Gatlinburg in the Smoky Mountains, where he plans to fish and hunt for a few weeks.

VAGUE All the columnists are commenting on the high cost of living. [*Who* are commenting? *Where* did comment appear?]

IMPROVED In the July 12 issue of the New York *Herald Tribune,* Walter Lippmann, George Sokolsky, and Robert Ruark discussed the recent advance in food prices.

VAGUE The Army team finally advanced the ball. [*How* did they do it?]

IMPROVED Adams, the Army quarterback, received the ball from center Jim Hawkins, retreated to his ten-yard line, and threw a pass to left-end Smith, who was tackled on the Army thirty-five-yard line.

VAGUE I think the speech was biased. [*Why?*]

IMPROVED Mr. Jones began his speech without any attempt to support his statement that the policies of the

Republican administration were a "total denial of the American way of life."

► EXERCISE 8. Substitute specific or emphatic words for general words in the sentences below.

1. The officer made a bad mistake.
2. My father looked at the report.
3. The author's criticism of Blake's work is very good.
4. The journey was made to obtain information concerning various aspects of the North American Indians.
5. It is my prime desire to like all my classes.

(3) *Vividness.* **Use figurative language whenever needed to create vividly the required imaginative or emotional impression.**

A figure of speech is the use of a word in an imaginative rather than in a literal sense. The two chief figures of speech are the simile and the metaphor. A *simile* is an explicit comparison between two things of a different kind or quality, usually introduced by *like* or *as:* "He sprang on the foe like a lion." A *metaphor* is an implied comparison: "He was a lion in the fight." (See sentences 2, 5, 8, and 10, in Exercise 6 above, for other examples of simile and metaphor.)

Other figures of speech are personification, metonymy, synecdoche, litotes, and hyperbole. To say that our college is an alma mater (fostering mother) is to *personify* an institution. In the words of *The American College Dictionary,* we often use "the name of one thing for that of another to which it has some logical relation" (*metonymy*), such as *scepter* for *sovereignty. Synecdoche,* which is similar to metonymy, puts a part for the whole or the whole for a part, as *fifty head* for *fifty cattle. Litotes* is the name for understatement, as in the remark,

"Picasso is not a bad painter." *Hyperbole* is deliberate overstatement or fanciful exaggeration: "The waves were mountains high."

A false sense of simplicity still blinds many contemporary writers to the importance of figurative language in everyday communication. Metaphors and similes are not, as is commonly supposed, merely the ornaments of poetry and old-fashioned oratory. They are essential to certain kinds of physical description and to the expression of feelings and states of mind. When a husband slumps into his chair after a hard day's work and says to his wife, "Thank goodness I'm out of that squirrel cage!" *squirrel cage* is not an ornamental word or an elegant variation. It is a very useful, although unoriginal, metaphor. His wife might respond with another figure of speech by saying, "I played bridge at the Women's Club. It was *suffocating.*" Both figures, *squirrel cage* and *suffocating,* are more effective than the conventional terms *job* and *dull.* Both terms express exactly how the man and his wife felt. The husband's work was confining and active; the wife's bridge game was unbearably dull.

Metaphor and simile are especially valuable because they are concrete and tend to point up essential relationships that cannot otherwise be communicated. (For faulty metaphors see Section 23c.)

► EXERCISE 9. Test the exactness and force of the metaphors and similes in the following sentences by attempting to state the same ideas literally.

1. Man is a wild beast, carnivorous by nature, and delighting in blood. —TAINE
2. That luncheon party . . . was the beginning of a new epoch in my life, but its details are dimmed for me and confused by so many others, almost identical

with it, that succeeded one another that term and the next, like romping cupids in a Renaissance frieze.
—EVELYN WAUGH, *Brideshead Revisited*

3. The fortnight at Venice passed quickly and sweetly—perhaps too sweetly; I was drowning in honey, stingless. —EVELYN WAUGH
4. The prince became flame to refute her.
—HENRY JAMES, *The American*
5. His face was like a human skull, a death's-head spouting blood. —HAZLITT
6. The soul is placed in the body like a rough diamond and must be polished or the luster of it will never appear. —DEFOE
7. Napoleon was the French Revolution on horseback.
8. O full of scorpions is my mind, dear wife.
—SHAKESPEARE, *Macbeth*
9. She was as graceful as a sow on ice.
10. The cloud emptied its bellyful of rain.

20b Use the exact idiom demanded by English usage.

Idioms are short, homely, vigorous expressions that grow up with a language and are peculiar to it. Such idioms as *for many a year, to center around,* or *to strike a bargain* cannot be analyzed or justified grammatically; and yet usage has made them the very heart of the language, suitable for either formal or informal occasions. The unabridged dictionaries treat many idiomatic phrases. See, for instance, the idioms built around *go* and listed after this word in your dictionary. (Note that an idiom—like a word—may be classified as *standard, colloquial, dialectal,* or *slang.*) Writers should be careful to use the exact phrasing for each idiom, not some unidiomatic approximation such as those listed below.

Unidiomatic	*Idiomatic*
accuse with	accuse of
acquitted from	acquitted of
all the farther	as far as
angry at	angry with
authority about	authority on
buy off of	buy from
comply to	comply with
desirous to	desirous of
die with	die of
equally as bad	equally bad
identical to	identical with
in accordance to	in accordance with
in search for	in search of
in the city Denver	in the city of Denver
in the summer 1947	in the summer of 1947
in the year of 1947	in the year 1947
independent from	independent of
off of	off
prior than	prior to
remember of	remember
seldom or ever	seldom if ever, seldom or never
superior than	superior to
treat on	treat of
vie against	vie with
wait on	wait for

► EXERCISE 10. In the following sentences make the idioms conform to standard English usage. If you are not sure whether a given phrase is idiomatic, consult an unabridged dictionary. Write *C* in place of each sentence that needs no revision.

1. The steamer collided against the tug.
2. Mother is vexed at Robert.
3. Your hat is identical to Jane's.

4. I finished high school in the year of 1946.
5. I shall try to comply to your request.
6. The destitute have need of help.
7. Divide up the apples among the children.
8. The child was born in the city Miami.
9. Robert has gone in search for a secondhand car.
10. I bought my car off of the man next door.
11. We plan on going to the seashore.
12. The boy soon became independent from his family.
13. The small child was unequal for the task.
14. She was oblivious to the presence of her friend.
15. I am glad the ordeal is over with.
16. I was not to be taken in by such trickery.
17. Mary seldom or ever misses a class.
18. The boy fell off of the pier.
19. He returned a week ago yesterday.
20. I was sick of a cold.

► EXERCISE 11. Consult an unabridged dictionary to determine what prepositions are idiomatically used with *agree, charge, compare, consist, deal, differ,* and *part.* Use each of these verbs correctly in two sentences, each with a different preposition.

► EXERCISE 12. In an unabridged dictionary study the idiomatic phrases treated under *catch, put, set, tie,* and *win.* Select three different idioms formed with each verb, and illustrate each idiom in a sentence.

20c Select fresh expressions instead of trite, worn-out ones.

Nearly all trite expressions were once striking and effective. *A bolt from the blue, acid test,* and *social whirl* are, in themselves, effective expressions. What you may not know is that excessive use has made them trite. They are now stock phrases in the language, automatic clichés that have lost their effectiveness.

To avoid trite phrases you must be aware of current usage. Catch phrases and slogans pass quickly from ephemeral popularity into the Old Words' Home. Glittering political shibboleths like *grass roots, pulse of public opinion, forgotten man, century of the common man* are notoriously short-lived. Commercial advertising also bestows its *kiss of death* on an honorable phrase. When a mattress company bids you *sleep in peace* or promises a *midsummer night's dream* on their *airy fairy beds,* when blankets are publicized as *soft as down* or *gentle as a baby's breath,* mark the italicized words as lost to good usage for your generation at least.

Some expressions, however, survive the wear of repeated usage. Proverbs, epithets from great writers like Shakespeare, quotations from the Bible will probably live until the English language dies out completely.

► EXERCISE 13. Construct sentences which contain acceptable substitutes for twenty of the hackneyed expressions listed below. In your sentences include within brackets the hackneyed expressions you replace. Be careful not to replace one hackneyed expression with another.

Some Hackneyed Expressions

a long-felt want
abreast of the times
after all is said and done
agree to disagree
all work and no play
along this line
as luck would have it
beat a hasty retreat
better late than never
bitter end
blushing bride
brave as a lion
brilliant performance
briny deep
budding genius
busy as a bee
by leaps and bounds
center of attraction

cold as ice
depths of despair
do justice to the occasion
doomed to disappointment
easier said than done
equal to the occasion
exception proves the rule
fair sex
fast and furious
filthy lucre
glittering generalities
goes without saying
green as grass
green with envy
heart's content
in all its glory
iron constitution
it stands to reason
last but not least
light fantastic
method in his madness
monarch of all I survey
Mother Earth
motley crowd
nipped in the bud
no sooner said than done
none the worse for wear
on the ball
partake of refreshments
poor but honest
powers that be
promising future
psychological moment
reigns supreme
royal reception
sadder but wiser
scratch the surface
sleep of the just
slow but sure
staff of life
stern realities
straight from the shoulder
sturdy as an oak
sumptuous repast
sweat of his brow
table groaned
this day and age
to the bitter end
too full for utterance
too funny for words
tower of strength
watery grave
wee small hours
where ignorance is bliss
white as a sheet
work like a Trojan
worse for wear
wreathed in smiles

► EXERCISE 14. Bring to class a list of hackneyed expressions used in a newspaper or magazine.

► OTHER EXERCISES ON EXACTNESS

A. Construct sentences to illustrate one of the exact meanings of each of the following words:

latent	universal	dense	distinguish
opinion	judgment	conclusion	enchanting
aspire	equivocal	tense	handsome
affiliation	flexible	reflection	temper

B. Improve the following sentences by correcting errors in idiom and by introducing words that are exact and unhackneyed.

1. I shall neither go or send an explanation.
2. We waited on Jane more than an hour.
3. I read a story where a poor man became a millionaire.
4. The poor man was in the depths of despair.
5. William would not except the appointment.
6. John could not leave without he finished his work.
7. Frank looked very funny when I told him that he had failed.
8. He made an illusion to his former position.

C. The following passage from *The Education of Henry Adams* is an excellent example of precise writing. Study the italicized expressions first with the aid of a dictionary and then in the context of the sentence and the paragraph. Substitute a synonym for each italicized word and compare its effectiveness with that of the original.

Adams, too, was Bostonian, and the Bostonian's uncertainty of *attitude* was as natural to him as to Lodge. Only Bostonians can understand Bostonians and thoroughly sympathize with the *inconsequences* of the Boston mind. His theory and practice were also *at variance.* He *professed* in theory equal distrust of English thought, and called it a huge *rag-bag* of *bric-a-brac,* sometimes *precious* but never sure. For him, only the Greek, the Italian or the French *standards* had claims to respect, and the barbarism of Shakespeare was as *flagrant* as to Voltaire; but his *theory* never *affected* his *practice.* He knew that his artistic standard was the illusion of his own mind;

that English disorder approached nearer to truth . . . than French *measure* or Italian *line,* or German *logic;* he read his Shakespeare as the *Evangel* of conservative Christian *anarchy,* neither very conservative nor very Christian, but *stupendously* anarchistic. He loved the *atrocities* of English art and society, as he loved Charles Dickens and Miss Austen, not because of their example, but because of their humor. He made no *scruple* of defying *sequence* and denying *consistency*—but he was not a Senator.[1]

D. Read the following paragraphs from Virginia Woolf's "The Patron and the Crocus." Notice Mrs. Woolf's fondness for doublets such as "*plausible* but utterly *impracticable* advice," "*subtle* and *insidious,*" "*instigator* and *inspirer,*" "*varied* and *vigorous.*" Show how these doublets contribute to exactness.

Young men and women beginning to write are generally given the plausible but utterly impracticable advice to write what they have to write as shortly as possible, as clearly as possible, and without other thought in their minds except to say exactly what is in them. Nobody ever adds on these occasions the one thing needful: "And be sure you choose your patron wisely," though that is the gist of the whole matter. For a book is always written for somebody to read, and, since the patron is not merely the paymaster but also in a very subtle and insidious way the instigator and inspirer of what is written, it is of the utmost importance that he should be a desirable man.

But who, then, is the desirable man—the patron who will cajole the best out of the writer's brain and bring to birth the most varied and vigorous progeny of which he is capable? Different ages have answered the question dif-

[1] From *The Education of Henry Adams* by Henry Adams. By permission of Houghton Mifflin Company.

ferently. The Elizabethans, to speak roughly, chose the aristocracy to write for and the playhouse public. The eighteenth-century patron was a combination of coffee-house wit and Grub Street bookseller. In the nineteenth century the great writers wrote for the half-crown magazines and the leisured classes. And looking back and applauding the splendid results of these different alliances, it all seems enviably simple, and plain as a pikestaff compared with our own predicament—for whom should we write? For the present supply of patrons is of unexampled and bewildering variety. There is the daily Press, the weekly Press, the monthly Press; the English public and the American public; the best-seller public and the worst-seller public; the highbrow public and the red-blood public; all now organized self-conscious entities capable through their various mouthpieces of making their needs known and their approval or displeasure felt. Thus the writer who has been moved by the sight of the first crocus in Kensington Gardens has, before he sets pen to paper, to choose from a crowd of competitors the particular patron who suits him best. It is futile to say, "Dismiss them all; think only of your crocus," because writing is a method of communication; and the crocus is an imperfect crocus until it has been shared. The first man or the last may write for himself alone, but he is an exception and an unenviable one at that, and the gulls are welcome to his works if the gulls can read them.[2]

E. Analyze one (or more) of the model paragraphs from Section 31 for choice of words.

---

[2] From *The Common Reader* by Virginia Woolf, copyright, 1925, by Harcourt, Brace and Company, Inc.; renewed, 1953, by Leonard Woolf. Reprinted by permission of the publishers.

▶ Wordiness and Useless Repetition

21

Avoid wordiness. Repeat a word or phrase only when it is needed to gain force or clearness.

Wordiness is an offense against exact usage. The exact word or expression says all that is necessary (see Section 20), neither too little (see 22) nor too much. We say too much:

a. When we use words or phrases that add nothing to the meaning.
b. When we use an unnecessarily elaborate sentence structure.
c. When we repeat words and phrases carelessly.

21a Omit words or phrases that add nothing to the meaning.[1]

Note how the following sentences are improved by the omission of the bracketed words.

[1] Bureaucratic jargon, called "gobbledygook," is often extremely wordy. See the examples on page 209.

1. The [architectural] design of the White House is basically [the same as] that of the Duke of Leinster's palace in Dublin.
2. [Architect] James Hoban, the designer of the White House, was a native of Dublin.
3. [It was] in 1792 [that] the cornerstone of the White House was laid.
4. The White House is [such] an impressive building, and [so] much in the spirit of its century.
5. The [usual] consensus [of the majority] is that George Washington did not cut down the cherry tree.
6. Thomas Jefferson was more democratic [to a greater degree] than most of his contemporaries.
7. When Andrew Jackson became President of the United States, the banks were close to [the point of] bankruptcy.
8. [The reason why] we honor Lincoln [is] because he saved the Union.
9. John Adams was very different [in various ways] from his predecessors.
10. The Federalist party was soon connected [up] with the new Republican movement.

SOME WORDY PHRASES As a [usual] rule; at ten P.M. [in the evening]; big [in size]; circulated [around]; combined [together]; co-operate [together]; first time [in my life]; Halloween [evening]; [important] essentials; [joint] partnership; meet [up with]; modern colleges [of today]; my [own] autobiography; round [in shape]; small [in size]; ten [in number]; total effect [of all this]; where . . . [at]; yellow [in color]

► EXERCISE 1. Strike out unnecessary words from the following sentences. Write *C* in place of each sentence that needs no revision.

1. It happened that my brother was stronger than I had expected him to be.

2. On our list are the names of many wealthy and influential citizens.
3. The marble columns were gray in color.
4. Mr. McConn divides into three groups, or classes, the students of today who go to modern colleges.
5. As a usual rule the legislature is filled with lawyers.
6. It was during the Renaissance that a very large number of words, many of them terms of scholarship, were then taken from the Latin.
7. My chief aim is to make life easier for the farmer.
8. After the play was over with, we walked home together.
9. I wish to refer you back to the first page.
10. We pondered in our minds how we might descend down to the bottom of the canyon.
11. In our modern universities of today, students have many numerous courses from which to choose.

21b If necessary, revise the structure of the sentence to avoid wordiness.

Caution: In order to understand **21b** you may need to review **Section 1, Sentence Sense,** especially pages 14-22.

An idea may be expressed in one of the four primary units of composition: a sentence, a clause, a phrase, or a word. Sometimes we waste many words in trying to make an idea clear. Note in the following series of examples how the fundamental idea (printed in italics) becomes successively sharper as the expression grows less wordy.

The mist hung like a veil. It obscured the top of the mountain. [Full sentences used to express the idea]

The mist *hung like a veil* and obscured the top of the mountain. [Part of a compound predicate]

The mist, *which hung like a veil,* obscured the top of the mountain. [Subordinate clause]
The mist, *hanging like a veil,* obscured the top of the mountain. [Participial phrase]
The mist, *like a veil,* obscured the top of the mountain. [Prepositional phrase]
The mist *veiled* the top of the mountain. [Word]

All of these sentences are acceptable, but they are not equally effective. Although any one of them may, at times, meet the special needs of the writer, the least wordy will normally be the most effective.

Practice reducing sentences to the simplest and shortest form, as in the following examples:

WORDY Another thing is good health. It is one of our great blessings. It may be had through proper diet and exercise. Rest is also desirable. [Four simple sentences—25 words]

BETTER The great blessing of good health may be had through proper diet, exercise, and rest. [Reduced to one simple sentence—15 words]

WORDY A new addition has been built at the side of the house, and this addition has been developed into a library. [Compound sentence—21 words]

BETTER An addition, built at the side of the house, has been developed into a library. [Reduced to a simple sentence containing a participial phrase—15 words]

WORDY When the Indians made tools, they used flint and bone. [Complex sentence—10 words]

BETTER The Indians made tools of flint and bone. [Reduced to a simple sentence—8 words]

WORDY There were six men who volunteered. [Complex sentence—6 words]

BETTER Six men volunteered. [Reduced to a simple sentence—3 words]

► EXERCISE 2. Revise the structure of the following sentences to correct wordiness.

1. Personally I believe it was the Spaniards rather than the Indians who first brought horses and ponies to America.
2. If any workers were disgruntled, they made their complaints to the man who was in charge as manager.
3. My uncle was a tall man. He had a long nose. Over his right eye he had a deep scar.
4. The grass was like a carpet. It covered the whole lawn. The color of the grass was a deep blue.
5. When anyone wants to start a garden, it is best to begin in the early part of the spring of the year.
6. Near the center of the campus of our university a new building has been erected, and it is constructed of red brick.

21c Avoid careless or needless repetition of a word or phrase.

Use repetition only to attain greater clearness (see 22b, 22c, 26b, 31b(3)) or emphasis (see 29e).

CARELESS Since the committee has already made three general *reports,* only the *report* dealing with promotions will be *reported* on today.

BETTER Since the committee has already made three general reports, it will submit today only its recommendations on promotions.

CARELESS It is *impossible* to ask me to do the *impossible.*

BETTER You cannot expect me to do the impossible.

Use a pronoun instead of needlessly repeating a noun. Several pronouns in succession, even in successive sentences, may refer to the same antecedent noun, so long as the reference remains clear.

NEEDLESS When Mr. Bevan temporarily lost his place in the Parliamentary party on that memorable day there were many people who thought that *Bevan* would be subsequently expelled from the party. After three weeks of fury and alarm, *Mr. Bevan* was saved by about the tenth of a gnat's eyebrow—that is to say, a compromise resolution was passed by only one vote. Thus for the first time in four years *Bevan's* enemies were defeated on a major issue and Mr. Bevan remains within the fold.

CORRECT When Mr. Bevan temporarily lost his place in the Parliamentary party on that memorable day there were many people who thought that *he* would be subsequently expelled from the party. After three weeks of fury and alarm, *he* was saved by about the tenth of a gnat's eyebrow—that is to say, a compromise resolution was passed by only one vote. Thus for the first time in four years *his* enemies were defeated on a major issue and Mr. Bevan remains within the fold. —HUGH MASSINGHAM [2]

► EXERCISE 3. Revise the following sentences to avoid careless repetition.

1. In 1923 Ruth batted .393, and he batted .378 the next year.
2. While driving, a good driver always takes care to obey the driving laws of the state he is driving through.
3. The practice of helping one's neighbors for the enjoyment of it is a very common practice.
4. In the last act of the play we find the explanation of the title of the play.
5. Early in the morning we set out for Jones Beach so that we could enjoy all the pleasures that that great playground affords.

---

[2] From "The Labor Party: A Study in Schizophrenia" by Hugh Massingham, *The New York Times Magazine,* May 15, 1955. Reprinted by permission of the author and the publisher.

▶ EXERCISES ON WORDINESS AND USELESS REPETITION

A. Make needed revision of the following sentences to correct wordiness and useless repetition. Write *C* in place of each sentence that needs no revision.

1. The National Gallery of Art, which is in Washington, D. C., and which contains the Mellon, Kress, and Widener collections of paintings and sculpture, is one of the largest marble structures in the entire world.
2. The reason why he went to Heidelberg College was because it was located in his home town of Tiffin, in the state of Ohio.
3. I wanted to visit the Sequoia National Park last summer, but I did not have the money required for such a long trip to California.
4. The radio announcer repeatedly kept saying, "Buy Peterson's Perfect Prawns," over and over and over again.
5. There were fifty people in the hospital ward who were among those who received great benefit from the new drug.
6. The reason that the National League has won so many All-Star games from the American League recently is due largely to the fact that the National League has had the larger number of home-run hitters and long-ball hitters.
7. The Finnish people, who are intensely independent by nature, always resist any attack upon the independence of their nation.
8. I had an advantage over the other contestants because of the fact that I had just looked up the word myself in a dictionary.
9. Just when, if at all, the Vikings came to America has not been determined and is unknown to us.

10. The St. Lawrence River Power Development Project will be under the supervision of a committee. This committee will be international in character. The project will cost almost $500,000,000.
11. The problem of charting the 3,200 miles of the Amazon is a difficult problem indeed.
12. He found the problem of discovering the legal status of the displaced persons an almost insoluble problem.
13. Are you going to go to class tomorrow?
14. In order that a man may apply to become a citizen of the United States he must make out an application stating his intention to become a citizen.

B. Rewrite the following passage to eliminate wordiness and useless repetition.

1. Samuel Clemens (Mark Twain) was born in 1835 at Florida, County of Monroe, State of Missouri; but while he was still quite young, his family moved to Hannibal, a small Mississippi River town, where Samuel as a boy spent the days of his youth, and he grew up to young manhood there. 2. In 1853 Samuel Clemens left this small Mississippi River town of Hannibal to see something of the world. 3. In his itinerant wandering during the next four years which followed, Clemens worked at the printing trade in printing shops of various cities in the East and Middle West from the Mississippi to the Atlantic seaboard. 4. In Cincinnati, Ohio, in the year of 1857 Clemens took passage on a river steamboat bound down the river for New Orleans, Louisiana. 5. On this trip down the river Clemens met the pilot who steered the boat, named Mr. Horace Bixby, who agreed for the sum of five hundred dollars in money to teach young Clemens (Mark Twain) the art of piloting boats up and down the river. 6. One may read of Mark Twain's experience as a cub pilot apprentice in his book which he wrote about it and called *Life on the Mississippi.*

▸ Omission of Necessary Words

22

Do not omit a word or phrase necessary to the meaning of the sentence.

Most faulty omissions in student writing may be traced to carelessness. To avoid such errors, proofread all compositions before submitting them to your instructor.

EXAMPLES We have learned the importance ^ using perfume. [Careless omission of the preposition *of*]

John had been there only ^ moment ago. [Careless omission of the article *a*]

I wish I ^ been able to play football at ^ university. [Careless omission of *had* (a part of the verb) and of the article *the*]

22a Do not omit an article, a pronoun, a conjunction, or a preposition that is necessary to make your meaning clear.

(1) Omitted article or pronoun

RIGHT A friend and helper stood at his side; *or,* His friend and helper stood at his side. [The friend and helper are the same person.]

RIGHT A friend and *a* helper stood at his side; *or,* His friend and *his* helper stood at his side. [To show that the friend and the helper are different persons, the article *a* or the pronoun *his* must be repeated.]

(2) Omitted conjunction

CONFUSING They noticed the young men who made up the crew were eager to start. [*Young men* can be momentarily mistaken for the object of *noticed.*]

BETTER They noticed *that* the young men who made up the crew were eager to start.

Note: The conjunction *that* is frequently omitted as an introduction to clauses when the omission is not confusing.

EXAMPLE He said he would go.

(3) Omitted preposition

AWKWARD The school burned down my last term.

BETTER The school burned down *during* my last term.

AWKWARD Mardi Gras he went to New Orleans.

BETTER *For* Mardi Gras he went to New Orleans.

Note: Some idiomatic phrases indicating time or place regularly omit the preposition. *Examples: Next summer* he will go to camp. They arrived *last week.* He will come *home.*

22b Do not omit a necessary verb or a necessary auxiliary verb.

AWKWARD The play is good and the characters interesting. [Singular *is* may be used with singular *play* but not with plural *characters.*]

BETTER The play is good and the characters *are* interesting. [The correct verb is supplied for *characters.*]

AWKWARD He never has and never will be an enemy of his country. [*Be* is the correct auxiliary for *will* but not for *has.*]

BETTER He never has *been* an enemy of his country, and he never will be. [The correct auxiliary is supplied for *has.*]

22c Do not omit words necessary to complete comparisons (or other constructions).

CONFUSING The equipment of a soldier is heavier than a sailor. [Did the soldier's equipment weigh more than an individual sailor?]

CLEAR The equipment of a soldier is heavier than *that* of a sailor.

CLEAR A soldier's equipment is heavier than a sailor's.

CONFUSING The scenery here is as beautiful as any other place. [Comparison of things not capable of comparison]

CLEAR The scenery here is as beautiful as *it is at* any other place.

CONFUSING I admire Shakespeare more than Goethe.

CLEAR I admire Shakespeare more than I *admire* Goethe; *or,* I admire Shakespeare more than Goethe *did.*

Note: Incomplete comparisons are a particularly common fault in advertising copy.

INCOMPLETE This filter tip screens out 50% more harmful tar products. [What two things are being compared?]

COMPLETE This filter tip screens out 50% more harmful tar products than a tea strainer would. *Or:* This filter tip screens out 50% more harmful tar products than it does bugs and flies. [Probably no advertiser would make either of these statements, but at least they do contain some definite information—which the incomplete comparison does not.]

INCOMPLETE You will agree that Crumpet Creek Dairy products are definitely better. [Better than what? Ditch water?]

COMPLETE You will agree that Crumpet Creek Dairy products are definitely better than ever before. *Or even:* You will agree that Crumpet Creek Dairy products are definitely better than ditch water.

Note, however, that once a frame of reference has been established, an intelligible comparison may be made without explicit mention of the second term of the comparison.

RIGHT It is not to be inferred that of this poetical vigor Pope had only a little, because Dryden had more [*than Pope had* is clearly understood without its being stated]; for every other writer since Milton must give place to Pope; and even of Dryden it must be said, that, if he has brighter paragraphs [*than Pope has* again is clearly enough understood], he has not better poems. . . . If the flights of Dryden . . . are higher, Pope continues longer on the wing. If of Dryden's fire the blaze is brighter, of Pope's the heat is more regular and constant. —SAMUEL JOHNSON

INCOMPLETE I have always preferred living in Chiengmai. [Preferred it to what?]

IMPROVED Though Bangkok is by far the larger place, I have always preferred living in Chiengmai.

INCOMPLETE When you first see Dr. Zeiss, you will be surprised at how different he is. [Different from whom or what?]

IMPROVED When you first see Dr. Zeiss, you will be surprised at what an unusual person he is. *Or:* When you first see Dr. Zeiss, you will be surprised at how much he has changed.

INCOMPLETE He is as old, if not older, than his cousin.

IMPROVED He is as old *as his cousin,* if not older.

Standard writing avoids such intensives as *so, such,* and *too* without the completing clause.

COLLOQUIAL I was so tired. She had such beautiful eyes. He was not too much interested in the lecture.

STANDARD I was so tired that I could not sleep. *Or:* I was extremely tired. She has such beautiful eyes that everyone admires them. He was not especially interested in the lecture.

► EXERCISES ON OMISSIONS

A. Rewrite the following sentences, supplying all words that are needed to make the meaning clear and unambiguous. Write *C* in place of each sentence that needs no revision.

1. Our new Hampton shirts last much longer.
2. Jim's wife and mother stood beside him at the trial.
3. You are as good as, if not better than, anyone else.
4. The prisoner had been hiding some place near Detroit.
5. He writes about the days he had neither food nor shelter.
6. William is so different from the others.
7. The lawyer had to prove whatever the witness said was false.
8. The spillway allows the water at the dam be kept at the same level.
9. He was so manly and so brave although only six years old.
10. I protested that I could not come.
11. I helped him more than James.

12. He never has and never will enjoy fishing.
13. Will you return the winter quarter?
14. The author writes more about the Hardy country than he does about Hardy.
15. I managed to add track and football my senior year.

B. Follow directions under A.

1. If Jack is in a profession he is not trained, he will not succeed.
2. Americans usually prefer beef.
3. He owned a very smart, if not the smartest, pony I ever saw.
4. She was so excited.
5. The plains are mostly given over to cattle raising but not farming.
6. The park is very attractive and enjoyed by all the children.
7. Yesterday the pilot and captain went ashore.
8. I always have and always will live in Chicago.
9. She was not too much interested in mathematics.
10. Chifford cars are longer, faster, more economical to operate.
11. Thanksgiving I went home.
12. The club was organized my first year in college.
13. The work of the farmer requires longer hours than a plumber.
14. William was more prejudiced against Henry than James.
15. In our state the winter is as mild as Louisiana.
16. Some people like cars with gear shifts much better.
17. I never have and never will enjoy eating spinach.
18. Some counties in Texas are larger than Delaware.
19. Fewer and fewer persons in United States are becoming farmers.
20. Do you prefer the country to the city?

EFFECTIVE SENTENCES

▶ Unity and Logical Thinking

The fundamental qualities of an effective sentence are unity, coherence, emphasis, and variety. Unity and coherence help to make a sentence logical and clear. Emphasis makes it forceful. Variety lends interest. Usually every good sentence contains all these equally necessary qualities of style. But for the purpose of study we may consider each quality separately. In this section and the next we shall present some of the problems of unity.

23

Avoid bringing into the sentence unrelated ideas or too many details. Complete each thought logically.

A sentence is unified when all its parts contribute to one clear idea or impression. In such a sentence, thought and expression are one, parts unite to form a perfect whole, and we say: "Here it is. We cannot alter a clause, a phrase, or even a word without disturbing the clarity of thought or the focus of the impression." Such a sentence is like a pane of clearest glass; we look through it, unconscious of its existence. But when an idea is not clear or an impression is somewhat fuzzy, the sentence becomes like a wall that stands between us and what the writer is trying to say.

We have already noted that a sentence lacks unity when it is a fragment (see Section 2), contains a "comma splice" (see 3), or is incomplete (see 22). We shall now note that a sentence also lacks unity:

a. When it combines unrelated ideas.
b. When it has excessive detail.
c. When it is mixed, obscure, or illogical.

23a Unrelated ideas should be developed in separate sentences. (If the ideas are related, they should be expressed in such a way that the relationship is immediately clear to the reader.)

UNRELATED Mr. Smith is my teacher and he has a large family.

IMPROVED Mr. Smith is my teacher. He has a large family. [Ideas given equal importance]

IMPROVED Mr. Smith, my teacher, has a large family. [Unity secured by subordination of one idea. See Section 24.]

UNRELATED The birds are numerous and the cherries seldom ripen. [Relationship not immediately clear]

IMPROVED The numerous birds pick most of the cherries before they ripen.

UNRELATED Ireland has a deep culture, but the country is out of the path of general travel. [Unity thwarted by a gap in the thought]

IMPROVED Ireland has a deep culture, but this culture is insufficiently appreciated because the country is out of the path of general travel.

▶ EXERCISE 1. Rewrite the following sentences to point up the implied relationship between the ideas.

1. The stocks continued to drop, and the war was not far off.
2. He came into the room, and immediately the situation explained itself.
3. Lee fell back on Richmond, so that Stuart was forced to retreat.

▶ EXERCISE 2. Rewrite the following sentences to achieve unity.

1. Mollusks which yield pearls are widespread, and pearl fishing is carried on in many parts of the world.
2. The foreman, speaking in gruff tones and seldom smiling, wore a gray coat.
3. Birds migrate to the warmer countries in the fall and in summer get food by eating worms and insects which are a pest to the farmer.

23b Excessive detail should not be allowed to obscure the central thought of the sentence.

Such detail, if important, should be developed in separate sentences; otherwise it should be omitted.

OVERLOADED When I was only four years old, living in an old Colonial house, little of which remains today, I could already walk the two miles that separated the house from the railroad station.

BETTER When I was only four years old, I could already walk the two miles between my house and the railway station. [If the writer considers other details important, he may write another sentence to include them: I was living in an old Colonial house, little of which remains today.]

OVERLOADED In 1788, when Andrew Jackson, then a young man of twenty-one years who had been living in the Carolinas, still a virgin country, came into Tennessee, a turbulent place of unknown opportunities, to enforce the law as the new prosecuting attorney, he had the qualities in him which would make him equal to the task.

BETTER In 1788, when Andrew Jackson came into Tennessee as the new prosecuting attorney, he had the necessary qualifications for the task.

OVERLOADED AND WORDY I have never before known a man who was so ready to help a friend who had got into difficulties which pressed him so hard. [Avoid this house-that-Jack-built construction: *who . . . who,* etc.]

BETTER I have never before known a man so ready to help a friend in trouble.

► EXERCISE 3. Recast the following sentences to eliminate excessive detail.

1. The boat, considered seaworthy ten years ago, but now in need of paint and repairs, as is so often true of things that should be discarded, moved out into the bay.
2. The captain asked for a volunteer, and the soldier picked up his pack, which weighed thirty pounds, and asked if he might go.
3. A course in business methods helps the young man to get a job in order that he may prove whether he is fitted for business and thus avoid postponing the test, as so many do, until it is too late.

Be careful to note that length alone does not make a sentence ineffective. Most good writers compose long sentences, sometimes of paragraph length, without loss of unity. The use of parallel structure, balance, rhythm, careful punctuation, well-placed connectives can bind a sentence into perfect unity. Observe the effective repetition (indicated by italics) in Winston Churchill's famous sentence:

> We shall go on to the end, *we shall fight* in France, *we shall fight* on the seas and oceans, *we shall fight* with growing confidence and growing strength in the air, *we shall defend* our Island, whatever the cost may be, *we shall fight* on the beaches, *we shall fight* on the landing grounds, *we shall fight* in the fields and in the streets, *we shall fight* in the hills; *we shall never surrender,* and even if, which I do not for a moment believe, this Island or a large part of it were subjugated and starving, then our Empire beyond the seas, armed and guarded by the British Fleet, *would carry on the struggle,* until, in God's good time, the New World, with all its power and might, steps forth to the rescue and the liberation of the old. —WINSTON CHURCHILL [1]

In the following sentence Henry James maintains unity by balancing the "grand hotel" with the "small Swiss pension." (Italics have been added.)

> The shore of the lake presents an unbroken array of establishments of this order, of every category, *from the "grand hotel" of the newest fashion,* with a chalk-white front, a hundred balconies, and a dozen flags flying from its roof, *to the small Swiss pension of an elder day,* with its name inscribed in German-looking lettering upon a pink or yellow wall and an awkward summer-house in the angle of the garden. —HENRY JAMES, *Daisy Miller*

23c Mixed, obscure, or illogical constructions should be avoided.

[1] From *Their Finest Hour* by Winston Churchill. By permission of Houghton Mifflin Company.

(1) Do not mix figures of speech by changing too rapidly from one to another.

MIXED This rebellion must be checked before it boils over. [Figure of spirited horse being reined in + figure of liquid becoming overheated]

BETTER This rebellion must be checked before it gets out of control (*or* runs away). [Figure of spirited horse carried throughout]

(2) Do not mix constructions. Complete each construction logically.

MIXED Because he was sick caused him to stay at home. [An adverb clause, a part of a complex sentence, is here mixed with the predicate of a simple sentence.]

CLEAR His sickness caused him to stay at home. [Simple sentence]

CLEAR Because he was sick he stayed at home. [Adverb clause retained; main clause added to complete the complex sentence]

MIXED A sonnet *is when* a poem has fourteen lines. [Avoid the *is when* or *is where* construction. A *when* clause, used as an adverb, cannot be substituted for a noun.]

LOGICAL A sonnet is a poem of fourteen lines.

MIXED To banish *is where* a person is driven out of his country. [Adverb clause misused as a noun]

LOGICAL To banish a person is to drive him out of his country.

(3) Make each part of the sentence agree logically with the other parts.

Often a sentence which contains no grammatical error is nevertheless absurd because of failure in logical agreement.

ILLOGICAL Many of the men were refusing to re-enlist and were returning home to their family. [It is almost impossible to suppose an army in which *many of the men* share among them only one *family*.]

LOGICAL Many of the men were refusing to re-enlist and were returning home to their families. [This is a far more likely statement of what the men were actually doing.]

ILLOGICAL George is a better player than the others are. [There is no logical basis for comparison; although George is *a player,* the others are not *a player,* but *players.*]

BETTER George is a better player than any of the others.

► EXERCISE 4. In each sentence select the parenthetical word or phrase which logical expression of the thought requires and give reasons for your choice.

1. (A new wing was, New wings were) added to the building in 1923 and 1949.
2. Do you men realize that your (career depends, careers depend) upon the work you are doing now?
3. The page preceding (each chapter, the chapters) contains an appropriate illustration.
4. Their (temperament was, temperaments were) as nearly alike as any two men's could have been.
5. Every evening this week we have had (a fire, fires) in our fireplace.
6. Besides that, we have needed an extra blanket on (each bed, the beds).
7. Upon completion of their (enlistment, enlistments) the men will be given travel pay to their (home, homes).
8. The Empire State Building is taller than (any, any other) building in New York.
9. The Empire State Building is taller than (any, any other) building in New Orleans.
10. Tourists are not permitted to bring their (camera, cameras) inside the area.

11. Does each of them understand the nature of (his assignment, their assignments)?
12. You children may take off your (mask, masks) now and come into the dining room for refreshments.

(4) Do not use the double negative.

ILLITERATE I don't want none.
STANDARD I don't want any.

ILLOGICAL The driver couldn't hardly miss the way.
LOGICAL The driver could hardly miss the way.

(5) Do not make illogical, poorly reasoned statements.

The final test of good writing is the soundness of its reasoning. You should make sure that all your sentences are well thought out and contain no fallacies in reasoning. Three fallacies that often occur in writing and speaking are (1) drawing an inference that does not follow from the evidence (called a *non sequitur*, "it does not follow"): "He's an honest boy; he'll make a success at anything he tries"; (2) obscuring the issue by reference to the man involved (called *argumentum ad hominem*, "argument to the man"): "He's a radical; his arguments against the assessment are worthless"; or especially (3) making a hasty generalization—jumping to a conclusion without a sufficient number of instances or examples: "None of my children will drink coffee; children don't like coffee."

► EXERCISES ON UNITY AND LOGICAL THINKING

A. Revise the following sentences as necessary to make them unified, logical, and clear.

1. Of course the other car was at fault: the driver was a woman.

2. Franklin D. Roosevelt was a victim of infantile paralysis, and he founded the National Foundation for Infantile Paralysis in 1938 in order to support scientific research as well as to give aid to thousands of sufferers.
3. The average farm wage for the calendar year 1910 was $21.22, including board, a small sum indeed compared with the monthly wage of $96.00 in 1947, although prices have also gone up at the same time.
4. You can't do but one thing at a time, so buckle down and consider your job of studying as better than a wage earner.
5. Alaska is a country for future colonization, and the people from the Dust Bowl have gone there to live.
6. There were over 78,000,000 cattle in the United States in 1948 and about 50 persons per square mile, with almost 15,000,000 bales of cotton being grown at the same time.
7. Being prompt helped win Jones a raise, so he went to the ball game, but, because the grounds were wet, caused the game to be postponed and he went home to celebrate privately.
8. Whole wheat, which is especially nourishing, is being used more and more, especially in some parts of the country, by the leading bakeries to improve the texture and food content of the bread.
9. One hardly knows what to do in the desperate condition he is.
10. To barter is when one exchanges one commodity for another.
11. Florida is a place where many people go for the winter.
12. The Continental Divide is a watershed extending from Mexico to Canada which is created by the Rocky Mountain range, and east of the Divide water flows to the Gulf of Mexico, while west of the Divide it flows to the Pacific Ocean.

13. The United States government owns 412,000,000 acres of land in the various states which consists of national parks and forests as well as Indian reservations and military posts which are expanded by lease during periods of national emergency.
14. I ate shrimp last night, and therefore I am sick today.

B. Use the following unified and logical sentences as models for sentences of your own. Do not imitate slavishly. Aim to reproduce the design or structure of the model sentence, not to copy the details. Especially be careful to avoid repeating expressions no longer in common use.

1. MODEL SENTENCE The human mind is capable of being excited without the application of gross and violent stimulants. —WORDSWORTH

   TOPIC The human heart

   EXAMPLE The human heart may be moved to deepest sympathy for human suffering without giving way to excessive sentimentality.

2. MODEL SENTENCE It is a truth universally acknowledged that a single man in possession of a good fortune must be in want of a wife. —JANE AUSTEN

   TOPIC A poor widow

3. MODEL SENTENCE He who would be a courtier under a king is almost certain to be a demagogue in a democracy. —JAMES FENIMORE COOPER

   TOPIC A thief in low and high society

4. MODEL SENTENCE I hate to see a load of bandboxes go down the street, and I hate to see a parcel of big words without anything in them. —HAZLITT

   TOPIC The excessive use of cosmetics

5. MODEL SENTENCE Character to a boy is a sealed book; for him a pirate is a beard, a pair of wide trousers, and a liberal complement of pistols. —R. L. STEVENSON

   TOPIC Frugality to a spendthrift

▶ Subordination

(An Aid to Unity)

24

Determine the most important idea of the sentence and express it in the main clause. Put lesser ideas in subordinate clauses, phrases, or words. Use co-ordination only for ideas of equal importance.

Note: Can you distinguish readily between phrases and clauses, between main clauses and subordinate clauses? Until you can do so you will have difficulty in understanding Section 24. If necessary, master first the fundamentals of the sentence treated under Section 1, **Sentence Sense,** especially **1d,** and then study **Subordination.**

The principle of subordination is of great importance in composition, since it is one of the best means of achieving sentence unity. The ability to discriminate between the main idea and the dependent idea is also a mark of maturity. As we develop the power of expression we discard *short, choppy sentences,* or a series of *brief main clauses connected by "and,"* in favor of the more precise complex sentence in which our ideas are properly subordinated.

A child will express himself somewhat like this:

I walked down the road. I saw a bird. It was in a tree. It was singing. [Short, choppy sentences—subordination lacking]

At a slightly older age the child might say:

I walked down the road, and I saw a bird, and it was in a tree, and it was singing. [*And*-sentence—subordination lacking]

A mature writer will express in the main clause of his sentence the idea he wishes to stress and will subordinate all other ideas by reducing them to a subordinate clause, a phrase, or a word.

As I walked down the road [subordinate clause], I saw a bird [main clause] singing [word] in a tree [phrase].

If the singing of the bird is more important than the seeing of the bird, the sentence might read:

A bird was singing in a tree as I walked down the road.

24a In general a related series of short, choppy sentences should be combined into longer units in which the lesser ideas are properly subordinated.

CHOPPY This is a wreck. It was formerly the stately Industrial Exhibition Hall. It is preserved deliberately as a reminder and symbol.

BETTER This wreck, formerly the stately Industrial Exhibition Hall, is preserved deliberately as a reminder and symbol. —ROBERT TRUMBULL[1]

[1] "Hiroshima—Ten Years After," *The New York Times Magazine,* July 31, 1955, p. 5.

CHOPPY Thousands of buildings met the same fate. This alone is now being preserved. It marks the center of the explosion. It is being preserved as a symbol. It symbolizes our wish that there be no more Hiroshimas.

BETTER "Of the thousands of buildings that met the same fate, this alone, marking the center of the explosion, is now being preserved to symbolize our wish that there be no more Hiroshimas." [2]

CHOPPY He stood there in his buckskin clothes. One felt in him standards and loyalties. One also felt a code. This code is not easily put into words. But this code is instantly felt when two men who live by it come together by chance.

BETTER As he stood there in his buckskin clothes, one felt in him standards, loyalties, a code which is not easily put into words, but which is instantly felt when two men who live by it come together by chance.

—WILLA CATHER

CHOPPY I was a little refreshed. I went up into the country. I resolved to deliver myself up to the first savages I should meet. I also resolved to purchase my life from them by some bracelets, glass rings, and other toys which sailors usually provide themselves with in those voyages. I had some of these trinkets with me.

BETTER When I was a little refreshed, I went up into the country, resolving to deliver myself to the first savages I should meet, and purchase my life from them by some bracelets, glass rings, and other toys which sailors usually provide themselves with in those voyages, and whereof I had some about me.

—JONATHAN SWIFT, *Gulliver's Travels*

---

[2] *Ibid.* (From a bronze plaque at the entrance of the building.)

► EXERCISE 1. Combine the following short sentences into longer sentences in which ideas are properly subordinated.

1. The miller was a large man. 2. He weighed well over two hundred pounds. 3. He wore a red beard. 4. It was thick and broad and was shaped like a spade. 5. On his nose grew a wart. 6. Red bristles sprouted out of the wart. 7. This miller was a quarrelsome man. 8. He was proud of his bull-like strength. 9. He missed no chance to display it. 10. He especially liked to show off by tearing down doors. 11. He would jerk them off their hinges. 12. He could also butt them to pieces with his head. 13. Sometimes there was no door convenient. 14. Then he would get attention in other ways. 15. He was a loud-mouth. 16. He always had a story ready to tell. 17. His stories were ones he had picked up in barrooms. 18. Usually they were filthy. 19. It didn't matter that decent people were nearby. 20. He would tell his story anyhow. 21. He had to make a noisy display of himself in one way or another. 22. He never ran out of ways of doing it. 23. He might not be able to find a door to wreck. 24. People sometimes wouldn't listen to his stories. 25. He played a bagpipe. 26. His behavior had its reward. 27. It kept him from being a very well-liked man.

24b Do not write *and, so,* or *but* sentences when one idea should be subordinated to another. Use co-ordination only for ideas of equal importance. (See also **30c**.)

INEFFECTIVE The weather was hot and (*or* so) I stayed at home. [Two main clauses]

BETTER Because the weather was hot [subordinate clause] I stayed at home.

ACCEPTABLE The offer was tempting, but I did not accept it. [Co-ordination used to stress equally the offer and the refusal]

USUALLY BETTER Although the offer was tempting, I did not accept it. [Stress on one of the two—the refusal]

INEFFECTIVE North Dakotans are sturdy and industrious, and they are mostly of Scandinavian and German stock, and they are working during this time of no immediate crisis on a promising plan to prevent future dust bowls.

BETTER Sturdy and industrious, mostly of Scandinavian and German stock, North Dakotans are working during this time of no immediate crisis on a promising plan to prevent future dust bowls. —TIME [8]

NEFFECTIVE I had always wanted to go to college, and I had always wished to become an engineer, and so I enrolled at the Carnegie Institute of Technology.

IMPROVED Because I had always wanted to enter college and prepare myself to become an engineer, I enrolled at the Carnegie Institute of Technology.

IMPROVED I enrolled at the Carnegie Institute of Technology to achieve my double purpose of attending college and becoming an engineer.

► EXERCISE 2. Revise the following sentences to subordinate the less important ideas.

1. Campanella has a good batting record, so pitchers treat him with respect.
2. We had just reached the bend in the road on our way home, and we saw a truckload of Boy Scouts crowded off the highway by an oncoming car.
3. First he selected a lancet and sterilized it, and then he gave his patient a local anesthetic and lanced the infected part.

[8] August 8, 1955, p. 16.

4. Father Latour was at a friend's house, and he saw two fine horses, and he induced the owner to part with them.
5. I graduated from high school, and then I worked in a bank, and so I earned enough to go to college.

The conjunctive adverbs *however, therefore,* and *consequently* are often used in transitions when subordination would be preferable. Main clauses linked by these conjunctive adverbs can usually be combined and the proper relationship indicated by a subordinating conjunction. Subordinating conjunctions express such relationships as cause (*because, since*), concession (*although*), time (*after, before, since, whenever, while, until*), place (*where*), or condition (*if, unless*).

CO-ORDINATION	I became increasingly uneasy; however, I kept my seat.
SUBORDINATION	Although I became increasingly uneasy, I kept my seat. [Subordination is usually better.]
CO-ORDINATION	Fred knows almost nothing about farming; therefore I do not expect him to enjoy much success.
SUBORDINATION	Since Fred knows almost nothing about farming, I do not expect him to enjoy much success.

► EXERCISE 3. Write twelve sentences to illustrate the twelve subordinating conjunctions listed above. Let each conjunction introduce a subordinate clause in which you express an idea of less importance than that in the main clause.

24c Do not place the main thought of the sentence in a subordinate clause (or construction).

FAULTY When we have made a good soldier out of a rookie, he has learned how to march, use his weapons, and respond to commands.

BETTER When a rookie has learned how to march, use his weapons, and respond to commands, we have made a good soldier out of him.

FAULTY William was only a substitute pitcher, winning half of his games.

BETTER Although William was only a susbtitute pitcher, he won half of his games.

FAULTY The rising water broke the dam, when the town was doomed.

BETTER When the rising water broke the dam, the town was doomed.

► EXERCISE 4. Revise each of the following sentences to give prominence to the main thought.

1. The insects eat the plant off just below the soil, stopping all growth.
2. I was at a lecture when our house burned down.
3. The man was asleep while his comrades planned to rob him.
4. One day I was musing on the pleasures of being idle when the thought struck me that complete idleness was hard work.
5. A cow kicked over a lantern, thus causing one of the world's great fires.

► EXERCISES ON SUBORDINATION

A. Revise the following sentences as necessary to give prominence to the main ideas and to subordinate less important ones.

1. Fishing is an exacting sport. One must use the right hook. The bait is also important. The weather must be propitious.

2. The gasoline tank sprang a leak, when all hope for a record flight was abandoned.
3. Throughout all the confusion the little boy had slept, and so he was unconscious of the worry and fear of those around him.
4. The room was large. There was very little furniture in it. It was a lonesome place. I decided not to stay.
5. The sun was very hot, causing the men to stop work.
6. The automobile pulled up at the station. It was just noon. The train had already discharged its passengers.
7. Mary was hurrying to the library when she lost the key to her room.
8. Mary was returning home, and she found her lost key.
9. Your letter came this morning, and I was just getting ready to write you, and so you will get a very prompt reply.
10. Henry was still in high school and his father died, and so he did not go to college.

B. Revise the following passage to achieve proper subordination.

1. I was walking down the street when I found a purse containing fifty dollars. 2. It was just noon. 3. Thousands of people were on the streets. 4. I could not find the owner. 5. I went into the neighboring stores, and I inquired of the shopkeepers whether anyone had lost the money, and I approached the policeman with the same question. 6. No one could say who had lost the money, and so I thought I was the rightful owner, having found the purse myself. 7. But my father did not approve my keeping the purse. 8. He asked me to advertise it. 9. He said I might use the daily paper. 10. Next day I ran an advertisement in the paper, and now a week has passed and I have had no answers, and so I think the money is really mine.

▸ Coherence: Misplaced Parts; Dangling Modifiers

25

Avoid needless separation of related parts of the sentence. Avoid dangling modifiers.

Note: Can you distinguish readily the various modifiers, the several parts of the sentence? Until you are able to do so, you may have difficulty in understanding Section 25. If necessary, master first the fundamentals of the sentence treated in Section 1, **Sentence Sense,** especially **1d;** then study **Coherence.** See also **Modifier** and **Modify** in Section 35, Grammatical Terms.

The meaning of an English sentence depends largely on the position of its parts. Usually these parts—especially the words, phrases, and subordinate clauses serving as modifiers—can be placed in various positions; and they should be placed to give just the emphasis or meaning desired. Note how the meaning in the following sentences changes according to the position of the modifier *only:*

She said that she loved *only* him. [She loved no one else.]
She said that *only* she loved him. [No one else loved him.]
She said *only* that she loved him. [She said nothing else.]

Normally the modifier should be placed as near the word modified as idiomatic English will permit.

Misplaced Parts

25a Avoid needless separation of related parts of the sentence.

(1) In standard written English, adverbs such as *almost, also, only, just, ever, before, even,* or *merely* are regularly placed immediately before the words they modify.

In spoken English, which tends to place these adverbs before the verb, ambiguity can be prevented by stressing the word to be modified.

AMBIGUOUS IN WRITING I *only* delivered the parcel. [Does *only* modify *parcel* or *delivered?*]

CLEAR I delivered *only* the parcel.

AMBIGUOUS He is *just* asking for a trifle.
CLEAR He is asking for *just* a trifle.

AMBIGUOUS Every soldier can*not* become a general. [Literally, no soldier can.]

CLEAR *Not* every soldier can become a general. [Some soldiers can.]

► EXERCISE 1. Place the adverbs in the following sentences immediately before the words they modify.

1. Some contemporary poets hardly show any interest in making their poems intelligible.
2. I only bet on the horse to take third place.
3. He took the penny home and polished it almost until it looked like new.
4. The man was only willing to sell a part of the farm.
5. He even works during his vacation.

(2) Phrases should be placed near the words they modify.

MISPLACED The boy says that he means to leave the country *in the first stanza.*

CLEAR The boy says *in the first stanza* that he means to leave the country.

MISPLACED He played a great part in the war with Mexico *as a statesman.*

CLEAR *As a statesman* he played a great part in the war with Mexico.

MISPLACED Heated arguments had often occurred *over technicalities in the middle of a game.*

CLEAR Heated arguments *over technicalities* had often occurred *in the middle of a game.*

► EXERCISE 2. Recast the following sentences to correct undesirable separation of related parts. Explain exactly what ambiguity each separation causes in each sentence.

1. King Arthur decided to punish those who opposed him for very good reasons.
2. The ship was stripped for action and ready for battle within an hour.
3. Romeo received word that Juliet was dead from another messenger.
4. The engineering work was a thing of beauty on all the large buildings.
5. He tells how Lincoln collected fees that his clients did not pay among other things.
6. My uncle wrote that he would arrive on Friday in his last letter.

(3) Clauses, especially relative clauses, should be placed near the words they modify. (See also 28a.)

AMBIGUOUS I placed the chair in the corner of the room *which I had recently purchased.* [The relative clause seems to modify *room.*]

CLEAR I placed in the corner of the room the chair *which I had recently purchased; or,* In the corner of the room I placed the chair *which I had recently purchased.*

AMBIGUOUS I saw the horse stop at the edge of the precipice *that had raced ahead.*

CLEAR I saw the horse *that had raced ahead* stop at the edge of the precipice.

(4) Avoid "squinting" constructions—modifiers that may refer either to a preceding or to a following word.

SQUINTING I agreed *on the next day* to help him.

CLEAR I agreed to help him *on the next day.*

CLEAR *On the next day,* I agreed to help him.

SQUINTING The tug which was whistling *noisily* chugged up the river.

CLEAR The whistling tug chugged *noisily* up the river.

CLEAR The tug whistled *noisily* as it chugged up the river.

(5) Avoid awkward splitting of infinitives or needless separation of subject and verb, and of parts of verb phrases.

AWKWARD You should now begin *to,* if you wish to succeed, *hunt* for a job.

IMPROVED If you wish to succeed, you should now begin *to hunt* for a job. [In general avoid the "split" infinitive unless it is needed for smoothness or emphasis.]

AWKWARD *I,* knowing all the facts, *want* to be excused.

IMPROVED Knowing all the facts, *I want* to be excused.

AWKWARD There stood the wagon which we *had* early last autumn *left* by the barn.

IMPROVED There stood the wagon which we *had left* by the barn early last autumn.

Dangling Modifiers

25b Avoid dangling modifiers.

Dangling[1] modifiers are verbal phrases (participial, gerund, infinitive) or elliptical clauses which do not refer clearly and logically to some word in the sentence. When these constructions come at the beginning of a sentence, they must refer to the subject of the sentence, as in the following examples:

PARTICIPLE *Taking* our seats, *we* watched the game.

GERUND After *taking* our seats, *we* watched the game.

INFINITIVE *To watch* the game, *we* took our seats.

ELLIPTICAL CLAUSE *When only a small boy, I* went with my father to Denver. [*I was* is implied in the elliptical clause.]

(1) Avoid dangling participial phrases.

DANGLING *Taking* our seats, the game started. [*Taking* does not refer to *game,* nor to any other word in the sentence.]

IMPROVED *Taking* (or *Having taken*) our seats, *we* watched the opening of the game. [*Taking* refers to *we,* the subject of the sentence.]

IMPROVED *After we had taken our seats,* the game started. [Participial phrase expanded into a clause]

DANGLING The evening passed very pleasantly, *eating* candy and *playing* the radio. [*Eating* and *playing* refer to nothing in the sentence.]

IMPROVED *We* passed the evening very pleasantly, *eating*

[1] The term "dangling" is applied especially to incoherent verbal phrases and elliptical clauses. But any misplaced word, phrase, or clause dangles in the sense that it is hanging loosely within the sentence.

candy and *playing* the radio. [*Eating* and *playing* refer to *we,* the subject of the main clause.]

(2) Avoid dangling gerund phrases.

DANGLING On *entering* the stadium, the size of the crowd surprises one. [*Entering* does not refer to any word in the sentence.]

IMPROVED On *entering* the stadium, *one* is surprised by the size of the crowd. [*Entering* refers to *one,* the subject of the sentence.]

(3) Avoid dangling infinitive phrases.

DANGLING *To write* well, good books must be read. [The understood subject of *to write* should be the same as the subject of the sentence.]

IMPROVED *To write* well, a *student* must read good books. [*To write* refers to *student,* the subject of the sentence.]

DANGLING *To run* efficiently, proper oiling is needed.

IMPROVED *To run* efficiently, the *machine* must be properly oiled.

Exceptions:

1. Participles, gerunds, and infinitives designating a general truth rather than the action of a specific person or thing may be used without relation to the main clause.

RIGHT Taking everything into consideration, the campaign was successful.

RIGHT To sum up, we all agreed to support the major.

RIGHT To judge from reports, all must be going well.

2. "Absolute" phrases, which consist of a noun or pronoun followed by a participle, are grammatically independent of the rest of the sentence and need not refer to its subject.

RIGHT *The game having ended,* we went home.

RIGHT *No one having objected,* the motion was passed.

(4) Avoid dangling elliptical clauses (or phrases).

An elliptical clause—that is, a clause with an implied subject and verb—"dangles" unless the implied subject is the same as that of the main clause.

DANGLING When only a small boy (*or* At the age of nine), my father took me with him to Denver. [*I was* is implied in the elliptical clause.]

IMPROVED When I was only a small boy (*or* When I was nine years old), my father took me with him to Denver. [Elliptical clause expanded]

IMPROVED When only a small boy (*or* At the age of nine), *I* went with my father to Denver. [Subject of the main clause made the same as the implied subject of the subordinate clause]

DANGLING Prepare to make an incision in the abdomen as soon as completely anesthetized.

IMPROVED Prepare to make an incision in the abdomen as soon as the patient is completely anesthetized.

► EXERCISE 3. Rewrite the following sentences to eliminate dangling modifiers. Write *C* in place of each sentence that needs no revision.

1. Anticipating no such difficulties as later developed, there was no provision in the Constitution for the admission of a new state as a slave state or as a free state.
2. After sitting there awhile, it began to snow.
3. By selecting the judges from both parties, the decisions are likely to give general satisfaction.
4. To grow good tomatoes, the vines should be supported by stakes.
5. Entering Chicago from the west, a whole network of stockyards is the first thing seen.
6. Darkness having come, we stopped for the night.

7. The meeting was adjourned by standing and repeating the pledge.
8. Having taken his seat, we began to question the witness.
9. In drawing up any system of classification, it is likely that there will be some overlapping.
10. Vaccination to prevent smallpox is required before entering the United States from a foreign country.

► EXERCISE 4. Many dangling modifiers may be eliminated by alternate methods. Revise at least half of the faulty sentences in Exercise 3 by a different method from that used in the first revision of the sentences.

► EXERCISES ON COHERENCE

A. Rewrite the following sentences to make them coherent. Write *C* in place of each sentence that needs no revision.

1. He was enchanted by the roast beef, causing him to tip the waiter inordinately.
2. That statement I do not find it possible to believe at this stage of the argument.
3. We found the house with no trouble after reaching Westwood.
4. After reaching Westwood, locating the house was no trouble.
5. She decided to most mischievously split her infinitives.
6. Being in a hurry to get away on our trip, our automobile was not overhauled.
7. The decision having been made, everyone was happy.
8. Having a broken arm and nose, I thought the statue was very ugly.
9. John and Robert had ridden several days without sleep in the rain.

10. While wondering about this phenomenon, the sun sank from view.
11. The slaves were unwilling to submit to his plans, thinking they could free themselves.
12. After taking only a few steps, I discovered that I had forgotten my keys.
13. You are, considering the whole affair, very fortunate.
14. The problem that bothered me was the selection of my courses upon entering college.
15. Located on a mountain top, this made it an ideal place for a summer resort.
16. Henry promised when he was on his way home to stop at the library.
17. To irrigate successfully, water must flow through carefully planned ditches.
18. The Browns returned this morning from their vacation in the mountains on the bus.
19. Before taking a first trip by air, the thought of flying frightens one.
20. The new members were asked to give the secretary their addresses.

B. Follow directions given under A.

1. My brother asked me on Wednesday to go with him.
2. The books on the first shelf are only reserved for three days.
3. Keep stirring the water into the mixture until pale green.
4. He only works when someone is around.
5. The evening passed pleasantly, talking about current events.
6. Feeling keenly about football, relations between the two schools became strained.
7. To tell the truth, very few people enjoyed the lecture.
8. To be a good engineer mathematics is a necessity.

▸ Parallelism

(An Aid to Coherence)

26

Parallel ideas should be expressed in parallel structure. Misleading parallels should be avoided.

Note: Can you distinguish readily the parts of speech, phrases and clauses, main clauses and subordinate clauses? Until you are able to do so you will have difficulty in understanding Section 26. If necessary, master first the fundamentals of the sentence treated in Section 1, Sentence Sense, especially 1c and 1d; then study Parallelism.

26a For the expression of co-ordinate (equal) ideas a noun should be paralleled with a noun, an active verb with an active verb, an infinitive with an infinitive, a subordinate clause with a subordinate clause, and so forth.

AWKWARD Let us consider the *origin* of engineering and *how engineering has progressed.* [Noun paralleled with a subordinate clause]

BETTER Let us consider the || *origin* and
|| *progress* of engineering.
[Noun paralleled with noun]

AWKWARD *Walking* and *to swim* are good exercise. [Gerund paralleled with infinitive]

BETTER || *Walking* and
|| *swimming* are good exercise.
[Gerund paralleled with gerund]

AWKWARD As a young man he *had been* in Africa, *fighting* in Greece, and *following* his general to India. [Verb paralleled with participles]

BETTER As a young man he || *had been* in Africa,
|| *had fought* in Greece, and
|| *had followed* his general to India.
[Verb paralleled with verbs]

AWKWARD He retired *respected* by his associates, *admired* by his friends, and *his employees loved him.* [Participles paralleled with a main clause]

BETTER He retired || *respected* by his associates,
|| *admired* by his friends, and
|| *loved* by his employees.
[Participle paralleled with participles]

RIGHT The dogmas || of the quiet past
are inadequate || to the stormy present.

—ABRAHAM LINCOLN

[Prepositional phrase paralleled with prepositional phrase]

RIGHT To say || *that* the character of real men cannot be completely known,
|| *that* their inner nature is beyond our reach,
|| *that* the dramatic portraiture of things is only possible to poetry,
is to say || *that* history ought not to be written.

—J. A. FROUDE

[Clause paralleled with clauses]

▶ EXERCISE 1. Indicate parallelism in the following sentences by an outline similar to that used above.

1. The example of this social pariah should have commended itself to Mr. Froude, for whom it is not enough that this woman should be made to suffer for a crime of which she was innocent—not enough that inhuman men should mock her infirmities in that awful moment—not enough that in her preparation for death she should be denied the consolations of her own faith—not enough that a religious bigot should be ordered to thrust himself between the victim and her Maker—not enough that she should receive vociferous assurance that her damnation was certain.

   —JAMES MELINE

2. Wit is a lean creature with sharp inquiring nose, whereas humor has a kindly eye and comfortable girth.

   —CHARLES S. BROOKS

3. We have seen the necessity of the Union, as our bulwark against foreign danger, as the conservator of peace among ourselves, as the guardian of our commerce and other common interests, as the only substitute for those military establishments which have subverted the liberties of the Old World, and as the proper antidote for the diseases of faction, which have proved fatal to other popular governments, and of which alarming symptoms have been betrayed by our own. —JAMES MADISON

▶ EXERCISE 2. Revise the following sentences to give parallel structure to co-ordinate ideas.

1. These illustrations will enable you to differentiate unintentional killing and killing with intent to kill.
2. Mr. Smith is fair in his grading but never giving anyone more than he earns.
3. The story is vivid, interesting, and one that appeals to every person.

4. His duties are cleaning up the cabins and to look after the boats.
5. She spends all her time shopping and on her studies.

26b Whenever necessary to make the parallel clear, repeat a preposition, an article, an auxiliary verb, the sign of the infinitive, or the introductory word of a long phrase or clause. (See also Section 22c.)

AWKWARD I admire Tennyson *for the ideals* in his poems but not *his style.*

IMPROVED I admire Tennyson || *for the ideals* in his poems
|| but not
|| *for his style.*

AWKWARD In the wreck the circus lost *a camel* and *elephant.*

IMPROVED In the wreck the circus lost || *a camel* and
|| *an elephant.*

OBSCURE He explained *that* the advertising campaign had been successful, business had increased more than fifty per cent, and additional capital was sorely needed.

CLEARER He explained || *that* the advertising campaign had been successful,
|| *that* business had increased more than fifty per cent, and
|| *that* additional capital was sorely needed.

► EXERCISE 3. Copy the following sentences, inserting the words needed to bring out the parallel.

1. The sentences are difficult to understand, not because they are long but they are obscure.

2. The child learns in nursery school to take his turn, to respect the rights of others, and take care of his materials.
3. They would lie on the battlefield for hours and sometimes days.

26c Correlatives (*either . . . or, neither . . . nor, both . . . and, not only . . . but also, whether . . . or*) should be followed by elements that are parallel in form.

POOR He was not only *kind* but also *knew* when to help people in trouble.
[Adjective paralleled with verb]

BETTER He was || *not only kind*
|| *but also helpful* to people in trouble.

POOR I debated whether *I should give* the beggar money or *to offer* him food.
[Subordinate clause paralleled with infinitive]

BETTER I debated || *whether to give* the beggar money
|| *or to offer* him food.

26d *Caution:* Do not use parallel structure for sentence elements not parallel in thought. Never use an awkward or unidiomatic expression for the sake of a parallel. Lack of parallel structure is preferable.

MISLEADING Our meetings were held on Friday afternoon, on Saturday morning, and on Saturday afternoon we started home.

CLEARER Our meetings were held on Friday afternoon and on Saturday morning. On Saturday afternoon we started home.

MISLEADING He discovered that the farm is well adapted to cotton and that it yields a bale to the acre. [Parallel structure used for ideas not co-ordinate]

CLEARER He discovered that the farm is well adapted to cotton, yielding a bale to the acre.

▶ EXERCISES ON PARALLELISM

A. Copy the following sentences, using parallel structure to express parallel ideas. Write *C* in place of each sentence that needs no revision.

1. He had long wondered whether he should go into his father's business or to start a small business of his own.
2. William is a boy with a good mind and who has the highest principles.
3. Someone has said that Americans cannot enjoy life without a TV set, an automobile, and a summer cottage.
4. My friend told me that the trip would be delayed but to be ready to start on Friday.
5. To learn to balance a ball, playing musical instruments, and riding horseback are some of the tricks a sea lion can perform.
6. A sea lion watches carefully the action of his fellows and how they obey their trainer.
7. He was quiet and in a serious mood after the talk.
8. He took up drinking, gambling, and killed several people.
9. I did not know whether I should go to some technical school or to enter a liberal arts college.
10. The real creed of a person should be living rather than in words.
11. The secretary must attend all meetings, call the roll, and keep the minutes.

12. When you have mastered the fundamentals of writing and after much practice, you will become a good writer.
13. People fall naturally into two classes: the workers and those who like to lean on others.
14. You will enjoy painting a favorite corner of the room, showing an armchair, drop-leaf table, and lamp.
15. Failure is due either to lack of preparation or inability to master the subject.

B. In the following sentence note how Newman develops the parallel between health and general education. Underline the words which bring out the parallelism. (This is an exceptional case of an exceedingly long sentence—203 words—which is maintained in perfect balance.)

Again, as health ought to precede labour of the body, and as a man in health can do what an unhealthy man cannot do, and as of this health the properties are strength, energy, agility, graceful carriage and action, manual dexterity, and endurance of fatigue, so in like manner general culture of mind is the best aid to professional and scientific study, and educated men can do what illiterate cannot; and the man who has learned to think and to reason and to compare and to discriminate and to analyze, who has refined his taste, and formed his judgment, and sharpened his mental vision, will not indeed at once be a lawyer, or a pleader, or an orator, or a statesman, or a physician, or a good landlord, or a man of business, or a soldier, or an engineer, or a chemist, or a geologist, or an antiquarian, but he will be placed in that state of intellect in which he can take up any one of the sciences or callings I have referred to, or any other for which he has a taste or special talent, with an ease, a grace, a versatility, and a success, to which another is a stranger. —JOHN HENRY NEWMAN

C. With Newman's structure as a guide, some students may wish to construct a shorter sentence on a subject such as the following: The game of football and the game of life; the course of a river and the course of history; military training and college education.

D. Indicate parallelism in the following sentence by underlining the words which bring out the parallelism.

To think nothing of symmetry and much of convenience; never to remove an anomaly merely because it is an anomaly; never to innovate except when some grievance is felt; never to innovate except so far as to get rid of the grievance; never to lay down any proposition of wider extent than the particular case for which it is necessary to provide; these are the rules which have from the age of John to the age of Victoria, generally guided the deliberations of our two hundred and fifty Parliaments. —THOMAS B. MACAULAY

E. With Macaulay's sentence as a guide, some students may wish to construct a similar sentence on a subject such as the following: American political practice; the rules of war; the conduct of a university.

F. Indicate parallelism in the passages quoted from Winston Churchill and Henry James in Section 23b.

▶ Point of View

(An Aid to Coherence)

27

Avoid needless shifts in point of view.

Sudden and illogical shifts in point of view tend to obscure the meaning and thus to cause needless difficulty in reading.

27a Avoid needless shifts in tense. (See also 7c.)

SHIFT The boy *closed* his book and *hurries* away to the playground. [A shift from past tense to present tense]

BETTER The boy *closed* his book and *hurried* away to the playground. [Both verbs in the past tense]

Note: When the historical present is used, as in summarizing plots of narratives, care will be needed to avoid slipping from the present tense into the past tense. *Example:* "Romeo *goes* in disguise to a Capulet feast, *falls* in love with Juliet, and *marries* her secretly. Just after his wedding he *is drawn* into a quarrel with the Capulets and *is banished* (not *was banished*) from Verona."

27b Avoid needless shifts in mood.

SHIFT First *rise* to your feet and then you *should address* the chairman. [A shift from imperative to indicative mood]

BETTER First *rise* to your feet and then *address* the chairman. [Both verbs in the imperative mood]

27c Avoid needless shifts in subject or voice.

A shift in subject often involves a shift in voice. A shift in voice nearly always involves a shift in subject.

SHIFT James liked fishing, but hunting was also enjoyed by him. [The subject shifts from *James* to *hunting*. The voice shifts from active to passive.]

BETTER James liked fishing, but he also enjoyed hunting. [One subject only. Both verbs active.]

SHIFT Mary took summer courses and her leisure hours were devoted to tennis. [The subject shifts from *Mary* to *hours*. The voice shifts from active to passive.]

BETTER Mary took summer courses and devoted her leisure hours to tennis. [One subject only. Both verbs active.]

SHIFT Paul hurried up the mountain path and soon the laurel came in sight. [The subject shifts from *Paul* to *laurel*.]

BETTER Paul hurried up the mountain path and soon caught sight of the laurel. [One subject only]

27d Avoid needless shifts in person. (See also 28c(3).)

SHIFT *We* have reached a point where *one* ought to face the possibility of a great and sudden change. [A shift from first to third person]

BETTER *We* have reached a point where *we* ought to face the possibility of a great and sudden change.

SHIFT *Students* will find the University Book Shop a great convenience. *You* need not leave the campus to purchase any school supplies *you* may need. [A shift from third to second person]

BETTER *The student* will find the University Book Shop a great convenience. *He* need not leave the campus to purchase any school supplies *he* may need.

27e Avoid needless shifts in number. (See also agreement of pronoun and antecedent, Section 6b.)

SHIFT *One* should be thoughtful of *their* neighbors. [A shift from singular *one* to plural *their*]

BETTER *One* should be thoughtful of *one's* neighbors.

SHIFT The United Nations *deserves* encouragement. Indeed, *they deserve* much more than that. [If *United Nations* takes a singular verb (*deserves*), it must not be referred to by a plural pronoun (*they*).]

BETTER The United Nations *deserves* encouragement. Indeed, *it deserves* much more than that.

27f Avoid needless shifts from indirect to direct discourse.

SHIFT My friend asked whether I knew the coach and will he be with the team. [Mixed indirect and direct discourse]

RIGHT My friend asked whether I knew the coach and whether he would be with the team. [Indirect discourse]

RIGHT My friend asked, "Do you know the coach? Will he be with the team?" [Direct discourse]

27g Maintain the same tone or style throughout the sentence.

INAPPROPRIATE Analysis of the principal obstacles to harmony in the United Nations reveals that Russia and her satellites refuse to *play ball* with the rest of the world. [A shift from formal to colloquial style. Substitute *co-operate,* or a similar word, for the italicized expression.]

INAPPROPRIATE After distributing the grass seed evenly over the lawn, rake the ground at least twice and then *gently bedew it* with fine spray. [The italicized expression is too "poetic" in a sentence with a prosaic purpose. Substitute *water it lightly*.]

INAPPROPRIATE A big *jazzy* moon bathed the sea in mellow light. [*Jazzy* and *mellow* clash. Substitute *harvest* for *jazzy*.]

INAPPROPRIATE It seemed to Juliet, as she gazed down from the balcony, that Romeo's face was as white as *the underside of a fish.* [The italicized expression clashes with the romantic beginning of the sentence.]

27h Maintain a consistent perspective throughout the sentence (and also throughout the larger elements of discourse).

FAULTY PERSPECTIVE From the top of the Washington Monument, the government offices seemed to be so many beehives, and the workers droned at their tasks behind long rows of desks. [The perspective shifts from the monument to the interior of government buildings.]

CONSISTENT PERSPECTIVE From the top of the Washington Monument, the government buildings seemed to be so many beehives, and it was easy to imagine the workers droning at their tasks behind long rows of desks.

ILLOGICAL *Standing in the valley,* I could see our troops at the crest of the hill and, on the other side of the ridge, the enemy in full retreat.

LOGICAL *From the airplane* I could see our troops at the crest of the hill and, on the other side of the ridge, the enemy in full retreat.

▶ EXERCISES ON POINT OF VIEW

A. In the following sentences correct all needless shifts in tense, mood, subject, voice, person, number, tone, or perspective. Write *C* in place of each sentence that needs no revision.

1. He said he had a convertible model in stock and would I like to try it out.
2. As I entered the building, I was overcome by its splendor of size, decoration, and furnishing, even of the smallest rooms.
3. Jane likes to cook, but house cleaning is not a pleasant occupation.
4. Each person has some distinctive mannerism of their own.
5. When she saw him in the room, she thinks that she is dreaming.
6. If there is little enthusiasm among the students, we might ask, "Why they should be enthusiastic?"
7. No matter what her mother may say, she always took the opposite view.
8. It is a book everyone should read, for you can derive much good from it.
9. Gentlemen, we have finished our discussion about balancing the budget; bear with me awhile until I have said a few words about budgeting the balance.

10. The foreign ministers held their powwow in Paris, and contrary to rumors, the peace pipe is passed around.
11. Pick the roses in the morning, and then they should be placed in water.
12. A vacation is enjoyed by all because it refreshes the mind and the body.
13. He told his aunt that there is someone in the room.
14. Every citizen should do his duty as they see it.
15. Aunt Jane spent her summers in Wisconsin, but Arizona is her favorite winter climate.
16. Later he attended a feast given by the Capulets, and there he meets Juliet.

B. Revise the following paragraph to avoid all needless shifts. If necessary, expand the paragraph.

1. From behind the desk the shopkeeper emerged and comes toward me. 2. He is a heavy-set man, and his brown tweed coat was badly worn. 3. An assistant gave me a chair and leaves the room, but not before he had welcomed us and even told me where one might find lodging. 4. "First, look around in this vicinity and then you should find a comfortable place in a nearby hotel," he says. 5. I hurried out of the shop and soon the hotel comes into view. 6. Be thankful for suggestions when offered you. 7. It usually helps one.

C. Follow the directions for B.

1. He was an artful old codger, it always had seemed to me. 2. He has a deceptively open face and his manner is that of a simple farmer. 3. He tried to appear humble and said that "I am opposed to all pretense." 4. Nevertheless he will let it be known that he has great influence with important people. 5. Take these impressions for what they are worth; it may help one in your dealings with this reptile.

▶ Reference of Pronouns

(An Aid to Coherence)

28

Make every pronoun refer unmistakably to a definite antecedent. (For agreement of pronoun and antecedent see Section **6b.**)

One of the principal obstacles to clear and immediate understanding is the faulty use of pronouns. *He, she, it; who, which, what; this, that; the same, such,* etc. can have meaning only if the antecedent noun is immediately obvious to the reader. Hence the writer should place all pronouns as close as possible to the antecedent. If, having done this, he finds that the reference of the pronoun is still not obvious, he should repeat the antecedent or use a synonym for it. If repetition proves awkward, he should recast his sentence.

28a Avoid ambiguous reference. Construct the sentence in such a way that the reader can easily distinguish between two possible antecedents.

AMBIGUOUS John told William that he had made a mistake. [Who made the mistake?]

CLEAR John said to William, "You have made a mistake."

CLEAR John said to William, "I have made a mistake."

CLEAR In talking to William, John admitted that he had made a mistake.

AWKWARD The books were standing on the shelf which needed sorting. [See also 25a(3).]

BETTER The books which needed sorting were standing on the shelf.

AMBIGUOUS It is hard for men to like many people who enjoy solitude. [See also 25a(3).]

CLEAR It is hard for men who enjoy solitude to like many people.

28b Avoid remote reference—reference to an antecedent (1) too far removed from the pronoun or (2) so placed in a subordinate construction that it is not central in the mind of the reader.

Make your meaning immediately clear to the reader. Save him the annoyance of searching about for the antecedent.

REMOTE The *lake* covers many acres. Near the shore water lilies grow in profusion, spreading out their green leaves and sending up white blossoms on slender stems. *It* is well stocked with fish. [The pronoun *it* is too far removed from the antecedent *lake.*]

IMPROVED . The *lake* is well stocked with fish. [Repetition of the antecedent *lake*]

VAGUE He sat by the little window all day and worked steadily at his translating. *It* was too small to give much light. [Temporarily confusing: antecedent of *it* not clear until reader finishes the sentence]

CLEAR He sat by the little window all day and worked steadily at his translating. The *window* was too small to give much light. [Repetition of the noun]

REMOTE When *Johnson's* club was organized, *he* asked Goldsmith to become a member. [Reference to antecedent in the possessive case]

IMPROVED When *Johnson* organized his club, *he* asked Goldsmith to become a member.

Caution: As a rule avoid pronoun reference to the title of a theme, or to a word in the title.

AWKWARD *He* and I enjoyed hiking. [The first sentence of a theme entitled, "Hiking with My Brother"]

BETTER My *brother* and I enjoyed hiking.

28c Use broad reference, if at all, only with discretion.

Informal English allows much latitude in the use of antecedents that must be inferred from the context. Even standard English accepts the general idea of a clause as an antecedent when the reference is unmistakable. But students who overuse *this, that, it,* or *which* to refer to the general idea of the preceding clause or sentence may be advised, as a means of insuring greater clarity, to make each of their pronouns refer to a specific substantive.

(1) Avoid reference to the general idea of a preceding clause or sentence unless the meaning is clear and unmistakable.

VAGUE William was absent from the first performance, which caused much comment. [*Which* has no antecedent.]

CLEAR William's absence from the first performance caused much comment. [Pronoun eliminated]

VAGUE The story referred to James, but Henry misapplied it to himself. This is true in real life. [*This* has no antecedent.]

CLEAR The story referred to James, but Henry misapplied it to himself. Similar mistakes occur in real life.

VAGUE When class attendance is compulsory, some students feel that education is being forced upon them. This may cause them to dislike college. [*This* has no antecedent.]

CLEAR When class attendance is compulsory, some students feel that education is being forced upon them. This feeling (*or* this compulsion) may cause them to dislike college.

(2) As a rule do not refer to a noun not expressed but merely inferred from some word.

VAGUE My mother is a music teacher. It is a profession I know nothing about.

CLEAR My mother is a music teacher, but the teaching of music is a profession I know nothing about.

VAGUE He wanted his teachers to think he was above average, as he could have been if he had used it to advantage.

CLEAR He wanted his teachers to think he was above average, as he could have been if he had used his ability to advantage.

(3) In standard (formal) writing avoid the use of the indefinite *it, you,* or *they*. Especially avoid the *you* habit.

AWKWARD If a person breaks the law you may be arrested. [See also 27d.]

COLLOQUIAL (OR STANDARD) If you break the law, you may be arrested. [Colloquial when *you* means "anyone"; standard when *you* is addressed to a specific person or persons]

STANDARD	If anyone breaks the law, he may be arrested. *Or,* Anyone breaking the law may be arrested.
COLLOQUIAL	In France *they* could not understand William.
STANDARD	In France William could not be understood.
AWKWARD	In the book *it* says that many mushrooms are edible.
IMPROVED	The book says that many mushrooms are edible.

Note: The pronoun *it* is correctly used in such idiomatic expressions as *it seems, it is cold, it is raining, it is useless to go,* and *it is five miles to town.*

28d Avoid the confusion arising from the repetition in the same sentence of a pronoun referring to different antecedents.

CONFUSING	Although *it* is very hot by the lake, *it* looks inviting. [The first *it* is the indefinite pronoun; the second *it* refers to *lake.*]
CLEARER	Although it is very hot by the lake, the water looks inviting.
CONFUSING	We should have prepared for our examinations earlier. *It* is too late to do *it* now.
CLEARER	We should have prepared for our examinations earlier. It is now too late to prepare.

▶ EXERCISE ON REFERENCE OF PRONOUNS

Reconstruct the following sentences as necessary to correct faults in reference. Write *C* in place of each sentence that needs no revision.

1. Howard was more intelligent than the average student, but he did not use it properly.
2. I did not even buy a season ticket, which was very disloyal to my school.

3. Her ladylike qualities were reflected in the graciousness of her manner. This was apparent in her every act.
4. Package wrapping has always been my job, because they say that I can do it better than anyone else.
5. When building roads the Romans tried to detour around valleys as much as possible for fear that flood waters might cover them and make them useless.
6. If you are taken to the courthouse, they will fine you.
7. In the article it states that the inland sea is salt.
8. Our language is rich in connectives which express fine distinctions of meaning.
9. One summer while visiting my grandparents I was attracted by three pigeons that decided to settle in their barn loft.
10. If all impurities are not removed from the iron, it will deprive steel of its ductility and prevent it from being rolled into bars or drawn into wire.
11. The speaker was eloquent, but he was annoyed by the intense heat in the auditorium.
12. My worst fault is the inability to express myself clearly in the presence of other people. But this is not true when I am with close friends.
13. I left home and hitchhiked to Chicago. This means of travel is not satisfactory, for it requires much waiting at the side of the road.
14. When the termite eggs are hatched, they grow wings and fly about the country in swarms.
15. Mary told Ann that she would be accepted as a member of the club.
16. The story awakens your interest in radium, which continues to the end of the book.
17. Visitors should heed the notice that is on the outside of the door.
18. Mary showed Jane that she had not made a mistake.

▶ Emphasis

29

Select words and arrange the parts of the sentence to give emphasis to important ideas.

Emphasis, expressing an idea as strongly as possible, is the third of four fundamental qualities of a good style: unity, coherence, emphasis, and variety.

As our ideas vary in importance, so our expression should vary in stress. Short factual statements and routine description or narration cannot always be varied for emphasis without doing violence to the natural order of the English language. It would be absurd for a policeman to describe a prisoner in this fashion: "Red was his hair, blue were his eyes, and on his nose sat a great brown wart." But in most types of writing, sentences may be rearranged to achieve emphasis without sacrificing naturalness of expression.

Emphasis may be gained through the use of concrete words and figurative language (Section 20), through economy of language (Section 21), and through the subordination of less important ideas (Section 24). We may also emphasize ideas:

a. By placing important words in the important positions at the beginning and end of the sentence.

b. By changing loose sentences into periodic sentences.
c. By arranging ideas in the order of climax.
d. By using the active instead of the passive voice.
e. By repeating important words.
f. By putting words out of their usual order.
g. By using balanced construction.
h. By abruptly changing the sentence length.

29a Gain emphasis by placing important words at the beginning or end of the sentence—especially at the end. Whenever possible tuck away in the middle of the sentence parenthetical expressions and other elements of minor importance.

WEAK The colonel will bluntly refuse, in all probability. [The weakest part of the sentence is given the most emphatic position—the end.]

EMPHATIC In all probability the colonel will bluntly refuse. [Strong end]

EMPHATIC The colonel, in all probability, will bluntly refuse. [Most emphatic—strong beginning and end]

WEAK He became an archbishop in his later years, however.

EMPHATIC In his later years, however, he became an archbishop.

WEAK Fallacies as gross as these may easily be detected by all men who can see an inch before them.

EMPHATIC All men who can see an inch before them may easily detect these gross fallacies. —DRYDEN

► EXERCISE 1. Gain emphasis by rearranging the parts of the sentences.

1. He had little success, but he was a tireless worker, if we may believe the reports.
2. The old man withdrew into his cabin for some good reason we must suppose.
3. He may become an expert accountant by a study of business methods at home.
4. A trailer saves hotel expense and can be moved about from place to place readily.
5. However, he could not redeem himself, in my opinion.

29b Gain emphasis by changing loose sentences into periodic sentences. (Section 29b is an extension of 29a.)

A sentence in which the main clause is either placed at the end or completed at the end is called *periodic;* one that makes a complete statement and then adds details is called *loose*. Both types of sentences are effective. The loose sentence, more commonly used, makes for informal writing and easy reading. But the periodic sentence, by holding the reader in suspense and reserving the main idea until the end, is more emphatic. Note the difference in tone in the following sentences.

LOOSE Practice daily if you want to become a good pianist. [A clear sentence]

PERIODIC If you want to become a good pianist, practice daily. [More emphatic]

LOOSE History has proved amply that mere numbers may be defeated by smaller forces who are superior in arms, organization, and morale.

PERIODIC That mere numbers may be defeated by smaller forces who are superior in arms, organization, and morale is amply proved by history.

Caution: Do not overuse the periodic sentence to the point of making your style unnatural. Variety is desirable. See Section 30.

► EXERCISE 2. Change the following loose sentences into periodic sentences. Note the gain in emphasis.

1. I attended his wedding, many years ago, on a beautiful June afternoon, in a little village near Cincinnati.
2. He returned to the camp when he found that he could be of no further assistance.
3. It was no concern of mine that he neglected his studies.
4. The workers were afraid to return until the dam had been repaired.
5. It never entered his mind to be dissatisfied with his dreary lodgings, to resent the purposelessness of his job, or to revolt against the complacent ignorance of his associates.

► EXERCISE 3. Examine typical pages from several prose writers (Swift, Newman, Conrad, or others) to determine the proportion of loose and periodic sentences.

29c Gain emphasis by arranging ideas in the order of climax.

UNEMPHATIC We could hear the roar of cannon, the shrieks of the wounded, and the crash of falling timbers

EMPHATIC We could hear the roar of cannon, the crash of falling timbers, and the shrieks of the wounded. [Climax reached in "shrieks of the wounded"]

UNEMPHATIC We have been spurned with contempt by the throne. Our supplications have been disregarded, and our remonstrances have produced additional violence and insult. Our petitions have been slighted.

EMPHATIC Our petitions have been slighted; our remonstrances have produced additional violence and insult; our supplications have been disregarded; and we have been spurned, with contempt, from the foot of the throne! —PATRICK HENRY

Note: A striking arrangement of ideas in reverse order of climax, called anticlimax, is sometimes used for comic effect.

> Not louder shrieks to pitying heav'n are cast,
> When husbands, or when lap-dogs, breathe their last.
> —POPE

► EXERCISE 4. Arrange the ideas of each sentence in what you consider to be the order of climax.

1. He left the city because of ill health, failure in business, and the loss of his club membership.
2. His confident manner, his knowledge of men, and his friendliness made him the logical man for the office.
3. Something must be done at once. The commission is faced with a deficit.
4. Give me death or give me liberty.
5. I gathered together the souvenirs of college days: my diploma, a textbook on mathematics, my fraternity pin, and a battered book bag.

29d Gain emphasis by using the strong active voice instead of the weak passive voice.

WEAK His grave was dug by his teeth.
STRONGER He dug his grave with his teeth.

WEAK Honey was gathered by the bee as it flitted from flower to flower.
STRONGER The bee, flitting from flower to flower, gathered honey.

Exception: If the receiver of the action is more important than the doer, the passive voice is more effective.

EMPHATIC Wheat is grown in Kansas.
EMPHATIC Any person who attempts to escape will be shot.

► EXERCISE 5. Substitute the active for the passive voice.

1. As the station is reached, the train is seen coming around a curve.
2. On her head was worn a beautiful green hat.
3. Paul was hesitant to enter the room, for he saw that a poster was being made by Jane.
4. On Sunday afternoon many fishermen may be seen trying their luck.
5. It was decided by the members that the meetings were to be held at their homes.
6. When the play was brought to an end, the actors were greeted with a loud burst of applause by the audience.
7. It is greatly feared by the citizens that adequate punishment will not be meted out to the lawbreakers by the jury.

29e Gain emphasis by repeating important words.

Note the great difference between the careless repetition in Section 21c and the effective repetition in the following passages.

EMPHATIC *wet* roads, *wet* fields, *wet* housetops; not a *beautiful,* scarcely a *picturesque* object met my eyes along the whole route; yet to me, *all* was *beautiful, all* was more than *picturesque.*

—CHARLOTTE BRONTË

EMPHATIC There is *no mistake;* there has been *no mistake;* and there shall be *no mistake.*

—DUKE OF WELLINGTON

EMPHATIC . . . that government of the *people,* by the *people,* for the *people,* shall not perish from the earth.
—ABRAHAM LINCOLN

EMPHATIC If it's *against the law* in the corner saloons, it is *against the law* in the country club, too.
—ADLAI STEVENSON

[See also the quotation from Winston Churchill in Section **23b.**]

► EXERCISE 6. From your reading, copy three passages in which emphasis is gained by the repetition of an important word or phrase.

29f Gain emphasis by putting a word or phrase out of its natural order.

EMPHATIC *Trust* her I dare not.

EMPHATIC *Never* did I think he would return alive.

EMPHATIC *Mutter* she does at times, but it is in solitary places that are desolate as she is desolate, in ruined cities, *and when the sun has gone down to his rest.*—DE QUINCEY. [Note how the italicized words are deliberately placed out of a natural order.]

Caution: This method of securing emphasis, if overused, will make the style distinctly artificial. And of course the order of the parts of the sentence should never be such as to make for ambiguity. (See **25a.**)

► EXERCISE 7. Copy from your reading and bring to class five passages in which emphasis is secured by putting a word or phrase out of natural order.

29g Use balance to gain emphasis.

A sentence is balanced when identical or similar grammatical structure is used to express contrasted ideas. A balanced sentence uses parallel structure (see Section 26) and emphasizes the contrast between parts of similar length and movement. Overuse of balance seems especially artificial.

UNBALANCED It is human to err, but to forgive is divine.

BALANCED To err is human, to forgive divine. —POPE

BALANCED You had better talk trifles elegantly to the most trifling woman, than coarse inelegant sense to the most solid man: you had better return a dropped fan genteelly, than give a thousand pounds awkwardly; and you had better refuse a favor gracefully, than grant it clumsily.
—CHESTERFIELD

BALANCED The notice which you have been pleased to take of my labours, had it been early, had been kind; but it has been delayed till I am indifferent, and cannot enjoy it; till I am solitary, and cannot impart it; till I am known, and do not want it.
—SAMUEL JOHNSON (to Chesterfield)

BALANCED Fools talk about each other, ordinary men about things, wise men about ideas.

► EXERCISE 8. Copy from your reading and bring to class five examples of the balanced sentence.

► EXERCISE 9. Copy all examples of balanced structure from Lincoln's Gettysburg Address (at the end of Section 1, pages 26-27).

► EXERCISE 10. Use balanced sentences to show the contrast between the following: Men and women, youth and age, success and failure.

► EXERCISES ON EMPHASIS

A. Rewrite the following sentences as necessary to give greater emphasis. Write *C* in place of each sentence that needs no revision.

1. The chairman will give his report after the meeting has been called to order.
2. The soldiers were outnumbered two to one, as you may have heard.
3. It was no fault of hers that the program was a failure.
4. If you cannot come, say so, by all means.
5. The zero hour had come. Already the armies were marching.
6. On the other hand, he had done the best he could, according to his story.
7. At any time I shall be ready, no matter how late the hour is.
8. He saw much to interest him: the Statue of Liberty, the art galleries, the tall buildings, and the crowds on the street.
9. Extension courses may be taken for credit during any period of the year, and of course, at any place of residence.
10. Scouting develops a boy morally, mentally, and physically.
11. Convince her against her will I cannot.
12. The storm broke in all its fury at the close of a hot day.
13. Mr. Brown knew that he had made wrong decisions, that he should apologize, that he had made a mistake.
14. I met her in Boston, many years ago, in a shop on Tremont Street, late in the fall.
15. Around her shoulders was draped a gorgeous Spanish shawl.
16. The art of the Indians was crude, but a great deal of originality was shown by some of them.
17. Her charm, her friendliness, her generosity, and her neat appearance made her a favorite with the girls.
18. As we approached the house, lights were turned on and faces appeared at the windows.

19. Make the most of it if this be treason.
20. The car overturned when we struck a rut in the road

B. The following sentences are unemphatic statements of certain general truths which are stated emphatically in well-known epigrams and proverbs. Rewrite each sentence to give emphasis. Aim particularly for *conciseness.* Then compare your sentence with the original epigram or proverb.

1. The most appropriate name for woman is "Frailty."
2. If you take care in your work at the beginning, you will save yourself nine times the trouble later on.
3. Americans are willing to spend millions of dollars for defense armament, but they will not give one cent to appease an unjust aggressor.
4. Some people know how much a thing costs in dollars and cents, but they have no estimate of its human or moral value.
5. If you do not curb the native tendency of children toward selfishness and bad social behavior, you will be responsible for bad citizens in the future.
6. People who are constantly moving from place to place accumulate few worldly possessions.
7. If you have something to do, you should act promptly at the propitious moment.
8. Success in life comes to those who move with the greatest speed.

▸ Variety

30

Vary the length and the structure of your sentences to make your whole composition pleasing and effective.

Note: Can you distinguish readily between main clauses and subordinate clauses, clauses and phrases, compound sentences and compound predicates? Until you are able to do so you will have little success in learning how to vary your sentences. If necessary, master first the fundamentals of the sentence treated in Section **1, Sentence Sense,** especially **1d**; then study **Variety.**

Except for the loose, stringy sentences in **30c**, this section deals only with *good* sentences. Throughout Section **30** you are cautioned against monotonous repetition of any one type of sentence, not because these sentences are grammatically wrong, but because they do not combine to form a pleasing and effective pattern. Even the best sentence can become boring if it follows a long series of sentences similar in design.

Comparison of the two passages in the following example will illustrate the value of variety. The sentences in these parallel passages are equally correct, and the diction is the same. But one passage is made up entirely of simple or compound sentences. The other passage contains a varied sentence structure which is much more effective.

NOT VARIED

I had not time to be of help. The wrestler dropped at last, and Alan leaped back to get his distance. He ran upon the others like a bull, and he roared, and he went along. They broke before him like water, and they turned, and they ran. One fell against another in their haste.

VARIED

But I had not time to be of help. The wrestler dropped at last; and Alan, leaping back to get his distance, ran upon the others like a bull, roaring as he went. They broke before him like water, turning, and running, and falling one against another in their haste.

—ROBERT LOUIS STEVENSON

30a Usually avoid a series of short, simple sentences. Vary the length. (See also Section 29h.)

CHOPPY I settled back to my place. I recharged the three pistols. I had fired them earlier. I kept watch with both eye and ear.

IMPROVED I settled back to my place, recharging the three pistols I had fired, and keeping watch with both eye and ear —ROBERT LOUIS STEVENSON

30b Avoid a long series of sentences beginning with the subject. Vary the beginning.

This type of sentence, like all others discussed in Section 30b, is good. It should be at the command of every writer. In fact, the best writers begin about half their sentences with the subject—far more than in any other one way.[1] But some students use this kind of beginning almost exclusively. To avoid overuse, they should vary the subject-first beginning:

(1) Chiefly by opening with an adverb or an adverb clause.

SUBJECT *The injured man* lay beside the road and waited patiently for help. [Beginning with the subject—an excellent method that should be used for perhaps half of one's sentences but not for nearly all of them]

ADVERB *Patiently* lying beside the road, the injured man waited for help.

ADVERB CLAUSE *While the injured man was waiting for help,* he lay patiently beside the road.

(2) By opening with a prepositional or a participial phrase.

PREPOSITIONAL PHRASE *Beside the road* lay the injured man, waiting patiently for help.

PARTICIPIAL PHRASE *Lying beside the road,* the injured man waited patiently for help.

(3) By opening with a co-ordinating conjunction such as *but, and, or, nor,* or *yet.*

Effective sentences can often begin with a co-ordinating conjunction, but only when the conjunction shows the proper relation of the sentence to the preceding sentence.

CO-ORDINATING CONJUNCTION *But* the injured man, lying beside the road, waited patiently for help. [The *but* makes a contrast with something in the preceding sentence, such as, "The young woman wept and wrung her hands."]

---

[1] In a study of sentence beginnings George Summey, Jr., *American Punctuation,* New York, 1949, pp. 166-71, finds 53 per cent with subject, 28 per cent with adverb or adverb clause, 9 per cent with co-ordinating conjunction, leaving 10 per cent for all other types of beginnings.

CO-ORDINATING CONJUNCTION *And* the injured man, lying beside the road, waited patiently for help. [The *and* makes a simple addition to the preceding sentence.]

► EXERCISE 1. Compose a good sentence that begins with the subject. Then revise the sentence to vary the beginning in as many ways as you can.

► EXERCISE 2. In a piece of prose assigned by your instructor, classify the beginnings of the sentences into the types designated above.

30c Avoid the loose, stringy compound sentence. (See also 24b.)

The ineffective compound sentence may be improved:

(1) By using a subordinate clause.

AIMLESSLY COMPOUND The Mississippi River is one of the longest rivers in the world, and in the springtime it often overflows its banks, and many people are endangered.

IMPROVED The Mississippi River, which is one of the longest rivers in the world, often endangers many people during the springtime by overflowing its banks.

(2) By using a compound predicate.

AWKWARD He put on his coat, and next he picked up his hat and cane, and then he hurried from the house.

BETTER He put on his coat, picked up his hat and cane, and hurried from the house.

(3) By using an appositive or other modifiers.

COMPOUND The town had a population of three thousand, and a tornado struck it, and it was practically demolished.

IMPROVED The town, with its three thousand people, was struck by a tornado and practically demolished.

COMPOUND He was the mayor of the town, and he was a genial fellow, and he invited the four young boys into his study.

IMPROVED The mayor of the town, a genial fellow, invited the four young boys into his study.

(4) By using phrases.

COMPOUND The streets were icy and we could not drive the car.

IMPROVED Because of the icy streets we could not drive the car.

COMPOUND You will reach your destination tomorrow, and then you can take a long rest.

VARIED After reaching your destination tomorrow, you can take a long rest.

30d Learn how to vary the conventional subject-verb sequence by occasionally separating subject and verb by words or phrases.

SUBJECT–VERB The auditorium is across from the park and it is a gift of the alumni. [A loose compound sentence]

VARIED The auditorium, across from the park, is a gift of the alumni.

SUBJECT–VERB The crowd sympathized with the visitors and applauded every good play. [A good sentence]

VARIED The crowd, sympathizing with the visitors, applauded every good play.

Caution: Avoid awkward or needless separation of subject and verb. See 25a(5).

30e Learn how to vary the usual declarative statement with an occasional question, exclamation, exhortation, or command.

STATEMENT	We will fight to the end.
QUESTION	Who of us will not fight to the end?
EXCLAMATION	Imagine our nation not fighting to the very end!
EXHORTATION	Let us fight, then, to the very end.
COMMAND	Fight on, fellow citizens, fight to the end.

► EXERCISES ON VARIETY

Point out the sentence variety in the following paragraphs.

A. 1. The only house I had been the owner of before, if I except a boat, was a tent, which I used occasionally when making excursions in the summer, and this is still rolled up in my garret; but the boat, after passing from hand to hand, has gone down the stream of time. 2. With this more substantial shelter about me, I had made some progress toward settling in the world. 3. This frame, so slightly clad, was a sort of crystallization around me, and reacted on the builder. 4. It was suggestive somewhat as a picture in outlines. 5. I did not need to go outdoors to take the air, for the atmosphere within had lost none of its freshness. 6. It was not so much within-doors as behind a door where I sat, even in the rainiest weather. 7. The *Harivansa* says, "An abode without birds is like a meat without seasoning." 8. Such was not my abode, for I found myself suddenly neighbor to the birds; not by having imprisoned one, but having caged myself near them. —HENRY DAVID THOREAU

B. 1. Man has humanized only one power machine—the steam locomotive engine. 2. All his other creations are mere monsters of speed, or efficiency, or ingenuity, or all three. 3. Perhaps the reason for this one exception is that the steam locomotive engine breathes and seems to have moods like those of humans; it takes conscious pride in its strength and its endless labors for mankind. 4. To see one of them at the end of its long journey, panting at a railway terminal—a deep, quiet *"tsoo-tsoo, tsoo-tsoo"*—is to be tempted to speak to it, to thank it for its faithful service. 5. But one never feels that way about a motorbus or an electric engine, purely mechanical things. —JAMES NORMAN HALL [2]

C. 1. It was never a pilot that started the idea that night falls. 2. A pilot knows that it does not. 3. It oozes up out of the ground, fills the hollows and low places with purple pools of shadow that spread and rise to the tops of the trees and the houses. 4. Long before the sky has darkened, the world below is swimming in night. 5. And then finally darkness begins washing up over the sky from the east, climbing over the zenith, closing down at last over the final gleams of the sunset. 6. Here and there stars begin to prick through, larger and more liquid than ever seen from the ground, and the moon, big and white, outlines the earth. 7. Below the plane, lights map the town, race along the roads, accenting but not relieving the blackness, for darkness clings to the ground. 8. Whatever light there is clings to the sky to the last. —ALMA HEFLIN [3]

---

[2] From *Under a Thatched Roof* by James Norman Hall. As condensed in *The Reader's Digest.* Used by permission of Houghton Mifflin Company.

[3] From *Adventure Was the Compass* by Alma Heflin McCormick, by permission of the author.

LARGER ELEMENTS

▶ The Paragraph

31

Make paragraphs unified and coherent; develop them adequately.

A paragraph is a distinct unit of thought—usually a group of related sentences, though occasionally no more than one sentence—of an essay, a story, or a chapter. Just as chapters mark the chief divisions of books, paragraphs mark the chief divisions of chapters. The paragraph has two functions in a composition. First, it is a physical break in the page that allows the reader to rest his eyes. Second, it is a logical break, which allows the reader to collect his thoughts. It serves as a signpost of an approaching curve in the avenue of thought; or it warns him that he must take a new avenue of thought. It announces a new time, place, person, or thing in the course of a narrative, a different point of view in description, a new step in an exposition, or an advance in argument. If the paragraph served only the former, physical function, the writer would need only to chop his composition up into blocks of convenient length. But because of the second function the writer must consider the paragraph as a unit of thought and organize it accordingly around a central idea. Indeed, the paragraph might be defined as a group of sentences related to a central thought.

Length. Expository or argumentative paragraphs in current books and magazines are usually from 50 to 250 words in length, with the average perhaps 100 words. Paragraphs tend to run longer in books and shorter in the narrow columns of newspapers. Shorter paragraphs are more frequent in narrative writing, especially dialogue, in which each speech is paragraphed separately.

Indention. The first lines of paragraphs are indented uniformly, about one inch in longhand and five spaces in typewritten copy.

31a Give unity to the paragraph by making each sentence contribute to the central thought.

A paragraph is said to have unity when each sentence contributes to the central thought. Any sentence that fails to contribute violates the unity of the paragraph and should be omitted. The central thought is usually expressed in a *topic sentence,* often the first sentence of the paragraph, though it may come anywhere within the paragraph. Sometimes it is not expressed at all but merely implied.

In the following unified paragraphs the central idea, when expressed, is indicated by italics.

1 *A cornfield in July is a sultry place.* The soil is hot and dry; the wind comes across the lazily murmuring leaves

laden with a warm, sickening smell drawn from the rapidly growing, broad-flung banners of the corn. The sun, nearly vertical, drops a flood of dazzling light upon the field over which the cool shadows run, only to make the heat seem the more intense. —HAMLIN GARLAND

[Topic stated first]

2 From time to time the American economic system has been solemnly declared on the verge of ruin because of protective tariff, because of free trade, taxation policies, the abandonment of gold, labor unions, trusts, foreign agitators, Wall Street manipulators—what a list of total calamities could be compiled since 1900! Yet the American economy in sober fact, save for small setbacks in 1907 and 1921, and the large one in 1929, has grown like a green bay tree, to become today the wonder and envy of the world. The helpful indexes have gone up—population, production, output of inanimate energy, output per man hour, literacy, health, longevity—all up, while the curves of disease, slum-dwelling, poverty, have gone down. More than half of all American farmers are now enrolled in conservation districts, with the result that we are even beginning to save our soil. This comparison is given not to show that American economic problems are solved, only that *the facts have consistently belied the predictions of the economists.* —STUART CHASE [1]

[Topic stated last]

3 A man in cuffless shirt-sleeves with pink arm-garters, wearing a linen collar but no tie, yawned his way from Dyer's Drug Store across to the hotel. He leaned against the wall, scratched a while, sighed, and in a bored way gossiped with a man tilted back in a chair. A lumber-wagon, its long

---

1 From *Power of Words*, copyright, 1953, 1954, by Stuart Chase. Reprinted by permission of Harcourt, Brace and Company, Inc.

green box filled with large spools of barbed-wire fencing, creaked down the block. A Ford, in reverse, sounded as though it were shaking to pieces, then recovered and rattled away. In the Greek candy-store was the whine of a peanut-roaster, and the oily smell of nuts. —SINCLAIR LEWIS [2]

[Topic implied: *Such were the activities in Main Street.*]

► EXERCISE 1. Point out, or supply, the topic sentences for paragraphs 6 and 15 on the following pages, or for other paragraphs assigned by your instructor.

Note the lack of unity in the faulty paragraph below. All the sentences are about Michigan in general, but they do not develop any specific topic.

FAULTY PARAGRAPH

Michigan is a hunter's paradise. Deer, quail, and other kinds of wild game abound in the piny woods of the upper peninsula. Michigan has perhaps more coast line than any other state in the Union, being practically surrounded by Lake Superior, Lake Michigan, and Lake Huron. Along the coast almost every cove affords an ideal location for vacation camps. The lakes that fashion the state into two peninsulas, the upper and the lower, abound in fish which are eagerly sought by fishermen for pleasure or profit.

[The topic shifts from (1) *hunter's paradise* to (2) *coast line* providing sites for *vacation camps* and then to (3) *fishermen.* Each of these ideas might well be developed in a separate paragraph. Another remedy would be to supply a topic sentence, such as *Michigan is a paradise for the lover of the out-of-doors,* to which each of the ideas might be made to contribute.]

---

2 From *Main Street* by Sinclair Lewis, copyright, 1920, by Harcourt, Brace and Company, Inc.; renewed, 1948, by Sinclair Lewis. Reprinted by permission of the publishers.

IMPROVED PARAGRAPH

4 *Michigan is a paradise for the lover of the out-of-doors.* Made up of two peninsulas, the upper and the lower, it probably has more coast line than any other state in the Union. In the waters of Lake Superior, Lake Huron, and Lake Michigan, which practically surround the state, teem fish, eagerly sought by fishermen for pleasure or profit. Here every cove affords an ideal location for vacation camps. Anyone who prefers hunting to fishing can find deer, quail, and other kinds of game in the piny woods of the upper peninsula. Surely Nature was in an extravagant mood when she created Michigan.

31b Give coherence to the paragraph by so interlinking the sentences that the thought may flow smoothly from one sentence to the next.

A paragraph is said to have coherence when the relationship between sentences is clear, when the transition from one sentence to the next is easy and natural. The reader should be able to follow the thought without difficulty. In order to secure this coherence, this easy flow of the thought from sentence to sentence, the writer should rely first of all on (1) arrangement of the sentences in a clear order, and then on the use of (2) pronouns referring to the preceding sentence, (3) repeated words or ideas, (4) transitional expressions, and (5) parallel structure.

(1) Arrange the sentences of the paragraph in a clear, logical order.

There are several common, logical ways to order the sentences in a paragraph; the choice of an appropriate order depends upon the writer's purpose and the nature of his material. Perhaps the simplest and best order is "time" order.

POOR ARRANGEMENT OF SENTENCES

After the death of Saul, David ruled Israel for forty years. Once he incurred the king's anger and was driven ignominiously from court. As a shepherd lad he had lived in the hills of Judea. He had vanquished the mighty Philistine with his slingshot. The sad-faced Saul was charmed with his songs. He was the sweetest singer in all Israel.

[Confused time order]

ORDERLY SEQUENCE OF SENTENCES

5 David, the shepherd lad who lived in the hills of Judea, was the sweetest singer in all Israel. It was he who charmed the sad-faced Saul with his songs. It was he, too, who vanquished the mighty Philistine with his slingshot. Later he incurred the anger of Saul and was driven from court. But upon Saul's death David came back and ruled Israel for forty years.

[David's (1) *youth in Judea,* (2) *experiences with Saul,* and (3) *reign over Israel*]

This paragraph about David is made clearer by rearrangement in time order. Narrative paragraphs lend themselves naturally to such arrangement, and other types of paragraphs often have a time element that makes possible and natural a chronological arrangement. For example, in explaining a process—how something is done or made—the writer can follow the process through, step by step, from beginning to end. The following paragraph uses time order in explaining the difference between soaps and detergents.

6 Soaps and detergents have a "split personality" molecular structure, having one end that wants to dissolve in oil and the other end compatible with water. This can be seen by pouring mineral oil and water into a glass, and adding first some sodium-hydroxide (lye) solution, and then some salad oil, such as corn or olive oil. The sodium hydroxide will mix with water, and the salad oil will mix with mineral oil, but the oil and water layers still won't mix. However, if soap is added, the two layers can be mixed to form a milky emulsion. Soap combines in one molecule the fatty structure of the salad oil with the sodium from the sodium hydroxide, and shares the solubilities of the two minerals. —J. P. MULLEN [3]

Sentences that have no evident time order can sometimes be arranged in "space" order, in which the paragraph moves from east to west, from west to east, from the near to the distant, from the distant to the near, from the left to the right, etc. This order is used especially for descriptive paragraphs. Note the movement from east to west in the following paragraph:

7 In New England woods the fiddlehead ferns were unfolding, and blankets of wisteria spread over the houses. Outside Santa Fe, ribbons of green laced the brown adobe on the flatlands, and here and there the full-flowering lilacs formed purple buttons. On riverbanks of the Northwest, wild rhododendrons, spiraling up to thirty feet, were spreading red and pink and white blooms two hands wide. *Spring was full-blown in the United States, and the nation's prevailing mood seemed to be as bright as its blossoms.* —TIME [4]

---

[3] From "How Modern Detergents Work" by J. P. Mullen, *Popular Mechanics,* August 1955.

[4] Reprinted by permission of *Time* Magazine; copyright Time Inc. 1955.

[One comprehensive sweep from *New England* in the extreme northeast to *Santa Fe* in the mid southwest and then on to the great *Northwest,* with the topic stated in the last sentence]

Another good arrangement of sentences is in order of "climax," according to which the least important idea is stated first and the others in order of increasing importance, as in the following paragraph:

8 A black spot on the bright surface of the nation had been a huge, jagged patch of drought, spreading over large areas of the west, south and southwest. But last week, on much of the parched land, rain fell. At Hale Center, Texas, clouds that swept up from the gulf dumped six inches of rain in two hours. In other Texas cities, men and women stood and let the rain soak them to the skin, while children played in the swirling waters of overflowing gutters. The day after Secretary of State Dulles made his television report on international affairs, the top headline in the Omaha *World-Herald* exulted: RAINS UP TO 3 INCHES SOAK STATE'S DRY AREA. —TIME [5]

[The first two sentences, taken together, state the topic: *The drought areas have been relieved by rains.* The last three sentences, developing the topic, rise to a climax: (1) *The rain fell in torrents;* (2) *the people were so happy that they "let the rain soak them to the skin";* and (3) *the rains even stole the headlines from the most significant world affairs.*]

Sometimes the movement within the paragraph may be from the general to the particular, from the particular to the general, or from the familiar to the unfamiliar. A paragraph may begin with a general statement which is then supported by particular details, or, reversing the

[5] Reprinted by permission of *Time* Magazine; copyright Time Inc. 1955.

process, it may begin with a series of details and conclude with a summarizing statement. Note the movement from the general to the particular in the following paragraph:

> 9 In the ten years we have been married, I have yet to see Maurine act deviously. Although caginess is presumed to be a prerequisite for politics, she has marched to the top of the ballot by blurting out exactly what is in her mind. When she was asked to back a bill allocating a portion of dog-racing revenues for 4-H clubs, Maurine scolded her constituents for tying a worthy cause to pari-mutuel gambling. The special interests which she has offended would terrify most politicians—utility companies, dairy farmers, the Bar-Tenders' Union, the fairs in all thirty-six Oregon counties, slot-machine operators, the Farm Bureau Federation, even the American Legion.
>
> —RICHARD L. NEUBERGER [6]

[The first sentence states the topic: *Maurine never acts deviously.* The second sentence begins the development with a general statement about her positive action. The third sentence shows specifically how she faced up to the 4-H clubs, and the fourth lists other special interests defied in the same way.]

Paragraphs 6, 7, 8, and 9 above illustrate four of many possible types of clear sentence arrangement within the paragraph. Any order of sentences, or any combination of orders, is satisfactory so long as it makes the sequence of thought clear. Proper arrangement of the sentences is the first, the basic, step to insure good transitions from sentence to sentence. All other steps presuppose that the sentences have first been arranged in the clearest possible order.

---

[6] From "My Wife Put Me in the Senate," *Harper's Magazine,* June 1955.

► EXERCISE 2. Analyze paragraphs 16 and 17 below to determine the order used.

(2) Link sentences by means of pronouns referring to antecedents in preceding sentences. (See also Section 28.)

In the following paragraphs italics are used to indicate the pronouns serving as links between sentences. Such pronouns should usually come near the beginning of the sentence if they are to be of much use in paragraph coherence.

10 There is still a good book to be written about the legend of the heroic West and the cowboy. The author would have to be a social philosopher as well as an historian. The legend has not been with us long. That West has had a very short history. *It* did not begin until the 'sixties, and *its* Homeric age was over before the century ended. *It* was created by a passing set of economic circumstances, by cheap open grazing-land in the Southwest, and good prices on the hoof in Kansas City. *It* could not survive the invention of barbed wire. Yet what a legend *it* has created! —J. B. PRIESTLEY [7]

11 The crew are divided into two divisions, as equally as may be, called the watches. Of *these* the chief mate commands the larboard, and the second mate the starboard. *They* divide the time between them. . . .

—RICHARD HENRY DANA, JR.

► EXERCISE 3. Underline the pronouns used to link sentences in paragraphs 21 and 33, or in any others assigned by your instructor. Check the antecedent (in a preceding sentence) to which each pronoun refers. Underline the pronouns used to link sentences in your last theme.

---

[7] From *Midnight on the Desert.* By permission of the author.

(3) Link sentences by repeating words or ideas used in the preceding sentences.

In the next paragraph below, note the repetition of the key word *cowboys,* or *cowboy,* as one method of linking the sentences. In paragraph 13 an idea is repeated by means of a summarizing word.

12 It was here in Arizona that I first met cowboys. Many of these *cowboys* now spend more time taking parties of ranch guests out for a morning ride than they do in rounding up cattle. Nevertheless, they are genuine *cowboys.* As a rule they have known nothing but ranch life, and they have all the accomplishments of the legendary *cowboy,* except perhaps that famous marksmanship with a Colt. When not at work they practice for forthcoming rodeos or entertain themselves, and you, with that melancholy music, those long lugubrious strains, for which all men who lead an active open-air life seem to have a strange passion. Sedentary men may need gay cynical little tunes, but the *cowboy,* the sailor, the soldier, and their kind ask for nothing better than a gloomy ballad of true love cut short by early death. The *cowboy,* who is a man of tradition, keeps the traditional tone in song, an odd and rather nasal little tone, which would drive any singing-master mad but somehow pleases the rest of us. —J. B. PRIESTLEY[8]

13 The steward is the captain's servant, and has charge of the pantry, from which every one, even the mate himself, is excluded. These *distinctions* usually find him an enemy in the mate. . . . —RICHARD HENRY DANA, JR.

[*Distinctions* repeats an idea rather than a word.]

► EXERCISE 4. In paragraphs 26 and 30, or in any others assigned by your instructor, underline each word or idea

[8] From *Midnight on the Desert.* By permission of the author.

that is repeated in order to link the sentences within the paragraph. In your last theme underline words or ideas that are repeated as a means of linking sentences.

(4) Link sentences by using such transitional expressions as the following.

ADDITION moreover, further, furthermore, besides, and, and then, likewise, also, nor, too, again, in addition, equally important, next, first, secondly, thirdly, *etc.*, finally, last, lastly

CONTRAST but, yet, and yet, however, still, nevertheless, on the other hand, on the contrary, after all, notwithstanding, for all that, in contrast to this, at the same time, although this may be true

COMPARISON similarly, likewise, in like manner

PURPOSE to this end, for this purpose, with this object

RESULT hence, therefore, accordingly, consequently, thus, thereupon, wherefore

TIME meanwhile, at length, immediately, soon, after a few days, in the meantime, afterward

PLACE here, beyond, near by, opposite to, adjacent to, on the opposite side

SUMMARY, REPETITION, EXEMPLIFICATION, INTENSIFICATION to sum up, in brief, on the whole, in sum, in short, as I have said, in other words, to be sure, as has been noted, for example, for instance, in fact, indeed, in any event

EXAMPLES

It is the unpunctual who are the slaves of time, which constantly rushes them to and fro with whips and scourges. *Further,* unpunctual persons are unmannerly. —ARNOLD BENNETT

[Note also the repetition of the word *unpunctual* as an aid to coherence.]

It was also in the great hall of the palace of the Olympian king that the gods feasted each day on ambrosia and nectar, their food and drink, the latter being handed round by the lovely goddess Hebe. *Here* they conversed of the affairs of heaven and earth. . . . —THOMAS BULFINCH

[Note also the use of the pronoun *they* as an aid to coherence.]

They fought with more pertinacity than bulldogs. . . . *In the meanwhile* there came along a single red ant. . . .
—HENRY DAVID THOREAU

► EXERCISE 5. In paragraphs 25 and 27, or in any others assigned by your instructor, underline all transitional expressions used to link sentences within the paragraph. In your last theme underline all transitional expressions used to link sentences.

(5) Link sentences by means of parallel structure—that is, by repetition of the sentence pattern.

Note how the following paragraph is made coherent by the parallel structure of the last four sentences.

14 In the minds and in the ideals of Americans we have untouched natural resources that need developing just as much as the material treasures still tucked away in unused patents, in undeveloped river valleys, and in the atomic nuclei. For the next war, if one is still required to iron out national vanities, we shall need not so much manpower as brain power and alertness. For the continuing fight against disease, we shall need trained technical skills and unlimited resources in laboratory equipment and service. For the advancement of knowledge generally, we need a deliberate plan to free contemplative men for quiet and respected contemplation. For the realization of "fuller and more fruitful employment and a fuller and more fruitful life" we need a National Science Foundation and a country-wide awareness that governmental support for knowledge-research is henceforth basic in the national policy.

—HARLOW SHAPLEY [9]

► EXERCISE 6. In paragraphs 10 and 21, or in any others assigned by your instructor, point out instances of parallel structure used to link sentences within the paragraph. Can you find instances in your own writing?

We have observed that easy transition from sentence to sentence within the paragraph depends on clear arrangement of the sentences and then on linking these sentences by means of pronouns, repeated words or ideas, transitional expressions, and parallel structure. Usually several of these aids to coherence are found in a single paragraph. In the following paragraph the linking devices are italicized and explained in brackets. Note that the order is from the general to the particular.

15 *They* [pronoun: transition from the preceding paragraph] haven't any ideological principles, or if they have, they don't show. *Their* [pronoun: reference to *they,* subject of previous sentence] only commitment as far as I can see is the well-being of the whole island. *They* [pronoun: reference to *their* and *they* in last two sentences] are not tied up in either Marxian or free-enterprise straitjackets. *They* [pronoun: reference to *they* in last sentence, with some parallel structure] can think without looking it up in the book; they are flexible and mentally free to think out what needs to be done. If business can meet a *need* [repetition of *needs*], fine. *But* [transitional expression: contrast with last sentence] *if business cannot* [parallel

[9] From "Status Quo or Pioneer," *Harper's Magazine,* October 1945.

with *if business can*], then let the government do it, or a co-operative, or a non-profit association. The main thing is to get *it* [pronoun: reference to *it* in the last sentence] done. *They* [pronoun: reference to *they* in preceding sentences] have achieved what you once called "ideological immunity."

—STUART CHASE [10]

► EXERCISE 7. In paragraph 32 below, point out all devices used to insure easy transition from sentence to sentence.

(6) Transitions between paragraphs.

Transitions from one paragraph to the next are even more necessary than those between sentences within the paragraph. The reader takes it for granted that all sentences in one paragraph are on the same topic. But the paragraph break signals a new topic or a new phase of the preceding one, and the reader wants to know at once what the new one is to be. In the three connected paragraphs (16, 17, and 18) below, note how each opening sentence ties in with the preceding paragraph and also indicates the direction in which the new paragraph is to go.

16 In Philadelphia, the advantage of a small car was recently illustrated in a court of law. A baffled cop had dragged before a magistrate the owners of two MGs which had both been parked in the motor space designed for a single vehicle. It was the view of the cop that this arrangement resulted in an illicit mulcting of the city at the rate of a dime an hour. The magistrate disagreed; he commended the drivers for their ingenuity.

---

10 From *Power of Words*, copyright, 1953, 1954, by Stuart Chase. Reprinted by permission of Harcourt, Brace and Company, Inc.

17 Another and no less precious asset arises not so much from size as from lighter and differently distributed weight. A small car is supremely handy in icy weather. It is almost never trapped by snow or mud, and it will almost never lose traction on a slippery grade. Its skids are rare and gentle. And its driver can enjoy the soul-satisfying experience of wending his way up a steep and snowy hill at an even speed among big cars which have skidded into the gutter or which lie helplessly athwart the highway.

18 For many of the more than a million Americans who own two or more cars, these and other advantages have dictated the choice of a small car as a supplement to the basic big car. The combination of, say, a station wagon and an MG provides a nice balance between capacity and chic and provides an escape from the status of a two-car family with all the financial and social implications it involves. A small car doesn't seem to be *exactly* a car; its sheepish owner can treat it as a gadget and explain that it costs next to nothing to operate.

—LAURENCE LAFORE, R. W. LAFORE, AND R. W. LAFORE, JR.[11]

The topics of the three paragraphs may be stated thus: (16) *Ease of parking small cars was recently illustrated in Philadelphia.* (17) *The light weight of small cars is especially advantageous in icy weather.* (18) *The small car needs hardly to be considered a "second" car.* The opening sentence of paragraph 16 refers, by *advantage,* to the previously discussed ease of parking small cars and also leads up to the illustration to be used in the paragraph. The next paragraph begins with *another . . . asset,* showing at once that an additional advantage of

11 From "The Small Cars: Fun on Wheels," *Harper's Magazine,* March 1955.

small cars is to be pointed out (at the same time that *another* calls attention to the one just discussed). And *these and other advantages* in the opening sentence of paragraph 18 ties in with what has preceded while leading to what is to follow.

► EXERCISE 8. Analyze for transitions between paragraphs the seven paragraphs of "Riveting a Skyscraper" in Section 32, pages 378-81.

31c Develop the paragraph adequately. Supply enough information to satisfy the reader but avoid excessively long paragraphs.

(1) Supply enough information to satisfy the reader.

Avoid short, inadequately developed paragraphs. A topic sentence is not in itself a paragraph. In ordinary writing a very short paragraph is sometimes used for emphasis or for transition between longer paragraphs. But a *series* of paragraphs each less than fifty words in length (except in dialogue and other special types of writing) suggests inadequate development of the thought. If such choppy paragraphs deal with the same topic, they should be combined into one or more longer paragraphs. If not, each paragraph should be given adequate development.

PARAGRAPHS THAT SHOULD BE COMBINED

The line of demarcation between capitalism and socialism is sharp and clear.

Capitalism is that form of organization in which the means of production—and by that is meant the machine and the funds required to utilize the machine—are controlled by private individuals or by privately owned organizations.

Under a socialistic regime the control of the means of production, the control of capital—for even socialists concede the need for capital—is by the group. Under capitalism the profits accrue to the private individual; under socialism, to the group.

[These three short paragraphs, read together, actually make one unified paragraph of ninety words and should be so written. Taken separately, the paragraphs are short and choppy; together they form a paragraph of average length developing a clearly stated topic sentence: *The line of demarcation between capitalism and socialism is sharp and clear.*]

PARAGRAPHS THAT SHOULD BE EXPANDED

During his first term of office President Roosevelt introduced many laws to promote national recovery. These laws covered all phases of the national life.

[The reader wants to know specifically what some of these laws were.]

My father had an interesting life. I remember the time he began to tell us about the incidents of his boyhood on a Texas ranch.

[Obviously some of the incidents should be related.]

The football game was much more like a movie than like real life. The most improbable things happened.

[Some of the improbable happenings should be mentioned, and the implied contrast between the movies and real life elaborated.]

Each of these short paragraphs begins with a promising topic sentence and then stops before supplying enough information to satisfy the reader. In other words, the paragraphs are not adequately developed.

Methods of Paragraph Development

Analysis shows that good paragraphs may be developed by many methods and by innumerable combinations of methods. No one method, or combination of methods, is better than another except as it happens to fit the needs of a given paragraph. The experienced writer is probably unaware of the method he is using. But even though the particular method of development makes little difference, it is highly important that the development be full enough to satisfy or convince the reader. The inexperienced writer can learn how to fill out his own paragraphs by studying the methods of professional writers. One very common method of paragraph development is by listing the particulars and details suggested by the topic sentence (in italics in the following paragraph).

PARTICULARS AND DETAILS

19 *My aunt was a tall, hard-featured lady, but by no means ill-looking.* There was an inflexibility in her face, in her voice, in her gait and carriage, amply sufficient to account for the effect she had made upon a gentle creature like my mother; but her features were rather handsome than otherwise, though unbending and austere. I particularly noticed that she had a very quick, bright eye. Her hair, which was gray, was arranged in two plain divisions, under what I believe would be called a mobcap; I mean a cap, much more common then than now, with sidepieces fastening under the chin. Her dress was of a lavender color, and perfectly neat, but scantily made, as if she desired to be as little encumbered as possible. I remember that I thought it, in form, more like a riding habit with the superfluous skirt cut off, than anything else. She wore at her side a gentleman's gold watch, if I might judge from its

size and make, with an appropriate chain and seals; she had some linen at her throat not unlike a shirt collar, and things at her wrists like little shirt wristbands. —CHARLES DICKENS

[Details of features and dress fill out the picture of the stern but not ill-looking person of the topic sentence.]

► EXERCISE 9. Supply specific details to complete one of the following: (1) The sergeant was stern without being cruel. (2) His expression advertised his sense of humor. (3) Our cook was in almost perpetual emotion.

20 *The captain, in the first place, is lord paramount.* He stands no watch, comes and goes when he pleases, and is accountable to no one, and must be obeyed in everything, without a question, even from his chief officer. He has the power to turn his officers off duty, and even to break them and make them do duty as sailors in the forecastle. Where there are no passengers and no supercargo, as in our vessel, he has no companion but his own dignity, and no pleasure, unless he differs from most of his kind, but the consciousness of possessing supreme power, and, occasionally, the exercise of it.

—RICHARD HENRY DANA, JR.

[The paragraph lists particulars or details in which the captain is indeed "lord paramount," as stated in the topic sentence.]

► EXERCISE 10. Develop a paragraph by listing some important details in support of one of the following topic sentences: (1) The sergeant is the backbone of the army. (2) The dean is an important administrative officer. (3) The modern farmer is a scientist.

21 *My second great fortune was Lily Bess Campbell, professor of English literature at the University of California in Los Angeles.* She taught me to think exactly, to say the precise truth as nearly as I could perceive it. She taught me

that there is vitality in logic, that there is logic in humor and in beauty, that in humor the greater the truth the funnier, that in lyricism the more consistent and clear the more moving. She made me brief a Shelley ode as though it were a legal argument. She taught me that a sentence was organic with bones and sinews and for this reason had life, that the power of logic was a passionate power and that Euclid and Grammar were one. And for the first time I recognized Pattern, which is Law as well as Magic. —AGNES DE MILLE [12]

[The paragraph lists nine particulars in which Professor Campbell proved to be a "great fortune." Note that in this paragraph and in paragraphs 19 and 20, the order of development is from the general to the particular.]

INSTANCES OR EXAMPLES

22 *It is important to remember that, in strictness, there is no such thing as an uneducated man.* Take an extreme case. Suppose that an adult man, in the full vigor of his faculties, could be suddenly placed in the world, as Adam is said to have been, and then left to do as he best might. How long would he be left uneducated? Not five minutes. Nature would begin to teach him, through the eye, the ear, the touch, the properties of objects. Pain and pleasure would be at his elbow telling him to do this and avoid that; and by slow degrees the man would receive an education which, if narrow, would be thorough, real, and adequate to his circumstances, though there would be no extras and very few accomplishments.

—THOMAS HENRY HUXLEY

[The topic sentence is developed by the one example, admittedly extreme, of a hypothetical modern Adam.]

► EXERCISE 11. Develop one of the following sentences by an example in the manner suggested by Huxley's

[12] From "The Valor of Teaching" by Agnes de Mille, *Atlantic Monthly,* June 1955.

paragraph: (1) No man is wholly fearless. (2) Even an illiterate man can be wise.

23 To those who did not know the U.S. or who did not look closely, the mood of May 1955 might be mistaken for fatuous euphoria. *But beneath the glass surface there was a deep undercurrent, a persistent concern for country.* In Kentucky's Pennyroyal, where farmers were just finishing their tobacco-setting, a middle-aged farm wife apologized for paying too little attention to world affairs, then demonstrated that she had a remarkably clear understanding of what has been going on. "There seems to be a little less fear around," she said. "Fear's sort of lost its power. I thought it was pretty good that Mr. Dulles seemed to have gained what he's been struggling so hard for. He's been trying so hard for footing and he seems to have got it." —TIME [13]

[The first sentence makes the transition from the preceding paragraph. The topic sentence (the second) is developed by the one example of the Kentucky farm wife.]

24 Disregarding the words and observing any considerable segment of economic behavior, *it is immediately apparent that activities are mixed, sometimes inextricably tangled.* The Tennessee Valley Authority, for instance, is owned by the federal government, but encourages new private enterprise throughout the Valley, sells much power to private power companies, co-operates closely with state and local governments. Great corporations take on functions closely resembling governmental powers, as Peter Drucker has pointed out, while many private businesses are subsidized by governments—for example, trucks on the highways. —STUART CHASE [14]

[The topic sentence is developed by several examples.]

---

[13] Reprinted by permission of *Time* Magazine; copyright Time Inc. 1955.

[14] From *Power of Words,* copyright, 1953, 1954, by Stuart Chase. Reprinted by permission of Harcourt, Brace and Company, Inc.

25 *Perhaps the most extraordinary quality the Mohammedan religion developed in Jolo is its fanaticism.* For years, no Moro would attend school for fear of "invisible conversion" to Christianity. As recently as 1940 the students of one of the schools killed all their non-Moro teachers for no reason that the authorities were ever able to discern. And even today, some people of Jolo will not ride in a car, simply because Christians introduced automobiles to the island. It is also a problem for Moros to go to the hospital, because, according to their reasoning, if they died, a Christian would touch them, and this is not to be borne. —FAUBION BOWERS [15]

[The topic sentence is developed by four instances or examples, each in a separate sentence.]

➤ EXERCISE 12. Select a suitable topic sentence and develop a paragraph; use several instances or examples.

COMPARISON OR CONTRAST

26 *France offers the world a picture the very opposite of England.* The words of English diplomacy are fuzzy, confusing and, all too often, meaningless; the vigor of English diplomacy springs from the way Englishmen understand each other and stand united in purpose without need of wordy persuasion. French diplomacy speaks in lucid, clear analysis, but it speaks for a people divided from village roots to sovereign assembly. Even France's diplomats are divided; it is doubtful whether ten out of a hundred of the professionals at the Quai d'Orsay are wholeheartedly agreed that their government's support of European Union makes sense.

—THEODORE H. WHITE [16]

[The topic sentence is developed by contrasting England (in one long sentence) with France (in two long sentences).]

---

[15] From "The Land-Locked Pirate of the Pacific," *Harper's Magazine,* June 1955.

[16] From *Fire in the Ashes: Europe in Mid-Century* by Theodore H. White, by permission of William Sloane Associates. Copyright 1953 by Theodore H. White.

27 *In all the countries of Europe I have visited there is a patent difference between metropolises and smaller towns.* In the provinces of France, or Austria, or Germany you notice the difference in every shop window, in every coffee house, in the universities themselves. When, for instance, you go from Paris to Lille or to Orleans or to Bordeaux the dresses, the books, the furniture you see in the windows will lag some months if not years behind those you were used to seeing in Paris. The hotels and restaurants will be more modest, uncomfortable, and rather shabby. Universities will lack the stimulating élan of the Sorbonne. *Nothing of this kind distinguishes Madison from, let us say, New York or Chicago.* Here you see just the same merchandise in the windows as in New York, the same neon lights, the same pictures in the same movie theaters, you read the same columns and comics in the local papers as in those of New York, and the university with its splended installations, its rich library, its almost luxurious Students' Union certainly does not fall behind any university I saw in New York, though it is smaller.

—PAUL SCHRECKER[17]

[The implied topic sentence, derived from the two italicized sentences, is: In Europe, but not in America, there is a patent difference between metropolises and smaller towns. European conditions (in three sentences following the first italicized sentence) are contrasted with American conditions (in one very long sentence following the second italicized sentence). Note that instances or examples are used to develop the separate parts of the contrast.]

► EXERCISE 13. Develop by contrast one of the following topics: (1) the service in a lunch wagon and in a hotel dining room; (2) the dialogue of a motion picture and the dialogue of Shakespeare; (3) the architecture of the Washington Monument and of the Lincoln Memorial; (4) the relative effectiveness of radio and television.

---

[17] From "American Diary," *Harper's Magazine,* July 1944.

28 It is because of this universality of athletic sports that *English training is briefer and less severe.* The American makes, and is forced to make, a long and tedious business of getting fit, whereas an Englishman has merely to exercise and sleep a trifle more than usual, and this only for a brief period. Our oarsmen work daily from January to July, about six months, or did so before Mr. Lehmann brought English ideas among us; the English 'varsity crews row together nine or ten weeks. Our football players slog daily for six or seven weeks; English teams seldom or never "practice," and play at most two matches a week. Our track athletes are in training at frequent intervals throughout the college year, and are often at the training-table six weeks; in England six weeks is the maximum period of training, and the men as a rule are given only three days a week of exercise on the cinder-track. To an American training is an abnormal condition; to an Englishman it is the consummation of the normal. —JOHN CORBIN [18]

[The topic sentence is developed by the five following sentences, each of which contrasts American and English methods of training athletes. The first states the contrast in general terms; the second deals with rowing; the third with football; the fourth with track; and the fifth makes a general summarizing contrast.]

Note that the last three paragraphs illustrate two different ways of making the contrast. In paragraphs 26 and 27 one side of the contrast is completely developed and then the other; in paragraph 28 both sides are contrasted in each sentence. Either way is good, and so is a combination of the two.

► EXERCISE 14. Develop one of the topics given in Exercise 13 according to the method used in paragraph 28.

[18] From *An American at Oxford,* Houghton Mifflin Company, 1902.

DEFINITION

29 *Well, what I mean by Education is learning the rules of this mighty game.* In other words, education is the instruction of the intellect in the laws of Nature, under which name I include not merely things and their forces, but men and their ways; and the fashioning of the affections and of the will into an earnest and loving desire to move in harmony with those laws. For me, education means neither more nor less than this. Anything which professes to call itself education must be tried by this standard, and if it fails to stand the test, I will not call it education, whatever may be the force of authority or of numbers upon the other side.

—THOMAS HENRY HUXLEY

[The topic sentence, a definition of education, is further defined and explained by the other sentences in the paragraph.]

30 *A guaranteed annual wage is money paid by an employer to people for all or some part of a year in which they are not making products.* The payments are part of the manufacturer's cost and hence part of the consumer's cost. If the manufacturer has ten employees but work for only eight, he must nevertheless recover in the price he gets for his product the payments he makes to his employees for hours they did not work, or he must go out of business. This is true of any employer, whether he has ten or ten thousand employees.

—LELAND HAZARD [19]

[The topic sentence defines "guaranteed annual wage," and the remaining sentences serve to refine and clarify this definition.]

31-32 *The Romancer is an artist who deliberately sets out with the intention of representing life as it is not —as he would like it to be, perhaps, and as on rare and heroic*

---

19 From "Can We Afford a Guaranteed Wage?" by Leland Hazard, *Atlantic Monthly,* March 1955.

occasions it is, when the fire of humanity burns at its highest and hottest. He represents a world which is like our own, in a sense, but unlike it in the respect that it is infinitely more exciting, more vigorous, more interesting, more profound —more beautiful, in fact, with that beauty which the perceptive eye realizes in nature as in art. The Romancer arrives at this effect by a deliberate selection of qualities and characteristics, by a deliberate heightening of certain values and depressing of others. He does not aim at the development of character, but at the presentation of sentiment, and his characters become, not inconsequent and inconsistent human beings, but types of qualities.

The Realist, on the other hand, aims at presenting life as it is, and character as it develops. He is not afraid, as the Romancer is, of depicting any emotion that might be misinterpreted in a well-bred person. He does not wish to emphasize the driving force of the world, but he wishes to show, in a panoramic kind of way, how lives as a matter of fact do work themselves out, how they triumph, how they collapse. Of course, the Realist has to use selection too, because one cannot treat life in the mass; but his aim is not to represent either life at a high level, or life at a low level. He tries to give the true flavor of it, with its broken hopes, its successes that are often more hollow than its failures, its stolid complacencies, its meaningless sufferings, its baffling mysteries. But the essence of the Realist's art is that he has no preconceived idea of what life ought to be or might be; his one aim is to present it as it is.

—A. C. BENSON

[This pair of paragraphs exemplifies both definition and comparison and contrast. Each begins with a topic sentence which defines the subject of the paragraph. The definition is then supported by details.]

► EXERCISE 15. Using Benson's method, define one of these sets of opposites: (1) the Easterner and the Westerner; (2) the leader and the follower; (3) the typical male undergraduate and the typical co-ed.

MISCELLANEOUS PARAGRAPHS

Many good paragraphs are developed not by any one specific method but by a combination of methods. Some good paragraphs almost defy analysis. The important consideration is not the specific method used but the adequacy of the development.

33 I have heard rumors of visitors who were disappointed. The same people will be disappointed at the Day of Judgment. In fact, the Grand Canyon is a sort of landscape Day of Judgment. It is not a show place, a beauty spot, but a revelation. The Colorado River, which is powerful, turbulent, and so thick with silt that it is like a saw, made it with the help of the erosive forces of rain, frost, and wind, and some strange geological accidents; and all these together have been hard at work on it for the last seven or eight million years. It is the largest of the eighteen canyons of the Colorado River, is over two hundred miles long, has an average width of twelve miles, and is a good mile deep. It is the world's supreme example of erosion. But this is not what it really is. It is, I repeat, a revelation. The Colorado River made it, but you feel when you are there that God gave the Colorado River its instructions. It is all Beethoven's nine symphonies in stone and magic light. Even to remember that it is still there lifts up the heart. If I were an American, I should make my remembrance of it the final test of men, art, and policies. I should ask myself: Is this good enough to exist in the same country as the Canyon? How would I feel about this man, this kind of art, these political measures, if I were near that Rim? Every member or officer of the Federal Government ought to remind himself, with triumphant pride, that he is on the staff of the Grand Canyon. —J. B. PRIESTLEY [20]

---

20 From *Midnight on the Desert* by J. B. Priestley. By permission of the author.

► EXERCISE 16. Pick out the topic sentence in paragraph 33. Show how Priestley effectively develops his central idea. Does he use a specific method or combination of methods of development?

34 I wonder why American towns look so much alike that I sometimes mix them up in my memory. The reference to the standard influence of mass production whose agents are the traveling salesman, the mail-order houses, the five-and-ten cent stores, the chain stores, the movies, is not sufficient. If you stay two days in Bologna and in Ferrara, or in Arles and in Avignon, you will never mix them up in all your life. But it may well happen that after you spend two days in St. Louis and in Kansas City the images of these towns soon merge into one. I think the real reason for this is that these towns have not yet had time enough to individualize and to crystallize visible local traditions of their own. Physiognomically speaking, children are much less differentiated from each other than grown people. —PAUL SCHRECKER [21]

► EXERCISE 17. Notice how paragraph 34 has been developed by asking the question *why*. Develop a paragraph by asking yourself: (1) why you really came to college; (2) why you go to the movies; (3) why you prefer your favorite magazine; (4) why you enjoy college football games.

35 After Colonel Carter was gone home I went to work on my new horse. The old one, the pony, I used only for business: to go to fires, to see my friends, run errands, and go hunting with my new shotgun. But the game that had all my attention was the breaking in of the colt, the beautiful

---

[21] From "American Diary," *Harper's Magazine*, July 1944.

cream-colored mare, who soon knew me—and my pockets. I carried sugar to reward her when she did right, and she discovered where I carried it; so did the pony, and when I was busy they would push their noses into my pockets, both of which were torn down a good deal of the time. But the colt learned. I taught her to run around a circle, turn and go the other way at a signal. My sisters helped me. I held the long rope and the whip (for signaling), while one of the girls led the colt; it was hard work for them, but they took it in turns. One would lead the colt round and round till I snapped the whip; then she would turn, turning the colt, till the colt did it all by herself. And she was very quick. She shook hands with each of her four feet. She let us run under her, back and forth. She was slow only to carry me. Following Colonel Carter's instructions, I began by laying my arm or a surcingle over her back. If she trembled, I drew it slowly off. When she could abide it, I tried buckling it, tighter and tighter. I laid over her, too, a blanket, folded at first, then open, and, at last, I slipped up on her myself, sat there a second, and as she trembled, slid off. My sisters held her for me, and when I could get up and sit there a moment or two, I tied her at a block, and we, my sisters and I, made a procession of mounting and dismounting. She soon got used to this and would let us slide off over her rump, but it was a long, long time before she would carry me. —LINCOLN STEFFENS [22]

► EXERCISE 18. The topic sentence of paragraph 35—"But the game that had all my attention was the breaking in of the colt, etc."—is developed chiefly by giving details in time order. In like manner expand one of the following topics: (1) how I spent all my time training my hound; (2) how I shot my first deer; (3) how we won the football game; (4) how I got my first job; (5) how I cooked my first dinner.

---

22 From *The Autobiography of Lincoln Steffens,* copyright, 1931, by Harcourt, Brace and Company, Inc.

▶ EXERCISE 19. Indicate an appropriate method of developing each of the following topic sentences:

1. The school is the servant of the individual, the family, and the community.
2. The guaranteed annual wage has aroused much controversy.
3. There is more than one reason why the college student should study English.
4. My roommate has helped me to understand myself.
5. The changing aspects of the seasons are as stimulating as they are restful.
6. The companionship of man and animals contains secrets as important as the companionship of man and man.
7. A circus has many mouths to feed.
8. Before talking about democracy we should at least say what democracy is not.
9. If you don't trust my judgment about the value of reading, let me quote a few authorities.
10. Some men think our great cities are monuments of progress; others say they are symptoms of social disease.
11. You can solve most problems by taking a walk.
12. Intelligence means the ability to discriminate.
13. The farmer has recently acquired great popular esteem.
14. To be self-reliant one must know one's predominant weakness as well as one's predominant strength.
15. Three men showed me the true meaning of patriotism.
16. The ability to think and the ability to write are closely allied.
17. Soil erosion is a menace to national security.
18. When the storm was over we all set to work in earnest.
19. It is necessary to read *Hamlet* at least three times.

20. Railroads are a romantic element of the industrial age.

► EXERCISE 20. Select a topic sentence and develop a paragraph by one or more of the following methods:

1. Particulars and details
2. Instances or examples
3. Comparison or contrast
4. Definition

(2) Avoid excessively long paragraphs.

In current writing, paragraphs seldom run to more than two or three hundred words, and the average is much shorter, perhaps not more than one hundred words. Whenever a writer finds that he needs more than 250 words to develop his central thought, he should, if possible, divide his material into two or more paragraphs. Let us notice, for example, how we may divide the following long paragraph, which Richard Steele wrote more than two hundred years ago when readers were less hurried than those of our generation.

36 1. When a good artist would express any remarkable character in sculpture, he endeavors to work up his figure into all the perfections his imagination can form, and to imitate not so much what is, as what may or ought to be. 2. I shall follow their example, in the idea I am going to trace out of a fine gentleman, by assembling together such qualifications as seem requisite to make the character complete. 3. In order to do this I shall premise in general, that by a fine gentleman I mean a man completely qualified as well for the service and good as for the ornament and delight of society. 4. When I consider the frame of mind peculiar to a gentle-

man, I suppose it graced with all the dignity and elevation of spirit that human nature is capable of. 5. To this I would have joined a clear understanding, a reason free from prejudice, a steady judgment, and an extensive knowledge. 6. When I think of the heart of a gentleman, I imagine it firm and intrepid, void of all inordinate passions, and full of tenderness, compassion, and benevolence. 7. When I view the fine gentleman with regard to his manners, methinks I see him modest without bashfulness, frank and affable without impertinence, obliging and complaisant without servility, cheerful and in good humor without noise. 8. These amiable qualities are not easily obtained; neither are there many men that have a genius to excel this way. 9. A finished gentleman is perhaps the most uncommon of all the great characters in life. 10. Besides the natural endowments with which this distinguished man is to be born, he must run through a long series of education. 11. Before he makes his appearance and shines in the world, he must be principled in religion, instructed in all the moral virtues, and led through the whole course of the polite arts and sciences. 12. He should be no stranger to courts and to camps; he must travel to open his mind, to enlarge his views, to learn the policies and interests of foreign states, as well as to fashion and polish himself, and to get clear of national prejudices, of which every country has its share. 13. To all these more essential improvements he must not forget to add the fashionable ornaments of life, such as are the languages and the bodily exercises most in vogue; neither would I have him think even dress itself beneath his notice.

A careful reading shows that this whole paragraph of 404 words develops Steele's concept of the ideal gentleman. The paragraph has unity; except for the excessive length, there would be no reason for dividing it. Fortunately it can (like most overlong paragraphs) be divided into shorter paragraphs, each developing a specific part of the general topic. Steele's long paragraph can be divided, without any rewriting, into three good paragraphs as follows:

FIRST PARAGRAPH (sentences 1-3) The method to be used in depicting the ideal gentleman and a general definition of him.

SECOND PARAGRAPH (sentences 4-7) The ideal gentleman's specific qualities of mind, heart, and manners.

THIRD PARAGRAPH (sentences 8-13) The education needed to develop these qualities.

If the long paragraph were thus divided into three, it would be much easier for the reader, both for his eye and for his comprehension. And each paragraph would be well unified, with good transitions from one to the other. Note especially the excellent transition to the third paragraph: "These amiable qualities are not easily obtained; neither are there many men that have a genius to excel this way."

▶ Planning and Writing the Whole Composition

The four units of composition, in an ascending order, are (1) the word—Sections 19-22, (2) the sentence—Sections 23-30, (3) the paragraph—Section 31, and (4) the whole composition—Section 32. Words make up the sentence, sentences make up the paragraph, and paragraphs make up the whole composition.

32

Arrange and express your ideas effectively.

It has long been a convention of rhetoric to divide all writing into four main types—exposition or explanation, the most common kind of nonfiction writing and the kind most frequently written by college students; argument, similar to exposition but written with the intention of convincing rather than simply explaining; narration; and description. Very seldom is description written independently. Usually it is only part of a composition in which one of the other types dominates. In fact, few compositions are a single form of discourse. Most are mixtures with one form predominant. Thus, a paper on "How to Drive a Car" would be primarily exposition but would also contain bits of description (perhaps of the steering mechanism) and narration (perhaps an anecdote about the author's first drive). Whatever form of discourse a paper may take, it does not fall into order by chance. *Order is the result of careful planning.*

32a Choose an appropriate subject and limit it properly.

A subject is appropriate:

1. If it appeals to you, or if you can develop an interest in it as you work on it.
2. If it is acceptable to the intended reader.

A subject is properly limited:

1. If you know enough about it or can learn enough in a reasonable period. (Subjects that require extensive reading should be reserved for the library paper. See Section 33.)
2. If the topic is not too broad to treat in the time or space at your command. "Amateur Photography" might be a satisfactory title for a paper of several thousand words; but if you must limit yourself to several hundred words, you will do better with "Developing a Film" or "The Growth of My Interest in Photography."

Let us suppose that you have chosen (or have been assigned) the subject, "My Home Town—Rushville," for a paper of five hundred words. Obviously, you cannot cover everything to be said about your town in five hundred words. You must therefore find a more limited topic. You may be particularly interested in the town's industry, but "The Industries of Rushville" is still too broad for your short paper. So you concentrate on a single industry—perhaps the chief industry, paper making. Your topic then becomes "The Paper Industry in Rushville."

Central Idea. At this stage you will find it helpful to set down, in a single sentence, a central or controlling idea for your paper, such as "Paper manufacturing in Rushville is an interesting process" or "The prosperity of Rushville depends chiefly upon its paper industry" or "The paper industry in Rushville is not an unmixed blessing." This statement, in a single sentence, of the central or controlling idea helps to limit the subject and especially helps determine the items to be included in the outline. If the central idea is not determined in the process of limiting the subject, it should be written out before the outline is completed and then used to test the contents of the outline.

If you wish later to write another paper on your home town, you may use as your central idea "Rushville has a good school system" or (more limited) "Rushville has a well-rounded high-school program." If you wish to convince your readers of the need for action—that is, if you wish to write an argument—you may use a central idea like one of these:

1. Rushville should have a technical night school.
2. Rushville should authorize bonds for new school buildings.

If you wish to interest your readers in the history of your home town, you will choose a central idea suitable for a narrative:

1. The early settlers in Rushville had many difficulties with the Indians.
2. Rushville had a minor but interesting part in the Civil War.

If your purpose is to give a vivid picture of Rushville and its surroundings, you might select a central idea that lends itself to description, such as "Rushville has an interesting setting in the mountains."

Your home town, then—and many other subjects, for that matter—may suggest good topics for your papers, whether you wish to explain (exposition), to convince (argumentation), to narrate events (narration), to describe (description), or to combine two or more of these forms of discourse. The four forms should be used either separately or freely in combination, according to the demands of the topic. A combination of exposition and description might be used, for example, in a paper with one of these central ideas:

1. Colonel Brown is our most distinguished citizen.
2. Old Tony is the most colorful individual in Rushville.

Each of the suggestions listed below is a suitable subject for a student paper. Some of the suggestions, as worded, may provide the exact title you need for your paper. In all likelihood, however, you will wish to limit the subject to the scope of your experience and to sharpen the wording for use as a title. (For the proper capitalization of titles, see Section **9c**.)

Suggestions for Written Work

HOME AND THE INDIVIDUAL

1. My home town
2. Being an elder brother (*or* elder sister, only child, etc.)
3. My favorite author (*or* book, poem, magazine, newspaper, radio program, television program, etc.)
4. My hobby and why I like it (hiking; photography; collecting stamps, old glass, coins, books, furniture, etc.)

5. Learning to swim (*or* play tennis, ride horseback, sail a boat, ride a bicycle, skate, play the saxophone, etc.)
6. The efficient or attractive kitchen (*or* bathroom, living room, bedroom, playroom, etc.)
7. Color schemes (*or* draperies, period furniture, etc.) in interior decorating
8. Milk (meat, vegetables, etc.) in the diet
9. Changes in men's (women's) clothing
10. Peacetime draft and its effect on the individual

SCHOOL AND COLLEGE

1. Differences between school and college
2. Freshman Week
3. College slang
4. Earning one's way
5. My first field trip
6. The course I find most practical (*or* difficult, interesting, etc.)
7. The student union
8. Campus politics
9. My roommate
10. My room at college
11. The writing laboratory
12. Using a microscope
13. Are examinations fair?
14. The honor system
15. How to be a cheer leader
16. What makes school spirit?
17. Why I am going to college
18. Duties of the quarterback (*or* halfback, fullback, etc.)
19. What is sportsmanship?
20. Life in a dormitory (*or* fraternity house, sorority house, etc.)

HISTORY, ECONOMICS, AND SOCIOLOGY

1. What do our taxes buy?
2. Peacetime military conscription
3. The third term for President
4. The State of Israel
5. The Monroe Doctrine today
6. Our Foreign Aid Program
7. The guaranteed annual wage
8. The Iron Curtain
9. How to appraise a used car
10. Socialized medicine
11. Today's teen-agers

12. The National Park Service
13. Reforestation
14. Causes of juvenile delinquency
15. Living in a housing development
16. Radio and television advertising
17. The parole system
18. Unemployment insurance
19. Sharecroppers
20. The right to strike (*or* compulsory arbitration)

SCIENCE AND MEDICINE

1. Atomic submarines
2. Wild plants and their uses in medicine
3. The prevention of forest fires
4. Vitamins from plants
5. Color television
6. Chemical warfare on insects (*or* DDT, etc.)
7. Yeasts and vitamins
8. Migration of wild ducks and geese
9. Blood plasma
10. Beneficial bacteria
11. Synthetic diamonds
12. Nylon (*or* rayon, dacron, etc.)
13. Amateur photography
14. The Salk vaccine
15. What is food allergy?
16. Penicillin (*or* streptomycin, aureomycin, sulfathiazole, etc.)
17. Space flight
18. Coal, the raw material of many products
19. Uses of uranium
20. Plastic surgery

FARM AND MACHINE

1. Soil erosion
2. How to grow tomatoes (*or* asparagus, strawberries, celery, dahlias, mushrooms, chrysanthemums, etc.)
3. Wild life on the farm
4. The apple, from tree to consumer
5. New car designs
6. Good seeds make good crops
7. Judging cattle
8. Making a tobacco bed
9. Curing tobacco
10. The work of the 4-H Club (*or* home demonstration work, etc.)

11. Frozen foods
12. Newsprint from Southern pine
13. Electricity in the modern home
14. Air conditioning every home
15. Soilless farming
16. Electric (*or* gas) refrigeration
17. Mining coal (*or* lead, copper, zinc, etc.)
18. Building a skyscraper (*or* road, canal, dam, ship, etc.)
19. The most wonderful machine I know
20. Advantages of living on a farm (*or* in the city, in a small town)

► EXERCISE 1. Select one subject from the preceding "Suggestions for Written Work," limit it as necessary to make it a suitable topic for an expository paper of five hundred words, and write a single sentence expressing the central idea for the paper. Choose a suitable title for the paper.

► EXERCISE 2. Follow directions given under Exercise 1, substituting "argumentative" for "expository."

► EXERCISE 3. Follow directions given under Exercise 1, substituting "narrative" for "expository."

32b Develop the outline during the preparation of the paper. (See also 33c.)

The outline is the blueprint of the composition. Just as the carpenter or the engineer follows his blueprint implicitly in order to avoid costly structural blunders, so the writer—especially the student writer—follows his outline carefully so that he may arrange his ideas effectively.

But blueprints can be changed and improved, and so can outlines. The writer should make the outline his helpful tool; he should not become its slave. He should keep the outline a growing, developing plan which he will not hesitate to change at any stage of his composition whenever he hits upon a way to improve it. He will naturally try to perfect his outline before he starts to write the paper, but the actual writing will almost certainly suggest a few desirable changes in the arrangement of details.

The first step in the preparation of an outline is the jotting down of ideas on the topic. The student should not hesitate to jot down a long list of ideas; and he should jot them down rapidly, without much concern for the proper order. When he begins to classify his ideas, he will find it easy to reject needless ones; he may find also that he needs to supplement his knowledge by further observation or reading.

Suppose, for example, a student has selected subject No. 18 on page 366, "Building a Skyscraper," and has limited this subject to "Riveting a Skyscraper." From his observation of riveters at work, or from his reading on the process of riveting, he may jot down the following items:

1. Throwing the rivets
2. The gun
3. Noise of the gun
4. The catcher and his can
5. The bucker-up and his dolly bar
6. Work of the gun-man
7. The furnace
8. Skill required in heating
9. The rivet boy's duties
10. Danger from dropped rivets
11. Danger to the riveters

12. Co-operation of the gang
13. The alignment of the holes for the rivet
14. The inserting of the heated rivet
15. The complicated task of completing the work
16. Silence of the gang during the work

On inquiry or further reading, additional information may be added, such as:

17. Essential unity of the gang
18. Replacements
19. Experience required
20. Insurance rates for members

At this point—if he has not done so before—the writer should set down in one sentence the central idea of his proposed paper. For a short paper on "Riveters" this controlling idea might well be: "Riveting requires skillful work under dangerous conditions." Such a statement of the scope and purpose of the paper will often suggest, as we have already observed, items to be discarded and others to be added.

The next step in putting together an outline is the grouping, or classification, of the miscellaneous items under a few main headings. A little thought will show that general information about the gang should be gathered under one heading, and that material on the three steps in the actual process of riveting ought to be grouped under other headings. The general information would logically come first, the three steps next. Thus there would be the following main headings:

I. Skillful co-ordination of a riveting gang of four
II. Preparation of the rivets
III. Passing of the red-hot rivets
IV. Securing the rivets in place

Arrangement of the miscellaneous details under these four headings, with further additions during the writing of the paper, gives the final outline as it appears below.

32c Make an outline of the type specified by your instructor.

The types of outlines most commonly used are (1) the topic outline, (2) the sentence outline, and (3) the paragraph outline. Many persons prefer the sentence outline because the use of complete sentences forces the writer to express himself with greater clarity. Topic outlines and sentence outlines have the same parts and the same groupings; they differ only in the fullness of expression. In the paragraph outline no effort is made to classify the material into major headings and subheadings: the topic of each paragraph is simply listed in the order in which it is to come.

Topic Outline:

RIVETING A SKYSCRAPER

CENTRAL IDEA Riveting requires skillful work under dangerous conditions.

I. Skillful co-ordination of a riveting gang of four
  A. Unity of the gang
  B. Replacements of members
  C. Necessity for skill, judgment, and experience

II. Preparation of the rivets
  A. Delivery to the furnace
  B. Precarious position of the furnace
  C. Work of the heater
    1. His equipment
    2. His skill

III. Passing of the red-hot rivets
  A. Need for throwing
  B. Receptacle used by the catcher
  C. Dangerous position of the catcher
  D. Skill of the catcher
  E. Silence during the whole process

IV. Securing the rivets in place
  A. Alignment of the holes
  B. Insertion of the rivet
  C. Precarious work of the bucker-up
  D. Hard work of the gun-man
    1. Use of the heavy gun
    2. Concussion and vibration
    3. Assistance from the catcher
    4. Interchange with the bucker-up

Sentence Outline:

RIVETING A SKYSCRAPER

CENTRAL IDEA Riveting requires skillful work under dangerous conditions.

I. Riveters work in well co-ordinated, skillful gangs of four.
  A. The gang works as a unit.
  B. Replacements are made by an overlapping of service.
  C. The gang must have skill, judgment, and experience.

II. The rivets must be prepared under difficult conditions.
  A. The rivets are brought to the furnace by the rivet boy.
  B. The furnace stands in a precarious position.
  C. The heater must have specialized equipment and skill.
    1. He must have special clothing and tongs.
    2. He must have skill in order to heat the rivets properly.

III. Passing the rivets from the furnace to the place where they are used is an exacting and dangerous process.

   A. Rivets must be thrown, sometimes under difficult conditions.

   B. The catcher receives them in a battered tin "cup."

   C. He stands in a dangerous position.

   D. Only his skill in catching red-hot rivets insures the safety of the persons below.

   E. The whole process of passing rivets is conducted silently and methodically.

IV. Securing the rivets in place requires the exercise of great strength, dexterity, and co-operation.

   A. The gun-man and the bucker-up align the holes from dangerous positions.

   B. The catcher inserts the red-hot rivet.

   C. The bucker-up braces himself with his dolly bar against the end of the rivet.

   D. The gun-man has the heaviest work.

      1. He must handle the heavy gun.
      2. He must endure great concussion and vibration.
      3. He usually is assisted by the catcher.
      4. He sometimes passes the gun to the bucker-up.

Paragraph Outline:

RIVETING A SKYSCRAPER

CENTRAL IDEA Riveting requires skillful work under dangerous conditions.

1. Riveters work in well co-ordinated, skillful gangs of four men.
2. Rivets must be heated with care.
3. The red-hot rivets must be thrown to the place where the riveting is being done.
4. The catcher, standing in a dangerous position, must have great skill.

5. The whole process of throwing and catching the rivets is carried on in silence.
6. The catcher, the gun-man, and the bucker-up co-operate in securing the rivet in place.
7. The work of the gun-man is the hardest.

32d Make sure that the outline covers the subject, that it treats of everything promised in the title.

An adequate outline is essential to a successful composition. The major headings (I, II, III, etc.) must be sufficient in number and in scope to satisfy the expectation aroused by the title. And each of these major headings must, in turn, be covered by its subheads just as the title is covered by the major headings. These subheads, however, should not be unduly detailed.

WRONG (titles not adequately covered by the major headings)

Geology of the United States
I. States east of the Mississippi
II. Texas

History of the United States
I. Period before 1800
II. Period from 1800 till 1860

RIGHT (titles properly covered)

Geology of the United States
I. States east of the Mississippi
II. States west of the Mississippi

History of the United States
I. Period before 1800
II. Period from 1800 till 1860
III. Period since 1860

It would also be proper to leave the main headings unchanged and to alter the titles to agree, thus: "Geology of Texas and the States East of the Mississippi" and "History of the United States before the Civil War." In the same way the student can revise the title of his paper, thus limiting it further, if he finds that his original topic cannot be covered adequately in the allotted space. The title and the major headings of the completed outline must have the same scope.

32e Make sure that the parts of the outline are logically arranged.

Logical arrangement is second in importance only to adequacy. If the outline is disorganized and ineffective, the paper that follows it will also be disorganized and ineffective. (See also Section 31b.)

(1) Do not scatter your ideas.

Related ideas should be brought together. As the student begins his outline he ought to jot down as many ideas on the topic as possible, hastily, without regard to order. But then he must group these under two or more major headings. Compare the first hasty jotting down of ideas on "Riveting a Skyscraper" (pages 367-68) with the groupings in the finished outline.

(2) Arrange the parts in a natural, easy order.

The problem of arrangement within the paper as a whole is much the same as that within each separate paragraph. (See pages 330-34.) The nature of the subject will suggest an appropriate arrangement, such as time order, space order, or order of climax.

(3) Do not allow headings to overlap.

Overlapping often occurs when a writer attempts a division according to more than one principle.

WRONG (overlapping)

History of the United States

I. Period before 1800 [Time]
II. The South [Space]
III. Negroes [Group]

RIGHT (division according to a single principle)

History of the United States

I. Period before 1800
II. Period from 1800 till 1860
III. Period since 1860

I. The North
II. The South
III. The West

I. Indians and original settlers
II. Negroes
III. Immigrants

(4) Do not co-ordinate any heading that should be subordinated. Do not subordinate any heading that should be co-ordinated.

WRONG

History of the United States before the Civil War

I. Period before 1800
  A. Period from 1800 till 1860
II. The War of 1812
III. The Monroe Doctrine

RIGHT

History of the United States before the Civil War

I. Period before 1800
II. Period from 1800 till 1860
  A. The War of 1812
  B. The Monroe Doctrine

(5) Do not allow single headings or subheadings to stand anywhere in the outline.

Headings and subheads stand for divisions, and a division denotes at least two parts. Therefore, each outline must have at least two main headings, I and II. If it has a subhead marked A, it must also have a B. If it has a subhead marked 1, it must also have a 2.

ILLOGICAL

History of the United States

I. Period before 1800

If the history continues after 1800 the outline should indicate it by another major heading. Otherwise the title should read, "History of the United States before 1800."

32f Check the outline for the formal details of (1) notation and indention and (2) parallel structure.

(1) In the outline use consistently one system of notation, and indent headings to indicate degrees of subordination.

Any intelligible system of notation is acceptable. The one used for the complete sentence outline and the topical outline in Section 32c is in very common use and may well be adopted. This system, it will be noted, is as follows:

I.	[Used for major headings]
A.	[Used for subheadings of the first degree]
B.	
1.	[Used for subheadings of the second degree]
2.	

Seldom will a short outline (or even a longer one) need subordination beyond the first or second degree. If it does, it may use "a," "b," "c," etc., for the third degree and (1), (2), (3), etc., for the fourth degree.

The indention, as well as the notation, should indicate the degree of subordination. Major headings (I, II, III, etc.) should be indented equally, subheadings of the first degree (A, B, C, etc.) should be indented more, and subheads of the second degree (1, 2, 3, etc.) should be indented still more. If a heading or subheading runs beyond the end of the line, it is given "hanging indention," as in the sentence outline above.

(2) Give parallel structure to parallel parts of the outline to make clearer the co-ordination of the parts. (See the full discussion of parallel structure under Section 26.)

WRONG

II. Preparation of the rivets
- A. Delivering to the furnace [Participle or gerund as the core of the topic]
- B. Precarious position of the furnace [Noun]
- C. The heater works hard. [Sentence]
  - 1. His equipment [Noun]
  - 2. Skillful [Adjective]

RIGHT

II. Preparation of the rivets
- A. Delivery to the furnace [Noun]
- B. Precarious position of the furnace [Noun]
- C. The work of the heater [Noun]
  - 1. His equipment [Noun]
  - 2. His skill [Noun]

The major headings (I, II, III, etc.) should be expressed in parallel structure, as should each group of subheads. But it is unnecessary to strive for parallel structure between different groups of subheads; for example, between A, B, C under I and A, B, C under II. Parallel structure is no problem in the complete sentence outline, for parallelism is insured by the requirement of complete sentences.

32g Write the paper from the outline.

Once you have checked your outline to make sure that it covers the subject (see 32d), is logically arranged (32e), and has proper notation, indention, and parallel structure (32f), you are ready to write the paper. You simply write a series of effective paragraphs, with good transitions between them (see 31), to cover all items in the outline, taking up each item in the order in which it comes in the outline. The actual writing of the paper will probably suggest a better arrangement for some of the details. If so, the proper changes should be made in the outline so that the finished paper and the outline will agree fully.

(1) The paragraphs in relation to the outline. Although the paragraphs must develop the headings (including the subheadings) of the outline in the exact order in which they come in the outline, there is no rule regarding the number of these headings a paragraph may cover. In a general way, however, the writer is limited by the need to make each paragraph a unit and to keep it from being unduly long or short. Let us notice, for example, how the seven paragraphs of "Riveting a Skyscraper" (see pages 378-81) are related to the topic outline (see page 369). The writer could secure unity for his first paragraph by treating only A ("Unity of the gang") under I, or by treating A, B, and C together since these three form a unit under I ("Skillful co-ordination of a riveting gang of four"). The deciding factor is usually the number of words needed for adequate treatment. Since only 235 words are required to treat A, B, and C together, a single paragraph is used. Similarly, the second paragraph of 215 words covers the whole of II. But since 420 words are needed to cover III, the writer uses three paragraphs. The first—130 words—covers A and B (throwing and catching the rivets), the second—202 words—covers C and D (the catcher's dangerous position and skill), and the third—88 words—covers E (the silence of the gang). It is possible to use A and B together in the same paragraph only because they form a unit, and the same is true of C and D. The last two paragraphs of the article cover IV, the first—168 words—covering A, B, and C as a unit, and the second—155 words—covering D.

► EXERCISE 4. Note that the following article on "Riveting a Skyscraper" follows the exact order of the topic (or sentence) outline. Note also how much of the article is covered by each heading and subheading, and indicate in the margin of the article the point at which the treatment of each begins.

RIVETING A SKYSCRAPER[1]

The most curious fact about a riveter's skill is that he is not one man but four: "heater," "catcher," "bucker-up," and "gunman." The gang is the unit. Riveters are hired and fired as gangs, work in gangs, and learn in gangs. If one member of a gang is absent on a given morning, the entire gang is replaced. A gang may continue to exist after its original members have all succumbed to slippery girders or the business end of a pneumatic hammer or to a foreman's zeal or merely to the temptations of life on earth. And the skill of the gang will continue with it. Men overlap each other in service and teach

[1] Reprinted by special permission from the October 1930 issue of *Fortune* Magazine; © 1930 by Time Inc.; all rights reserved under International and Pan-American Copyright Conventions.

each other what they know. The difference between a gang which can drive 525 inch-and-an-eighth rivets in a working day and a gang which can drive 250 is a difference of co-ordination and smoothness. You learn how not to make mistakes and how not to waste time. You learn how to heat a rivet and how not to overheat it, how to throw it accurately but not too hard, how to drive it and when to stop driving it, and precisely how much you can drink in a cold wind or a July sun without losing your sense of width and the balance of a wooden plank. And all these things, or most of them, an older hand can tell you.

The actual process of riveting is simple enough—in description. Rivets are carried to the job by the rivet boy, a riveter's apprentice whose ambition it is to replace one of the members of the gang—which one, he leaves to luck. The rivets are dumped into a keg beside a small coke furnace. The furnace stands on a platform of loose boards roped to steel girders which may or may not have been riveted. If they have not been riveted there will be a certain amount of play in the temporary bolts. The furnace is tended by the heater or passer. He wears heavy clothes and gloves to protect him from the flying sparks and intense heat of his work, and he holds a pair of tongs about a foot-and-a-half long in his right hand. When a rivet is needed, he whirls the furnace blower until the coke is white hot, picks up a rivet with his tongs, and drives it into the coals. His skill as a heater appears in his knowledge of the exact time necessary to heat the steel. If he overheats it, it will flake, and the flakes will permit the rivet to turn in its hole. And a rivet which gives in its hole is condemned by the inspectors.

When the heater judges that his rivet is right, he turns to face the catcher, who may be above or below him or fifty or sixty or eighty feet away on the same floor level with the naked girders between. There is no means of handing the rivet over. It must be thrown. And it must be accurately thrown. And if the floor beams of the floor above have been laid so that a flat trajectory is essential, it must be thrown with considerable force. The catcher is therefore armed with a smallish, battered tin can, called a "cup," with which to catch the red-hot steel. Various patented cups have been put upon the market from time to time, but they have made little headway. Catchers prefer the ancient can.

The catcher's position is not exactly one which a sportsman catching rivets for pleasure would choose. He stands upon a narrow platform of loose planks laid over needle beams and roped to a girder near the connection upon which the gang is at work. There are live coils of pneumatic tubing for a rivet gun around his feet. If he moves more than a step or two in any direction, he is gone; and if he loses his balance backward he is apt to end up at street level without time to walk. And the object is to catch a red-hot iron rivet weighing anywhere from a quarter of a pound to a pound and a half and capable, if he lets it pass, of drilling an automobile radiator or a man's skull 500 feet below as neatly as a shank of shrapnel. Why more rivets do not fall is the great mystery of skyscraper construction. The only reasonable explanation offered to date is the reply of an erector's foreman who was asked what would happen if a catcher on the Forty Wall Street job let a rivet go by him around lunch hour. "Well," said the foreman, "he's not supposed to."

There is practically no exchange of words among riveters. Not only are they averse to conversation, which would be reasonable enough in view of the effect they have on the conversation of others, but they are averse to speech in any form. The catcher faces the heater. He holds his tin can up. The heater swings his tongs, releasing one handle. The red iron arcs through the air in one of those parabolas so much admired by the stenographers in the neighboring windows. And the tin can clanks.

Meantime the gun-man and the bucker-up have prepared the connection—aligning the two holes, if necessary, with a drift pin driven by a sledge or by a pneumatic hammer—and removed the temporary bolts. They, too, stand on loose-roped boards with a column or the beam between them. When the rivet strikes the catcher's can, he picks it out with a pair of tongs held in his right hand, knocks it sharply against the steel to shake off the glowing flakes, and rams it into the hole, an operation which is responsible for his alternative title of sticker. Once the rivet is in place, the bucker-up braces himself with his dolly bar, a short heavy bar of steel, against the capped end of the rivet. On outside wall work he is sometimes obliged to hold on by one elbow with his weight out over the street and the jar of the riveting shaking his precarious balance. And the gun-man lifts his pneumatic hammer to the rivet's other end.

The gun-man's work is the hardest work, physically, done by the gang. The hammers in use for steel construction work are supposed to weigh around thirty pounds and actually weigh about thirty-five. They must not only be held against the rivet end, but held there with the gun-man's entire strength, and for a period of forty to sixty seconds. (A rivet driven too long will develop a collar inside the new head.) And the concussion to the ears and to the arms during that period is very great. The whole platform shakes, and the vibration can be felt down the column thirty stories below. It is common practice for the catcher to push with the gun-man, and for the gun-man and the bucker-up to pass the gun back and forth between them when the angle is difficult. Also on a heavy rivet job the catcher and the bucker-up may relieve the gun-man at the gun.

(2) Effective beginnings and endings. Seldom does a short paper need a formal introduction or conclusion. Usually it is wise to begin promptly and to end as soon as the last topic has been adequately treated. Even when some part of the outline is to serve as an introduction or conclusion it should not be called merely "introduction" or "conclusion" but should be given a more informative heading.

Note the lack of any formal beginning or ending in the effective short article (see above) on "Riveting a

Skyscraper." The longer library paper on "The French Horn: Its Development and Use" (see pages 429-48) also begins promptly with a striking fact that arouses the reader's interest at the same time that it starts the development of the topic. The last paragraph rounds out the paper by emphasizing the great improvement in the French horn since its humble origin. The last paragraph serves as a brief and effective conclusion, but it is not called "conclusion" in the outline.

▶ EXERCISES ON OUTLINING AND WRITING

A. Make (1) a topic outline, (2) a sentence outline, and (3) a paragraph outline on the subject used for Exercise 1 above. Then check your outlines with the principles set forth in 32d-f.

B. Write a 500-word paper based on the topic outline prepared for Exercise A.

C. Revise the paper written for Exercise B, using the following check list. Follow through on one point at a time. (If you make many errors in grammar, etc., you should follow the more detailed check list on page 94.)

1. Have I stated my central idea clearly, and have I developed it adequately in the paper?
2. Is my paper correct as regards manuscript form, grammar and mechanics, punctuation, and spelling?
3. Is the diction standard, exact, concise? (See Sections 19-22.)
4. Are the sentences as effective as possible? (See Sections 23-30.)
5. Are the paragraphs properly developed? (See Section 31.)
6. Does the outline follow exactly the final version of the paper? (If not, revise the outline to fit the paper.)

Student Papers—with Analyses

The writer should always remember that the content, or subject matter, of his paper is first in importance. Because much student writing is filled with errors in grammar, spelling, and punctuation (as in the student paragraph reproduced on pages 96-97), the instructor's comments often must be limited to mechanical corrections. The student should overcome his deficiencies in grammar, spelling, and mechanics as rapidly as possible so that he and the instructor may give fuller attention to the more important problems of content and organization, as illustrated in the comments on the following specimen student papers.

(1) COFFEE

A definition might be given to coffee that would explain what this drink does to a person's system. I would define coffee as a drink that contains caffeine and is drunk in the early morning to soothe a person's shattered nerves.

Another interesting fact about coffee is that no matter how high the price may go, a person will always pay the required amount. If coffee does lift in price, people at first grumble about how they are not going to pay the price. But a little later you might hear the same person asking a friend to have a cup of coffee with him.

Coffee outranks all other beverages in demand. A great many people drink whiskey, wine, and beer, but they will always choose a cup of coffee after they have taken a few drinks of some alcoholic beverage to dispose of their hangover.

Coffee, along with smoking cigarettes, is an essential drink to nervous people, to people who drink alcoholic beverages, and most of all to husbands whose wives are expecting babies. Nervous people take this drink to soothe their nerves and stimulate themselves. People who drink take it to rid themselves of hangovers. And husbands who are pacing the floor because their wives are expecting babies must have a cup of coffee in their hand to keep themselves from chewing their fingernails off up to their elbows. Therefore, coffee is the essential drink in our everyday environment.

Comment on Content and Composition: Your paper shows some planning, but not nearly enough. As a first rough draft it might have served very well for development into a good paper. But you have left it full of inconsistencies.

In paragraph 1 you propose to define coffee according to what it does to a person's system. But you never do. Instead you describe it as a beverage "drunk in the early morning to settle a person's shattered nerves." That is what it is *supposed* to do to the *nerves.* We never are told what it *does* to the *system.*

But paragraph 2 immediately disregards the "early morning" and "shattered nerves" limit you put on coffee drinking and shows two friends—obviously later in the day—drinking coffee, not for shattered nerves, but apparently out of mere sociability. Furthermore, you begin the paragraph with the words "another interesting fact." No interesting fact has preceded it.

Paragraph 3 may be consistent enough with the morning-nerves limit; but look at the way you have stated the matter. Has the alcohol been taken to dispose of the hangover?

In paragraph 4 your phrasing suggests that smoking cigarettes is also "an essential drink." Further on you imply (if your first-paragraph description still holds) that the birth pangs of expectant fatherhood occur only in the early morning. And your last sentence indicates that early morning every day finds us in a state either of shattered nerves, post-alcoholism, or maternity-corridor vigilance.

Surely these states do occur. But you yourself must know that they are accountable for very little of the coffee an average coffee drinker consumes in his lifetime. Yet you indicate that they are *the* causes. You need to pay more attention to the logical consistency of your entire paper.

Suggestions for Improvement: Concentrate on a central idea for the whole paper. You might be able to use the concluding statement that you have here; but modify it, since *essential* is too strong a word to fit the facts. Then choose a more specific title—one which contains or suggests the central idea of the paper and no more. Next eliminate anything you have written that is not a development of the central idea: paragraph 2 will probably have to go. Make an outline of what you have left. You will probably see that the outline needs revising. Revise it; and then rewrite the paper.

(2) IGNORANCE IS BLISS

Have you ever been to a mountainous country and noticed how happy the people are? That is usually because they have had very little schooling and are just too dumb to get along in the outside world. They are happy just sitting around the porch on the general store and shooting the breeze. Their homes as a rule are old weather-beaten shacks and the furniture is that which has been handed down from their grandparents. These people enjoy that life and are not educated enough to strive for any better things in life. You will always find them laughing, talking, and joking. "What is wrong with this life?" you ask. Well, if they were not quite so ignorant, they might have a longer life span and a much cleaner life. People in big cities are not half as happy-go-lucky as the mountaineers, but they have very nice homes and much cleaner habits.

I can't help noticing the unfriendly attitude of the

teachers and students. Everyone seems to be in too much of a hurry to ever speak. I have never seen so many sour faces in all my life. This fact seems to prove my statements and goes as further evidence to prove that ignorance is bliss. You have to have a lot of knowledge to get into a college, and it seems that people in a university would be called an educated group. The people in college are always worried about getting ready for a big test, and if they fail it they are downhearted. They never seem happy. But the mountaineers are always happy and never seem to worry about a thing. Therefore ignorance must be bliss.

Comments: Your paper breaks off in the middle, where suddenly you begin to discuss college people without any indication of a reason for the shift. You need to provide some sort of transition. Furthermore, although you mention three groups —mountaineers, people in big cities, and college people—you neglect altogether to develop any discussion of the middle group.

Your arguments suffer from the two faults in logic known as "begging the question" and "false cause."

An argument "begs the question" when it assumes as already proven that which it sets out to prove. You set out to prove that ignorance is the cause of bliss. Yet, without proving it, you make the initial assumption that mountaineers are happy "usually *because* they have had very little schooling and are just too dumb to get along in the outside world."

An argument uses "false cause" when, finding two facts to exist simultaneously, it assumes without sufficient evidence that one is the cause of the other. You produce no evidence to show that, when ignorance and bliss are found together, the one has caused the other.

Actually the facts which common experience shows—your own experience included, if you would only examine it—are that some ignorant mountaineers are altogether miserable and that some college people are quite happy. Bliss, therefore, does not require ignorance to produce it; and bliss may be entirely lacking where ignorance is plentifully present.

This same analysis can be applied to your argument concerning college people.

Suggestions for Improvement: The only assumptions which the facts will support are that among mountaineers many who are happy are also ignorant and that among college people who are in pursuit of learning many are also miserable. And the only safe conclusion is that there *may* therefore be some relationship between ignorance and bliss.

Rewrite the paper with these cautions in mind; provide a suitable transition to introduce your second argument; and eliminate mention of city people unless you are going to develop an additional argument using their circumstances as supporting evidence.

(3) ATHLETICS: MORE WORK THAN PLAY

Athletics to the average participant may be more work than play. The star acquires a love for the game because he is given recognition for his playing and people look up to him as a marvel. But to the average athlete the steady grind of practice soon becomes old. He works and plays hard, but all his efforts are in vain because the star is getting all the recognition for the whole team's work.

When people watch a football game, they watch the man with the ball. Most of them never see the vicious block which was thrown by one of the linemen. And when the paper comes out the day following the game, the back who ran the touchdown is given all the credit. But nothing is said about the lineman who threw the block which set up the touchdown. The back receives the glory; and glory is the "play" that comes from athletics.

The man who does all the handling of the ball is getting the play from the game; the man who is there only to aid the player with the ball to score is doing only work. Football, for a man who never gets his hands on the ball, will then be nothing but work, if he is not given recognition for his playing.

The man who gets recognition after a hard-fought game does not mind the next week's practice, because he may repeat himself in the next game and again he may receive much glory. The boy who is not mentioned will be exactly the opposite; he will hate the week's practice that is to follow. The practice will be all work and no play.

The best example of a boy who works hard on a team and receives no recognition is the center on a football team. He makes the pass to the back, who runs his heart out for the glory. The backfield man will get his glory when the writing concerning the game comes out in the paper. But the center is never mentioned for his precision passes to the backs.

This unfairness could be remedied if the newspaper writers, coaches, and spectators would let it be known in some way that they knew the noncarrying man on the team had played a great game and that he was also responsible for the winning of the game. Athletics then would automatically become more play than work. But as it is at the present time, athletics for most players is more work than play.

Comments and Suggestions for Improvement: This paper begins well and ends well. It is only in the middle part that it is somewhat less than satisfactory.

Good as your beginning is, however, it would improve the paper as a whole if you would indicate, both in your title and very early in your first paragraph, that you are going to discuss football particularly and not athletics generally.

Your second and fourth paragraphs make good use of devices of paragraph development: the second introduces concrete examples to bear out the more generalized comments made earlier; and the fourth very effectively uses the element of contrast.

But there is little if anything said in your third paragraph that is not adequately said elsewhere. Your paper would gain rather than lose if you omitted this paragraph altogether.

Likewise, your fifth paragraph does over again what is already sufficiently done in your second. You make exactly the same point, using the center as an example, as you had already made using the blocking lineman. The fifth paragraph can be eliminated as well as the third.

Then, with a very slight transition furnished to lead into your final paragraph, you will have a well and compactly built argument. As your paper stands now, it is slowed down by the surplus it is carrying. Condition it down; work some of the fat off it. That is about all it needs.

(For the use of numbers or symbols in the correction of errors in grammar, mechanics, punctuation, spelling, etc., see Section 8, pages 96-97.)

▶ Library Paper

33

Learn how to use the library as you prepare a library paper.

In writing the usual expository paper, as explained in Section 32, you have already faced some of the problems of the library paper (also called a research, a reference, or a term paper)—that is, a paper based on materials to be found in the library, with references to the sources of information. You have, for example, already considered the problems of finding and limiting a subject (32a), of making an outline (32b-f), and of writing the paper from the outline (32g). Your only new problems will be (1) finding in the library the needed sources of information and listing these in a bibliography; (2) taking notes from which the paper can be written; and (3) using footnotes to show the exact sources of information.

Section 33 treats these new problems in some detail (and the other problems briefly) by following through the five steps in the preparation of a library paper:

a. Selecting and limiting the subject. (See p. 391.)
b. Preparing the bibliography. (See pp. 391-412.)
c. Making the outline. (See pp. 412-15).
d. Taking notes. (See pp. 415-19.)
e. Writing the paper—with footnotes. (See pp. 420-28.)

Each of these steps is illustrated in the preparation of a sample library paper, which is then given in full at the end of the section.

33a Select and limit the subject. (Follow the general suggestions given under Section 32a.)

Let us suppose that a student is interested in the general field of music and has limited his subject to the orchestra. But since this is still a subject broad enough for a book, he decides to limit himself further to one of the many instruments in the orchestra, selecting the one in which he has a special interest—the French horn. This topic is sufficiently limited for adequate treatment in a paper of two or three thousand words, the length most frequently used for library papers.

► EXERCISE 1. List three general fields in which you have some interest. Then by process of limitation derive three topics (1) which are suitable for library papers of two or three thousand words each and (2) in which you have a special interest. The subject headings and the cross references in the card catalogue or the *Readers' Guide* (see 33b below) may suggest subjects and possible limitations of them.

33b Prepare the bibliography (and learn your way about the library).

The bibliography lists sources of information—such as books, pamphlets, and articles—from which the student will draw the material for his paper on the French horn. Throughout his college career he will be called upon to write papers for which he will need to prepare bibliographies. To teach the student how to get needed information readily from the library is perhaps the chief purpose of the library paper. As he begins his search, he tries to determine whether he can find enough material on his specific topic and, if so, writes down the most promising titles, thus making up a preliminary bibliography. (Later he will probably drop from the list some books and articles that prove of little value, and will add useful references as he discovers them. The final bibliography will include only those works that help in the writing of the paper—usually those cited in the footnotes.)

Keys to the Library

The chief keys to information in the library are (1) the card catalogue, (2) the indexes to periodicals, and (3) the general reference books.[1]

(1) Learn how to use the card catalogue.

The card catalogue is the index to the whole library. It lists all books and all bound magazines, whether they are housed in the stacks, on the open shelves of the reference room, or in any other part of the building. In many libraries one general card catalogue lists all books owned by the university and indicates whether the book is kept in the general library or with some special collection in another building.

Usually the card catalogue consists of cards 3 x 5 inches in size, arranged alphabetically in drawers. These may

[1] Although the card catalogue and the periodical indexes are the chief keys to the library, the student may find it best to start with reference books, especially with articles in general encyclopedias which give a brief survey of his topic, often including a short bibliography.

be "author" cards, "title" cards, or "subject" cards; for in most libraries each book is listed—in its proper alphabetical place—once according to its author, again according to its title, and yet again according to its subject or subjects. Let us take, for example, *Thesaurus of Orchestral Devices,* by Gardner Read. If the student writing on "The French Horn" wishes to determine whether his library has this book, he may look under the name of the author—Read, Gardner. But if he does not know the author's given name, he may save time by looking for the book under the title—*Thesaurus of Orchestral Devices.* This is given on what is called a title card, which is identical with the author card except for the typewritten title at the top. The subject card is also the same except for the typewritten subject (normally in red or in capital letters) at the top. The typewritten call number,[2] usually in the upper left-hand corner, shows ex-

[2] From the Library of Congress system for the classification of books. In the United States most libraries use either this system or the Dewey Decimal system. The Library of Congress uses the following main classes:

A	General Works	M	Music
B	Philosophy, Religion	N	Fine Arts
C	History	P	Language and Literature
D	Foreign History	Q	Science
E, F	American History	R	Medicine
G	Geography, Anthropology	S	Agriculture
H	Social Sciences	T	Technology
J	Political Science	U	Military Science
K	Law	V	Naval Science
L	Education	Z	Library Science, Bibliography

The Dewey Decimal system has the following main classes:

000	General Works	500	Natural Science
100	Philosophy	600	Useful Arts
200	Religion	700	Fine Arts
300	Sociology	800	Literature
400	Philology	900	History

actly where the book is shelved and must be written out on a "call slip" when the book is requested for use. All three cards are furnished by the Library of Congress as a convenience for libraries throughout the country. Let us note what printed information is given on these carefully prepared cards. (See the three cards reproduced below and on page 395.)

MT70
.R37 Read, Gardner, 1913–
Thesaurus of orchestral devices. New York, Pitman Pub. Corp. [1953]
xxi, 631 p. music. 25 cm.

1. Instrumentation and orchestration. 2. Musical instruments. I. Title.

MT70.R37 781.632 53—13253
Library of Congress [54n10]

MT70 Thesaurus of orchestral devices.
.R37 Read, Gardner, 1913–
Thesaurus of orchestral devices. New York, Pitman Pub. Corp. [1953]
xxi, 631 p. music. 25 cm.

1. Instrumentation and orchestration. 2. Musical instruments. I. Title.

MT70.R37 781.632 53—13253
Library of Congress [54n10]

MT70 .R37	INSTRUMENTATION AND ORCHESTRATION.
	Read, Gardner, 1913–
	Thesaurus of orchestral devices. New York, Pitman Pub. Corp. [1953]
	xxi, 631 p. music. 25 cm.
	1. Instrumentation and orchestration. 2. Musical instruments. I. Title.
	MT70.R37 781.632 53—13253
	Library of Congress [54n10]

First comes the author's name, surname first, followed by the date of his birth, 1913. Absence of a second date shows that the author was still living when the card was printed in 1953. Then follow the title of the book, the place of publication, the name of the publisher, and the date. The brackets around this date indicate that the year of publication does not appear on the title page but has been supplied from some other source, usually the copyright date on the back of the title page. The next line shows that the book contains 21 prefatory pages followed by 631 pages, that it contains musical scores, and that it is 25 centimeters high. The lines some distance below suggest that, in addition to the author and title cards, the book should have two subject cards. (Only the first of the two subject cards is reproduced here.) The next line furnishes the Library of Congress call number for the book, then the Dewey Decimal classification number, and finally the number by which the card may be ordered from the Library of Congress. The last line names the publisher of the card (Library of Congress) and gives a special code number.

Of the three kinds of cards, the reader will probably begin by consulting the subject cards. Since a book may be listed under any one of various subjects, depending upon its primary interest, he should not be discouraged if he fails to find all he wants under the first subject consulted. He should look, next, under related subjects. Works not listed under "Agriculture" may appear under "Farming," or "Gardening," or "Soils." Especially helpful are the cards giving cross references to other subjects under which the reader should look. Under "Agriculture," for example, might appear a card reading "Agriculture, see also Agronomy." Works not listed under "Vitamins" but nevertheless important to that subject might appear under "Nutrition," or "Foods," or "Diet." The student writing the paper on "The French Horn" may find works not listed under "French horn" or "Horn" under "Musical instruments," "Wind instruments," or "Instrumentation and orchestration." Even so general a subject as "Music" might list books that treat of the French horn. And of course the student should not overlook the cross references (*see also* cards) at the end of the subject cards on the plain subject "Music," where he will find many cross references to such subjects as "Bands," "Concertos," "Jazz music," and "Opera."

THE ORDER OF THE CARDS

It is not enough, especially in a large library, to know that the cards are arranged alphabetically. Hundreds of cards may be listed under a single heading such as "England," "Lincoln," or "Washington." The reader who knows the principles of arrangement will save much time in finding what he wants.

Cards for subjects. Cards on a single subject are arranged alphabetically according to the name of the author, which appears on the line immediately below. Subdivisions of a subject are usually arranged alphabetically.

EXAMPLE Michigan
Michigan—Agriculture
Michigan—Biography
Michigan—Constitutional convention
Michigan—University

But subdivisions of history are arranged chronologically.

EXAMPLE Mexico—History—Conquest, 1519-1540
Mexico—History—Spanish colony, 1540-1810
Mexico—History—Wars of Independence, 1810-1821
Mexico—History—European intervention, 1861-1867

Names or titles beginning with abbreviations. Abbreviations are usually filed as if they were spelled out. Instead of *Mc* look for *Mac;* instead of *Dr.* look for *Doctor;* instead of *St.* look for *Saint;* etc.

"Short before long." In the catalogue a short word followed by other words always comes before a longer word of which the short word is a part. *Post office* comes before *Postage.*

EXAMPLE Post
Post office
Postage
Postal

(1) Person, (2) place, (3) title. When the same word names a person or place or begins a title, the order is: person, place, title.

EXAMPLE Lincoln, Abraham [Person]
Lincoln, Nebraska [Place]
Lincoln and Seward, by Gideon Welles [Title]

(1) Books by a person, (2) books about a person. Books written by a person come first; books written about a person follow. Various editions of an author's work are listed chronologically with collections first and single works second in alphabetical order.

EXAMPLE Shakespeare, William. Works
Shakespeare, William. Hamlet
Shakespeare, William. Macbeth
Shakespeare, William. A life of William Shakespeare, by Sidney Lee

(1) Saints, (2) popes, (3) kings, (4) others. Saints, popes, and kings are listed in this order by their first names, followed by the surnames of other persons. Kings are listed by countries.

EXERCISES ON USE OF THE CARD CATALOGUE

Use the card catalogue of the library to do the following exercises. In Exercises A-E, investigate either 1, 2, or 3 as directed by your instructor. (The assignments are varied, and may be varied even further by the instructor, to avoid undue wear on any one book.)

A. Does the library have a copy of one of the following:

1. *Uranium and Atomic Power,* by Jack A. DeMent
2. *Peace of Soul,* by Fulton J. Sheen
3. *Patterns of Culture,* by Ruth Benedict

[You should answer this question by looking in the card catalogue either under the author or under the title. You should look under both before deciding that the book is not in the library, for sometimes a card may be misplaced or temporarily removed. Note that librarians do not italicize titles and that they capitalize only the words that would be capitalized in ordinary writing.]

B. How many books by (1) Jack A. DeMent, (2) Fulton J. Sheen, or (3) Ruth Benedict does the library have?

[Look for the author cards. Distinguish between author and subject cards. Do not count the same book twice.]

C. Find the card for the book you are investigating under the subject indicated as follows:

1. For *Uranium and Atomic Power* under "Uranium"
2. For *Peace of Soul* under "Apologetics—20th Cent."
3. For *Patterns of Culture* under "Society, Primitive"

How many cards does the library have under this subject heading? Are there subheadings? [If the cards are very numerous, estimate the number instead of counting them.]

D. Find the card for the book you are investigating under the subject indicated as follows:

1. For *Uranium and Atomic Power* under "Radioactivity"
2. For *Peace of Soul* under "Catholic Church—Apologetic Works"
3. For *Patterns of Culture* under "Anthropology"

How many cards does the library have under this subject heading? Do you find any subheadings?

E. Find the card for the book you are investigating under the subject indicated as follows:

1. For *Uranium and Atomic Power* under "Atomic Bomb"
2. For *Peace of Soul* under "Conversion"
3. For *Patterns of Culture* under "Zuni Indians"

Are there any subheadings? Are there any cross references to other subjects?

F. List a few of the subheadings under "Education." In what order are they arranged? List a few of the subheadings under "U.S.–History." In what order are they arranged?

G. Does your library classify its books according to the Dewey Decimal system or the Library of Congress system?

(2) Learn how to use indexes to periodicals.

A periodical is a magazine or newspaper. Magazines are usually issued weekly, biweekly, monthly, or quarterly; newspapers, daily or weekly. For the convenience of those who wish to consult the recent issues, magazines are often kept for a few months or possibly a year on open shelves or racks; then they are bound into volumes, each of which commonly includes the issues of six months or a year. These bound volumes may be kept on the open shelves in the reference room, in a special periodical room, or in the stacks. The general card catalogue lists all periodicals in the library and often indicates where each may be consulted. But a more convenient special card catalogue to periodicals is often kept in the reference room or periodical room, or at the circulation desk.

Contents of periodicals are listed in periodical indexes (printed volumes) which are kept continually up to date. These printed indexes do for articles in periodicals what the card catalogue does for books in the library: an article can be found under author, subject, or title (in some cases). And subjects such as "French horn," "Wind instruments," "Musical instruments," or "Music," with the many cross references, can be followed through just as in the card catalogue. The chief indexes are mentioned below, with the years covered by each.

INDEXES TO PERIODICALS

GENERAL

Poole's Index. 1802-1906.
Nineteenth Century Readers' Guide. 1890-1899.
Readers' Guide. 1900–.
Book Review Digest. 1905–.
International Index. 1907–.
New York Times Index. 1913–.

SPECIAL

Agricultural Index. 1916–.
Art Index. 1929–.
Bibliographic Index. 1937–.
Catholic Periodical Index. 1930–.
Dramatic Index. 1909–.
Education Index. 1929–.
Engineering Index. 1884–.
Index Medicus. 1879-1926; *Quarterly Cumulative Index Medicus*. 1927–.
Index to Legal Periodicals. 1908–.
Industrial Arts Index. 1913–.
Music Index. 1949–.
Psychological Index. 1894-1936.
Public Affairs Information Service. 1915–.
Technical Book Review Index. 1917-1929; 1935–.

[See also the indexes to the various abstracts, such as *Biological Abstracts*, 1926–, *Chemical Abstracts*, 1907–, and *Psychological Abstracts*, 1927–.]

These indexes are compiled as soon as possible after the periodicals appear. The *Readers' Guide* (an index to over one hundred magazines of general interest) is only a few weeks behind the appearance of the articles. From time to time the issues of the *Readers' Guide* indexes covering single months or short periods of a few months are combined into longer units, and finally into a volume covering more than a year. The earlier volumes cover as many as five years, as will be seen from the following list.

Readers' Guide

I	1900-1904	XII	July, 1939–June, 1941
II	1905-1909	XIII	July, 1941–June, 1943
III	1910-1914	XIV	July, 1943–April, 1945
IV	1915-1918	XV	May, 1945–April, 1947
V	1919-1921	XVI	May, 1947–April, 1949
VI	1922-1924	XVII	May, 1949–March, 1951
VII	1925-1928	XVIII	April, 1951–March, 1953
VIII	1929–June, 1932	XIX	April, 1953–February, 1955
IX	July, 1932–June, 1935		
X	July, 1935–June, 1937		
XI	July, 1937–June, 1939		

A reader wishing to find all references to a given subject listed by the *Readers' Guide* would have to look through each of the larger volumes and the smaller ones covering the most recent months or month. Usually he is concerned only with articles that have appeared during a certain period, and he looks accordingly in the volumes covering that period.

► EXERCISES ON INDEXES TO PERIODICALS

Do the following exercises as a means of learning how to use indexes to periodicals. (The dates may be changed to avoid undue wear on any one reference book.)

A. On a rough drawing of the floor plan of the reference room (or periodical room) indicate where the indexes to periodicals may be found. Indicate also the locations of any special list or catalogue of periodicals and any unbound or bound periodicals that may be kept in the room.

B. Pick any volume of the *Readers' Guide* from IV through XIX and see how many articles on the League of Nations are listed in it. Are more listed for the period 1919-1921 or for the period May, 1949–March, 1951?

C. Investigate 1 or 2 or 3 as directed by your instructor. Do both indexes list the same articles?

1. How many articles on "Plastic coating" are listed by the *Readers' Guide* for April, 1953–February, 1955? How many by the *Industrial Arts Index* for 1954 only?
2. How many on "Silicones" by the *Readers' Guide* for April, 1951–March, 1953? How many by the *Industrial Arts Index* for 1952 only?
3. How many on "Transistors" by the *Readers' Guide* for May, 1949–March, 1951? How many by the *Industrial Arts Index* for 1950 only?

D. Investigate 1 or 2 or 3 as directed by your instructor. Do both indexes list the same articles?

1. How many articles on "Skunks" are listed by the *Readers' Guide* for May, 1945–April, 1947? How many by the *Agricultural Index* for October, 1945–August, 1948?
2. How many on "Airplanes in insect control" by the *Readers' Guide* for July, 1943–April, 1945? How many by the *Agricultural Index* for October, 1942–September, 1945?
3. How many on "Hybridization" by the *Readers' Guide* for July, 1939–June, 1941? How many by the *Agricultural Index* for October, 1939–September, 1942?

E. Consult the *New York Times Index* to determine the date of the conferring of knighthood on Prime Minister Winston Churchill (or any other significant event assigned by your instructor). [Since all important newspapers report events on the same day, the *New York Times Index* is a useful guide to all newspapers.]

(3) Learn how to find and use reference books.

Dictionaries, encyclopedias, atlases, and other books especially helpful for reference are usually kept on the open shelves of the reference room, where students may use them directly without the trouble of having them brought from the stacks. Each of these books is listed in the card catalogue, and the call number will often aid in finding the book. The student should learn the general location of the chief classes of reference books in order that he may turn to them without loss of time. For a detailed list of such books, with a short description of each, he should consult Constance M. Winchell's *Guide to Reference Books.*[3] A few of the more important reference books are listed below (with abbreviated entries).

GENERAL DICTIONARIES (UNABRIDGED)

Century Dictionary and Cyclopedia. 12 vols. 1911.
Dictionary of American English. 4 vols. 1938-1944.
New Standard Dictionary. 1947.
Oxford English Dictionary. 12 vols. and supplement. 1933. Originally issued as *A New English Dictionary.* 10 vols. and supplement. 1888-1933.
Webster's New International Dictionary. 1934, 1950.

SPECIAL DICTIONARIES

Allen, F. S. *Allen's Synonyms and Antonyms.* 1938.
Crabb, George. *Crabb's English Synonyms.* 1945.
Fowler, H. W. *Dictionary of Modern English Usage.* 1926.
Horwill, H. W. *Dictionary of Modern American Usage.* 1935.
Partridge, Eric. *Dictionary of Slang and Unconventional English.* 1949.
Roget's Thesaurus of Words and Phrases. 1947.

---

[3] Seventh ed., 1951, with supplements.

Webster's Dictionary of Synonyms. 1942.
Wentworth, Harold. *American Dialect Dictionary.* 1944.
Wright, Joseph. *English Dialect Dictionary.* 6 vols. 1898-1905.

GENERAL ENCYCLOPEDIAS

Collier's Encyclopedia. 20 vols. 1949-1951.
Columbia Encyclopedia. 1950, 1953.
Encyclopedia Americana. 30 vols. 1955.
Encyclopædia Britannica. 24 vols. 1954.
Lincoln Library of Essential Information. 1950, 1953.
New International Encyclopaedia. 27 vols. 1922-1930.

SPECIAL ENCYCLOPEDIAS

Adams, J. T. *Dictionary of American History.* 6 vols. 1940.
Bailey, L. H. *Cyclopedia of American Agriculture.* 4 vols. 1907-1909.
Bryan's Dictionary of Painters and Engravers. 5 vols. 1903-1905.
Catholic Encyclopedia. 17 vols. 1907-1922. New edition, 1936—.
Encyclopædia of the Social Sciences. 15 vols. 1930-1935.
Grove's Dictionary of Music and Musicians. 9 vols. 1954.
Harper's Encyclopedia of Art. 2 vols. 1937.
Hastings, James. *Dictionary of the Bible.* 5 vols. 1898-1904.
Hastings, James. *Encyclopaedia of Religion and Ethics.* 13 vols 1908-1927.
Hutchinson's Technical and Scientific Encyclopedia. 4 vols. 1935-1936.
Jewish Encyclopedia. 12 vols. 1925.
McLaughlin, A. C., and A. B. Hart. *Cyclopedia of American Government.* 3 vols. 1914. Reprint, 1949.
Monroe, Paul, *Cyclopedia of Education.* 5 vols. 1911-1913.
Monroe, W. S. *Encyclopedia of Educational Research.* 1950.
Munn, Glenn G. *Encyclopedia of Banking and Finance.* 1949.
Thompson, O. *International Cyclopedia of Music and Musicians.* 1949.
Thorpe, Sir Thomas. *Dictionary of Applied Chemistry.* 9 vols. 1937-1949.

Universal Jewish Encyclopedia. 10 vols. 1939-1943.
Van Nostrand's Scientific Encyclopedia. 1947.

ATLASES AND GAZETTEERS

Collier's New World Atlas and Gazetteer. 1953.
Columbia Atlas. ed. John Bartholomew. 1954.
Columbia Lippincott Gazetteer of the World. 1952.
Encyclopædia Britannica World Atlas. 1954.
Hammond's Ambassador World Atlas. 1954.
Rand-McNally Commercial Atlas. 1949.
Times (London) *Atlas of the World.* 5 vols. 1955–.
Webster's Geographical Dictionary. 1949.

YEARBOOKS—CURRENT EVENTS

American Yearbook. 1910-1919. 1925–.
Americana Annual. 1923–.
Annual Register. 1758–.
Britannica Book of the Year. 1938–.
Information Please Almanac. 1947–.
New International Year Book. 1907–.
Statesman's Year-Book. 1864–.
Statistical Abstract of the United States. 1878–.
University Debaters' Annual. 1915–.
Whitaker's Almanack. 1869–.
World Almanac. 1868–.

BIOGRAPHY

Current Biography. 1940–.
Dictionary of American Biography. 20 vols. and index. 1928-1937. Supplement.
Dictionary of National Biography. (British.) 24 vols. Indexes and supplements. 1937-1939 reprint.
International Who's Who. 1935–.
Kunitz and H. Haycraft. *American Authors, 1600-1900.* 1938.
Kunitz. *British Authors of the Nineteenth Century.* 1936.

Kunitz and H. Haycraft. *Twentieth Century Authors.* 1942. Supplement, 1955.

Kunitz and H. Haycraft. *British Authors before 1800.* 1952.

Webster's Biographical Dictionary. 1943, 1953.

Who's Who. 1848–.

Who's Who in America. 1899–.

LITERATURE

Apperson, G. L. *English Proverbs and Proverbial Phrases.* 1929.

Baker, E. A. *Guide to the Best Fiction.* 1932.

Bartlett's Familiar Quotations. 1955.

Bateson, F. W. *Cambridge Bibliography of English Literature.* 4 vols. 1941.

Brewer's Dictionary of Phrase and Fable. 1953.

English Association. *Year's Work in English Studies.* 1920–.

Gayley, C. M. *Classic Myths in English Literature and in Art.* 1939.

Granger, Edith. *Index to Poetry and Recitations.* Fourth ed., 1953.

Harper's Dictionary of Classical Literature and Antiquities. 1897.

Hart, James D. *Oxford Companion to American Literature.* 1948.

Harvey, Sir Paul. *Oxford Companion to Classical Literature.* 1937.

Harvey, Sir Paul. *Oxford Companion to English Literature.* 1946.

Millett, Fred B., J. M. Manly, and Edith Rickert. *Contemporary British Literature.* 1935.

Millett, Fred B. *Contemporary American Authors.* 1940.

Modern Humanities Research Association. *Annual Bibliography of English Language and Literature.* 1920–.

Sears, Minnie Earl, and Marian Shaw. *Essay and General Literature Index,* 1900-1954.

Spiller, Robert E., and others. *Literary History of the United States.* 3 vols. 1948.

Stevenson, B. E. *Home Book of Quotations.* 1947.
Trent, W. P., and others. *Cambridge History of American Literature.* 4 vols. 1917-1921.
Ward, A. W., and A. R. Waller. *Cambridge History of English Literature.* 15 vols. 1907-1927.

▶ EXERCISES ON REFERENCE WORKS

Do the following exercises as a means of locating some of the more important works of reference and of acquainting yourself with them.

A. Draw the floor plan of the reference room of your library, indicating the location of the most important books of reference. Indicate, for example, the locations of (1) unabridged dictionaries, (2) general encyclopedias, (3) atlases, and (4) the *Dictionary of National Biography* or some other collection of short biographies.

B. Trace the history of one of several words assigned by your instructor (such as *starve, mustard, answer, lady, tobacco*) and quote several passages to illustrate various uses of the word. [Consult the *Oxford English Dictionary.*]

C. When the new Congress convened in 1953 or in 1955 (or in any year assigned by your instructor) what were the respective strengths of the political parties in the two legislative houses? Official census data of late 1952 or 1953 (or any other year assigned) showed what estimated population for the United States? [Consult one or more of the yearbooks.]

D. Locate in atlases several good maps of either (1) Formosa, (2) Kenya, or (3) Bikini. State where you find each map.

E. Look up in a general encyclopedia the article on "Engraving," "Isotopes," or "Franciscans." Then look up the same subject in the appropriate special encyclopedia. Name the two encyclopedias in which the articles are found and indicate very briefly the relative usefulness of the articles.

Bibliographical Form

(4) Follow accepted usage in organizing your bibliography.

While the student is learning how to use the card catalogue, the periodical indexes, and general reference books, he should write out the titles that seem most promising for his library paper. He should put each item on a separate card (3 x 5 or 4 x 6 inches in size) so that he can readily drop or add a card and can arrange the list alphabetically without copying. He should write in ink and follow *exactly* and consistently the bibliographical form he is directed to use. The form illustrated by the models below (and by the footnote forms on pages 421-25) is based on the revised style sheet of the Modern Language Association (MLA). Note that the author's name, when given, always comes first; otherwise the title.

MODEL BIBLIOGRAPHICAL ENTRIES

BOOKS

Anderson, Virgil A. *Training the Speaking Voice.* New York: Oxford University Press, 1942.[4]

Duverger, Maurice. *Political Parties.* Translated from the French by Barbara and Robert North. New York: John Wiley & Sons, Inc., 1954. [A translation]

---

[4] Note that the entry falls into three units separated by periods: (1) the author's name; (2) the title; (3) the facts of publication—place, publisher, date. Another common bibliographical form uses commas between all parts, thus:

Anderson, Virgil A., *Training the Speaking Voice,* New York, Oxford University Press, 1942.

Menard, Henry W., "Fractures in the Pacific Floor," *Scientific American, CXCIII* (July, 1955), 36-41.

Hervey, George F., and Jack Hems. *Freshwater Tropical Aquarium Fishes.* London: Batchworth Press, 1952. [Two authors]

Johnson, R. U., and C. C. Buel, editors. *Battles and Leaders of the Civil War.* 4 volumes. New York: The Century Company, 1887-88. [Edited work]

McConnell, F. J., and others. *The Creative Intelligence and Modern Life.* Boulder: The University of Colorado Press, 1928. (University of Colorado Semicentennial Series, 1877-1927. Vol. V.) [A book by more than two authors; also a book in a series]

Prescott, William Hickling. *History of the Reign of Philip the Second, King of Spain.* Edited by John Foster Kirk. 3 volumes. Philadelphia: J. B. Lippincott & Company, 1871. [Author and editor]

Scott, Sir Harold. *Scotland Yard.* New York: Random House, 1955.

MAGAZINES AND NEWSPAPERS

Curti, Merle. "Intellectuals and Other People." *American Historical Review,* LX (January, 1955), 259-282.

Menard, Henry W. "Fractures in the Pacific Floor." *Scientific American,* CXCIII (July, 1955), 36-41.

Salisbury, Harrison E. "Farm Goals Cited by Soviet Official." New York *Times,* August 24, 1955, p. 1 ff.[5]

"Will the Credit Medicine Be Enough?" *Business Week* (August 13, 1955), pp. 26-28.

ENCYCLOPEDIAS

"Jackson, Andrew." *Encyclopædia Britannica,* 1954, XII, 851-853.

Lee, Edwin A. "Vocational Education." *Encyclopedia Americana,* 1950, XXVIII, 160-161. [A signed article]

[5] Note that page numbers are preceded by *p.* for *page.* The initials *p.* and *pp.* are not used when the volume number in Roman numerals precedes the date in parentheses, as for the first two items under "Magazines and Newspapers."

BULLETINS AND PAMPHLETS

Standards of Practice for Radio Broadcasters of the United States of America. Washington: The National Association of Radio and Television Broadcasters, 1954.

Velvetbean Caterpillar, The. Dept. of Agriculture, Bureau of Entomology and Plant Quarantine Leaflet No. 348. Washington: Government Printing Office, 1953.

UNPUBLISHED THESIS

Blair, Carolyn L. "Browning as a Critic of Poetry." M.A. thesis, University of Tennessee, 1948.

The models given above, with hanging indention, show the proper form for the entries in the final bibliography, which is to be written out and submitted as a part of the library paper. On the separate bibliography cards, the same form may be used; or the author, title, and facts of publication may be written on separate lines as in the following specimen. (The library call number in the lower left-hand corner will save the trouble of looking in the card catalogue again when the book is needed.)

Scott, Sir Harold.
Scotland Yard.
New York: Random House, 1955.

HV
8198
L753
1955

The form of the bibliographical models given above (referred to as MLA style) is commonly used by books and periodicals in languages and social sciences. Scientific periodicals tend to use boldface Arabic numerals for the volume number and to place the date at the end. Indexes to periodicals employ a compact form, but one not commonly used in books or periodicals and consequently not suitable as a model. The card catalogue is also unsuitable as a guide, since it capitalizes only the first word and the proper names in book titles and publication data.

Whatever bibliographical form a writer adopts, he should give due heed to the three divisions of each entry: the author's name (if it is given), the title, and the facts of publication. He should take great pains to be consistent, each time using commas, periods, italics (underlining), and quotation marks exactly as they are called for by his model. This model will usually be suggested by the periodical, the organization, or the department for which the paper is being written. If the instructor does not specify a form, the student may adopt the commonly used form illustrated above. The items may be classified in some logical way, such as "Books" and "Periodicals," or arranged in a single alphabetical list, as in the bibliography on pages 448-49.

► EXERCISE 2. Prepare a preliminary bibliography of at least ten items on the topic selected for your library paper. Include, if possible, two books, two general reference books, and two articles from periodicals.

33c Prepare the outline.

[Follow the general directions given under Section **32b-f**. But the outline for the library paper will need even more change and development than the outline for the ordinary exposition. You must write down at least a few tentative headings to guide your first note-taking; then the extensive reading and note-taking required to find material for the paper will show many ways to develop the headings into a complete outline.]

After completing a preliminary bibliography and a minimum of general reading on his subject (an encyclopedia article and parts of one or two other works may suffice), the student writing on "The French Horn" will make a preliminary outline that will give direction to his investigation. This tentative outline will enable him to discard irrelevant material from his bibliography and to begin spotting valuable passages on which he will want to take notes. There is nothing but frustration in store for anyone who attempts to take notes without knowing what he is looking for.

The student should be careful, however, not to become a slave to his preliminary outline. For although the outline will direct his reading, his reading will almost certainly suggest ways in which the outline may be improved. No outline should be regarded as complete until the research paper has been finished. As the student takes notes, he will probably revise his original outline frequently, adding subheads to it, changing subheads to major headings, perhaps dropping some headings entirely. After some general reading, he might make out an outline such as the following:

First Preliminary Outline

THE FRENCH HORN

I. History of the horn
   A. Early horns
   B. Modern horns

II. Characteristics of the French horn
III. Musical scores featuring the French horn
IV. Noted players of the French horn—Dennis Brain, etc.
V. The French horn in the twentieth century

With this rough and incomplete outline as a guide, the student is ready to begin his note-taking (see 33d below). While reading and taking notes he will write into the first outline each desirable addition or change as it occurs to him. He will soon drop Topic III, "Musical scores," on discovering that it is too technical for his paper; and he may decide to omit IV, "Noted players," on the grounds that he can write a better paper by limiting himself to "The French Horn: Its Development and Use." At this point, while the outline is still fluid, it will be helpful to the student if he can make a precise statement, in a single sentence, of the central or controlling idea of his paper, such as: "The French horn has evolved from a humble origin and has won a secure place in modern orchestras." After a few days the developing outline might look somewhat as follows:

Second Preliminary Outline

THE FRENCH HORN: ITS DEVELOPMENT AND USE

CENTRAL IDEA The French horn has evolved from a humble origin and has won a secure place in modern orchestras.

I. Origin and development of the instrument
 A. Early horns
  1. Roman
  2. Saxon
 B. Seventeenth- and eighteenth-century horns
 C. Nineteenth-century horns

II. Characteristics of the instrument
   A. Dimensions
   B. Quality of tone
III. The French horn in orchestras
   A. Seventeenth century
   B. Eighteenth century
   C. Nineteenth century
   D. Twentieth century

33d Take notes.

After the student has done enough broad reading on his subject to make a first tentative outline, he is ready (as we have already observed) to begin note-taking. He should learn how to find and evaluate useful passages with a minimum of time and effort. Seldom will a whole book, or even a whole article, be of use as subject matter for any given research paper. To find what is needed for his paper, the student writing on "The French Horn" must turn to many books and articles, rejecting most of them altogether and using from others only a section here and there. He cannot take the time to read each book carefully. He must use the table of contents of the book and its index, and he must learn to scan the pages rapidly until he finds the passages he needs.

One important consideration always is the reliability of the source. Does the author seem to know his subject? Does he have an official position that implies competence? Do others speak of him as an authority? Is he prejudiced? Is the work recent enough to give the information needed?

The best and most common way to take notes is to use cards or paper sheets of uniform size, usually 3 x 5 or

4 x 6 inches. Each card contains a single note with a heading keyed to significant words in the outline—not to the notation (IA, II, IIIC, etc.), which is especially subject to change. If the research paper is to use the customary footnotes, each card must also show the source of the note and the exact page or pages of the source.

Let us suppose that the student preparing the library paper on "The French Horn" has spotted the three passages quoted below and on the following page. Compare each of these passages with the note taken from it.

> In *Saxon* times horns were used by the huntsmen and in battle, and carried by the peaceful traveler as well, to make known his presence. An ancient law stated that "if a man come from afar or a stranger go out of the highway, and he neither shout or blow a horn, he is to be accounted a thief, either to be slain or to be redeemed." [6]

> *Early horns - Saxon*
>
> *The early Saxons used horns in the hunt, in battle, and in traveling. According to ancient law any stranger or anyone off the highway was required to cry out or sound his horn to insure himself against being slain or taken for ransom as a thief.*
>
> *Edgerly, p. 263.*

(For the use of this note in the finished library paper, see footnote 8, page 433.)

[6] Beatrice Edgerly, *From the Hunter's Bow* (New York, 1942), p. 263.

Thus we find the ancient Romans in the centuries immediately preceding our era with a varied assortment of what we should call "Military Brass." [7]

Early horns - Roman

The ancient Romans were using brass horns as early as the first century B. C.

Forsyth, p. 68.

(For the use of this note in the finished library paper, see footnote 5, page 432.)

The first two notes above are carefully written abbreviations of their sources, expressed by the student in his own phraseology. Since the words are his own, he is free to write them in his paper just as they stand or to adapt them further when he uses the note. A comparison of the notes with the finished paper shows that he adapts the first note but uses the second one exactly as written.

It became apparent, however, that the most valued attribute of the horn—its characteristic warmth and dark beauty of tone—could not be supplied by the high-pitched B♭ horn, whatever else it had to recommend it. Today this problem seems to have reached a workable solution with the invention of the double horn.[8]

[7] Cecil Forsyth, *Orchestration* (New York, 1947), p. 68.
[8] Walter Piston, *Orchestration* (New York, 1955), p. 233.

Characteristics - tonal quality

The quality of the French horn most valued is "its characteristic warmth and dark beauty of tone."

Piston, p. 233.

(For the use of this note in the finished library paper, see footnote 27, page 440.)

The last note of the three is taken partly in the words of the original since the student wishes to quote from the passage.

Quotations. Very seldom should a student write a note that is merely a quotation. Too many quotations in the library paper suggest a lack of mastery of the subject. And besides, the more a student quotes, the less practice he gets in composition. A quotation must be a very telling and important one before a student is justified in using it in his paper. Occasionally, however, a student will discover such a passage. When he does, he should take down the passage verbatim—that is, write every word, every capital letter, every mark of punctuation exactly as in the original. Then he should enclose the quoted passage in quotation marks. When a note-taker quotes, he should quote accurately. When he is not quoting, he should use his own phraseology, getting entirely away from that of the original.

Plagiarism. Any failure to acknowledge borrowed material is a serious offense called plagiarism. If a borrowed idea is expressed in the writer's phraseology, a footnote reference to the source is sufficient. If it is in the phraseology of the source, it should be put in quotation marks and also acknowledged in a footnote. Usually any conscious quotation (except well-known or proverbial passages) of three or four connected words or more should be placed in quotation marks.

► EXERCISE 3. Use the fifth paragraph of the model library paper at the end of Section 33 to write a short note of fewer than forty words. [Be careful to avoid the phraseology of the source. Write two or three effective sentences to express the gist of the paragraph.]

► EXERCISE 4. Use the same paragraph to write a longer note, perhaps three-fourths the length of the source. [Avoid entirely the phraseology of the source. Include more details than the shorter note of Exercise 3 permitted. Make the sentences as effective as you can.]

► EXERCISE 5. Make a paraphrase of the first paragraph of the library paper. [Avoid entirely the phraseology of the source. A paraphrase is approximately the same length as the source and should be expressed in equally effective sentences.]

► EXERCISE 6. Read carefully the paragraph by Harlow Shapley reprinted on pages 338-39. First write, in a single sentence, the central idea of the paragraph. Then write a note half as long as the paragraph. Finally write a note approximately as long as your source. [Avoid entirely the phraseology of the source. Choose your words carefully. Give variety to your sentences.]

33e Use the outline, the bibliography, and the notes to write the library paper. (Follow the general suggestions given under Section 32g.)

After the outline has been made as complete as possible and after a large number of notes have been taken —notes covering every major section of the outline and every subsection—the student is ready to begin writing. He will arrange his notes in the order of the outline and then use them as the basis of his paper, section by section. Naturally he will have to expand some parts, to cut others; and especially will he need to provide transitional sentences and even transitional paragraphs. He must write the material in the best way he can—in his own style, in his own words.

Since the bulk of the material consists of notes which the student has taken down from others, he should, of course, give proper credit. To do so, he makes use of footnotes. The number needed will vary with the paper. Every quotation must have its footnote, and so must all the chief facts and opinions drawn from others. Usually from two to six footnotes per page will be needed for proper documentation of the average library paper.

The footnote form used for making the first reference to a source (the primary footnote) is similar to, but not identical with, the bibliographical entry: The footnote has a normal paragraph indention; the author's name comes in normal order with surname last; commas replace periods between author, title, and facts of publication; and the exact page of the source is given. When the same title is referred to a second time (a secondary footnote), the entry is much briefer. Below are shown the forms that might be taken by a single title as it appears in (1) the bibliography, (2) the first footnote reference, and (3) the second or any later footnote reference.

1. BIBLIOGRAPHICAL ENTRY

Forsyth, Cecil. *Orchestration*. New York: The Macmillan Company, 1947.

[See the bibliography for the completed library paper, page 448.]

2. PRIMARY FOOTNOTE

[5] Cecil Forsyth, *Orchestration* (New York, 1947), p. 68.

[The form for the first reference to this book. See the library paper, footnote 5, page 432.]

3. SECONDARY FOOTNOTES

[25] Forsyth, p. 117.

[The form for any later reference to this book—provided it is not cited in the footnote *immediately* preceding. See footnote 25, page 439.]

[26] *Ibid.*

[The form for reference to the same book, and the same page, cited in the footnote *immediately* preceding. See footnote 26, page 439.]

[38] *Ibid.*, p. 77.

[The form for reference to the same book, but not the same page, cited in the footnote immediately preceding. See footnote 38, page 442.]

If the bibliography contains a book by Cecil Forsyth and one by William Forsyth, a secondary reference would be "C. Forsyth" or "W. Forsyth." If there are two books by the same author, the title of each is cited.

ABBREVIATIONS

Some abbreviations used in footnotes are as follows (those from Latin usually written in italics):

c. or *ca.* (*circa*)	about (*ca.* 1550)
cf. (*confer*)	compare [The English *see* is more common.]
ch., chs.	chapter, chapters
ed.	edited by, edition, editor
f., ff.	and the following page, pages
ibid. (*ibidem*)	in the same place
l., ll.	line, lines
loc. cit. (*loco citato*)	in the place cited
ms., mss.	manuscript, manuscripts
n.d.	no date given
n.p.	no publisher given
op. cit. (*opere citato*)	in the work cited
p., pp.	page, pages
rev.	revised
tr., trans.	translated by
vol., vols.	volume, volumes

MODEL FOOTNOTES—PRIMARY FORMS

BOOKS

[1] Virgil A. Anderson, *Training the Speaking Voice* (New York, 1942), p. 11.

[2] Maurice Duverger, *Political Parties,* trans. from the French by Barbara and Robert North (New York, 1954), p. 114. [A translation]

[3] George F. Hervey and Jack Hems, *Freshwater Tropical Aquarium Fishes* (London, 1952), p. 44. [Two authors]

[4] R. U. Johnson and C. C. Buel, eds., *Battles and Leaders of the Civil War* (New York, 1887-88), I, 9. [Edited work; also a work in several volumes]

[5] General James Longstreet, "Our March Against Pope," in *Battles and Leaders of the Civil War,* ed. R. U. Johnson and C. C. Buel (New York, 1887-88), II, 516. [Contributing author in an edited work]

[6] F. J. McConnell and others, *The Creative Intelligence and Modern Life,* University of Colorado Semicentennial

Series, V (Boulder, Colo., 1928), pp. 29-30. [A book by more than two authors; also a book in a series]

[7] William Hickling Prescott, *History of the Reign of Philip the Second, King of Spain*, ed. John Foster Kirk (Philadelphia, 1871), III, 87.

[8] Sir Harold Scott, *Scotland Yard* (New York, 1955), p. 101

MAGAZINES AND NEWSPAPERS

[9] Merle Curti, "Intellectuals and Other People," *American Historical Review*, LX (January, 1955), 279-280.

[10] Henry W. Menard, "Fractures in the Pacific Floor," *Scientific American*, CXCIII (July, 1955), 36.

[11] Harrison E. Salisbury, "Farm Goals Cited by Soviet Official," New York *Times*, August 24, 1955, p. 1. [A signed news story]

[12] Louisville *Times*, June 4, 1938, p. 16 [An unsigned news story]

[13] "Will the Credit Medicine Be Enough?" *Business Week* (August 13, 1955), pp. 26-27. [An unsigned magazine article]

ENCYCLOPEDIAS

[14] "Jackson, Andrew," *Encyclopædia Britannica*, 1954, XII, 853. [An unsigned encyclopedia article. The title here is given as "Jackson, Andrew" because it is found listed alphabetically under *J* and not under *A* in the encyclopedia.]

[15] Edwin A. Lee, "Vocational Education," *Encyclopedia Americana*, 1950, XXVIII, 160. [A signed encyclopedia article. Note the variant spellings: *Encyclopædia* for the *Britannica; Encyclopedia* for the *Americana*.]

BULLETINS AND PAMPHLETS

[16] *Standards of Practice for Radio Broadcasters of the United States of America* (Washington, 1954), p. 18.

[17] *The Velvetbean Caterpillar*, Department of Agriculture, Bureau of Entomology and Plant Quarantine Leaflet No. 348 (Washington, 1953), p. 3.

UNPUBLISHED THESIS

[18] Carolyn L. Blair, "Browning as a Critic of Poetry" (M.A. thesis, University of Tennessee, 1948), p. 41.

MODEL FOOTNOTES—SECONDARY FORMS

The secondary footnotes follow the order in which the works cited appear in the listing of Model Footnotes —Primary Forms.

BOOKS

[19] Anderson, p. 11. [20] Duverger, pp. 113-114.

[It is permissible to place extremely short footnotes two, and even three, on a line, so long as there is no appearance of overcrowding.]

[21] Hervey and Hems, p. 41. [22] Johnson and Buel, I, 5.
[23] Longstreet, II, 515. [24] McConnell and others, p. 28.
[25] Prescott, III, 125.
[26] *Ibid.* [Same work, same volume, and same page as in footnote immediately preceding]
[27] *Ibid.*, II, 94-95. [Same work (Prescott's), but a different volume]
[28] *Ibid.*, p. 95. [Same work, same volume, but only one page this time]
[29] *Ibid.*, III, 125. [Same work, but back to a volume not cited in the *immediately* preceding footnote]
[30] Scott, p. 133.
[31] Prescott, III, 127. [An *ibid.* here would refer to Scott's work, not Prescott's.]
[32] Scott, p. 133.

MAGAZINES AND NEWSPAPERS

[33] Curti, p. 279. [34] Menard, p. 39. [35] Salisbury, p. 1.
[36] Salisbury, "Farm Goals Cited by Soviet Official," p. 1. [This is the form that would have to be used if Salisbury had furnished more than one of the sources included in your bibliography.]

[37] Harrison E. Salisbury, p. 1. [This is the form that would have to be used if another author also named Salisbury were included in your bibliography.]

[38] Louisville *Times*, p. 16. [Proper if only one article from this newspaper is used. If more than one are used, the secondary form is the same as the primary. See footnote 12.]

[39] "Will the Credit Medicine Be Enough?" p. 27.

ENCYCLOPEDIAS

[40] "Jackson, Andrew," pp. 851-852. [It is possible that a research paper may use articles with identical titles from several different encyclopedias. In that case, the proper secondary footnote form would be as follows (footnote 41).]

[41] "Jackson, Andrew," *Encyclopædia Britannica*, pp. 851-852. [The year of publication and the volume number are cited in your primary footnote and need not be repeated here.]

[42] Lee, p. 160.

BULLETINS AND PAMPHLETS

[43] *Standards of Practice for Radio Broadcasters of the United States of America*, p. 17.

[44] *The Velvetbean Caterpillar*, p. 3.

UNPUBLISHED THESIS

[45] Blair, p. 38.

Final Outline and Paper, with Footnotes. After the student has written the first draft of his paper on "The French Horn," complete with footnotes, he will read it over carefully, correcting all errors in spelling, mechanics, and grammar, and making sure that the arrangement is logical and that the writing is as clear, concise, and pleasing in style as he can possibly make it. He will probably rewrite some sentences, strike out others, and add still others. His outline, which has developed steadily throughout the note-taking and the first draft of the paper, should now be in its final form. It has served primarily, of course, as a guide to the writing of the paper; but it will also serve, if copied in its final stage, as a guide to the contents of the paper.

With his first draft corrected and revised, and with his outline put in its final form, the student will write the final draft of his paper. He will use a typewriter if possible; if not, he will use pen and ink, taking pains to write legibly and neatly.

Final Bibliography. We have already noticed that the student assembles a preliminary bibliography early in his research. As he pursues his investigation, he eliminates some items and adds others. Not until he has completed his paper can he know the items that should make up his final bibliography. Now, with his writing completed, he may look through his footnotes. Every book or article appearing even once in a footnote belongs in his bibliography. His instructor may ask him to include everything that he has examined, whether he has actually used it in his writing or not. In that case his bibliography may have, instead of a dozen items, as many as fifty or a hundred. But, on the whole, the best practice is to include only items which have actually been used. Once the student has determined the items that should be included, he can easily arrange the bibliography cards and copy them, either in one alphabetical list or in a classified list.

The completed library paper consists of four units:

1. Title page, giving title, author's name, instructor's name, and course number, and also place and date of writing.
2. Outline, serving as the table of contents (numbered with small Roman numerals if it occupies more than one page).

3. **Text of the paper, with footnotes.**
4. **Bibliography, on a separate page or pages numbered with the text (with Arabic numerals).**

Students are often asked to submit, along with the completed paper, the materials used in the preparation of the paper: (1) one of the preliminary outlines, (2) the notes, on cards, (3) the rough draft of the paper, with footnotes, and (4) the bibliography, on cards.

The Sample Library Paper. In the preceding part of this section you have observed how a student has prepared, step by step, a library paper on the French horn. Gradually he limited his subject to the topic, "The French Horn: Its Development and Use," with the central or controlling idea: "The French horn has evolved from a humble origin and has won a secure place in modern orchestras."

As you come to read the completed paper on the following pages, note the adequate development of this central idea in twenty-seven paragraphs covering the three major divisions of the outline. The paper begins without any separate or formal introduction, with (I) the origin and development of the French horn, giving thirteen paragraphs to this important part of the topic. Next come (pages 438-41) four paragraphs on (II) the characteristics of the instrument, then the final ten paragraphs on (III) the use of the horn in orchestras. The last paragraph rounds out the paper by referring to the remarkable progress of the French horn "since its conch-shell beginning." But this paragraph is chiefly concerned with the secure place won by the horn in the modern orchestra. Therefore the author lets the paragraph come under the third major division of his outline instead of providing a fourth division: conclusion.

Adequate documentation is provided by 52 footnotes. Of these, numbers 1, 2, 4, 5, 9, 10, 11, 14, 24, 27, 28, 31, 33, 35, 50, and 51 (one for each of the 16 items in the bibliography) are primary footnotes—that is, first references to the source. The 36 other footnotes are secondary—that is, second or later references to the source—and in addition, footnote 33 includes both a secondary and a primary footnote.

By checking any or all of the 52 footnotes with the source, the reader can test the accuracy of the documentation and observe the methods used. To make such checking easier for footnotes 5, 8, and 27, the sources of these footnotes are quoted above on pages 416-17 along with the three notes taken by the student. A comparison of the source, the note taken, and the material used in the completed paper shows (1) that credit is carefully given in each instance for the material used, (2) that the phraseology is that of the author, not the source, except in the one instance (footnote 27) in which quotation marks are used, and (3) that the passage in quotation marks follows the source *exactly.*

The sample library paper follows on pages 429-48.

The French Horn: Its Development and Use

By Jack Howard Wilson

A Freshman Library Paper

Prepared for Professor Stewart

English 113, Section 36

Knoxville

The University of Tennessee

May 9, 1955

OUTLINE

Central Idea: The French horn has evolved from a humble origin and has won a secure place in modern orchestras.

I. Origin and development of the instrument

A. Early horns

1. Shells and animal horns

2. Biblical horns

3. Roman cornua

4. Saxon and medieval horns

B. Innovations of the seventeenth and eighteenth centuries

C. The valve horn of the nineteenth century

II. Characteristics of the instrument

A. Dimensions of the instrument

B. Quality of tone

C. Difficulties of performance

III. Use of the instrument in orchestras

A. Seventeenth century

B. Eighteenth century

C. Nineteenth century

1. Beethoven and his contemporaries

2. Brahms

3. Tchaikovsky

D. Twentieth century

The ancestors of the modern French horn may be traced back to the earliest days of man, when conch shells picked up from the seashore were used for horns.[1] Other primitive horns were made from the horns of cattle, oxen, and deer. These instruments of prehistoric times—which could sound but one or two rough, indefinite tones[2]--may be classified properly as noise makers, for the sounds they made were not musical.

One of these early horns, the Hebrew ram's horn or <u>shophar</u>, is still used in Jewish temple rites. This very pure-sounding horn is mentioned in the Bible over one hundred times. The priests blew on the shophar when the walls of Jericho tumbled down.[3] Another forerunner of the French horn found in the Bible is the cornet mentioned by Daniel as the first instrument in King Nebuchadnezzar's orchestra. "Cornet" is the rendering in the King James Version, but the Revised Standard Version is probably more accurate in the

---

[1]Beatrice Edgerly, <u>From the Hunter's Bow</u> (New York, 1942), p. 4.

[2]"Horns," <u>Encyclopaedia Britannica</u>, 1954, XI, 750.

[3]Edgerly, p. 144.

translation "horn," since the Oriental orchestras of those days probably began playing with a call or flourish from the horn. The other instruments followed, each playing individually.[4]

The ancient Romans were using brass horns as early as the first century B. C.[5] These cornua (the Latin word for "horns") were of three types: (1) the tuba, a straight trumpet; (2) the J-shaped lituus carried by horse soldiers; and (3) the buccina, a curved brass horn that wound around the player's body.[6] These horns were not used as musical instruments, but they were excellent for sounding fanfares.[7]

Saxon England used the animal horn in hunting, and in battle to rally troops or frighten the enemy. For a stranger or any man off the main highway, it was a means of identification. Such a person was supposed to cry out or sound his horn to show that he was not a thief. If he did not

---

[4]Curt Sachs, The History of Musical Instruments (New York, 1940), pp. 83-85.

[5]Cecil Forsyth, Orchestration (New York, 1947), p. 68.

[6]Edgerly, pp. 135-136.

[7]"Horns," XI, 750.

properly identify himself to residents, he ran the risk of being slain.[8]

The nobles of the Middle Ages had little to do but fight and hunt. At first they used animal horns (as in Saxon England) to signal their soldiers and hunting companions. Later they discovered that they could get more and clearer tones from a brass horn. The hunting horn that was developed for them was a marked improvement over the animal horn, but it was still very simple. It was a circular tube carried with the arm through the coil and the weight on the shoulder. It produced a few more tones than the animal horn.[9]

Although the hunting horn of the Middle Ages immediately preceded the hand horn, the two horns bore only faint resemblance to each other. The bell (the mouth of a wind instrument from which the sound comes) of the hunting horn was held on a level with, or slightly above, the player's head.[10]

---

[8]Edgerly, p. 263.

[9]George W. Andrews, editor, Musical Instruments, IV, in The American History and Encyclopedia of Music, W. L. Hubbard, editor-in-chief, 10 volumes (New York, 1908), IV, 143.

[10]Kathleen Schlesinger, "Horns," Encyclopaedia Britannica, 1911, XIII, 701.

In a picture from Galpin's Old English Instruments of Music, the circular horn has a funnel-shaped bell. England took the lead in developing the hunter's horn that was to become the French horn in seventeenth-century France.[11]

We cannot be positive about the details of this change. We do know that the hunter's horn was used in an undeveloped form in the early seventeenth century. A century later it had become the hand horn, with a lengthened tube and a narrow, partly cylindrical bore. Its cup-shaped mouthpiece had been replaced by a funnel-shaped one. No longer did it sound like a bugle or a piercing trumpet. It had a smooth, mellow sound similar to the modern French horn. Thus, by the end of the seventeenth century the horn had undergone many changes and improvements.[12]

In the middle of the eighteenth century Hampel of Dresden increased the number of notes possible for the French horn by inventing the practice of stopping. He had tried to soften its blaring sound

---

[11]Karl Geiringer, Musical Instruments (New York, 1945), p. 81.

[12]Sachs, p. 384.

by using a mute, but this had lowered the pitch of the notes. When he inserted his hand into the bell as a mute, he discovered that he could then produce many intermediate tones otherwise unobtainable on a natural horn.[13] Although these stopped tones were odd-sounding, the practice of stopping spread, and the horn gradually gained a place in the orchestra. But many musicians strongly objected to the admission of a rough and unrefined instrument which had so recently been a huntsman's horn.[14]

Composers, however, approved this orchestral newcomer, and the horn assumed a prominent position in French orchestras. Because these orchestras accompanied the French ballet popular in eighteenth-century England, the English began to call the hand horn "the French hunting horn." The "hunting" part was later dropped, and the name "French horn" has been accepted in most countries.[15] Today, some patriotic musicians of other countries refer to it simply as the "horn."

In the second half of the eighteenth century

---

[13]Andrews, p. 66.

[14]Arthur Elson, Orchestral Instruments and Their Use (Boston, 1922), p. 211.

[15]Forsyth, p. 69.

much attention was given to the improvement of the French horn. To increase its range, U-shaped crooks were inserted into the middle of the instrument; the result was the "inventions-horn."[16] Another type, the natural horn, differed from the inventions-horn in that the crooks were inserted at the end nearest the mouthpiece. By making the crooks of various lengths, these newer horns could be changed to play in any key. The disadvantage was that both types required some time to change crooks. A composer writing for either instrument had to give it several measures' rest if he wrote a change of key.[17]

Charles Clagget, an Englishman, secured a British patent in 1788 for a third type of French horn that he thought would end this problem. He united two horns (one in D, one in E flat), and he put separate openings for a mouthpiece in each horn. This gave the player eighteen open tones and many stopped ones. The player transferred the mouthpiece from one horn to the other to play the necessary notes. The invention did not prove

---

[16]Geiringer, pp. 175-176.

[17]Andrews, p. 126.

popular; most players continued to use the earlier types. The nineteenth century saw Clagget's idea carried even further. "Omnitonic" horns that played in every key were produced. The player chose his key by manipulating a small dial, but this instrument was too heavy, and the action of the dial was too slow.[18]

Then in 1815 came the solution to the problem of increasing the notes of a French horn. Blühmel of Silesia and Stölzel of Berlin applied the valve principle to the French horn. Others improved on their system, but all of these improvements involved either piston or rotary valves. Sachs' explanation of the valve's action is one of the clearest and simplest:

> The piston has an up-and-down action. When in rest, the piston disconnects the additional crook and allows the wind to pass directly through the main tube. When the piston is pressed down, on the contrary, the direct passage is barred, and the wind is forced to make the detour through the additional crooks before re-entering the main tube.
>
> In rotary valves, connection and disconnection are effected by a revolving cylinder. The player, however, does not need to make a rotary movement; he presses a key, the

---

[18]Sachs, p. 426.

vertical motion of which is transformed into rotation.[19]

The invention of valves was the most important single step in the development of the French horn. In a musical instrument valves have three functions: (1) they enable a performer to produce the notes of a complete scale; (2) they enable him to transpose the key; and (3) they correct faults or imperfections in the timbre. The three valves on a French horn may be used in a variety of combinations to supply all the tones of the chromatic scale.[20]

The four main parts of the modern French horn are the body, crooks, mouthpiece, and slides. The body is a tube, approximately seven and one-third feet long, coiled in a circular manner. At the end of this tube is a bell with a diameter of eleven or twelve inches. Its crooks can be inserted or taken out to vary the length of the tube and the pitch and key.[21] The various types of horns and the rarely played "Wagner tubas" are the only brass wind instruments that use a funnel-

---

19 *Ibid.*, pp. 426-427.

20 Andrews, pp. 66-67.

21 "Horns," XI, 749.

shaped mouthpiece.[22] The tuning slides are U-shaped tubes which can be pulled out or pushed in to tune the instrument exactly.[23] Unlike the crooks, they are permanent parts of the horn. The old natural horn produced open and stopped tones. The open sounds produced by the old natural horn were beautiful and sonorous, but the closed sounds were dull and rough.[24] On the valve horn, all tones are open. It has incorporated the best features of the hand horn instead of merely replacing it.[25]

Many people have tried to describe the tone quality of the French horn. Although they hear suggestions of different sounds, almost all agree that its timbre is unusually beautiful. Forsyth says that "the Horn differs materially from all other brass instruments. It is, indeed, at a higher artistic level altogether."[26] Walter Piston writes

---

[22]Forsytn, p. 89.

[23]"Horns," XI, 749.

[24]Hector Berlioz, A Treatise upon Modern Instrumentation and Orchestration, trans. from the French by Mary Cowden Clarke (London, 1858), p. 130.

[25]Forsyth, p. 117.

[26]*Ibid*.

of the horn's "characteristic warmth and dark beauty of tone."[27] Mason describes its tone quality as "unforgettable"[28] and believes that it has varied and unlimited possibilities. When played loudly, the horn is sonorous and blaring; yet it may be mysterious or poetic in soft passages. Andrews points out that this "genial instrument" adds warmth to an orchestra when used in pairs.[29]

Men will go on trying to capture these beautiful tones and put them down on paper, but there are some things that will never be adequately described. The master of nineteenth-century orchestration, Berlioz, speaks with authority and feeling on this subject: "The horn is a noble and melancholy instrument. . . . It blends easily with the general harmony; and the composer--even the least skilful--may, if he choose, either make it play an important part, or a useful but subordinate one."[30]

---

[27]Walter Piston, Orchestration (New York, 1955), p. 233.

[28]Daniel Gregory Mason, The Orchestral Instruments and What They Do (New York, 1909), pp. 70-71.

[29]Andrews, pp. 85-86.

[30]Berlioz, p. 140.

Because the French horn has a difficult range of four octaves,[31] it is practically impossible for a player to alternate high and low notes or parts. For the sake of convenience, horn music is written in four parts. The first and third horn players execute the high parts; the second and fourth, the low parts. Thus most horn players specialize in either high- or low-range playing.[32] Even the first and third horn players have difficulty playing high passages for any length of time because their lips must be extremely tense to play high notes. A French horn player must be a musician with an excellent ear, and he must have his tone definitely in his mind before he can produce it.[33] No other brass instrument is as demanding as the French horn.

The use of some form of the horn in orchestras can be traced as far back as the seventeenth century. Cavalli and Lulli, Italian composers and conductors, used the natural horn in some of

---

[31]Gardner Read, <u>Thesaurus of Orchestral Devices</u> (New York, 1953), p. 90.

[32]Piston, p. 227.

[33]Andrews, p. 127; "Young Man with a Horn," <u>Time</u>, LXII (July 6, 1953), 38-39.

their operas. Toward the end of the century, Reinhard Keiser, the founder of the German opera, employed two horns in one of his works. Handel continued to improve the horn part in his scores.[34]

In the eighteenth century the hand horn came into more general use. Bach wrote horn parts for several cantatas. Horns also sounded salutes to royal figures or depicted pastoral scenes.[35] In 1757 Gossec wrote obbligato parts for two horns and two clarinets in two operatic arias, and thus for the first time the horn was played in the Paris orchestra.[36] During this period Haydn and Mozart regularly employed two French horns in their orchestras.[37] It is interesting to note, however, that none of these earlier composers made much use of stopped tones.[38]

Beethoven devoted more attention to the horn than had any previous composer. Most of his

---

[34]Schlesinger, "Horns," XIII, 704.

[35]Charles Sanford Terry, Bach's Orchestra (London, 1932), pp. 46-47.

[36]Elson, p. 211.

[37]Forsyth, p. 120.

[38]*Ibid*., p. 77.

symphonies contained elaborate horn parts in spite of the limitations of the hand horn. He used almost as many stopped tones as open ones. The wide and difficult ranges of his horn parts and his love of high horn passages make his treatment of the instrument unique.[39]

Beethoven's contemporaries and later composers took a hint from this German genius. Weber was a master at original, poetic, and complete use of the French horn. The horns seem to speak in his three best works, Oberon, Euryanthe, and Der Freischütz.[40] In Der Freischütz he obtains round, full, pure horn tones by writing open tones for horns in F and C.[41] He uses as many as eight horns in his opera, Preciosa.[42] Schubert and Mendelssohn wrote sparingly but effectively for the horn. At times Wagner produced lavish horn parts. His "Ride of the Valkyries" demands eight horns,[43] and in the first act of Tannhäuser

---

39 Ibid., pp. 121-123.

40 Berlioz, p. 140.

41 Mason, pp. 67-68.

42 Forsyth, p. 132.

43 Elson, p. 215.

he wrote for sixteen horns.[44] Some composers used the stopped tones of the natural horn to emphasize special effects. In Gounod's Faust they depict evil. Wagner gets some baleful and effective tones in Götterdämmerung. In Massenet's "Angelus" from Scenes Pittoresques, the horn represents an old, cracked village bell. Berlioz employs the horn and the harp to imitate a full-toned bell in his Harold in Italy.[45]

The composers already mentioned wrote largely for the hand horn. Many nineteenth-century composers disliked the new valve horns. They knew that the difference intended by earlier composers between open and closed sounds might be neglected by players of the new instruments.[46] At first the orchestras ignored valve horns because of their imperfections. But by 1850 they were used as much as the hand horns, and near the end of the century, the valve horns triumphed.[47] However, their orchestral parts have remained

---

[44]Forsyth, p. 132.

[45]Elson, pp. 217-218.

[46]Berlioz, p. 141.

[47]Geiringer, p. 228.

characteristically the same as those of the limited natural horn.[48]

Of the later nineteenth-century composers who wrote for the valve horn, Tchaikovsky and Brahms stand out as exponents of the French horn as a solo instrument.[49] Brahms had played it in his early days at Hamburg. He had come to love it and showed his feeling for the instrument by writing important parts for it in such works as his <u>First Orchestral Serenade</u>, <u>First</u> and <u>Second Symphonies</u>, and <u>Second Piano Concerto</u>. He even wrote a trio for piano, violin, and French horn, but this beautiful work is rarely played because of the unusual combination of instruments.[50]

Tchaikovsky used the horn for solos, accompaniment, and sustaining harmony. Of the horn part in Tchaikovsky's <u>Fifth Symphony</u> Huneker gives a picturesque description: "But what an impassioned romance the French horn sings in the second movement! It is the very apotheosis of a

---

[48]Forsyth, p. 127.

[49]Mason, p. 73.

[50]Walter Niemann, <u>Brahms</u>, trans. from the German by Catherine Alison Phillips (New York, 1941), pp. 271-272.

night of nightingales, soft and seldom footed dells, a soft moon and dreaming tree-leaves. Its tune sinks a shaft into your heart and hot from your heart comes a response. . . ."[51]

Entering into the twentieth century, we find many changed conditions in the musical world. The greatest musical composers of our period write vocal, not instrumental, music. There are a number of good composers, but we have no twentieth-century Brahms, Beethoven, or Bach. In the best of our instrumental music--in the scores of Stravinsky, Hindemith, and Bartók--we find the French horn securely holding its place and receiving attention in almost every arrangement.[52]

The repertoires of our modern symphony orchestras consist largely of eighteenth- and nineteenth-century music. There are generally in any symphony orchestra five or six versatile horn players who can play melody, accompaniment, or sustaining harmony equally well. In the popular-music or dance band, the French horn is usually in the background and rarely gets a chance

---

[51]James Huneker, Mezzotints in Modern Music (New York, 1905), pp. 121-122.

[52]Read, p. 90.

to solo. Exceptions to this practice are made by the bands of Hugo Winterhalter and Mitch Miller, which quite often feature the French horn. Leroy Anderson, composer of semi-classical music, favors the French horn in his compositions. Almost any high school band has two French horn players, but four is a more usual number, and five or six horns are not uncommon. The number of horns in college bands, as in high school bands, depends on the size of the organization. While the horn is of little value in a marching band, it is virtually indispensable to a concert band.

The French horn has made remarkable advances since its conch-shell beginning. It has become a respected member of most musical organizations. Because of its unique tonal quality, it is used as a solo instrument for special effects. And it makes a very pleasing contribution to any band or orchestra, whatever part it plays. We wonder how the many musicians who have contributed in earlier centuries to the development and use of the French horn would feel if they could see and hear it in its modern form. They would be surprised, no doubt, but the surprise would be a pleasant one.

-18-

BIBLIOGRAPHY

Andrews, George W., editor. Musical Instruments, IV, in The American History and Encyclopedia of Music, W. L. Hubbard, editor-in-chief. 10 volumes. New York: Irving Squire, 1908.

Berlioz, Hector. A Treatise upon Modern Instrumentation and Orchestration. Translated from the French by Mary Cowden Clarke. London: Novello and Company, 1858.

Edgerly, Beatrice. From the Hunter's Bow. New York: G. P. Putnam's Sons, 1942.

Elson, Arthur. Orchestral Instruments and Their Use. Boston: The Page Company, 1922.

Forsyth, Cecil. Orchestration. New York: The Macmillan Company, 1947.

Geiringer, Karl. Musical Instruments. New York: Oxford University Press, 1945.

"Horns." Encyclopaedia Britannica, 1954, XI, 749-750.

Huneker, James Gibbons. Mezzotints in Modern Music. New York: Charles Scribner's Sons, 1905.

Mason, Daniel Gregory. The Orchestral Instruments and What They Do. New York: H. W. Gray Company, 1909.

Niemann, Walter. Brahms. Translated from the German by Catherine Alison Phillips. New York: Alfred A. Knopf, 1941.

Piston, Walter. Orchestration. New York: W. W. Norton & Company, 1955.

Read, Gardner. Thesaurus of Orchestral Devices. New York: Pitman Publishing Corporation, 1953.

-19-

Sachs, Curt. The History of Musical Instruments. New York: W. W. Norton & Company, 1940.

Schlesinger, Kathleen. "Horns." Encyclopaedia Britannica, 1911, XIII, 697-706.

Terry, Charles Sanford. Bach's Orchestra. London: Oxford University Press, 1932.

"Young Man with a Horn." Time, LXII (July 6, 1953), 38-39.

▸ Letters

34

Letters should follow the forms prescribed by usage.

Business letters are preferably typewritten on one side only of sheets 8½ by 11 inches in size. These sheets are folded either (1) once horizontally and twice in the other direction to fit an envelope about 3½ by 6½ inches in size or (2) twice horizontally to fit an envelope about 4 by 10 inches in size.

Personal letters and social notes are commonly written by hand on note paper—a four-page sheet to be folded once horizontally for insertion in a matching envelope; or on club paper—a sheet about 7¼ by 11 inches, to be folded twice horizontally to fit a matching envelope 3¾ by 7½ inches. Both sides of the sheets may be used.

34a Business letters should follow prescribed usage with respect to the six essential parts:

(1) Heading.
(2) Inside address.
(3) Salutation (or greeting).
(4) Body of the letter.
(5) Complimentary close.
(6) Signature.

MODEL BUSINESS LETTER

1 1288 Catawba Street
Columbia 2, Missouri
May 3, 1955

2 Mr. J. W. Rice
Editor of the Rushville News
122 East Market Street
Rushville, Missouri

3 Dear Sir:

4 Mr. Erskine Freeman, of your City Room, has mentioned to me your regular practice of employing two student reporters every summer. I am now majoring in journalism at the University of Missouri, and I should like, therefore, to apply for one of those positions for this next summer.

By the end of this college year I shall have completed three quarters of the university program in journalism. Included in this work are two courses in reporting and one in copyreading. Before I began my college work, I had served four years as sports editor of my high school newspaper, where I learned some of the fundamentals of page make-up. Last year I was awarded the Missouri Press Association Scholarship for journalism.

I have permission to refer you to my employer of the last three summers:

Mr. George Armour
Armour Drug Store
Rushville, Missouri

and to the professors under whom I have taken courses in journalism:

Dr. James D. Turner
Professor of Journalism
University of Missouri
Columbia, Missouri

Dr. John M. Cain
Assistant Professor of Journalism
University of Missouri
Columbia, Missouri

I shall be in Rushville after June 6 and should appreciate an opportunity to call at your office for an interview at your convenience.

5 Very truly yours,

6 *Donald Burke*
Donald Burke

(1) The heading must give the full address of the writer and the date of the letter.

The heading is usually blocked as in the model, but it may be indented.

BLOCKED	860 Fremont Street Bessemer, Alabama March 22, 1946	[End punctuation is regularly omitted with the blocked heading.]

INDENTED	860 Fremont Street
	    Bessemer, Alabama
	        March 22, 1946
		[End punctuation is usually omitted with the indented heading.]

Either of these forms may be used. The important thing is to be consistent—to adopt one form and to use it throughout the heading, the inside address, and the outside address.

If there is a letterhead (which supplies the address), the date may be written either under the letterhead or flush with the right margin, as in the heading of the model business letter on page 451.

(2) The inside address (identical with the address to appear on the envelope) must give the name and the full address of the person to whom the letter is written.

The inside address must be consistent with the heading. That is, it must be (1) blocked or (2) indented in accordance with the form adopted for the heading. The inside address is typed flush with the left margin about four spaces lower than the heading.

(3) The salutation (or greeting) should be consistent with the tone of the letter and with the complimentary close.

The salutation is written flush with the left margin two spaces below the inside address and is followed by a colon. The following salutations are used:

For men	*For women*
Dear Sir:	Dear Madam:
My dear Sir: [More formal]	My dear Madam: [More formal]
Dear Mr. Smith:	Dear Mrs. Smith:
My dear Mr. Smith: [More formal]	My dear Mrs. Smith: [More formal]
Gentlemen:	Ladies:

Note: The masculine salutation is used to address an organization or an individual whose name the writer does not know.

For the proper form of salutation in letters to government officials, ecclesiastical dignitaries, etc., see *Webster's New International Dictionary,* Second Edition, pp. 3012-14; *The American College Dictionary,* Text Edition, p. xxxiii; *Webster's New World Dictionary,* pp. 1717-19.

In salutations and addresses, abbreviations are generally disapproved except for *Mr.* (plural, *Messrs.*), *Mrs.* (plural, *Mmes.*), and *Dr.*

MODEL ADDRESSED ENVELOPE

```
Donald Burke
1288 Catawba Street
Columbia 2, Missouri



        Mr. J. W. Rice
        Editor of the Rushville News
        122 East Market Street
        Rushville, Missouri
```

(4) The body of the letter should follow the principles of good writing.

Typewritten business letters are usually single-spaced, with double spacing between paragraphs. All paragraphs (1) should be indented equally, as in the model business letter on page 451, or (2) should begin flush with the left-hand margin. The subject matter should be well organized and paragraphed, but the paragraphs will frequently be shorter than in ordinary writing. The style should be clear and direct. Indirect, abbreviated, or outdated phrasing should be avoided.

INDIRECT	Your kind favor . . . Your esteemed favor . . .
BETTER	Your letter . . .
INDIRECT	I beg to inform you that we have . . . I beg to send . . . Permit us to report that we now supply . . . I wish to apply . . .
BETTER	We have . . . I send . . . We now supply . . . I apply . . .
ABBREVIATED	Yours of the 5th instant . . . Hope to have . . . Enclose check for six dollars.
BETTER	Your letter of May 5 . . . We hope to have . . . I enclose a check for six dollars.
OUTDATED	Hoping to receive . . . Wishing you success . . . Trusting you will be pleased . . .
BETTER	We hope to receive . . . We wish you success . . . I trust you will be pleased . . .

(5) The complimentary close should be consistent with the tone of the letter and with the salutation.

Ordinary business letters addressed to strangers beginning with the usual *Dear Sir,* etc., should close with *Yours truly, Yours very truly,* or *Very truly yours.* Professional letters, or business letters addressed to an individual with such an opening as *Dear Mr. White,* may well close with the more friendly *Yours sincerely, Sincerely yours, Sincerely, Faithfully yours,* or *Cordially yours.*

(6) The signature should be written by hand directly below the complimentary close.

If the name does not appear in the letterhead, it may be typed just below the signature. Ordinarily, neither professional titles nor degrees should be used with the signature, but the writer's official capacity may be indicated:

WRONG *James M. Smith, LL.D.*
PERMISSIBLE *James M. Smith*
President

A married woman should sign her own name (*Mary Hughes Black,* not *Mrs. John K. Black*). In business letters her status is indicated by the use of parentheses as follows:

CORRECT *Mary Hughes Black*
(Mrs. John K. Black)
CORRECT *(Mrs.) Mary Hughes Black*

34b Personal letters and informal social notes follow in general the form of business letters.

Friendly letters usually omit the inside address. If it is included, it may be placed either at the beginning or at the end of the letter flush with the left margin.

The salutation is usually followed by a comma instead of the more formal colon. As in the business letter, the salutation should be in keeping with the complimentary close and with the tone of the letter. A letter beginning with *Dear Mr. Brown* may close with *Sincerely yours, Yours sincerely,* or *Cordially yours.* A more familiar salutation and complimentary close may be justified by the intimacy of the correspondents.

The body of the letter will vary greatly with the occasion and with the personality of the writer. An easy, informal style is best.

34c Formal social notes—announcements, invitations, answers to invitations—follow very definite conventions.

For the rare occasions when formal notes are required, engraving or handwriting (not typing) is the rule. Formal notes are always written in the third person. They have no inside address, no salutation, no complimentary close, and no signature. The writer's street address and the month and the date may be placed below at the left. Every word (except the street number and the abbreviations *Mr., Mrs.,* and *Dr.*) is spelled out in full. Acceptances and regrets follow the form of the invitation closely, repeating the hour and date to insure understanding. The verb used in the reply is always in the present tense.

▶ EXERCISES ON LETTERS

A. Write the following business letters:

1. Request the circulation manager of your newspaper to send your paper to a new address.
2. Ask the manager of a New York hotel to reserve a room for you.

3. Call the attention of your representative in the city government to some needed repairs in a street near your home.
4. Apply for a position that you are competent to fill. Be sure to include the following: (a) a brief description of the job desired—be specific; (b) your qualifications, including age, schooling, and experience; (c) at least three references—people who know you well and are able to evaluate your ability; (d) a request for an interview. See the model business letter on page 451
5. Explain to your employer why you must resign your position at the end of the year.
6. Recommend to your employer (to fill the position you must resign) a young man or woman with whom you have worked.
7. Request permission of a former employer to use his name as a reference in applying for a new position.
8. Ask a local radio station to give more time to classical music (or dance music, sports, plays, news, etc.).
9. Read the editorials in a recent issue of your newspaper and write the editor commending (or objecting to) one or more of his views.

B. Write the following personal letters:

1. Invite a friend to spend a week end in your home.
2. Accept an invitation to spend a week end with a friend.
3. Answer a friend's inquiry about the course in dramatics (or chemical engineering, astronomy, political science, etc.) in your college.
4. Congratulate a friend in another college on his election to some class office (or on any other honor).
5. Introduce a friend to one of your former classmates who lives in a distant city.
6. Thank a friend for a birthday (or wedding, etc.) gift
7. Cheer a friend who has been sick in the hospital and is now convalescing.

▶ Grammatical Terms

35

Consult the following list as needed for explanations of grammatical terms.

Absolute. An absolute expression is one that is grammatically independent of the rest of the sentence. Usually it consists of a noun or pronoun followed by a participle, a construction often called the **nominative absolute.**

The game having ended, the crowd went home.

Abstract noun. See **Noun.**

Active voice. See **Voice.**

Adjective. A word (one of the eight parts of speech) used chiefly to modify (*i.e.,* describe or limit) nouns.

Descriptive adjective: *honest* man, *white* pony, *blue* sky, *waving* flag.

Limiting adjective: *my* book, *its* nest, *his, her, our, your, their* property (possessive); *that, this* house, *these, those* apples (demonstrative); *whose* cap? *which* coat? *what* dress? (interrogative); the boy *whose* dog was lost (relative); *one* pear, *three* plums, *first* robin, *third* sparrow (numerical); *a* street, *an* avenue, *the* park (article).

See also Section 4, **Adjectives and Adverbs.**

Adjective clause. A subordinate clause used as an adjective.

The man *who is honest* will succeed.

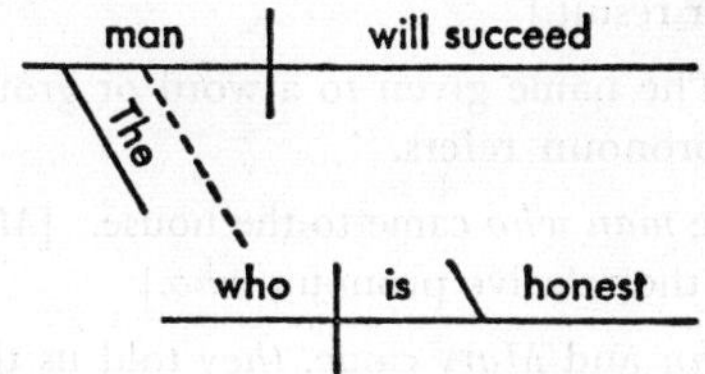

[The clause, equivalent to the adjective *honest,* modifies the noun *man.*]

Adverb. A word (one of the eight parts of speech) used chiefly to modify (*i.e.,* qualify or limit) a verb, an adjective, another adverb, or even a sentence as a whole. An adverb indicates time (*now, then, today*), place (*here, there, outside*), manner (*calmly, quickly, clearly*), or degree (*very, somewhat, only*).

Stand *here.* [*Here* modifies the verb *stand.*]
Stand beside the *very* old clock. [*Very* modifies the adjective *old.*]
Stand *very quietly.* [*Very* modifies the adverb *quietly,* which modifies the verb *stand.*]
Certainly you may be seated. [*Certainly* modifies the sentence as a whole.]

See also Section 4. **Adjectives and Adverbs.**

Adverb clause. A subordinate clause used as an adverb.

I shall leave the house *after she comes.*

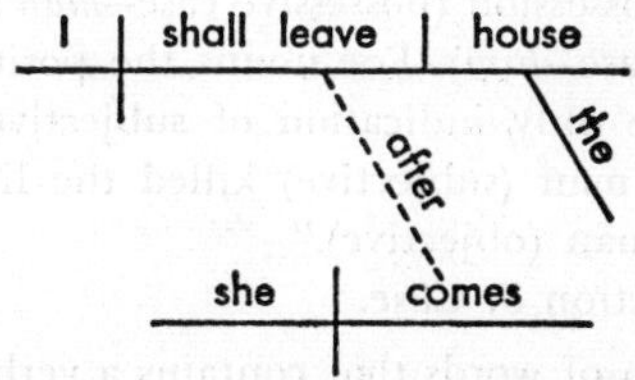

[The adverb clause *after she comes* modifies the verb *shall leave* and indicates time. Adverb clauses may also indicate place, manner, cause, purpose, condition, concession, comparison, or result.]

Antecedent. The name given to a word or group of words to which a pronoun refers.

This is the *man who* came to the house. [*Man* is the antecedent of the relative pronoun *who*.]

When *John* and *Mary* came, *they* told us the facts in the case. [*John* and *Mary* are the antecedents of the personal pronoun *they*.]

Appositive. A noun or any other substantive set beside another substantive and denoting the same person or thing. See also Section **12d(2).**

Dr. Smith, our *dentist,* is visiting *England,* his native *country.* [*Dentist* is in apposition with *Dr. Smith,* and *country* is in apposition with *England.*]

Article. Articles are usually classed as adjectives. The definite article is *the.* The indefinite articles are *a* and *an.*

Auxiliary. A verb that is used to form various tenses of other verbs. *Have, may, can, be, shall, will, must, ought,* and *do* are the common auxiliaries.

I *shall* go.
He *was* sent away.
He *has been* promoted.

Case. The inflectional form of a noun (*man's*) or pronoun (*he, his, him*) to show such relations as subject (subjective case–*he*), possession (possessive case–*man's, his*), or object (objective case–*him*). For nouns the position in the sentence is the only indication of subjective and objective case. "The man (subjective) killed the lion." "The lion killed the man (objective)."
See also Section **5, Case.**

Clause. A group of words that contains a verb and its subject and is used as a part of a sentence. A clause may be main (independent, principal) or subordinate (dependent).

(1) A main (independent, principal) clause can stand by itself as a simple sentence.

The moon rose and *the stars came out.* [Two main clauses, either of which can stand by itself as a simple sentence]

(2) A subordinate (dependent) clause cannot stand alone. It is used as a noun, an adjective, or an adverb.

That he will run for office is doubtful. [Noun clause: a subordinate clause used as the subject of the sentence]

See also Section **1d, Sentence Sense.**

Collective noun. See **Noun.**

Colloquial. Appropriate for conversation and informal writing rather than for formal writing.

Common noun. See **Noun.**

Comparison. The change in the form of an adjective or adverb to indicate degrees of superiority in quality, quantity, or manner. There are three degrees: positive, comparative, and superlative.

EXAMPLES	*Positive*	*Comparative*	*Superlative*
	good	better	best
	high	higher	highest
	quickly	more quickly	most quickly

See also **Inflection.**

Complement. A word or words used to complete the sense of the verb, the subject, or the object. The complement may be an object, a predicate noun, or a predicate adjective.

OBJECTS

John gave the *boy* a *book.* [*Book* is the direct object; *boy* is the indirect object.]

PREDICATE NOUNS

Samuel was a good *child* [The predicate noun *child,* referring to the subject *Samuel,* is also called the predicate complement, the **subjective complement,** or the **predicate nominative.**]

He called the man a *hero.* [*Man* is the direct object. The noun *hero,* referring to *man,* is called the **objective complement** or the **predicate objective.**]

PREDICATE ADJECTIVES

The boy is *obedient.* [The predicate adjective *obedient,* referring to the subject *boy,* is also called the **subjective complement** or the **predicate complement.**]

Jack colored the egg *blue.* [*Egg* is the direct object. The predicate adjective *blue,* referring to *egg,* is also called the **objective complement** or the **predicate objective.**]

Complete predicate. See **Predicate.**

Complex sentence. See **Sentence.**

Compound sentence. See **Sentence.**

Compound-complex sentence. See **Sentence.**

Concrete noun. See **Noun.**

Conjugation. A grouping of verb forms to indicate **tense,** voice, mood, number, and person. See the conjugation of the irregular verb *to see* in Section 7. See also **Inflection.**

Conjunction. A word (one of the eight parts of speech) used to connect words, phrases, or clauses. There are two kinds, co-ordinating conjunctions and subordinating conjunctions.

(1) **Co-ordinating conjunctions** connect words, phrases, and clauses of equal rank: *and, or, but, for, either . . . or, neither . . . nor.*

(2) **Subordinating conjunctions** connect subordinate clauses with main clauses: *if, although, since, in order that, as, because, unless, after, before, until, when, whenever, where, while, wherever,* etc.

Conjunctive adverb. An adverb which serves also to connect or relate main clauses: *however, therefore, nevertheless, hence, then, besides, moreover, thus, otherwise, consequently, accordingly,* etc.

Construction (Syntax). The grammatical functions of words, phrases, or clauses in the sentence.

Co-ordinate, co-ordinating. Of equal rank. For example, two nouns, two subordinate clauses, or two main clauses.

Copula (Copulative verb, linking verb). A verb used to express the relation between the subject and the predicate noun or predicate adjective. "He *is* merry." The chief copulative verbs are *be, become, seem, appear* and verbs pertaining to the senses.

Declension. See **Inflection.**

Demonstrative adjective. See **Adjective.**

Demonstrative pronoun. A pronoun that points out. "*This* is good; *that* is bad."

Dependent clause. See **Clause.**

Descriptive adjective. See **Adjective.**

Diagraming. An arrangement of words on lines to show relationships within the sentence. Various forms are used. Any form is serviceable if it helps the student to understand the sentence. A diagram is only a means to an end, not an end in itself. One form of diagraming in common use is illustrated below.

The very feeble woman carefully placed the cakes on the shelf.

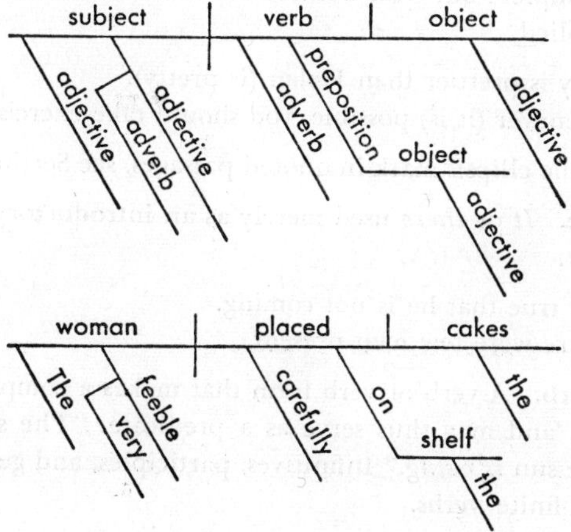

To decide was difficult.

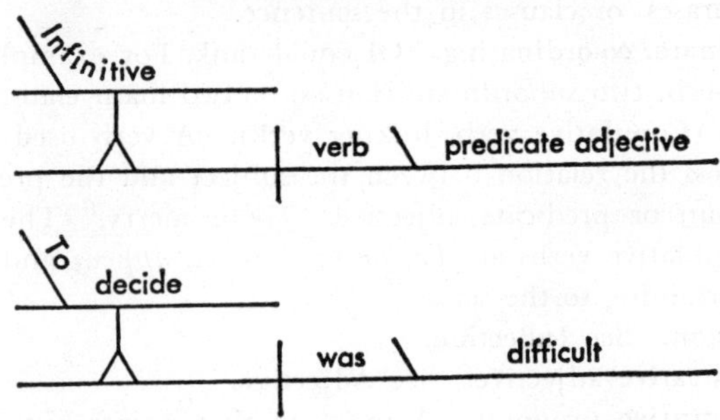

See other diagrams under **Adjective clause, Adverb clause, Gerund, Modify, Noun clause, Sentence,** and especially in Section **1, Sentence Sense.**

Direct address (Nominative of address, vocative). A noun or pronoun used parenthetically to direct a speech to a definite person.

I hope, *Mary,* that you will go. *Mary,* close the door.

Direct object. See **Object.**

Ellipsis (Elliptical expression). An expression grammatically incomplete but clear because omitted words can be readily supplied.

Mary is prettier than Helen (is pretty).
Whenever (it is) possible, you should take exercise.

For the ellipsis mark in quoted passages, see Section **17a(3).**

Expletive. *It* or *there* used merely as an introductory word or filler.

It is true that he is not coming.
There were few men present.

Finite verb. A verb or verb form that makes a complete assertion and may thus serve as a predicate. "The sun *rose.*" The sun *is rising.*" Infinitives, participles, and gerunds are not finite verbs.

Gerund. A form of the verb used as a noun and ending in *-ing.* The gerund should be carefully distinguished from the present participle (a verbal adjective), which also ends in *-ing.*

Swimming is enjoyable.

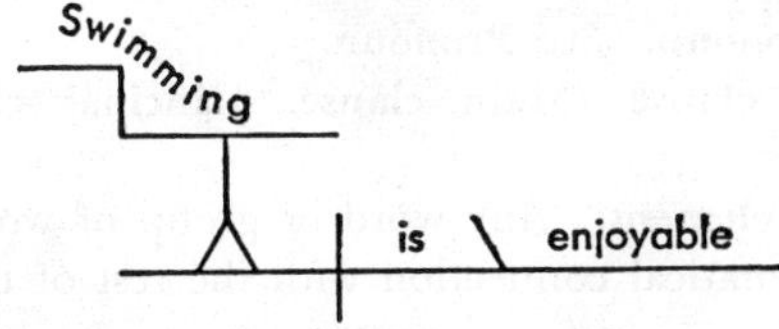

[Gerund—verbal noun used as subject]

The boy *swimming* against the current was exhausted.

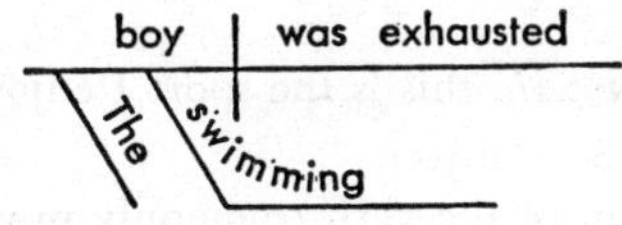

[Present participle—verbal adjective modifying the noun *boy*]

Since the gerund is a noun, it may function as subject (as in the sentence given above), as object of a verb ("I enjoy *swimming*"), as object of a preposition ("By *swimming* he reached shore"), as a predicate noun ("My chief recreation is *swimming*"), or as an appositive ("My chief recreation, *swimming,* has some disadvantages"). The gerund, like a noun, may be modified by an adjective: "*Skillful* swimming saved his life."

But the gerund shows its verbal origin by its ability to take an object ("Swimming the *horse* across the stream was difficult") or to be modified by an adverb ("By swimming *rapidly* he escaped").

Gerund phrase. See **Phrase.**

Idiom. An expression in good use that is peculiar to a language. (Idioms sometimes violate established rules of grammar, but are nevertheless sanctioned by usage.)

I have known him for *many a year.*

Do you *remember saying that* you were tired?

Indefinite pronoun. See **Pronoun.**

Independent clause (Main clause, principal clause). See **Clause.**

Independent element. Any word or group of words that has no grammatical connection with the rest of the sentence.

DIRECT ADDRESS I hope, *William,* that you can go.

DIRECTIVE EXPRESSION The whole family, *we hope,* will come.

ABSOLUTE EXPRESSION *Darkness having come,* he slipped away.

INTERJECTION *Ah,* this is the sport I enjoy.

Indirect object. See **Object.**

Infinitive. A form of the verb commonly preceded by *to* and used as a noun, an adjective, or an adverb. After certain verbs the *to* is often omitted: "He helped (*to*) *make* the kite." "He dared not (*to*) *go* away."

USED AS A NOUN

To walk was a pleasure. [Subject]
He began *to open the box.* [Object of verb]
Her wish was *to see him leave.* [Predicate noun]
He was about *to leave.* [Object of preposition]

USED AS AN ADJECTIVE

I have work *to do.* [*To do* modifies the noun *work.*]

USED AS AN ADVERB

He enlisted *to become an aviator.* [The infinitive modifies the verb *enlisted.*]

The infinitive shows its verbal origin by its ability to take a subject ("I asked *him* to go"), to take an object ("I wanted to pay *him*"), or to be modified by an adverb

("I asked him to drive *slowly*"). Note that the subject of the infinitive is in the objective case.

Infinitive phrase. See **Phrase.**

Inflection. A change in the form of a word to show a change in meaning or in relationship to some other word or group of words. The inflection of nouns and pronouns is called **declension:** *man, man's, men, men's; I, my, me,* etc. The inflection of verbs is called **conjugation;** that of adjectives and adverbs is called **comparison.**

Intensive pronoun. See **Pronoun.**

Interjection. A word (one of the eight parts of speech) expressing emotion and having no grammatical relation with other words in the sentence. "*Oh,* I can hardly believe it." "*Whew!* That was a narrow escape."

Interrogative pronoun. See **Pronoun.**

Intransitive. See **Verb.**

Irregular verb. See **Strong verb.**

Limiting adjective. See **Adjective.**

Linking verb. See **Copula.**

Main clause (Independent clause, principal clause). See **Clause.**

Modifier. Any word or group of words that describes or qualifies another word or group of words. See **Modify.**

Modify. To describe or qualify the meaning of a word or group of words. In a diagram modifiers are attached to the words they modify.

A very old man hobbled slowly along the road.

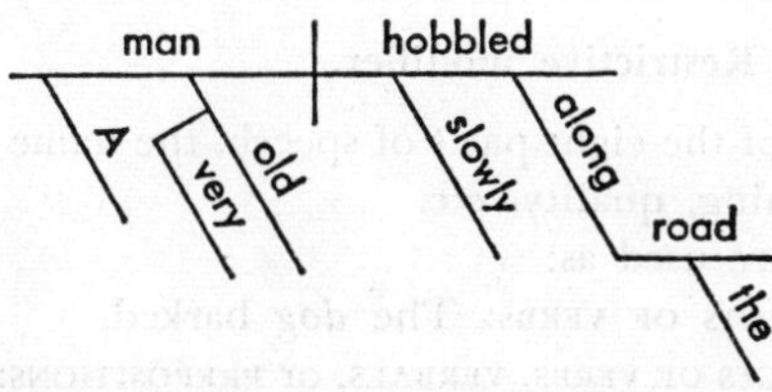

[*A* and *old* modify *man; very* modifies *old; slowly* and *along the road* modify *hobbled; the* modifies *road.*]

Mood (Mode). The form of the verb that is used to indicate the manner in which the action is conceived. English has indicative, imperative, and subjunctive moods. See Section **7.**

The **indicative mood** states a fact or asks a question.

The sun *is* shining.
Is the sun shining?

The **imperative mood** gives a command or makes a request.

Release the prisoners.
Walk carefully.

The **subjunctive mood** expresses a doubt, a condition contrary to fact, a wish or regret, a concession, a supposition.

I wish that Mother *were* here.
If I *had* my way, you would not go.
If I *should be gone,* wait for me.

Nominative. Equivalent to **Subjective.** See **Case.**
Nominative absolute. See **Absolute.**
Nominative of address. See **Direct address.**
Nonrestrictive modifier. A nonessential modifier. A phrase or clause which could be omitted without changing the essential meaning of the sentence.

The airplane, *which is now being manufactured in large numbers,* is of immense commercial value.

See also **Restrictive modifier.**

Noun. One of the eight parts of speech, the name of a person, place, thing, quality, etc.
Nouns are used as:
(1) SUBJECTS OF VERBS: The *dog* barked.
(2) OBJECTS OF VERBS, VERBALS, OR PREPOSITIONS: He opened the *door* to let the *dog* into the *house.*
(3) PREDICATE NOUNS: She was his *secretary.*

(4) APPOSITIVES: Mr. Brown, our *neighbor,* is sick.
(5) NOMINATIVES OF ADDRESS: *Mary,* will you help us?
(6) PREDICATE OBJECTIVES (OBJECTIVE COMPLEMENTS): He called the man a *traitor.*

Nouns are classified as:

(1) COMMON OR PROPER.

A **common noun** is the name applied to any one of a class of persons, places, or things: *man, woman, city, state, chair, bed.*

A **proper noun** is the name applied to a specific individual, place, or thing: *Henry Ford, Jane Addams, New Orleans, Texas,* the *Parthenon,* the *Washington Monument.*

(2) COLLECTIVE.

A **collective noun** is a name applied to a group: *band, flock, jury, army.* See Section **6a(7)** and **6b(3)**.

(3) CONCRETE OR ABSTRACT.

A **concrete noun** names something that can be perceived by one or more of the senses: *water, trees, man, river.*

An **abstract noun** names a quality or general idea: *love, ambition, hate, pity.*

Noun clause. A subordinate clause used as a noun. It may be used as subject, direct object, appositive, predicate nominative, object of a preposition.

Whoever comes will be welcome. [Subject]
I hope *that he will recover.* [Object of the verb]

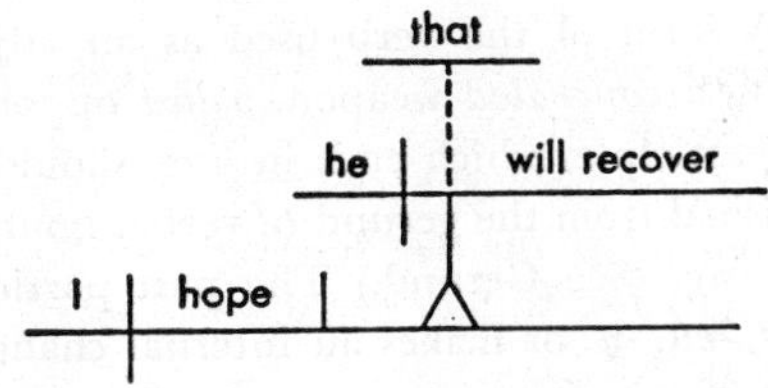

The hope *that he might win* upheld him. [Appositive]
This is *what I asked for.* [Predicate nominative]
I shall spend the money for *whatever seems best.* [Object of the preposition *for*]

Number. The change in the form of a verb, a noun, or a pronoun to designate one (*singular*) or more than one (*plural*).

Object. A noun or pronoun (or a phrase or clause used as a noun) that receives the action of a transitive verb or follows a preposition.

Direct object. Any noun (or its equivalent) that receives the action of a transitive verb.

He raked *leaves.* [Noun]
He supplied *whatever was needed.* [Clause used as a noun]

Indirect object. Any noun (or its equivalent) that receives indirectly the action of the verb.

He gave *me* an apple. [*Apple* is the direct object, *me* the indirect object, of the verb *gave.* It is usually possible to substitute for the indirect object a prepositional phrase with *to.*]

Object of a preposition. Any noun (or its equivalent) following a preposition. See **Preposition.**

He walked into the house. [*House* is the object of the preposition *into.*]

Objective complement. See **Complement.**

Participial phrase. See **Phrase.**

Participle. A form of the verb used as an adjective. "The *rising* sun, a *concealed* weapon, a *lost* opportunity." The present participle, which ends in *-ing,* should be carefully distinguished from the gerund (a verbal noun), which also ends in *-ing.* (See **Gerund.**) The past participle ends in *-ed, -d, -t, -en, -n,* or makes an internal change.

PRESENT PARTICIPLES concealing, losing, rising, singing.
PAST PARTICIPLES concealed, lost, risen, sung.

Parts of speech. The eight classes into which most grammarians group words according to their uses in the sentence: *verb, noun, pronoun, adjective, adverb, conjunction, preposition,* and *interjection.* Each of these is discussed separately in this section. It is important to note that *part of speech* is determined by function. The same word is often used as several different parts of speech.

Passive voice. See **Voice.**

Person. Changes in the form of verbs and pronouns which indicate whether a person is speaking (first person), is spoken to (second person), or is spoken about (third person).

FIRST PERSON *I* see the boy.
SECOND PERSON Can *you* see the boy?
THIRD PERSON *He* sees the boy.

Personal pronoun. See **Pronoun.**

Phrase. A group of related words which lacks subject and verb and is used as a single part of speech.

Prepositional phrase:

The man *with red hair* is my brother. [Adjective]
My brother lives *in the city.* [Adverb]

See also **Preposition.**

Participial phrase:

The door *leading to the porch* is open. [Adjective]

See also **Participle.**

Gerund phrase:

Reckless driving along the highways is responsible for many wrecks. [Substantive]

See also **Gerund.**

Infinitive phrase:

To err is human. [Substantive]

See also **Infinitive.**

Verb phrase:

He *has been employed* for a year. [Verb]

Predicate. The part of the sentence comprising what is said about the subject. The **complete predicate** consists of the verb (the **simple predicate**) along with its complements and modifiers.

He *runs* through the house. [*Runs* is the simple predicate; *runs through the house* is the complete predicate.]

Predicate adjective, predicate complement, predicate nominative, predicate noun, predicate objective. See **Complement.**

Preposition. A word (one of the eight parts of speech) used to show the relation of a noun (or noun-equivalent) to some other word in the sentence.

He ran *with* the team. [The preposition *with* shows the relation of the noun *team* to the verb *ran*.]
The bird is *in* the tree.
The man walked *into* the house.
The man *of* the house is absent.

Prepositional phrase. See **Phrase.**

Present tense. See **Tense.**

Principal clause (Main clause, independent clause). See **Clause.**

Principal parts. The forms of any verb from which the various tenses are derived: (1) present stem (infinitive), (2) past tense, and (3) past participle.

EXAMPLES	see	saw	seen
	take	took	taken
	love	loved	loved

Pronoun. A word (one of the eight parts of speech) used instead of a noun.

Personal pronouns: *I, you, he, she, it.* See the declension under Section 5, **Case.**

Interrogative pronouns: *who, which, what.*

Relative pronouns: *who, which, that.*

Demonstrative pronouns: *this, that, these, those.*

Indefinite pronouns: *each, either, any, anyone, some, someone, one, no one, few, all, everyone,* etc.

Reciprocal pronouns: *each other, one another.*

Reflexive pronouns: *myself, yourself, himself,* etc.

You hurt *yourself.*
He ruined *himself.*

Intensive pronouns: *myself, yourself, himself,* etc.

I *myself* will go.
You *yourself* should go.

Proper adjective. An adjective formed from a proper noun, as *Spanish* from *Spain.*

Proper noun. See **Noun.**

Reciprocal pronoun. See **Pronoun.**

Reflexive pronoun. See **Pronoun.**

Regular verb. See **Weak verb.**

Restrictive modifier. An essential modifier. A phrase or clause which cannot be omitted without changing the essential meaning of the sentence.

Men *who are industrious* will succeed.

See also **Nonrestrictive modifier.**

Sentence. A unit of expression that may stand alone. A complete sentence contains a verb (predicate) and its subject, with or without modifiers. (For the incomplete sentence see pages 32-33.) Sentences are classified structurally as (1) simple, (2) compound, (3) complex, or (4) compound-complex.

(1) **Simple sentence.** A sentence containing but one main clause and no subordinate clauses.

Birds fly. [Simple sentence]

Birds and bats fly. [Simple sentence with compound subject]

Birds and bats swoop and fly. [Simple sentence with compound subject and compound predicate.]

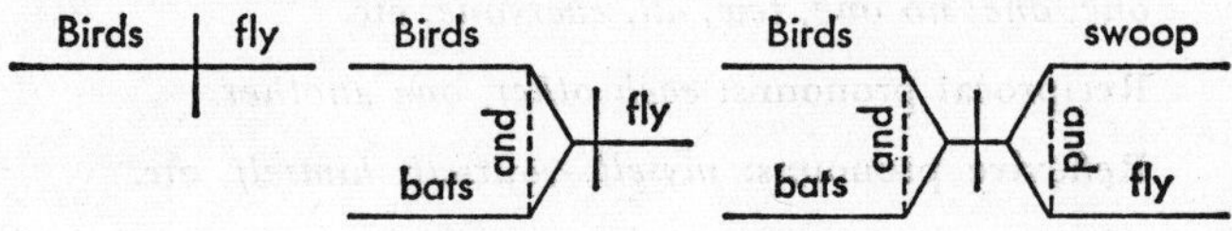

(2) **Compound sentence.** A sentence containing two or more main clauses but no subordinate clauses.

The moon rose and the stars came out.

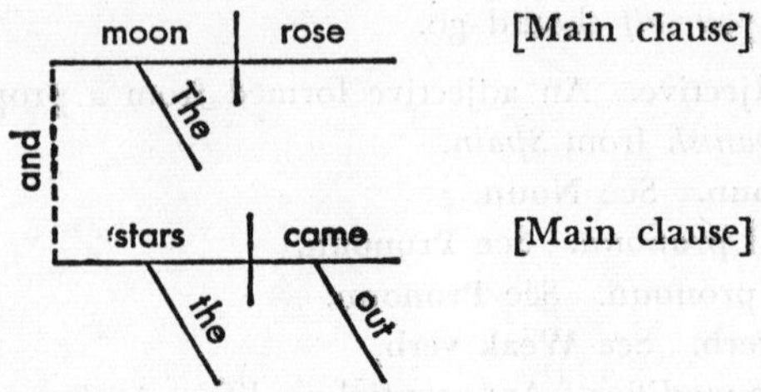

(3) **Complex sentence.** A sentence containing one main clause and one or more subordinate clauses.

Birds fly when they are startled.

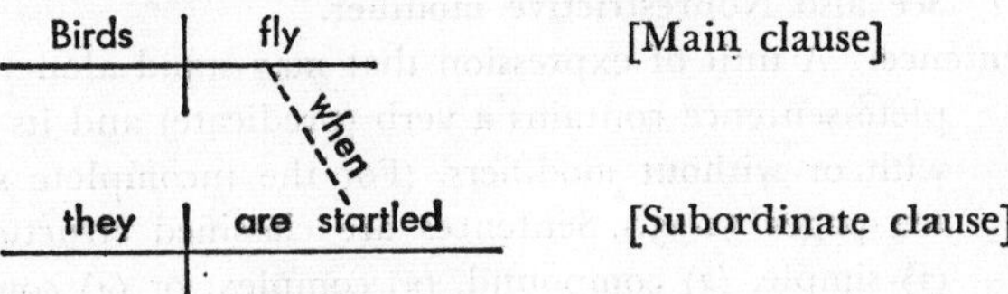

(4) **Compound-complex sentence.** A sentence containing two or more main clauses and one or more subordinate clauses.

Engines roared overhead and a bomb fell where we had stood.

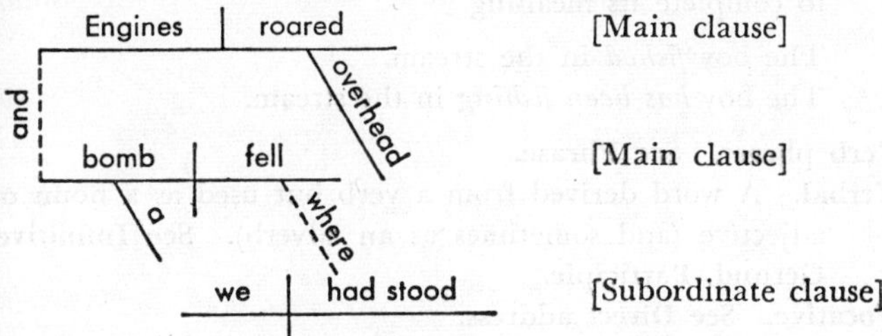

Simple predicate. See **Predicate.**

Simple sentence. See **Sentence.**

Strong verb (Irregular verb). A verb that forms its principal parts by vowel change: *ring, rang, rung; see, saw, seen.*

Subject. The person or thing (in a sentence or a clause) about which an assertion is made.

The *dog* barked at the car.

Subjective. See **Case.**

Subjective complement. See **Complement.**

Subjunctive. See **Mood.**

Subordinate clause. A dependent clause. See **Clause.**

Substantive. Any word or group of words used as a noun. Substantives may be nouns, pronouns, phrases (especially gerund or infinitive phrases), or noun clauses.

Syntax. Sentence structure. See **Construction.**

Tense. Change in the form of the verb to indicate the time of the action. There are six tenses: *present, past, future, present perfect, past perfect, future perfect.* See also Section **7.**

Transitive. See **Verb.**

Verb. A word or word group (one of the eight parts of speech) used to assert action, being, or state of being.

Transitive verb. A verb with a receiver of the action (object) to complete its meaning. See **Object.**

The boy *sold* his bicycle.
The boy *has sold* his bicycle.

Intransitive verb. A verb without a receiver of the action to complete its meaning.

The boy *fished* in the stream.
The boy *has been fishing* in the stream.

Verb phrase. See **Phrase.**

Verbal. A word derived from a verb but used as a noun or adjective (and sometimes as an adverb). See **Infinitive, Gerund, Participle.**

Vocative. See **Direct address.**

Voice. Distinction in the form of the verb to indicate whether the subject of the verb acts (active voice) or is acted upon (passive voice). See Section 29d.

Weak verb (Regular verb). Any verb that forms its principal parts by adding *-ed, -d,* or *-t* to the infinitive: *love, loved, loved; sweep, swept, swept.*

▸ Index

[Numbers in **boldface** refer to rules; other numbers refer to pages. A colon is used after each boldface number to indicate that the following pages refer to the rule or the part of the rule concerned. An *ex* indicates that appropriate drill exercises are included. An *n* indicates reference to a footnote.]

GRAMMAR

1 ss **Sentence Sense**

a Recognizing verbs
b Recognizing subjects (and objects)
c Recognizing all parts of speech
d Recognizing phrases and clauses
e Recognizing types of sentences

2 frag **Fragmen**

a Phrase
b Subordinate clause
c Other fragments

5 ca **Case**

a Subject of verb
b Predicate complement
c Possessive noun, pronoun
d Possessive with gerund
e *Of* phrase
f Object of verb, etc.
g Object, etc., of infinitive

6 agr

a Subject and verb
(1) Intervening word
(2) Subjects joined by *and*
(3) Subjects joined by *or*, etc.
(4) Subject following verb
(5) Relative pronoun
(6) *Each, either*, etc.
(7) Collective nouns

MECHANICS

8 ms **Manuscript**

a Proper materials
b Arrangement on page
c Legibility
d Revision
e Record of errors
f Syllabication

9 cap **Capital**

a Proper names
b Titles preceding name, etc.
c Titles of books, etc.
d *I* and O
e Beginning of sentence, etc.
f Unnecessary capitals

PUNCTUATION

12 ,/ **The Comma**

a Main clauses
b Introductory clauses, phrases
c Series; co-ordinate adjectives
d Nonrestrictive elements
e Misreading

13 O **Superfluou Comma**

a Subject and verb, etc.
b Words, phrases joined by *and*
c Slight parenthesis
d Restrictive elements
e First item of series, etc.

16 "/ **Quotation Marks**

a Direct quotations
b Titles
c Special words
d Overuse
e Position with other marks

17 **The Period an**

a ./ Period
b ?/ Question mark
c !/ Exclamation point
d :/ Col
e —/ Das

DICTION

19 g **Good Use**

a Use of dictionary
b Colloquialisms
c Slang and jargon
d Dialectal words
e Illiteracies
f Obsolete and archaic words
g Technical words
h Fine writing, etc.
i **Glossary**

20 e **Exactnes**

a Exact words
b Idioms
c Fresh expressions

EFFECTIVE SENTENCES

23 u **Unity and Logical Thinking**

a Unrelated ideas
b Excessive detail
c Mixed, obscure, or illogical constructions

24 sub **Subordinatio**

a Short, choppy sentences
b *And* sentences
c Subordination of main thought

27 pv **Point of View**

a Tense
b Mood
c Subject or voice
d Person
e Number
f Indirect and direct discourse
g Tone or style
h Perspective

28 ref **Reference o Pronoun**

a Ambiguous
b Remote antecedent
c Broad
d Repeated pronoun with different antecedents